P9-DTI-607

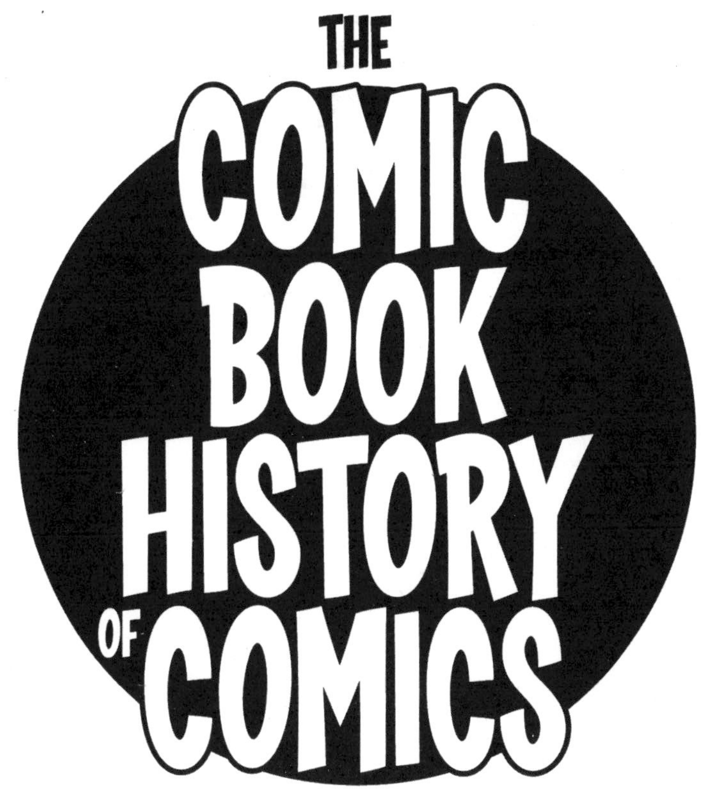
THE
COMIC
BOOK
HISTORY
OF COMICS

BY FRED VAN LENTE AND RYAN DUNLAVEY

Ted Adams, CEO & Publisher
Greg Goldstein, President & COO
Robbie Robbins, EVP/Sr. Graphic Artist
Chris Ryall, Chief Creative Officer/Editor-in-Chief
Matthew Ruzicka, CPA, Chief Financial Officer
Alan Payne, VP of Sales

The IDW logo is registered in the U.S. Patent and Trademark Office. IDW Publishing, a division of Idea and Design Works, LLC. Editorial offices: 5080 Santa Fe St., San Diego, CA 92109. Any similarities to persons living or dead are purely coincidental. With the exception of artwork used for review purposes, none of the contents of this publication may be reprinted without the permission of Idea and Design Works, LLC. Printed in Korea. IDW Publishing does not read or accept unsolicited submissions of ideas, stories, or artwork.

INTRODUCTION

COMICS HISTORY IS IMPORTANT TO COMICS. The medium has been shaped and re-shaped since its start by how contemporary creators and readers come to understand their past. A key reason superheroes became the dominant genre in North American comic books in the late 20th Century is because fans of those works established a way of looking at comics history through masked and/or goggled eyes. The popular idea of a "Golden Age," "Silver Age," and "Bronze Age" of comic books fails as a meaningful measure of comics content by any reasonable standard. Worse, it limits that content to a single genre, and re-casts the historical developments of an entire medium into a series of meaningful events in superhero comics publishing. Histories that embrace a wider view of important works, historians that might even dare engage with forms like the comic strip or ventures outside of the English-speaking world, have done so mostly by making their works counter-narratives. So much of what comics is, and can be, has been treated as the yellow boxes at the corners of comic book panels offering up a sly suggestion from an editor or publisher instead of the content of the panels themselves.

We need different histories. This is a good one.

The Comic Book History Of Comics abandons the idea of One Great Narrative—that a truth is out there to flatter whatever present we choose to embrace. Instead, its authors engage a whirlwind of competing ideas and points of view on what made comics into Comics and trust in the power of their insights and the form itself to make sense of what they discover. They pound through the unlikely story that results with the vigor of creators on a deadline. The end result is a remarkably generous look at the comics medium, with something close to equal time split between creators and businessmen, what comics clicked and maybe why this was so, artistic movements of all kinds, and legal wrangling with the shared aim of profit by ownership. You might not agree with every argument that gets made, but you'll grasp the point of their inclusion, and respect the number of times you're forced to stop and consider something with which you're unfamiliar.

The temptation is to make a point of this being a work in comics form but, after authors like Scott McCloud (on comics theory) and Larry Gonick (on history of all sorts), making a comics history out of comics seems less revolutionary and more a choice of the "I guess no one's done that before" variety. I'd argue the primary virtues on display here can be found in the willingness of the authors to make as many specific points as possible in the service of fashioning an amenable, broader view. It's good to be reminded about the Yellow Kid, but it's downright vital we learn about the way *Yellow Kid* made sense of time on the newspaper page. Seeing his journey to underground comix stardom pays deserving homage to Robert Crumb's iconic status, but it's not a mistake that we see what was happening in Austin with college humor magazines before we move on to Cleveland. Comic stores are rightly cast as both an artistic safe haven and as players in a lengthy saga of tragic, sometimes self-inflicted, wounds.

If comics is an elephant to be described by a series of blind men looking at individual, hard-to-connect parts, Fred Van Lente and Ryan Dunlavey have both stepped back and come closer, giving you the benefit of perspective but also a key insight of a detail or two when that can make just as big of a difference. We need to know that comics is an elephant, a living organism with a lifespan and purpose; we also benefit from learning how the skin on the front leg feels and how the comic that sensation represents might have been sold in the shops in 1985.

Details and perspective: it's how a comic is built. It's how this comics history was formed. Enjoy it.

Tom Spurgeon
March 2012

*Tom Spurgeon runs the web site http://www.***comicsreporter***.com/. Tom has written about comic strips, comic books and editorial cartoons for various publications since 1982. He worked for five years, 1994-1999, as Managing Editor and then Executive Editor of the lauded and controversial industry trade magazine* **The Comics Journal***. The magazine won several industry awards under his stewardship.*

LEGALESE!

THIS COMIC BOOK IS A WORK OF ***HISTORICAL SCHOLARSHIP.*** ALL TRADE NAMES, PRODUCT NAMES AND TRADEMARKS AND COPYRIGHTS OF THIRD PARTIES, INCLUDING ANY TRADEMARKED AND/OR COPYRIGHTED CHARACTERS, ARE REFERENCED OR REPRESENTED FOR HISTORICAL, SCHOLARLY, AND EDUCATIONAL "FAIR USE" PURPOSES ONLY OR, WHERE APPLICABLE, THE PURPOSES OF PARODY AND/OR IDENTIFICATION.

NO SPONSORSHIP, ENDORSEMENT OR AFFILIATION BY OR WITH THOSE THIRD PARTIES EXISTS OR SHOULD BE IMPLIED.

"ART"
SUPPLIES

THE ***VIEWS AND OPINIONS*** EXPRESSED IN THIS COMIC BOOK ARE ***SOLELY*** THOSE OF ***FRED VAN LENTE*** AND ***RYAN DUNLAVEY*** AND DO ***NOT*** REFLECT THE VIEWS OR POSITIONS OF THE OWNERS AND/OR PUBLISHERS OF THE COMICS AND PRODUCERS OF OTHER MEDIA WHICH ARE REFERRED TO IN THIS COMIC BOOK.

POPEYE © KING FEATURES SYNDICATE, INC. AND ™ HEARST HOLDINGS, INC.

MUTT & JEFF © AND ™ H. C. FISHER

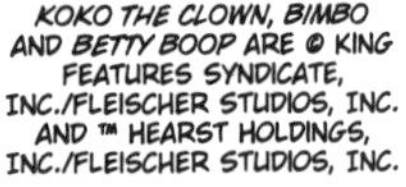

KOKO THE CLOWN, BIMBO AND *BETTY BOOP* ARE © KING FEATURES SYNDICATE, INC./FLEISCHER STUDIOS, INC. AND ™ HEARST HOLDINGS, INC./FLEISCHER STUDIOS, INC.

TARZAN IS © AND ™ E.R.B., INC.

BUCK ROGERS IS © AND ™ THE DILLE FAMILY TRUST.

THE SHADOW AND DOC SAVAGE ARE © AND ™ ADVANCE MAGAZINE PUBLISHERS INC.

ZORRO IS © AND ™ ZORRO PRODUCTIONS, INC.

THE SPIRIT IS © AND ™ THE ESTATE OF WILL EISNER.

MORTICIA ADDAMS & UNCLE FESTER ARE © & ™ THE TEE & CHARLES ADDAMS FOUNDATION.

TALES FROM THE CRYPT & TWO-FISTED TALES ARE © & ™ WILLIAM M. GAINES, AGENT, INC.

POGO THE POSSUM IS © & ™ OGPI

SUPERMAN, BLUE BEETLE, *ACTION COMICS, YOUNG ROMANCE,* THE SANDMAN (BOTH VERSIONS), BOY COMMANDOS, CAPTAIN (*SHAZAM!*) MARVEL, WONDER WOMAN, GREEN LANTERN, FLASH, BATMAN, ROBIN, THE RIDDLER, THE ATOM, ALFRED E. NEWMAN, *MAD* MAGAZINE, THE DC BULLET, THE BATMOBILE, GREEN ARROW, THE JOKER, DARKSEID, LEX LUTHOR, JIMMY OLSEN, THE BOTTLE CITY OF KANDOR, SUPERDUPERMAN, SWAMP THING, BLACKHAWKS, PLASTIC MAN, DR. MANHATTAN, NITE OWL, CAPTAIN ATOM, THE QUESTION, THE COMEDIAN, PEACEMAKER, OZYMANDIAS, THUNDERBOLT AND *WATCHMEN* ARE ™ AND © DC COMICS.

SNOW WHITE & THE SEVEN DWARVES, MICKEY MOUSE, *SILLY SYMPHONIES,* THE THREE LITTLE PIGS, "WHO'S AFRAID OF THE BIG, BAD WOLF?". "STEAMBOAT WILLIE," PINOCCHIO, BAMBI, GOOFY, THUMPER, FLOWER AND *IT'S A SMALL WORLD* ARE ™ AND © THE WALT DISNEY COMPANY.

CAPTAIN AMERICA, HUMAN TORCH, KA-ZAR, THE SUB-MARINER, GEN. "THUNDERBOLT" ROSS, THE FANTASTIC FOUR, THE THING, THE INVISIBLE WOMAN, MR. FANTASTIC, SPIDER-MAN, DR. OCTOPUS, THE HULK, THOR, THE WATCHER, THE X-MEN, DR. STRANGE, DAREDEVIL, CAPTAIN AMERICA, AVENGERS, NICK FURY, GALACTUS, THE SILVER SURFER, M.O.D.O.K., GHOST RIDER, IRON MAN, DR. DOOM, THE MARVEL "M", HOWARD THE DUCK, BLADE, CAPTAIN BRITAIN, CAPTAIN MARVEL (THE OTHER ONE), MARVELMAN, AND, OF COURSE, PATSY WALKER ARE ™ AND © MARVEL CHARACTERS, INC.

ARCHIE, BETTY, THE SHIELD, THE BLACK HOOD, THE COMET, ROY THE SUPER BOY, JUGHEAD, MR. WITHERS, AND JOSIE AND THE PUSSYCATS ARE ™ AND © ARCHIE COMICS, INC.

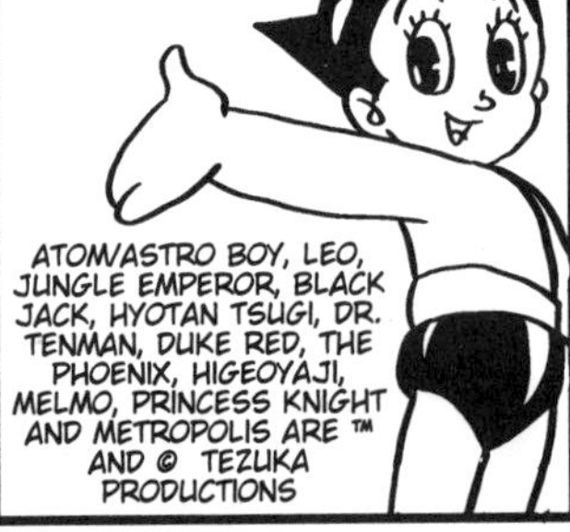

ATOM/ASTRO BOY, LEO, JUNGLE EMPEROR, BLACK JACK, HYOTAN TSUGI, DR. TENMAN, DUKE RED, THE PHOENIX, HIGEOYAJI, MELMO, PRINCESS KNIGHT AND METROPOLIS ARE ™ AND © TEZUKA PRODUCTIONS

DENNIS THE MENACE IS © AND ™ HANK KETCHUM ENTERPRISES, INC.

RICHIE RICH IS © AND ™ CLASSIC MEDIA.

KRAZY KAT, IGNATZ, SGT. SNORKEL & GEN. HALFTRACK ARE © AND ™ KING FEATURES SYNDICATE.

TINTIN & MILOU ("SNOWY") ARE TM AND © 2012 CASTERMAN, BELGIUM.

THE FABULOUS FURRY FREAK BROTHERS ARE TM AND © 2011 GILBERT SHELTON.

DICK TRACY IS © AND ™ TRIBUNE MEDIA SERVICES, INC.

SAD SACK IS © AND ™ SAD SACK INC.

FRITZ THE CAT, MR. NATURAL, FLAKEY FOONT, SNOID, ANGELFOOD MCSPADE, "KEEP ON TRUCKIN'" ARE TM AND © R. CRUMB.

SPAWN IS © & ™ TODD MACFARLANE

MAUS IS © & ™ ART SPIEGELMAN

SPIDER JERUSALEM IS © & ™ WARREN ELLIS & DARICK ROBERTSON

JUDGE DREDD IS © & ™ REBELLION DEVELOPMENTS LTD.

JESSE CUSTER IS ™ AND © GARTH ENNIS & STEVE DILLON

CAPTAIN HARLOCK IS ™ & © LEIJI MATSUMOTO

ELFQUEST IS ™ & © WARP GRAPHICS, INC.

ACTION PHILOSOPHERS IS ™ & © RYAN DUNLAVEY & FRED VAN LENTE

BONE IS ™ & © JEFF SMITH

TEENAGE MUTANT NINJA TURTLES ARE ©2012 VIACOM INTERNATIONAL INC.

GODZILLA IS ™ & © TOHO CO., LTD.

GATCHAMAN IS ™ & © TATSUNOKO

PIKACHU IS ™ & © NINTENDO/POKEMON

VOLTRON IS ™ & © WORLD EVENTS PRODUCTIONS

ZIGGY IS ™ & © ZIGGY AND FRIENDS, INC.

CHEECH WIZARD IS ™ & © THE ESTATE OF VAUGHN BODE

TRASHMAN IS ™ AND © SPAIN (A/K/A MANUEL RODRIGUEZ)

KORGI IS ™ & © CHRISTIAN SLADE
PERSEPOLIS IS ™ & © MARJANE SATRAPI

PEANUTS IS ™ & © PEANUTS WORLDWIDE LLC

CAPTAIN VICTORY & THE GALACTIC RANGERS IS ™ & © THE ESTATE OF JACK KIRBY

THE FAMILY DOG ™ & © 1992 AMBLIN TELEVISION, INC. AND UNIVERSAL CITY STUDIOS, INC.

ZIPPY THE PINHEAD IS ™ AND © BILL GRIFFITH

ANY OMISSION OR INCORRECT INFORMATION SHOULD BE TRANSMITTED TO THE PUBLISHER SO IT CAN BE RECTIFIED IN ANY FUTURE EDITION OF THE MATERIAL CONTAINED HEREIN.
Dear Morons,

THIS BOOK WAS PUBLISHED BY **IDW PUBLISHING,** A DIVISION OF IDEA & DESIGN WORKS, LLC 5080 SANTA FE STREET, SAN DIEGO, CA 92109

THE COMIC BOOK HISTORY OF COMICS IS COPYRIGHT © 2012 ***RYAN DUNLAVEY*** AND ***FRED VAN LENTE***. ALL RIGHTS RESERVED.

ORIGINALLY PUBLISHED BY EVIL TWIN COMICS AS COMIC BOOK COMICS ISSUES #1-6.

FIRST PRINTING MAY 2012. PRINTED IN KOREA.

ISBN 978-1-61377-197-6
15 14 13 12 1 2 3 4

Funnies get Famous

October 18, 1896...

...WAS, ALL THINGS CONSIDERED, A FAIRLY ***UNREMARKABLE*** DAY, AS DAYS GO...

...SOMEBODY TRIED TO KILL THE KING OF ***SPAIN*** BY LAYING ***DYNAMITE*** IN FRONT OF THE ROYAL LOCOMOTIVE AS IT CHUGGED TOWARD ***MADRID...***

(THE GOVERNMENT BLAMED INDEPENDENCE-MINDED ***CUBANS.***)

...AN ACCUSED BURGLAR NAMED ***JAMES SWEENEY*** SLIPPED THROUGH THE BARS OF HIS CELL AND ***WALKED OUT*** OF THE BROOKLYN JAIL WHERE HE HAD BEEN AWAITING TRIAL...

(MUST BE HOW HE GOT INTO HIS VICTIMS' ***HOMES*** SO EASILY.)

...IN ***BUDAPEST***, DUE TO AN UNACCOUNTABLE ***BLUNDER*** BY HIS OPPONENT, A ***DR. NOA*** WON HIS MATCH IN THE TENTH ROUND OF THE INTERNATIONAL ***CHESS*** TOURNAMENT...

(THOUGH MR. ***CHAROUSEK*** REMAINED IN THE ***LEAD.***)

...AND ***WILLIAM RANDOLPH HEARST*** PUBLISHED THE FIRST ISSUE OF THE ***AMERICAN HUMORIST***, A COLOR SUPPLEMENT TO THE ***NEW YORK JOURNAL*** THAT FEATURED SOMETHING THAT HAD NEVER BEEN SEEN ***BEFORE...***

...SOMETHING THAT WOULD ***CHANGE THE LIVES*** OF EVERY SINGLE PERSON HOLDING THIS BOOK, EVEN THOUGH ***NO ONE***, NOT EVEN HEARST ***HIMSELF***, SUSPECTED IT AT THE TIME...

INNOVATION: IMITATION OF LIFE!

...FOR THE *HUMORIST* CONTAINED THE FIRST MODERN ***COMIC STRIP:*** RICHARD F. OUTCAULT'S *THE YELLOW KID!*

AS HISTORIANS BILL BLACKBEARD AND MARTIN WILLIAMS WRITE, THE *KID* EARNS THIS DISTINCTION BECAUSE:

WHY IS DE COLORED SUPPLEMENT OF DE SUNDAY JOURNAL LIKE DE YALLER KID'S BEST GAL? — CAUSE ITS A PEACH

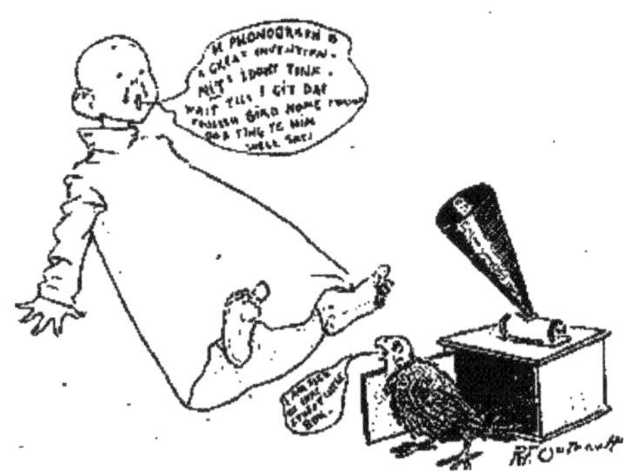

"THE WHOLE POINT OF THE VAUDEVILLE GAG DEPENDED ON THE DIALOGUE BETWEEN THE KID AND THE PARROT, AND THAT WAS THE FIRST TIME THIS HAD OCCURRED IN A GRAPHIC WORK WHICH ALSO MET THE OTHER PREREQUISITES OF THE STRIP FORM."

SATIRICAL PICTURES IN PRINT IN AND OF THEMSELVES WERE NOTHING ***NEW***. IN FACT, THEY'RE NEARLY AS OLD AS THE PRINTING PRESS ***ITSELF***, WHICH WAS INVENTED IN 1440.

THE ENGRAVING AT LEFT BY GERMAN ARTIST ***ERHARD SCHÖN*** DEPICTING RELIGIOUS REFORMER ***MARTIN LUTHER*** AS THE LITERAL ***INSTRUMENT OF SATAN*** IS BELIEVED TO BE THE ***FIRST*** POLITICAL CARTOON... PUBLISHED IN THE ***1500s!***

PICTURES ***TALKING*** INSIDE THE CONFINES OF ***WORD BALLOONS*** WERE NOTHING NEW ***EITHER;*** AS SEEN BELOW, ***THAT*** DEVICE HAD BEEN USED SINCE AT LEAST THE ***18TH*** CENTURY.

D—n it, how he nicks 'em
Oh! this cursed Ograbme.

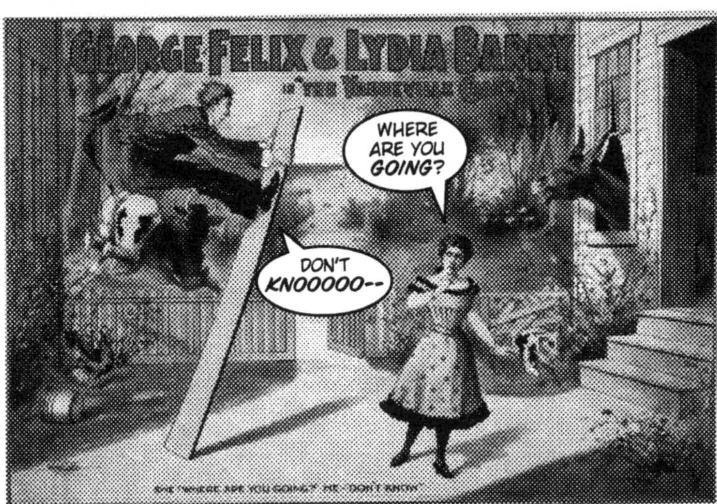
WHERE ARE YOU GOING?
DON'T KNOOOOO--

BUT WHILE PREVIOUS "PROTO-COMICS" MAY HAVE HAD ***SUCCESSIVE IMAGES*** AND/OR ***DIALOGUE***, OUTCAULT'S INNOVATION WAS TO MERGE THE TWO TOGETHER INTO A NARRATIVE CADENCE THAT RENDERED A FACSIMILE OF ***REAL LIFE*** AS IT WAS LIVED BY HIS ***READER...***

...OR, AT THE VERY LEAST, COPIED THE RAT-A-TAT, BACK-AND-FORTH ***COMEDY ROUTINES*** COMMON IN THE ***VAUDEVILLE THEATRE*** OF THE DAY.

IT IS ***DIFFICULT*** FOR US TO WRAP OUR BRAINS AROUND HOW ***REVOLUTIONARY*** THIS CHANGE WAS, SINCE WE ALL ***GREW UP*** IN A WORLD ALREADY FULLY ***MADE*** BY IT.

HERE WE'VE TRIED TO IMAGINE JUST HOW ***DIFFICULT*** IT WOULD BE TO REPRODUCE THE MOST ***FAMOUS*** VAUDEVILLE ROUTINE ***OF ALL TIME*** IN THE STYLE OF COMICS, ***PRE***-OUTCAULT...

"THEY SURE GIVE BALLPLAYERS FUNNY NAMES THESE DAYS"

DUNCE
"I DON'T KNOW is on THIRD"
"WHAT is on SECOND"
MON
13
"WHO is on FIRST"
"TOMORROW is PITCHING"

...IN WHICH A SERIES OF ***HUMOROUS DRAWINGS*** WERE ARRAYED ON A PAGE, LINKED BY A ***SIMILAR THEME***, PERHAPS, BUT WITH NO ***NECESSARY*** CONNECTION ***BETWEEN*** THEM.

THEY WERE NOT YET ***"SEQUENTIAL"*** ART IN THE SENSE OF THE TERM COINED BY THE LEGENDARY ***WILL EISNER***...

If I'm going to play on your team, Fred, you should tell me all the players' names.
I'd be happy to, Ryan. Though you should know they sure give ballplayers funny names these days.
How so?
Well, let's see, we have on the bags, Who's on first, What's on second, I Don't Know is on third...
That's what I wanna know.
I say Who's on first, What's on second, I Don't Know's on third—
Are you the manager?
Yes.
And you don't know your guys' names?
Of course I do!
Then who's on first?
Yes.

...UNTIL OUTCAULT PIONEERED ***EXCHANGES*** BETWEEN CHARACTERS IN THE FORM OF "LIVE" ***DIALOGUE,*** LIKE ***THIS...***

I mean the fellow's name.
Who.
The guy on first.
Who.
The first baseman.
Who.
The guy playing—
Who is on first!
I'm asking you who's on first!
That's the man's name.
That's who's name?
Right.
WELL GO AHEAD AND TELL ME!!!
You just did.

...THEREBY INJECTING INTO THE MEDIUM THAT *A PRIORI* "SUBJECTIVE CONDITION" THE GREAT PHILOSOPHER ***IMMANUEL KANT*** WROTE IS ***REQUIRED*** FOR THE VERY ***CONCEPT*** OF "SEQUENCE": ***TIME!***

Look. You got a first baseman?
Certainly.
Who's on first?
That's right.
When you pay the first baseman every month, who gets the money?
Every penny.
AAAAAAAAAAA RRRRRRRRRRR GGGGGGGGGGG!

SEE HOW ***EASY*** IT IS TO DO A VAUDEVILLE ROUTINE IN ***THIS*** STYLE, WHICH MIMICS THE RHYTHMS OF ***SPEECH?*** THE CHANGE IS AS ***SIMPLE*** AND AS ***PROFOUND*** AS THE DIFFERENCE BETWEEN MERELY ***LOOKING*** AT PICTURES ... AND ***READING*** THEM!

Yellow Kid
YELLOW KID CIGARETTES
-KOF! -HACK!

HOWEVER ONE WISHES TO ***DEFINE*** THE DIFFERENCE, THE PROOF THAT SOMETHING ***BIG*** HAD HAPPENED WAS IN THE PUBLIC ***REACTION*** TO IT: THE YELLOW KID BECAME AN INSTANT ***CULTURAL PHENOMENON***. HIS BUCKTOOTHED MUG APPEARED ON BOOKS, SHIRTS, TINS OF "GINGER WAFERS," BOWLING PINS... THERE WERE EVEN YELLOW KID ***CIGARETTES***!

OUTCAULT HAD ***CREATED*** THE KID IN *"HOGAN'S ALLEY,"* A SERIES OF SLUM VIGNETTES HE DREW FOR THE *NEW YORK WORLD*... BUT HEARST LURED HIM TO THE *JOURNAL* WITH A HUGE BUMP IN ***SALARY***!

THE PUBLISHER MADE A ***SHREWD*** INVESTMENT: THE *JOURNAL'S* CIRCULATION ***EXPLODED*** ALONG WITH THE KID'S POPULARITY!

WOE! ME IZ A PRODUCT OF A BROKE-IN HOME

OUTCAULT'S OLD BOSS AND HEARST'S ARCH-NEMESIS, ***JOSEPH PULITZER***, CLAIMED ***HE*** OWNED THE RIGHTS TO THE NAME ***"HOGAN'S ALLEY,"*** HOWEVER, AND HIRED AN ARTIST TO ***CONTINUE*** THE STRIP AFTER ITS CREATOR'S DEFECTION!

FOR ALMOST A ***YEAR*** THE KID APPEARED IN PULITZER'S *WORLD* AND HEARST'S *JOURNAL* ***SIMULTANEOUSLY...***

....LEADING MORE ***RESPECTABLE*** (AND ***LOWER-SELLING***) DAILIES TO REFER TO THEM CONTEMPTUOUSLY AS THE ***"YELLOW KID PAPERS"***...

...AND THE BRAND OF SENSATIONALISTIC, JINGOISTIC ***MUCKRAKING*** THEY PRACTICED -- PARTICULARLY IN THE HYSTERIA-FUELED LEAD-UP TO THE ***SPANISH-AMERICAN WAR*** OF 1898 -- WAS DUBBED ***"YELLOW JOURNALISM!"***

OUTCAULT'S SUCCESS WAS NOT LOST ON ***OTHER*** NEWSPAPER ARTISTS, LIKE HENRY CONWAY ***"BUD"*** FISHER, SPORTS-PAGE ILLUSTRATOR FOR THE *SAN FRANCISCO CHRONICLE* AND ***HORSERACING JUNKIE***.

YEESH, I BET ***OUTCAULT*** DOESN'T HAVE TO SWEAT ***LOSSES*** LIKE THIS...

HEY, ***WAIT*** A MINUTE... WHAT IF ***I*** TRIED A CARTOON?
ONE ABOUT THE ***PONIES***-- IT CAN RUN ON THE ***RACING FORM PAGE!*** I CAN EVEN GIVE ***BETTING TIPS!***

WHILE MOST COMICS IN THOSE DAYS (AS OUR ***PREVIOUS*** PAGES ATTEST) WERE VERTICAL, AMORPHOUS ***BLOBS***, FISHER CHOSE TO ARRANGE HIS PANELS ***HORIZONTALLY*** ACROSS THE PAGE LIKE ***THIS***, SO, HE SAID...

..."I WOULD GET A PROMINENT POSITION ACROSS THE TOP OF THE SPORTING PAGE, WHICH I DID, AND THAT PLEASED MY VANITY."

THE CHRONICLE'S EDITOR RESISTED THE FORMAT AT FIRST BECAUSE HE FEARED IT WOULD BE DIFFICULT TO READ.

BUT FISHER'S A. MUTT, WHICH PREMIERED ON NOVEMBER 15, 1907, GREATLY INCREASED COMICS' READABILITY!
INNOVATION: THE STRIP!
THE STANDARDIZATION OF PANEL BORDERS RENDERED EACH INDIVIDUAL PICTURE AN UNMISTAKABLY DISTINCT UNIT.

A ***SIMILAR*** ACHIEVEMENT HAD BEEN ACHIEVED IN ***WRITING*** WITH THE STANDARDIZATION OF ***PUNCTUATION MARKS*** (THEMSELVES INVENTED AROUND THE ***9TH CENTURY***) THAT ACCOMPANIED THE RISE OF THE ***PRINTING PRESS***, ALLOWING WORDS TO BE SEPARATED INTO DISTINCT ***SENTENCES*** AND ***PHRASES*** WITH PERIODS, COMMAS, AND THE LIKE.

THE HILARIOUS A. MUTT WAS AN OVERNIGHT HIT, SO HEARST PULLED AN "OUTCAULT" AND LURED FISHER AWAY TO HIS SAN FRANCISCO EXAMINER WITH MORE DOUGH.
$
EXAMINER

RIGHT BEFORE DEFECTING, FISHER SNUCK INTO THE CHRONICLE ENGRAVING ROOM AND ETCHED A COPYRIGHT SLUG IN HIS NAME ONTO THE PLATE OF HIS FINAL STRIP FOR THEM!
HEH, HEH...

FISHER'S DEFENSE OF HIS COPY-RIGHTS PAID OFF. HIS STRIP MADE HIM SO RICH...
...HE SOON OWNED THE LARGEST STABLE OF RACEHORSES IN THE U.S.!

BY THAT TIME, FISHER HAD GIVEN MUTT A ***SIDEKICK***, AND THE STRIP BECAME KNOWN AS *MUTT & JEFF*.

IMPRESSED BY FISHER'S SUCCESS IN 'FRISCO, HEARST STARTED RUNNING M&J IN HIS PAPERS ACROSS THE COUNTRY, MULTIPLYING ITS POPULARITY!
FUNNIES

THIS PRACTICE, KNOWN AS "SYNDICATING," ASSURED FANS THEY'D ALWAYS GET THEIR FUNNIES... NO MATTER WHERE THEY LIVED!
FUNNIES

BY 1913, HEARST NEEDED A NEW SUBSIDIARY OF HIS NEWSPAPER EMPIRE TO CONTROL SYNDICATION OF ALL HIS MANY STRIPS.

THE HEAD OF THE COMPANY, ***MOSES KOENIGSBERG***, ULTIMATELY NAMED IT AFTER A SHORTENED VERSION OF HIS OWN NAME: ***"KING."*** SOON THE RIGHTS TO ***ALL*** COMIC STRIPS IN THE MAJOR AMERICAN DAILIES WOULD BE CONTROLLED BY A HANDFUL OF POWERFUL ***"SYNDICATES"*** LIKE HEARST'S ***KING FEATURES!***

FAME AND FORTUNE CONTINUED TO LURE ARTISTS FROM OTHER FIELDS INTO STRIP CARTOONING.
WINSOR MCCAY, FOR INSTANCE, STARTED OUT AS A SIGN PAINTER FOR A DIME MUSEUM IN CINCINNATI.
TWO-HEADED BEARDED SNAKE WOMAN

HIS DREAMS OF A RAREBIT FIEND WAS SOON JOINED BY LITTLE NEMO IN SLUMBERLAND, AMONG THE MOST BELOVED OF ALL THE EARLY STRIPS.
~URP!~

THE TITLE TOT'S SURREAL ADVENTURES WHENEVER HE CLOSED HIS EYES ENCOURAGED HIS CREATOR TO ADD A NEW TECHNIQUE TO THE ARTIST/STORYTELLER'S ARSENAL...

INNOVATION: PAGE LAYOUT AS NARRATIVE TOOL!

1
...HE BEGAN TO VARY PANEL SIZES TO GIVE VISUAL EMPHASIS TO HIS NARRATIVE!
LITTLE PANELS TO FOCUS IN ON SMALL, INTIMATE ACTIONS...
2
...BIG PANELS FOR DRAMATIC ACTIONS OR EPIC REVEALS!
ARTISTS LEARNED THEY COULD PACE CARTOON STORIES TO THEIR OWN INTERNAL RATE JUST AS WRITERS COULD USE DIFFERENT PHRASE AND SENTENCE LENGTH TO SET AN INTERNAL CADENCE FOR THEIR PROSE!
3
LIKE MANY SUPERSTAR CARTOONISTS, MCCAY PERFORMED HIS OWN LIVE VAUDEVILLE ACT, KNOWN AS "CHALK-TALKING," THRILLING PACKED HOUSES BY AGING A SKETCH FROM CHILDHOOD TO OLD AGE IN MINUTES WHILE AN ORGANIST PLAYED "SWEET MYSTERY OF LIFE!"
4
WINSOR McCAY LIVE!
SOLD OUT!
LITTLE NEMO
HE ACTUALLY MISSED THE OPENING OF THE BROADWAY MUSICAL VERSION OF LITTLE NEMO BECAUSE HE WAS PERFORMING IN THE THEATER ACROSS THE STREET!
5
THIS MOVEMENT-OBSESSED ARTIST REALIZED HE COULD JUICE UP HIS ACT BY INCORPORATING THE NEW MEDIUM OF MOTION PICTURES: BETWEEN 1912 AND 1914, MCCAY PAINSTAKINGLY DREW, THEN PHOTO-GRAPHED, 10,000 DRAWINGS OF A LOVABLE DIPLODOCUS TO CREATE GERTIE THE DINOSAUR...
6
...AN ANIMATED FILM THAT WAS PROJECTED NEXT TO MCCAY DURING HIS LIVE SHOW SO HE COULD APPEAR TO INTERACT WITH THE CREATURE!
BE A GOOD GIRL, GERTIE, AND BOW TO THE AUDIENCE!
GERTIE EXPRESSES BOREDOM, SPITE, SADNESS, FRIVOLITY, EXCITEMENT, SELF-CONSCIOUSNESS... MARKING THE SHORT AS THE BIRTH OF "CHARACTER" ANIMATION!

UNFORTUNATELY, HEARST, MCCAY'S PUBLISHER, BELIEVED THE QUALITY OF HIS STRIPS HAD BEGUN TO DECLINE BECAUSE OF HIS EXTRACURRICULAR ACTIVITIES.
"CITIZEN KANE" BULLIED THEATER OWNERS INTO DROPPING MCCAY'S ACT!
LITTLE NEMO

FEW OF MCCAY'S FELLOW EARLY ANIMATORS SHARED HIS BORDERLINE OBSESSIVE-COMPULSIVE DISORDER ATTENTION TO DETAIL.
THE MOVEMENT IN THEIR FILMS WAS CRUDE, SHUDDERY AND OFTEN DIFFICULT FOR AUDIENCES TO FOLLOW.
?!?

WALDEMAR KAEMPFFERT, EDITOR OF POPULAR SCIENCE MAGAZINE, GOT SO DISGUSTED BY THE QUALITY OF A CARTOON HE SAW IN 1915 THAT HE COMPLAINED TO HIS ART DIRECTOR:
"MAX, YOU'RE A BRIGHT YOUNG MAN. YOU'RE AN ARTIST, YOU UNDERSTAND MECHANICS...YOU'VE GOT A SCIENTIFIC MIND.
"SURELY YOU CAN COME UP WITH SOME IDEA, SOME WAY TO MAKE ANIMATED CARTOONS LOOK BETTER, SMOOTHER, MORE LIFELIKE."

MAX FLEISCHER'S DAD HAD BEEN AN AMATEUR INVENTOR, AND MAX HAD INHERITED HIS KNACK FOR GADGETRY.
TAKING UP HIS BOSS'S CHALLENGE, MAX SPENT THE NEXT TWO YEARS LABORING ON HIS "ROTOSCOPE," A DEVICE THAT PROJECTED A STRIP OF MOVIE FILM ONTO A FLAT PLATE OF GLASS ONE FRAME AT A TIME.
AN ARTIST COULD THEN SET A PIECE OF PAPER OVER THE GLASS AND TRACE EACH PHOTOGRAPH INDIVIDUALLY.

WHEN ALL THE DRAWINGS WERE THEN RE-FILMED, THEY PRODUCED COMPLETELY SMOOTH ANIMATION!
MAX'S FIRST FEW ROTOSCOPED "OUT OF THE INKWELL" SHORTS, STARRING KOKO THE CLOWN (WHO, IN HIS PRE-ANIMATED LIVE-ACTION INCARNATION, WAS ORIGINALLY MAX'S YOUNGER BROTHER DAVE), SOON LAUNCHED THE WORLD-FAMOUS FLEISCHER STUDIOS!

WHAT DOES FLEISCHER HAVE IN COMMON WITH OUTCAULT, FISHER, MCCAY, AND OUR OTHER EARLY INNOVATORS?
HE ALSO STARTED OUT AS A NEWSPAPER CARTOONIST, AT THE BROOKLYN DAILY EAGLE!
BUT NEWSPAPERS WERE NOT THE ONLY...OR EVEN THE PRIMARY MASS MEDIUM THAT INFLUENCED OUR MAIN SUBJECT!
EXTRA! EXTRA!
NEW MEDIA INVENTED DAILY
WILL MAKE US OBSOLETE
NEWSPAPER MEN: "WE'RE SCREWED"

AMAZING Spicy SCIENCE MYSTERY STORIES!

AROUND ***1929***, IN THE CRIME- AND POVERTY-INFESTED ***JEWISH GHETTO*** OF NEW YORK'S ***LOWER EAST SIDE***, 12 YEAR-OLD JACOB ***"JACK"*** KURTZBERG WAS DASHING HOME TO HIS FAMILY'S TENEMENT APARTMENT ON ***SUFFOLK STREET*** IN A TORRENTIAL ***DOWNPOUR...***

?

"I SPOTTED THIS ***MAGAZINE*** FLOATING DOWN THE ***GUTTER*** AND ***JUMPED*** FOR IT, AND SAVED IT JUST BEFORE IT WASHED INTO THE ***SEWER***," HE'D REMEMBER AS AN ADULT.

"SOME GUY DIDN'T WANT TO BE ***SEEN*** WITH IT."

"SOMETHING ON THE COVER I HAD NEVER ***SEEN*** BEFORE--THE COVER WAS ***AMAZING! SPACE SHIPS*** AND FUTURISTIC ***CITIES***."

WONDER
STORIES
10¢
"AT THAT MOMENT, SOMETHING GALVANIZED IN MY BRAIN."

YOUNG JACK HAD FALLEN UNDER THE SPELL OF THE PULP MAGAZINE--THE DOMINANT FORM OF MASS GENRE PROSE FICTION IN AMERICA SINCE 1896.
IN THE SAME YEAR AS THE BIRTH OF THE COMIC STRIP, PUBLISHER FRANK A. MUNSEY DECIDED TO CUT COSTS BY SWITCHING TO NEWLY INVENTED HIGH-SPEED PRINTING PRESSES AND CHEAP, GRAINY PULP PAPER, DECLARING...
..."THE STORY IS WORTH MORE THAN THE PAPER IT IS PRINTED ON!"
WOOD PULP
THE INEXPENSIVE NEW PROCESS ALLOWED MUNSEY TO SLASH THE COVER PRICE ON HIS FICTION MAGAZINES FROM A DIME DOWN TO A NICKEL!
THE AFFORDABLE FORMAT WAS A HUGE HIT. NUMEROUS PUBLISHERS BEGAN CRANKING OUT PULP MAGAZINES AT A PRODIGIOUS RATE IN EVERY CONCEIVABLE GENRE!
EACH BI-MONTHLY OR QUARTERLY ISSUE WAS, ON AVERAGE, 128 PAGES AND FEATURED ONE LEAD NOVEL OF 60,000 WORDS ALONG WITH 20,000 WORDS OR SO OF BACK-UP SHORT STORIES.
THE SHEER VOLUME OF PULPS--SOME 250 TITLES WERE ON THE STANDS AT ANY GIVEN TIME--MEANT THAT OVER 20 MILLION WORDS OF NEW FICTION GOT CRANKED OUT EVERY MONTH!
THOUGH PROSE, THE STORIES WERE HEAVILY ILLUSTRATED. SEXY DAMSELS IN DISTRESS--PARTICULARLY IN THE SOFT-PORN "SPICY" PULPS--WERE A BIG PART OF THEIR APPEAL!
BUT THE SCIENCE FICTION PULP--INCLUDING THE ONE JACK RESCUED--WAS THE NEAR-EXCLUSIVE PURVIEW OF ONE HUGO GERNSBACK, A WOULD-BE INVENTOR AND IMMIGRANT FROM LUXEMBOURG.
CALLING ALL GEEKS AND NERDS! COME IN, GEEKS AND NERDS! DESTINY IS CALLING!
GERNSBACK MADE MOST OF HIS MONEY SELLING RADIO PARTS THROUGH THE MAIL AND POPULARIZING AMATEUR WIRELESS AS A HOBBY.

GERNSBACK FOUNDED THE FIRST MAGAZINE DEDICATED SOLELY TO "SCIENTIFICTION" (AS HE CALLED IT), AMAZING STORIES, IN 1928 ...
... BECAUSE HE SINCERELY BELIEVED THAT IN SCIENCE FICTION WAS TO BE FOUND THE GUIDEPOSTS TO A BETTER FUTURE IN REAL LIFE!
"THE PRESENT ORDER OF CIVILIZATION IS HIGHLY UNSCIENTIFIC..."
(HERE MR. GERNSBACK MODELS HIS TELE-EYEGLASSES FOR US, WHICH HE PATENTED IN 1936...NO JOKE!)
"...AND WHEN WE CONTEMPLATE OUR CYCLES OF PROSPERITY, FOLLOWED BY CYCLES OF ABJECT DEPRESSION, EVERY THINKING INDIVIDUAL MUST COME TO THE CONCLUSION THAT WE HAVE FAILED SOMEWHERE.
"WHEN PEOPLE ARE STARVING IN THE MIDST OF PLENTY...
"...WHEN FOR THE FIRST TIME IN THE HISTORY OF THE HUMAN RACE IT BECOMES POSSIBLE FOR HUMANITY TO LABOR BUT A SHORT FRACTION OF ITS TIME AND HAVE LEISURE FOR A LARGER PERCENTAGE OF ITS TIME...
"...THEN, INDEED, WE KNOW THAT SOMETHING MUST BE DONE ABOUT IT!"
THE GREAT DEPRESSION HAD JUST SETTLED LIKE A BURIAL SHROUD OVER AMERICA, AND GERNSBACK'S IDEALISTIC EDITORIALS IN HIS SF MAGS STRUCK A CHORD WITH MANY, MANY YOUNG PEOPLE!
THIS SAME YEAR ALSO SAW TWO PULP HEROES LEAP FROM PURPLE PROSE TO THE FUNNIES PAGE:
PHILIP NOWLAN'S BUCK ROGERS, WHO HAD JUST PREMIERED THE YEAR BEFORE IN AMAZING STORIES...
...AND EDGAR RICE BURROUGHS' TARZAN, WHO FIRST SWUNG OUT OF THE JUNGLE IN MUNSEY'S ALL-STORY IN 1912.
AMAZING STORIES
THE ALL-STORY
FUNNIES
BOTH HAD COMIC STRIPS ABOUT THEM BEGIN ON JANUARY 7, 1929!

INNOVATION: ILLUSTRATION VS. CARTOONING

BEFITTING THEIR NON-COMEDIC SUBJECT MATTER, THESE NEW "ADVENTURE" STRIPS ALSO FEATURED A MORE REALISTIC ILLUSTRATION STYLE OF DRAWING (FROM RICHARD CALKINS AND HAL FOSTER, RESPECTIVELY)...
...INFLUENCED BY PULP ARTISTS SUCH AS GERNSBACK'S BEST, A FORMER ARCHITECT NAMED FRANK R. PAUL.
VS.

JACK WOULD LATER SAY THAT HE BECAME AN ARTIST INSTEAD OF A WRITER BECAUSE HE COULDN'T SPELL!
INSPIRED BY PAUL-ILLUSTRATED PULPS AND THE ADVENTURE STRIPS THAT SPAWNED FROM THEM, HE BEGAN DRAWING EVERYWHERE!

JACK'S PARENTS ENCOURAGED HIS ARTISTIC PURSUITS AS AN ALTERNATIVE TO THE ENDEMIC STREET GANGS IN THE LOWER EAST SIDE. THE JEWS FOUGHT THE IRISH--JEWS FROM DIFFERENT BLOCKS FOUGHT EACH OTHER!
THE BOYS USED ANYTHING HANDY AS A WEAPON IN THESE VICIOUS BRAWLS -- INCLUDING CORN ON THE COB STOLEN FROM STREET VENDORS!

VIOLENCE WAS SUCH A PART OF JACK'S EARLY LIFE THAT HE LATER CLAIMED HE WOULD TAKE THE SUBWAY TO DIFFERENT NEIGHBORHOODS AND PICK FIGHTS JUST TO SEE WHAT OTHER KIDS' COMBAT STYLES WERE LIKE!
HMMM...YOUR UPPERCUT IS BETTER THAN THE KIDS IN BROWNSVILLE... BUT YOUR ROUNDHOUSE NEEDS WORK! I'D SUGGEST SPENDING TIME IN THE SOUTH BRONX!
OVERALL, I RATE FOREST HILLS A "6.5"!

THE KURTZBERGS ENROLLED JACK IN ART CLASSES AT THE LEGENDARY EDUCATIONAL ALLIANCE, A FREE SCHOOL THAT WOULD ALSO TRAIN PAINTERS BEN SHAHN AND MARK ROTHKO!
UNFORTUNATELY, IN HIS FIRST CLASS HE USED UP ALL THE CHALK BEFORE THE OTHER STUDENTS HAD A CHANCE TO DRAW!

THOUGH JACK'S ASTOUNDING SPEED WOULD LATER MAKE HIM A LEGEND...
...IT GOT HIM KICKED OUT OF THE EDUCATIONAL ALLIANCE!

MEANWHILE, IN CLEVELAND...
...ANOTHER GERNSBACK DEVOTEE, GRADUATING SENIOR JERRY SIEGEL, PEDDLED HIS HOMEMADE, TYPED-UP PULP MAGAZINE.

IN 1929, SIEGEL PRODUCED WHAT HISTORIANS BELIEVE TO BE THE FIRST "FAN MAGAZINE," OR "FANZINE"...
SCIENCE FICTION
The Advance Guard of Future Civilization

...BUT BEYOND TRADING IT VIA MAIL WITH OTHER GERNSBACKIANS SCATTERED ACROSS THE COUNTRY, NOTHING MUCH CAME OF IT.

SF'S *THIRD* ISSUE CONTAINED A SIEGEL STORY ENTITLED ***"REIGN OF THE SUPERMAN"*** THAT HAD BEEN HEAVILY INFLUENCED BY PHILIP WYLIE'S 1930 ALLEGORICAL NOVEL *GLADIATOR*.

THOUGH NOT REALLY *PULP* (WYLIE WAS AN EDITOR AT THE *NEW YORKER*), *GLADIATOR* TELLS THE LIFE STORY OF A MAN FROM AN ISOLATED *FARM* COMMUNITY WHO IS INJECTED IN THE WOMB BY HIS SCIENTIST FATHER WITH A SERUM THAT GIVES HIM THE PROPORTIONATE STRENGTH OF AN *INSECT*.*

BULLETS BOUNCE *OFF* HIM, HE CAN OUTRUN *TRAINS*, HE CAN LEAP OVER ***BUILDINGS***.

*: YES, *REALLY*.

AS A BOY, HIS PARENTS ENCOURAGE HIM TO PRETEND TO BE ***MEEK*** SO REGULAR PEOPLE WON'T BE SCARED OF HIS ***STRENGTH*** -- SO HE BUILDS A ***FORTRESS*** IN THE WOODS WHERE HE CAN FIND SOME ***SOLITUDE*** AND BE HIMSELF.

SCIENCE FICTION WAS ENTIRELY WRITTEN BY SIEGEL UNDER VARIOUS PSEUDONYMS AND ILLUSTRATED BY CLASSMATE ***JOE SHUSTER***, A SHY, NEARSIGHTED, BODYBUILDING-OBSESSED TRANSPLANT FROM ***TORONTO*** HE HAD MET WHILE WORKING ON THE SCHOOL ***NEWSPAPER***.

IN *SIEGEL'S* "REIGN OF THE SUPERMAN," A HOMELESS MAN RECRUITED FROM A *BREADLINE* IS SUBJECTED TO A BIO-PERFECTION PROCESS, THEN USES HIS VAST *PSYCHIC* POWERS FOR *WORLD DOMINATION.*

THE NATIONS OF THE GLOBE TRY TO UNITE *AGAINST* HIM, BUT THE SUPERMAN BROADCASTS *"THOUGHTS OF HATE"* TO MAKE THEM TURN ON *EACH OTHER!*

THE SUPERMAN GETS *SO* OUT OF HAND THAT *GOD HIMSELF* FINALLY HAS TO TAKE HIM OUT.

NOW IF YOU'D JUST LISTENED TO *ME* THAT GOD WAS *DEAD*, YOU WOULDN'T BE *IN* THIS MESS!

OBVIOUSLY *THIS* "SUPERMAN" WAS HEAVILY INFLUENCED BY HIS *NAMESAKE*, THE SUPERIOR BEING ("ÜBERMENSCH") IN THE PHILOSOPHY OF GERMANY'S *FRIEDRICH NIETZSCHE*.

SOON EVEN THE INEXPENSIVE *PULPS* BEGAN TO FEEL THE PINCH OF THE *DEPRESSION.* LESSER FIRMS WENT OUT OF BUSINESS ... THOSE THAT REMAINED SLASHED *TITLES!*

BREAD FOR THE POOR

"REIGN OF THE SUPERMAN" AND SIEGEL'S OTHER SCIENCE FICTION STORIES EARNED HIM NOTHING BUT REJECTION SLIPS FROM THE STRUGGLING PULPS.
WHILE IN THE LOWER EAST SIDE, BEN, PATRIARCH OF THE KURTZBERG CLAN, GOT LAID OFF FROM HIS JOB IN THE IMMIGRANT "RAG TRADE!"
I KNOW YOU'RE SUPPOSED TO START PRATT IN THE FALL, JACK...
...BUT NOW YOU GOT TO GET A JOB AND HELP SUPPORT THE FAMILY. I'M SORRY.

FORTUNATELY, HOWEVER, THE KURTZBERGS' EARLY NURTURING OF JACK'S ARTISTIC SKILLS PAID OFF. HE QUICKLY LANDED A JOB THAT COULD SUPPORT THE WHOLE FAMILY...
...AT TIMES SQUARE'S FLEISCHER STUDIOS!

TOON FEUD

AS THE **SOUND ERA** IN MOTION PICTURES WAS DAWNING, THE FIELD OF THE **ANIMATED SHORT FILM** WAS AN INTENSELY COMPETITIVE **WAR OF ATTRITION** IN WHICH TWO CREATIVE TITANS, **MAX FLEISCHER** AND **WALT DISNEY**, PLAYED THE ROLES OF **OPPOSING GENERALS**.

HA HA
HA HA
HA HA
HA HA

MANHATTAN-BASED **FLEISCHER STUDIOS** HAD **DOMINATED** THE SILENT ERA WITH ITS GOOFY, BLACK-AND-WHITE SLAPSTICKS AND DECIDEDLY IMMIGRANT, **URBAN** HUMOR...

TOOT! TOOT!
IT'S MAKIN' NOISES!!

...BUT DISNEY'S **HOLLYWOOD** STUDIO HAD MADE THE FIRST POPULAR **SOUND** CARTOON, **"STEAMBOAT WILLIE,"** WHICH CATAPULTED **MICKEY MOUSE** TO SUPERSTARDOM.

AW, YEAH! MESS BLUTO UP!!

MAX **STRUCK BACK** BY SECURING, THROUGH HEARST'S **KING** SYNDICATE, THE FILM RIGHTS TO ELZIE SEGAR'S COMIC STRIP *THIMBLE THEATRE*, STARRING **POPEYE THE SAILOR**. THE CARTOONS WERE A SMASH HIT, DUE IN NO SMALL PART TO THE FLEISCHER BROTHERS' BIZARRE HOOK THAT POPEYE GAINED **SUPER-STRENGTH** WHEN HE ATE **SPINACH**.

OOOH! TCHAIKOVSKY!

BY THE MID-1930s POPEYE HAD PUT A SIGNIFICANT **DENT** IN MICKEY'S POPULARITY, BUT DISNEY OUT-INNOVATED MAX **AGAIN**, SECURING EXCLUSIVE RIGHTS TO A THREE-COLOR **TECHNICOLOR** PROCESS THAT HE SHOWCASED IN HIS SUMPTUOUS **"SILLY SYMPHONIES"** SERIES.

THOUGH THIS STRUGGLE APPEARS AT FIRST GLANCE TO LEND ITSELF TO ***EASY STEREOTYPES:*** JEW VS. GOY ... IMMIGRANT VS. ***NATIVE*** ... GRITTY ***EAST*** COAST VS. SUNNY ***WEST*** ... THERE WAS A NOT-INSIGNIFICANT ***DIFFERENCE***:

AUSTRIAN IMMIGRANT MAX HAILED FROM A DECIDEDLY MIDDLE-CLASS BACKGROUND. HIS FATHER OWNED AN NYC TAILOR SHOP THAT SPECIALIZED IN WOMEN'S RIDING HABITS. HE BOASTED ROCKEFELLERS, VANDERBILTS AND ASTORS AMONG HIS CLIENTS!

BUT NATIVE MIDWESTERNER DISNEY SUFFERED THROUGH A CHILDHOOD ALMOST DICKENSIAN IN ITS POVERTY. THE FAMILY FOLLOWED HIS FATHER FROM STATE TO STATE IN ONE FAILED BUSINESS VENTURE AFTER ANOTHER.
IN KANSAS CITY, WALT WORKED AS A DELIVERY BOY FOR HIS DAD'S PAPER ROUTE.
SUCCUMBING AT TIMES TO THE GRUELING HOURS HE WOULD PASS OUT IN CHIN-HIGH SNOWDRIFTS DURING THE PUNISHING MISSOURI WINTERS!

LIKE MANY WHO ESCAPE CRUSHING POVERTY, DISNEY WAS FILLED WITH AN INDOMITABLE DRIVE TO SUCCEED AT ALL COSTS -- AND TO KEEP FIRM CONTROL OF HIS OWN DESTINY WHILE DOING SO.
WHEN HE COULDN'T FIND SOUND FIRMS UP TO HIS STANDARDS, HE FOUNDED HIS OWN RECORDING STUDIO!
WHEN HE FELT HIS STAFF'S ARTISTIC SKILLS WEREN'T UP TO SNUFF, HE PAID FOR DRAWING INSTRUCTORS TO COME TEACH THEM FOR FREE ON STUDIO PROPERTY!
(PART OF HIS LEGACY IS LA'S WALT DISNEY CONCERT HALL!)
(DISNEY ALSO FUNDED THE CALIFORNIA INSTITUTE OF THE ARTS IN HIS WILL!)

THOUGH DISNEY KEPT SCORING POPULAR AND CRITICAL SUCCESSES WITH SHORTS LIKE "THE THREE LITTLE PIGS" (ITS THEME, "WHO'S AFRAID OF THE BIG, BAD WOLF?" BECAME AN ANTI-DEPRESSION ANTHEM), HE SPENT SO MUCH MONEY PERFECTING HIS FILMS THAT THE STUDIO FAILED TO BREAK EVEN.
BILL
DISNEY STUDIOS

NOT UNAWARE OF WALT'S MONEY TROUBLES, MAX BELIEVED HIS CHEAPER, MORE COST-CONSCIOUS WAY OF PRODUCING CARTOONS WOULD ULTIMATELY SEAL FLEISCHER STUDIOS' VICTORY. HE LIKED TO SAY:
"YOU CAN'T EAT MEDALS!"
VARIETY
DISNEY=GOD?

FLEISCHER STUDIOS OCCUPIED FOUR FLOORS OF 1600 BROADWAY AND EMPLOYED ABOUT 250 PEOPLE. ONE OF THE YOUNGEST WAS OUR HERO, JACK KURTZBERG.
IN OUT

ANY ILLUSIONS JACK MIGHT HAVE HAD ABOUT THE GLAMOUR OF CREATING CINEMATIC MAGIC WERE QUICKLY DISPELLED.
THE FLEISCHERS IMPOSED A STRICT HIERARCHY ON THEIR ARTISTS IN WHAT WAS KNOWN AS THE "HEAD ANIMATOR" SYSTEM.

THE FORMER KOKO, MAX'S BROTHER DAVE, A FLEISCHER PRODUCER, WOULD GIVE A ROUGH PLOT TO THE HEAD ANIMATOR, WHO WOULD BREAK IT INTO SCENES.

EXPERIENCED ANIMATORS DREW THE CRUCIAL, OR "KEY" POSES IN ANY GIVEN SCENE...

...WHILE APPRENTICE ARTISTS CALLED "IN-BETWEENERS" DREW ALL THE FIGURES THAT LED UP TO -- THEN AWAY FROM -- THE KEY POSES.

JACK WAS AN IN-BETWEENER. ALL HE DREW WAS MOVEMENT.
"I HATED IT," HE REMEMBERED. "IT REMINDED ME OF THE SWEATSHOPS WHERE MY FATHER WORKED."
BUT HIS $15-A-WEEK PAYCHECK WAS TOO CRITICAL TO HIS FAMILY'S SURVIVAL TO EVEN CONTEMPLATE QUITTING!

THE FLUID, ANARCHIC COMBAT OF A POPEYE CARTOON WAS PRODUCED IN A RIGID, TEDIOUS PROCESS BY HUNDREDS OF LOW-WAGE WORKERS.
"THE SUPER-STRENGTH AND ACTION (ARE) ABSOLUTELY SENSATIONAL! THIS IS REALLY GREAT, BUT...

"...WHAT IF IT FEATURED A STRAIGHT ADVENTURE CHARACTER?"
WHILE FLEISCHER POPEYES INSPIRED JERRY SIEGEL TO CONSIDER NEW FORMS OF DRAWN VIOLENCE IN CLEVELAND...

...IN NEW YORK A REAL-LIFE LABOR BATTLE COMMENCED! IN 1937 OVER 100 FLEISCHER EMPLOYEES JOINED THE COMMERCIAL ARTISTS' AND DESIGNERS' UNION. MAX SAW THEIR DEMANDS (PAID SICK LEAVE & VACATIONS, REDUCING THE 45-HOUR WORK WEEK) AS AN UNFORGIVEABLE BETRAYAL!
HE REFUSED TO RECOGNIZE THE CADU AND FIRED FIFTEEN LABOR ORGANIZERS!

ON MAY 7, THE REMAINING UNIONISTS DECLARED A STRIKE AND BLOCKED THE STUDIO ENTRANCE!
"I'M POPEYE THE UNION MAN..."
I MAKE MILLIONS LAUGH BUT THE REAL JOKE IS OUR SALARIES
CAN'T GET MUCH SPINACH FOR $15/WEEK

WHEN NON-UNION ANIMATORS TRIED TO CROSS THE PICKET LINES AND ENTER THE STUDIO A FIGHT BROKE OUT.
THE NYPD TRIED TO MOVE THE LINES BACK, THEN THINGS REALLY GOT UGLY. TWO THOUSAND GAWKERS GATHERED TO CHEER ON THE ENSUING RIOT, WHICH ENDED ONLY WHEN TEN ARTISTS WERE HAULED OFF IN A PADDY WAGON.
THE NEWLY-CREATED NATIONAL LABOR RELATIONS BOARD HAD TO COME IN AND NEGOTIATE A SETTLEMENT, WHICH MAX RELUCTANTLY AGREED TO ON OCTOBER 13...

...JUST IN TIME TO ABSORB THE ***THUNDERING SHOCK*** THAT WAS WALT'S LATEST--AND MOST ***DECISIVE***--SALVO AGAINST HIS RIVALS; A PROJECT THAT HAD BEEN IN DEVELOPMENT FOR ***SO LONG*** (SINCE ***1933***) IT WAS DERIDED THROUGHOUT HOLLYWOOD AS ***"DISNEY'S FOLLY"***:

A ***FEATURE-LENGTH CARTOON*** ENTITLED *SNOW WHITE AND THE SEVEN DWARFS.*

NOTE: ALL ACTUAL REJECTED DWARF CONCEPTS FROM SNOW WHITE!
Jaunty
Tubby
Puffy
Chesty
Blabby
Dirty
Awful
Scrappy
Biggo Ego
Shorty

WALT'S DRIVE TOWARD PERFECTION ***INTENSIFIED*** DURING THE MAKING OF *SNOW WHITE.*
HE ***"CAST"*** ANIMATORS TO WORK ON CHARACTERS HE THOUGHT REFLECTIVE OF THEIR INDIVIDUAL ***PERSONALITIES***, FOR EXAMPLE.

WALT'S STAFF WAS UNDER SUCH INTENSE ***PRESSURE*** TO OUTDO THEMSELVES WITH THE ***REALISM*** OF THE ANIMATION...
...THAT, ***IRONY OF IRONIES***, THEY USED FLEISCHER'S ***ROTOSCOPE*** PROCESS IN SEVERAL KEY SCENES!

THE ARGUMENT ***AGAINST*** CARTOON FEATURES HAD ALWAYS BEEN THAT THEY WOULDN'T BE ABLE TO SUSTAIN AUDIENCE ***INTEREST***...

...BECAUSE THE PUBLIC WOULDN'T BE ABLE TO ***IDENTIFY*** WITH ***DRAWN*** CHARACTERS THE WAY THEY DO WITH ***LIVE ACTORS*** -- THEY COULDN'T FEEL ***REAL EMOTION*** FOR ***CARTOON PEOPLE*** AND THEIR DRAMATIC STRUGGLES!

?
?

WHEN SNOW WHITE OPENED ON DECEMBER 21, 1937, IT BLEW THAT MISCONCEPTION OUT OF THE WATER.
AT THE PREMIERE, THE AUDIENCE--WHICH INCLUDED SCREEN LEGENDS CLARK GABLE AND CAROLE LOMBARD--STARTED BAWLING DURING SNOW'S FUNERAL SCENE!

DISNEY'S DEIFICATION WAS COMPLETE.
CRITICS HAILED SNOW WHITE AS CINEMA'S MOST IMPORTANT ACHIEVEMENT SINCE GRIFFITH'S BIRTH OF A NATION.
THE DAILY WORKER PRAISED THE DWARVES AS A "MINIATURE COMMUNIST SOCIETY"!

IN WALT WE TRUST
MORE IMPORTANTLY, FROM THE POINT OF VIEW OF THE OTHER STUDIOS, SNOW WHITE BECAME HISTORY'S HIGHEST GROSSING FEATURE!*
* THOUGH GONE WITH THE WIND WOULD SURPASS IT IN 1940.

FLEISCHER STUDIOS' DISTRIBUTOR, PARAMOUNT, HAD ALWAYS RESISTED MAX'S PLEAS FOR A FEATURE-LENGTH CARTOON.
NOW, HOWEVER, STUDIO HEAD ADOLPH ZUKOR DEMANDED ONE!
TO QUICKLY CRANK OUT A FULL-LENGTH MOVIE, MAX WOULD HAVE TO TRIPLE HIS STAFF.
STILL SMARTING FROM THE STRIKE, HE DECIDED TO RELOCATE HIS STUDIO FROM LABOR-FRIENDLY NEW YORK...

...TO PRO-MANAGEMENT MIAMI, WHICH OFFERED MAX GENEROUS TAX INCENTIVES TO BUILD A $300,000 COMPLEX THERE. DESPITE HIS EARLIER MISGIVINGS, JACK CONSIDERED RELOCATING TO FLORIDA ALONG WITH A LOT OF THE OTHER EMPLOYEES...
...BUT HIS MOTHER REFUSED TO LET HIM GO.

ON MAY 27, 1938, THE MANHATTAN DOORS OF FLEISCHER STUDIOS CLOSED FOR GOOD, LEAVING SCORES OF CARTOONISTS LIKE JACK KURTZBERG OUT OF WORK...
...AWAITING A NEW MEDIUM TO SUPPORT THEM!
WILL SATIRIZE FOR FOOD

NEW ACTION FUN

FOR OVER ***THREE DECADES*** AMERICAN CHILDREN HAD BEEN THROWING OUT EVERY ***OTHER*** SECTION OF THE NEWSPAPER TO GET THEIR HANDS ON THE ***FUNNIES.***

BUT IT WASN'T UNTIL THE ***DEPRESSION*** THAT THE PUBLISHING INDUSTRY FINALLY FIGURED OUT THE ***BEST WAY*** TO CUT OUT THE ***REST*** OF THE PAPER AND OFFER A PERIODICAL THAT WAS NOTHING ***BUT*** FUNNIES DIRECTLY ***TO*** CHILDREN.

STYLE
WORLD
FUNNIES
SPORTS

IN 1929, GEORGE T. DELACORTE'S ***DELL PUBLISHING*** ATTEMPTED AN ALL-COMICS TITLE SIMPLY CALLED ***THE FUNNIES***, BUT IT WAS NEARLY AS ***BIG*** AS A SUNDAY COLOR SECTION AND LOOKED LIKE AN ***INCOMPLETE*** NEWSPAPER SITTING ALONE ON THE STANDS. ***THE FUNNIES'*** REWARD FOR CONFUSING THE CONSUMER WAS A SWIFT DEMISE.

THEN IN 1933 THE ***EASTERN COLOR PRINTING COMPANY*** OF WATERBURY, CONNECTICUT, WHICH PRODUCED MOST OF THE ***COLOR SUNDAY FUNNIES*** FOR THE BIG NORTHEAST PAPERS...

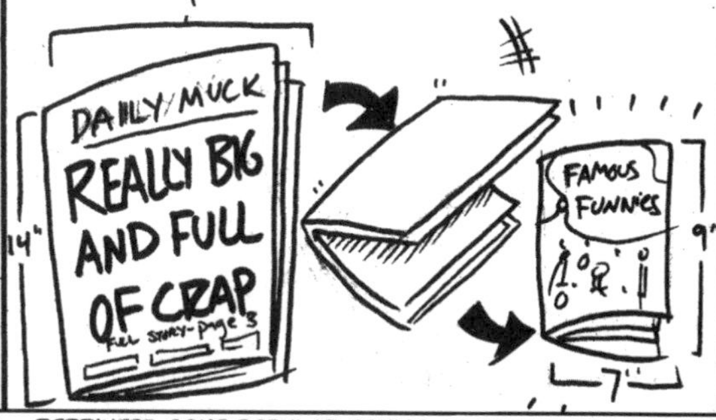
9"
DAILY MUCK
REALLY BIG AND FULL OF CRAP
FULL STORY-page 3
14"
FAMOUS FUNNIES
9"
7"

...REPRINTED SOME POPULAR COMICS AS BROADSIDES FOR THE *PHILADELPHIA LEDGER* THAT HAD BEEN SHOT DOWN TO 7"X9"... ROUGHLY THE SIZE OF A TABLOID NEWSPAPER ***FOLDED OVER.***

FISHER'S *MUTT & JEFF* HAD BEEN SELLING WELL IN COLLECTED ***"COMIC STRIP BOOKS"*** SINCE 1911 (AT STRIP ***DIMENSIONS*** -- THE BOOKS WERE ***18"*** WIDE), AND EASTERN WAS CURIOUS TO SEE IF AN ***ANTHOLOGY*** OF MULTIPLE STRIP REPRINTS MIGHT ***APPEAL*** IN A MORE ***MANAGEABLE*** SIZE CLOSER TO THE *LEDGER* BROADSIDES.

EASTERN SALESMAN ***MAXWELL C. "CHARLIE" GAINES*** CONVINCED ***PROCTER & GAMBLE*** TO USE THIS EXPERIMENTAL "COMIC BOOK," ***FUNNIES ON PARADE***, AS A MAIL-IN ***GIVEAWAY.***

ITS ***10,000-COPY*** PRINT RUN WAS EXHAUSTED IN A MATTER OF ***WEEKS.***

SOAP
SOAP
SOAP
SOAP

INTRIGUED, GAINES SLAPPED ***10-CENT*** STICKERS ON A COUPLE DOZEN INDIVIDUAL COPIES OF EASTERN'S ***SECOND*** GIVEAWAY, *FAMOUS FUNNIES: A CARNIVAL OF COMICS*, AND DROPPED THEM OFF AT VARIOUS ***NEWSSTANDS*** AROUND NEW YORK ONE FRIDAY.
NEWS

THEY ALL SOLD OUT BY THE FOLLOWING MONDAY!
NEWS
SOLD OUT!
SMELLING SALES, EASTERN TEAMED WITH DELACORTE'S DELL TO PRODUCE A REGULAR FAMOUS FUNNIES SERIES BEGINNING IN 1934. FISHER'S MUTT & JEFF WOULD GRACE THE COVER, MAKING THEM THE FIRST-EVER COMIC BOOK HEADLINERS!
M & J'S REPRINT RIGHTS, ALONG WITH THE RIGHTS TO ALL THE OTHER POPULAR COMICS IN THE COUNTRY, WERE, OF COURSE, STILL HELD IN THE HANDS OF THE ALL-POWERFUL SYNDICATES.
AFTER DELL AND EASTERN WENT THEIR SEPARATE WAYS, DELL BEGAN POPULAR COMICS, A SERIES FEATURING MOSTLY STRIPS OWNED BY THE CHICAGO TRIBUNE SYNDICATE (DICK TRACY, THE GUMPS, LITTLE ORPHAN ANNIE, ETC.)
HEY KIDS, COMICS!
HAH HAH! WHOOOO'S YOUR DADDY? WHO'S YOUR DADDY?
EYE IZ A PRIZ'NER
DELL, EASTERN AND OTHERS QUICKLY TIED UP THE COMIC BOOK RIGHTS TO ALL THE ESTABLISHED STRIPS!
BUT ONE MAN HAD THE COURAGE TO STAND AGAINST THE MIGHTY SYNDICATES--A CAVALRY OFFICER WHO HAD BRAVED THE FIRE OF PANCHO VILLA'S BANDITOS IN MEXICO--
--A MAN WHO HAD BEEN COURT-MARTIALED FOR DENOUNCING NEPOTISM IN THE U.S. MILITARY -- WHO LATER SURVIVED AN ASSASSINATION ATTEMPT FOR EXPOSING THE SAME!
THAT MAN WAS MAJOR MALCOLM WHEELER-NICHOLSON! PULP AUTHOR ...LOVER...PUBLISHER... WITNESS TO THE THE TREATY OF VERSAILLES...
...AND PERPETUALLY BROKE!
NICHOLSON FOUNDED NATIONAL ALLIED PUBLISHING TO APE FAMOUS FUNNIES' SUCCESS AND SAVE HIS FORTUNES.

BUT NICHOLSON MADE UP FOR WHAT HE LACKED IN CASH FLOW WITH CHUTZPAH:
WHO NEEDS ESTABLISHED STRIPS? I'LL BUY NEW, ORIGINAL PROPERTIES FOR MY COMIC BOOKS!
BUMPA-BUMPA-BUMPA-BUMPA-BAAAAAAAA!!!
C'MON, MEN! WHO'S WITH ME? CHARRRRGE!!
WELL, AT FIRST, PRETTY MUCH NOBODY WAS WITH HIM.
NICHOLSON TITLES LIKE NEW FUN AND NEW COMICS SHOWCASED CRUDE IMITATIONS OF NEWSPAPER STRIPS THAT WERE POORLY DRAWN AND POORLY WRITTEN...
OW. I'M DED.
...AND THE CREATORS WERE PAID PRETTY POORLY, TOO.
TWO OF NICHOLSON'S MORE PROMISING FREELANCERS WERE CLEVELAND'S OWN JERRY SIEGEL AND JOE SHUSTER.
DISCOVERING IN THE NASCENT WORLD OF ORIGINAL COMIC BOOK STORIES A LESS COMPETITIVE FIELD THAN THAT OF THE PULPS, THE WRITER/ARTIST TEAM BEGAN CRANKING OUT ADVENTURE STRIPS LIKE "HENRI DUVAL OF FRANCE, FAMED SOLDIER OF FORTUNE" FOR NICHOLSON.
NEVERTHELESS, THE BOYS' LOYALTY TO THEIR NEW MEDIUM ONLY WENT SO FAR.
FUN
THEIR REAL OPINION OF NICHOLSON'S PRODUCT IS DEMONSTRATED BEST BY THE FACT THAT THEY AVOIDED SELLING WHAT THEY FELT WAS THEIR BEST PROPERTY TO THE MAJOR.
THE INSPIRATION FOR IT, SIEGEL WOULD LATER SAY, CAME TO HIM IN THE MIDDLE OF THE NIGHT.
PERHAPS THE REVELATION WAS AS SIMPLE AS THAT HE COULD ACHIEVE FLEISCHER-STYLE CARTOON VIOLENCE IN A MORE REALISTIC SETTING...
...WITH A PROTAGONIST WHO, LIKE WYLIE'S GLADIATOR, GAINED A POPEYE-ESQUE SUPER-PHYSIOGNOMY NOT THROUGH SPINACH, BUT SCIENCE FICTION -- PERHAPS A DISPLACED ALIEN LIKE EDGAR RICE BURROUGHS' OTHER PULP HIT, "JOHN CARTER OF MARS."
SIEGEL CLEVERLY MERGED THIS FORMULATION WITH ANOTHER TROPE...

...INTRODUCED BY ANGLO-HUNGARIAN AUTHOR BARONESS ORCZY IN HER 1903 PLAY THE SCARLET PIMPERNEL.
THE MYSTERIOUS TITULAR FIGURE RESCUES ARISTOCRATS FROM THE FRENCH REVOLUTION'S GUILLOTINE, SPIRITING THEM TO SAFETY ACROSS THE ENGLISH CHANNEL WITH THE HELP OF HIS NETWORK OF SECRET AGENTS (COLLECTIVELY KNOWN AS "THE LEAGUE OF THE SCARLET PIMPERNEL").
HIS NOM DE GUERRE COMES FROM HIS SYMBOL --AN INNOCUOUS WILDFLOWER-- HE LEAVES IN NOTES TAUNTING THE REVOLUTIONARY AUTHORITIES.

NONE BUT HIS LEAGUE KNOWS THAT THE PIMPERNEL IS REALLY BRITISH ARISTOCRAT SIR PERCY BLAKENEY, WHO ADOPTS A FOPPISH, FRIVOLOUS PERSONA TO THROW PARISIAN PURSUERS OFF HIS SCENT.
"WE SEEK HIM HERE, WE SEEK HIM THERE, THOSE FRENCHIES SEEK HIM EVERYWHERE.
"IS HE IN HEAVEN? IS HE IN HELL?
"THAT DEMMED, ELUSIVE PIMPERNEL!"
THIS SEMINAL INSTANCE OF A "SECRET IDENTITY" IN LITERATURE SPAWNED NUMEROUS IMITATORS...

...NOTABLY PULP WRITER JOHNSTON MCCULLEY, WHO, UPON MOVING TO THE LOS ANGELES AREA, BECAME FASCINATED BY SPANISH ADOBE RUINS NEAR HIS HOME.
"THEY ARE SAYING THAT SR. ZORRO HAS PAID A VISIT HERE... CAN YOU NOT TELL ME?
"BUT I PRAY YOU MAKE NOT THE TALE TOO BLOODY. I CANNOT SEE WHY MEN MUST BE VIOLENT!"
HIS 1919 NOVELLA THE CURSE OF CAPISTRANO (ORIGINALLY SERIALIZED, LIKE TARZAN, IN MUNSEY'S ALL-STORY) INTRODUCES THE BLAKENEY-ESQUE DON DIEGO VEGA, A SPANISH NOBLEMAN IN 1810'S CALIFORNIA THAT APPEARS TO BE A COWARDLY DANDY.

BUT MCCULLEY PUT AN AMERICAN SPIN ON THE PIMPERNEL'S CLASS ALLEGIANCES: VEGA'S ALTER EGO, ZORRO ("FOX" IN SPANISH), IS A SAVIOR OF THE PEOPLE, FOILING THE EVIL SCHEMES OF THE CORRUPT COLONIAL ESTABLISHMENT.
SILENT MOVIE STAR DOUGLAS FAIRBANKS SAW CAPISTRANO AS THE PERFECT VEHICLE FOR HIS SIGNATURE ACROBATIC DERRING-DO: CO-WRITING THE ADAPTATION HIMSELF, FAIRBANKS STARRED IN THE 1920 BOX OFFICE SMASH THE MARK OF ZORRO.
IT WAS FAIRBANKS WHO INTRODUCED SUCH VISUAL ELEMENTS TO THE ZORRO MYTHOS AS HIS DISTINCTIVE COSTUME AND THE INITIAL HE CARVES AS HIS CALLING CARD.

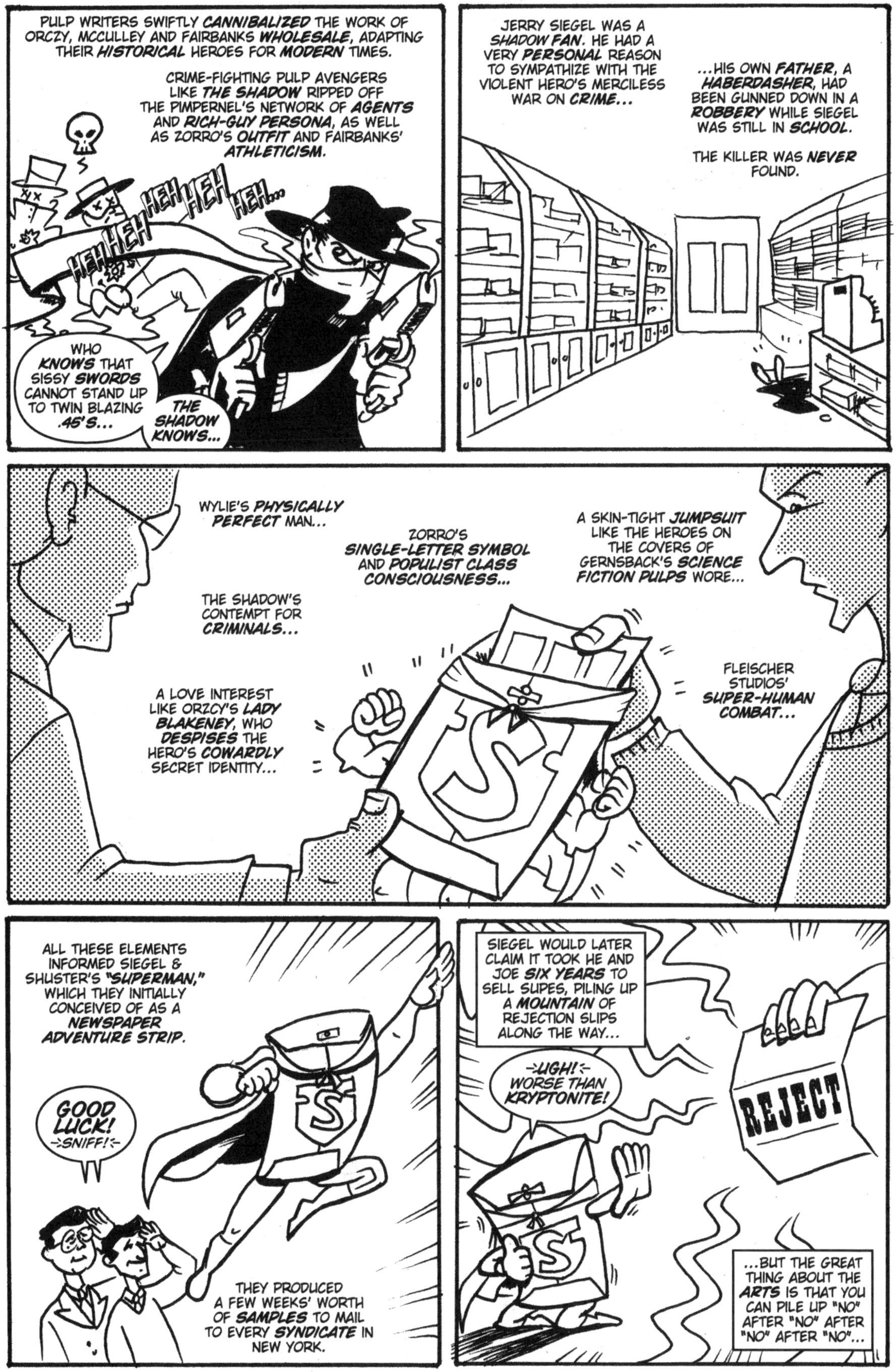

PULP WRITERS SWIFTLY **CANNIBALIZED** THE WORK OF ORCZY, MCCULLEY AND FAIRBANKS **WHOLESALE**, ADAPTING THEIR **HISTORICAL** HEROES FOR **MODERN** TIMES.

CRIME-FIGHTING PULP AVENGERS LIKE **THE SHADOW** RIPPED OFF THE PIMPERNEL'S NETWORK OF **AGENTS** AND **RICH-GUY PERSONA**, AS WELL AS ZORRO'S **OUTFIT** AND FAIRBANKS' **ATHLETICISM**.

HEH HEH HEH HEH HEH...

WHO **KNOWS** THAT SISSY **SWORDS** CANNOT STAND UP TO TWIN BLAZING **.45'S...**

THE SHADOW KNOWS...

JERRY SIEGEL WAS A **SHADOW FAN**. HE HAD A VERY **PERSONAL** REASON TO SYMPATHIZE WITH THE VIOLENT HERO'S MERCILESS WAR ON **CRIME...**

...HIS OWN **FATHER**, A **HABERDASHER**, HAD BEEN GUNNED DOWN IN A **ROBBERY** WHILE SIEGEL WAS STILL IN **SCHOOL**.

THE KILLER WAS **NEVER** FOUND.

WYLIE'S **PHYSICALLY PERFECT** MAN...

THE SHADOW'S CONTEMPT FOR **CRIMINALS...**

A LOVE INTEREST LIKE ORZCY'S **LADY BLAKENEY**, WHO **DESPISES** THE HERO'S **COWARDLY** SECRET IDENTITY...

ZORRO'S **SINGLE-LETTER SYMBOL** AND **POPULIST CLASS CONSCIOUSNESS...**

A SKIN-TIGHT **JUMPSUIT** LIKE THE HEROES ON THE COVERS OF GERNSBACK'S **SCIENCE FICTION PULPS** WORE...

FLEISCHER STUDIOS' **SUPER-HUMAN COMBAT...**

ALL THESE ELEMENTS INFORMED SIEGEL & SHUSTER'S **"SUPERMAN,"** WHICH THEY INITIALLY CONCEIVED OF AS A **NEWSPAPER ADVENTURE STRIP**.

GOOD LUCK! -SNIFF!-

THEY PRODUCED A FEW WEEKS' WORTH OF **SAMPLES** TO MAIL TO EVERY **SYNDICATE** IN NEW YORK.

SIEGEL WOULD LATER CLAIM IT TOOK HE AND JOE **SIX YEARS** TO SELL SUPES, PILING UP A **MOUNTAIN** OF REJECTION SLIPS ALONG THE WAY...

-**UGH!**- **WORSE THAN KRYPTONITE!**

REJECT

...BUT THE GREAT THING ABOUT THE **ARTS** IS THAT YOU CAN PILE UP "NO" AFTER "NO" AFTER "NO" AFTER "NO"...

...'CAUSE ALL YOU REALLY NEED IS ONE "YES." SIEGEL & SHUSTER'S "YES" CAME FROM THE MCCLURE SYNDICATE, WHICH HAD BEEN FOUNDED BY NONE OTHER THAN MAXWELL C. GAINES TO PACKAGE COMIC BOOKS!
GEEZ, THIS IS REALLY OUT THERE... BUT NATIONAL WANTS STRIPS FOR THEIR NEW ACTION COMICS...
...AND THEY'LL BUY ANYTHING...

IRONICALLY, SIEGEL & SHUSTER WOUND UP AT THE ONE COMPANY THEY HAD BEEN TRYING TO AVOID!
THE GOOD NEWS, HOWEVER, WAS THAT NICHOLSON WAS SO IN DEBT TO INDEPENDENT NEWS, HIS DISTRIBUTOR, THAT HE HAD LOST CONTROL OF HIS COMPANY.
CARTOONIST BOB KANE -- ANOTHER FLEISCHER VETERAN -- FOUND THIS OUT THE HARD WAY WHEN HE SHOWED UP TO COLLECT $300 THE MAJOR OWED HIM!
UH...
...HELLO?

THE BAD NEWS WAS THAT THE NEW OWNERS OF NATIONAL, INDEPENDENT NEWS'S HARRY DONENFELD AND JACK LIEBOWITZ, WERE NOT THRILLED TO HEAR THEIR EDITOR HAD AGREED TO PUBLISH "SUPERMAN" IN COMIC BOOK FORM.
WHAT IS THIS GARBAGE?!
ACTION COMICS

No. 1
ACTION COMICS
A MAN THROWING A CAR AROUND LIKE IT'S A TOY?! WE'LL BE LAUGHING STOCKS!
I NEVER WANT TO SEE THIS "SUPERMAN" ON THE COVER OF ACTION COMICS AGAIN!

EVEN THOUGH ACTION COMICS #1 PROMPTLY SOLD OUT, THE MAN OF STEEL DID NOT RETURN TO THE COVER UNTIL #7.
BY THAT TIME, ACTION WAS SELLING MORE THAN DOUBLE THE AVERAGE COMIC BOOK TITLE!
!

NATIONAL FINALLY FIGURED OUT THAT KIDS WEREN'T GOING TO THE NEWSSTAND ASKING FOR ACTION COMICS. THEY WERE DEMANDING...
NEWS
SUPERMAN!
SUPERMAN!!
SUPERMAN!!!

SUPES' ***METEORIC RISE*** TOOK THE PUBLISHING INDUSTRY SO THOROUGHLY BY ***SURPRISE*** IT WOULD TAKE ALMOST A ***FULL YEAR*** FOR IMITATORS TO BEGIN SPRINGING UP IN EARNEST...

...WITH ONE NOTABLE EXCEPTION...
STAFF ARTIST AND ART DIRECTOR WANTED for major comic book company. Contact Mr. Roberts, 480 Lexington Ave., NYC.
HMMM...
SINCE LEAVING FLEISCHER STUDIOS, JACK KURTZBERG HAD BEEN FREELANCING AS A CARTOONIST FOR VARIOUS SMALL SYNDICATES AROUND THE CITY.

FOR HIS FAMILY'S SAKE, THOUGH, HE WAS LOOKING FOR THE STABILITY OF A FULL-TIME JOB LIKE HE HAD HAD AT FLEISCHER.
AND THIS ADDRESS WAS THE SAME AS NATIONAL, PUBLISHERS OF SUPERMAN!

OF COURSE, MAYBE JACK DIDN'T NOTICE HE WAS BEING DIRECTED TO A FLOOR DIFFERENT FROM NATIONAL'S...
H-HELLO...
...ARE YOU MR. ROBERTS?

THE NAME'S FOX, SERGEANT. VICTOR FOX. "I'M THE KING OF THE COMICS!
"THIS MAY BE A KIDS' FIELD, BUT WE'RE NOT PLAYING SCHOOL HERE WITH CHALK ON A BLACKBOARD.
"I'VE GOT MILLIONS OF DOLLARS TIED UP IN THIS INDUSTRY. NOW WHAT MAKES YOU THINK YOU CAN HANDLE THIS JOB, PROTECT MY INVESTMENTS?"

INDUSTRY LEGEND HAD IT THAT FOX HAD BEEN A WALL STREET HIGH ROLLER, RUINED IN THE MARKET CRASH.
HE WAS REDUCED TO TAKING THE LOWLY JOB OF NATIONAL'S ACCOUNTANT.

HE REALIZED BEFORE LIEBOWITZ OR DONENFELD -- OR EVEN SIEGEL & SHUSTER -- WHAT A MEGA-HIT SUPERMAN WAS!
HE PROMPTLY QUIT HIS JOB, ROUNDED UP BACKERS, AND RENTED OFFICE SPACE IN THE SAME BUILDING AS HIS EX-EMPLOYERS!
!

FOX HIRED UNIVERSAL PHOENIX FEATURE SYNDICATE, A TINY PACKAGER FOUNDED BY WUNDERKIND WILL EISNER, TO PRODUCE HIS FIRST SUPER HERO "CREATION"...
..."WONDERMAN"? AREN'T WE...UH...
...GONNA GET SUED FOR THIS?
WHO'S WRITIN' THE CHECKS, SERGEANT?!
WONDER MAN

WHEN NATIONAL PREDICTABLY SLAPPED A LAWSUIT ON FOX, HE TOLD EISNER THAT UNIVERSAL PHOENIX WOULD NEVER RECEIVE THE $3,000 HE OWED THEM UNLESS EISNER LIED ON THE STAND AND CLAIMED WONDERMAN WAS HIS IDEA.
Cease&Desist

EISNER INSTEAD TESTIFIED TRUTHFULLY. NATIONAL WON; WONDERMAN WAS NO MORE. FOX SWORE REVENGE BY HIRING EISNER'S ARTISTS AWAY FROM HIM.
HE TOOK OUT THE AD AS "MR. ROBERTS" SO EISNER WOULDN'T CATCH ON, HOPING TO LAND ONE OF THE PHOENIX ARTISTS HE ADMIRED...

..."WILLIS B. RENSIE," "W. MORGAN THOMAS," "ERWIN WILLIS"...NOT REALIZING THESE WERE ALL PSEUDONYMS FOR EISNER HIMSELF, USED TO MAKE HIS SHOP LOOK BIGGER THAN IT WAS!
PHONY EDITORS TRYING TO HIRE FAKE ARTISTS...
...WELCOME TO THE COMIC BOOK INDUSTRY!

JACK HAD BRIEFLY FREELANCED FOR UNIVERSAL PHOENIX IN 1938.
SO! YOU'RE ONE OF BILLY EISNER'S BOYS, HUH?
NOT ANY-MORE! YOU'RE HIRED!

JACK'S DUTIES AT FOX FEATURE SYNDICATE INCLUDED SUCH HIGHLY CREATIVE TASKS AS ERASING PENCIL LINES OFF INKED ART, PASTING UP HOUSE ADS AND ADDING THE PRICE TO COVER ART...
"I DON'T WANT NO REMBRANDTS; I WANT PRODUCTION!"
BACK IN THE SWEAT-SHOP! -GROAN!-
...SINCE FOX OUTSOURCED ALL HIS COMIC BOOK ARTWORK TO UNIVERSAL PHOENIX!

HOWEVER, EISNER LEFT THE COMPANY HE FOUNDED LATER IN 1939 WHEN HE WAS OFFERED THE OPPORTUNITY TO PRODUCE A SYNDICATED COMIC BOOK SUNDAY SUPPLEMENT FOR NEWSPAPERS SO THEY COULD CAPITALIZE ON THE SUPERMAN TREND.
UNIVERSAL PHOENIX
THAT SUPPLEMENT, THE SPIRIT, WOULD SET A NEW STANDARD FOR SOPHISTICATION IN THE MEDIUM AND CATAPULT EISNER TO LEGENDARY STATURE!
EISNER

EISNER HAD BEEN SERVING AS FOX'S DE FACTO EDITOR, REQUIRING "THE KING" TO HIRE A REPLACEMENT.
MEET YOUR NEW BOSS, SERGEANT: JOE SIMON! HE'S A COLLEGE BOY FROM SYRACUSE!
HE OUGHTA BRING SOME CLASS TO THIS PLACE!

SIMON IMPRESSED FOX WITH A GLOWING RECOMMENDATION ON THE STATIONARY OF THE SYRACUSE HERALD, WHERE HE SERVED AS A SPORTS CARTOONIST...
(...SIGNED, SIMON NEGLECTED TO MENTION, BY THE HERALD COPY BOY.)
UTILITY

THE BAMBOOZLED FOX ENTRUSTED SIMON WITH SHEPHERDING THE ADVENTURES OF FOX'S LESS ACTIONABLE SUPERMAN WANNABE, THE BLUE BEETLE, WHO AT LEAST HAD A PRACTICAL REASON FOR DONNING AN OUTLANDISH OUTFIT TO BEAT UP CRIMINALS...
IT'S GIULIANI TIME!
...HE WAS A COP IN HIS CIVILIAN IDENTITY, SO THAT MASK MUST HAVE HELPED CUT DOWN ON POLICE BRUTALITY COMPLAINTS.

THOUGH SIMON HAD A WEALTH OF EXPERIENCE IN SPORTS CARTOONING, WHICH RELIED HEAVILY ON PHOTO REFERENCE AND STOCK POSES, HE HAD ALMOST NO BACKGROUND IN THE CREATIVE ART OF COMICS STORYTELLING, WHICH REQUIRED THE ARTIST TO CONJURE COMPOSITIONS USING (MOSTLY) PURE IMAGINATION.
IT DIDN'T TAKE HIM LONG, HOWEVER, TO SEE THAT HIS STAFF ARTIST POSSESSED...
...UNIQUE GIFTS.

SIMON HAD BEEN DRAWING FOR OTHER COMIC BOOK PUBLISHERS ON THE SIDE, AND QUICKLY FOUND HIMSELF WITH MORE WORK THAN HE COULD HANDLE. BUT JACK KURTZBERG REMAINED AS SPEEDY AS EVER--THANKS, NO DOUBT, TO THE PHYSICAL CONFIDENCE HE HAD PICKED UP ON THE MEAN STREETS OF THE LOWER EAST SIDE!

WHAT NONSENSE IS THIS, SERGEANT?!?
BLUE BEETLE COMICS
WHICH... PARTICULAR NONSENSE ARE YOU REFERRING TO, MR. FOX?

I TOLD YOU I WANTED AN EXPLOSION ON THE THIRD PANEL OF EVERY FIRST PAGE!
I THOUGHT THAT WAS MORE OF A, UH, ROUGH GUIDE-LINE...
NO! SALES FIGURES DON'T LIE! WE GET A BUMP EVERY TIME WE PUT A BLOW-UP THERE!
Look out!
BOOM!

I KNOW WHAT I'M DOING, SERGEANT! I'M THE KING OF THE COMICS!!
SLAM!
I GOTTA GET OUT OF THIS NUTHOUSE!

C'MON, JACK! BETWEEN YOUR SPEED AND MY BUSINESS SENSE, WE'D MAKE A KILLING STRIKING OUT ON OUR OWN, FREELANCE!
NO WAY, JOE--YOU'RE NOT LIKE ME! I GOT A FAMILY TO SUPPORT!

MAYBE... MAYBE IF I COULD GET A SALARY JOB AT A BETTER RATE AT ANOTHER PUBLISHER...
YOU WORRY TOO MUCH! LET ME TAKE CARE OF IT.
THERE'S TOO MUCH MONEY IN THIS RACKET NOT TO TRY!

INNOVATION:
SUPER HEROES
INDEED, STARTING IN 1940, THE SUPERMAN IMITATORS PROLIFERATED FASTER THAN A SPEEDING BULLET. EVERY STRUGGLING PULP PUBLISHER AND STRIP ARTIST WANNABE ATTEMPTED TO STRIKE IT RICH COPYING SIEGEL & SHUSTER'S SUCCESS.
THAT YEAR SAW THE NUMBER OF NEW COMIC BOOK TITLES BALLOON TO 150 AND THE NUMBER OF NEW COMIC BOOK PUBLISHERS RISE BY SIXTEEN, DOUBLING 1939'S TOTAL.
WHATEVER YOU MAY THINK ABOUT THE INHERENT MERITS OF SUPER HEROES, WITHOUT A NEW GENRE UNIQUE TO THIS NEW MEDIUM, THE COMIC BOOK INDUSTRY SIMPLY COULD NOT HAVE HAD THE FINANCIAL WHEREWITHAL TO BREAK FREE OF DEPENDENCY ON THE SYNDICATES AND BECOME A CREATIVE FORCE ON ITS OWN.
TIGHTY
Whitey
JOE CONVINCED JACK TO RENT OUT AN OFFICE WITH HIM NOT FAR FROM FOX WHERE THEY COULD WORK ON FREELANCE PROJECTS ON THE SLY.
I KNOW IT'S NOT MUCH OF A HOME-AWAY-FROM-HOME...
...BUT I GUESS IT'LL HAVE TO DO, EH, KURTZBERG?
THE ONE YOU KNEW AS JACK KURTZBERG IS NO MORE.
I CAN'T LET FOX FIND OUT WHAT WE'RE DOING--HE'D CAN ME FOR SURE...

...SO SAY HELLO TO
JACK KIRBY!

JACK KIRBY

JACK ADMIRED TOUGH-GUY IRISH-AMERICAN MOVIE STARS LIKE **JAMES CAGNEY** AND **RONALD REAGAN**, AND "KIRBY" SOUNDED SUFFICIENTLY **GAELIC** (AND *NOT-JEWISH*).

AAHH!!
BRRING!
BRRING!
LEAP!

BRRING!
BRRING!

IS "JACK KIRBY" GOING TO ANSWER THE *PHONE*?
DON'T! IT MIGHT BE *FOX!*
BRRING!
BRRING!

AMERICA ♥'S COMICS
IN THE BEGINNING, NOBODY (EXCEPT, PERHAPS, SIEGEL & SHUSTER) WAS SURE THE SUPER HERO FAD WOULD LAST. SKITTISH PUBLISHERS FARMED OUT THE ACTUAL CREATION OF COMIC BOOK MATERIAL TO PACKAGERS KNOWN AS "SHOPS."
"ARTISTS SAT LUMPED IN CROWDED ROOMS, KNOCKING IT OUT FOR THE PAGE RATE," PULITZER PRIZE-WINNING CARTOONIST JULES FEIFFER WRITES OF A TYPICAL SHOP.
"PENCILING, INKING, LETTERING IN THE BALLOONS FOR $10.00 A PAGE, SOMETIMES LESS; WORKING FROM YELLOW TYPE SCRIPTS WHICH ON THE LEFT DESCRIBED THE ACTION, ON THE RIGHT GAVE THE DIALOGUE.
"THE WORK WAS RELENTLESS. SOME MEN WORKED IN BULLPENS DURING THE DAY; FREELANCED AT NIGHT."
BUT: "WE WERE A GENERATION. WE THOUGHT OF OURSELVES THE WAY THE MEN WHO BEGAN MOVIES MUST HAVE.
"WE WERE OUT TO BE SPLENDID--
"--SOMEHOW."

NEW COMIC BOOK PUBLISHERS AND THE SHOPS THAT ***SERVICED*** THEM SPRUNG UP LIKE ***MUSHROOMS*** ACROSS MANHATTAN!

P
H
T
F
a
2
N
S
1
Q
3
L
C
D
A
M

GOLDEN-AGE "SHOPS"			
1	**Eisner & Iger, a/k/a Universal Phoenix**	202 E. 44th St.	*Wonder Comics*
2	**Funnies, Inc.**	49 W. 45th St.	*Human Torch, Sub-Mariner*
3	**Harry "A" Chesler**	276 5th Ave.	*Daredevil, Catman*

GOLDEN AGE PUBLISHERS				
a	**Ace Magazines**	1940-1956	23 W. 47th St.	*Super-Mystery, Four Favorites*
A	**All-American Comics (Later E.C.)**	c. 1940-1956	225 Lafayette St.	*Green Lantern, Flash, Wonder Woman*
C	**Centaur Publishing**	1938-1942	220 5th Ave.	*Amazing Man, Amazing Mystery*
D	**Dell Publishing**	1936-1973	261 5th Ave.	*Walt Disney's Comics and Stories*
F	**Fawcett Publishing Co.**	1940-1953	1501 Broadway	*Captain Marvel, Whiz Comics*
H	**Harvey Comics**	1941-1994	67 W. 47th St.	*Green Hornet, Black Cat Comics*
L	**Lev Gleason Publications**	1939-1956	114 E. 32nd St.	*Crime Does Not Pay*
M	**M.L.J. Magazines (Later Archie)**	1939-	60 Hudson St.	*Pep Comics, Archie*
N	**National Peridocial Publications (Later D.C.)**	1935-	480 Lexington Ave.	*Superman, Batman*
P	**Prize Publications**	1940-1963	1790 Broadway	*Prize Comics, Frankenstein*
Q	**Quality Comics**	1939-1956	369 Lexington Ave.	*Blackhawks, Spirit*
S	**Street & Smith Publications**	1940-1949	122 E. 42nd St.	*Shadow, Doc Savage*
T	**Timely (Later Marvel)**	1939-	330 W. 42nd St	*Captain America, Marvel Mystery*

THE FLY-BY-NIGHT INDUSTRY TEEMED WITH WEIRDOS, GRIFTERS, ***HUSTLERS***.
SHOP VET ***GIL KANE*** REMEMBERS THAT THE JANITOR IN ONE PACKAGER WHERE HE WORKED WAS A ***PIMP*** WHO BROUGHT GIRLS UP TO THE STUDIO TO PLY THEIR TRADE!

ONE SHOP OWNER, HARRY "A" CHESLER, TOLD PEOPLE THAT THE ***"A"*** IN HIS NAME STOOD FOR ***"ANYTHING!"*** HE WOULD TEASE THE ARTISTS EVERY PAYDAY:
"WELL, HOW MUCH DO YOU ***NEED*** THIS WEEK?"

BUT THIS WAS STILL THE ***DEPRESSION***, SO THE ARTISTS, MOST BARELY OLDER THAN ***TEENAGERS***, MOST BORN OF IMMIGRANTS, ALMOST TO THE MAN ***JEWISH***, WERE HAPPY FOR THE WORK.
BULLPENS BRED ***FOXHOLE*** CAMARADERIE-- ***PRANKS*** ABOUNDED.
THEY'D SET AN ARTIST'S TURPENTINE-LOGGED RAG FOR BRUSHES ON ***FIRE*** -- OR THEY'D ENCIRCLE HIS DRAWING TABLE WITH RUBBER CEMENT, THEN SET ***THAT*** ON FIRE.

STILL: "NOBODY WAS ***PROUD*** OF BEING A COMIC BOOK ARTIST," ADMITS SHOP VET JOE KUBERT. "MATTER OF FACT, IT WAS A COUPLE OF STEPS ***BELOW*** DIGGING DITCHES."
SO WHAT DO YOU ***DO*** FOR A LIVING?
I'M A, UH--*COUGH!*-- ***COMMERCIAL ARTIST***...
KA-POW! COMIX

KUBERT:
"SYNDICATION WAS ***RECOGNIZED*** SUCCESS. IF YOU COULD GET TO DO A SYNDICATED STRIP, MY GOD, ***THAT*** WAS THE ANSWER."

PAY TO: JOE COMIX
DATE: July
BIG BUCK$!
$$$!
SIGNED: Sam Syndicate

EVEN THE ***ARTISTS*** THOUGHT OF COMIC BOOKS AS ***TEMPORARY!***

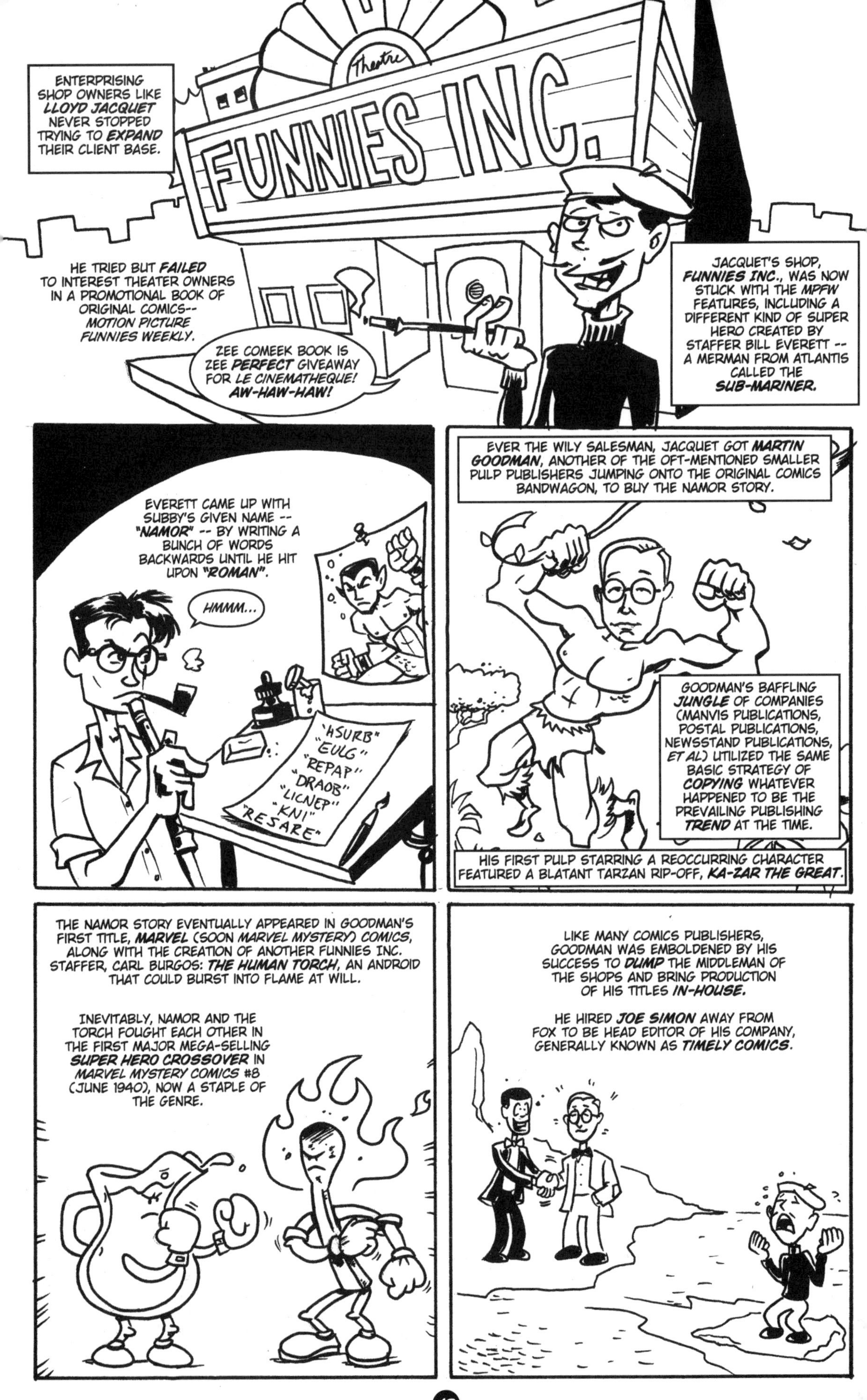

ENTERPRISING SHOP OWNERS LIKE LLOYD JACQUET NEVER STOPPED TRYING TO EXPAND THEIR CLIENT BASE.
Theatre
FUNNIES INC.
HE TRIED BUT FAILED TO INTEREST THEATER OWNERS IN A PROMOTIONAL BOOK OF ORIGINAL COMICS-- MOTION PICTURE FUNNIES WEEKLY.
ZEE COMEEK BOOK IS ZEE PERFECT GIVEAWAY FOR LE CINEMATHEQUE! AW-HAW-HAW!
JACQUET'S SHOP, FUNNIES INC., WAS NOW STUCK WITH THE MPFW FEATURES, INCLUDING A DIFFERENT KIND OF SUPER HERO CREATED BY STAFFER BILL EVERETT -- A MERMAN FROM ATLANTIS CALLED THE SUB-MARINER.
EVERETT CAME UP WITH SUBBY'S GIVEN NAME -- "NAMOR" -- BY WRITING A BUNCH OF WORDS BACKWARDS UNTIL HE HIT UPON "ROMAN".
HMMM...
"HSURB"
"EULG"
"REPAP"
"DRAOB"
"LICNEP"
"KNI"
"RESARE"
EVER THE WILY SALESMAN, JACQUET GOT MARTIN GOODMAN, ANOTHER OF THE OFT-MENTIONED SMALLER PULP PUBLISHERS JUMPING ONTO THE ORIGINAL COMICS BANDWAGON, TO BUY THE NAMOR STORY.
GOODMAN'S BAFFLING JUNGLE OF COMPANIES (MANVIS PUBLICATIONS, POSTAL PUBLICATIONS, NEWSSTAND PUBLICATIONS, ET AL) UTILIZED THE SAME BASIC STRATEGY OF COPYING WHATEVER HAPPENED TO BE THE PREVAILING PUBLISHING TREND AT THE TIME.
HIS FIRST PULP STARRING A REOCCURRING CHARACTER FEATURED A BLATANT TARZAN RIP-OFF, KA-ZAR THE GREAT.
THE NAMOR STORY EVENTUALLY APPEARED IN GOODMAN'S FIRST TITLE, MARVEL (SOON MARVEL MYSTERY) COMICS, ALONG WITH THE CREATION OF ANOTHER FUNNIES INC. STAFFER, CARL BURGOS: THE HUMAN TORCH, AN ANDROID THAT COULD BURST INTO FLAME AT WILL.
INEVITABLY, NAMOR AND THE TORCH FOUGHT EACH OTHER IN THE FIRST MAJOR MEGA-SELLING SUPER HERO CROSSOVER IN MARVEL MYSTERY COMICS #8 (JUNE 1940), NOW A STAPLE OF THE GENRE.
LIKE MANY COMICS PUBLISHERS, GOODMAN WAS EMBOLDENED BY HIS SUCCESS TO DUMP THE MIDDLEMAN OF THE SHOPS AND BRING PRODUCTION OF HIS TITLES IN-HOUSE.
HE HIRED JOE SIMON AWAY FROM FOX TO BE HEAD EDITOR OF HIS COMPANY, GENERALLY KNOWN AS TIMELY COMICS.

THE FIRST PROJECT SIMON BROUGHT TO GOODMAN WAS A PATRIOTIC SUPER HERO, "CAPTAIN AMERICA." HIS CREATION WAS UNIQUE FOR, AS SIMON SAID, "WE STARTED OFF WITH THE VILLAIN, AND BUILT THE SUPER HERO CHARACTER AROUND HIM."
IN 1940 THERE WAS NO GREATER REAL-LIFE VILLAIN THAN GERMAN DICTATOR ADOLF HITLER, WHOSE NAZI ARMIES HAD ALREADY CONQUERED HALF OF EUROPE.
EUROPE
THE COVER TO CAPTAIN AMERICA COMICS #1 WOULD BEAR THE MOST EXPLICITLY POLITICAL COVER OF ANY COMICS TITLE YET, DEPICTING ITS TITULAR HERO PUNCHING A FOREIGN HEAD OF STATE IN THE FACE!
GOODMAN LOVED THE IDEA AND WANTED TO RUSH CAP OUT AS SOON AS POSSIBLE, BECAUSE:
"THE BASTARD IS ALIVE AND IN THE CENTER OF A VERY EXPLOSIVE SITUATION! HE COULD GET KILLED--EVEN WHEN OUR BOOK IS ON THE PRESSES."
AND THAT COULD HURT SALES! GET CRACKING, SIMON!
THE DEADLINE MARTIN'S GIVEN US IS PRETTY RIDICULOUS. I THINK WE'RE GOING TO HAVE TO HIRE MORE ARTISTS.
AND CUT INTO MY PAGE RATE? NUTS TO THAT!
WHAT ARE YOU GONNA DO? DRAW ALL SIXTY-FOUR PAGES YOURSELF?!?
WATCH ME!
SIMON DID END UP HIRING ADDITIONAL ARTISTS, BUT HIS PARTNER, JACK KIRBY, DID MANAGE TO PENCIL THE BULK OF THE MATERIAL AT HIS USUAL BLINDING SPEED.
RUN FOR YOUR LIVES! HE'S GONNA BLOW!
"THE PRESSURE WAS TREMENDOUS," KIRBY WOULD RECALL. "I WAS PENCILING AT A BREAKNECK SPEED, AS MANY AS NINE PAGES A DAY.
"I GUESS THAT WAS THE REASON MY FIGURE-WORK BEGAN TO TAKE ON A DISTORTED LOOK.
"MY INSTINCTS TOLD ME THAT A FIGURE HAD TO BE EXTREME TO HAVE POWER."

INNOVATION:
THE KIRBY STYLE
"I FEEL THAT ACTION AND GRACEFUL MOVEMENT SYMBOLIZE BEAUTY AND LIFE!!
"ACROBATIC CHARACTERS ARE THE PERFECT INSTRUMENT TO CONVEY THIS!!"
KIRBY MANAGED TO FUSE TOGETHER THE TWO DOMINANT FORMS OF STORYTELLING ART IN AMERICA -- NEO-REALISTIC PULP ILLUSTRATION AND THE ABSTRACT CARICATURE OF NEWSPAPER STRIP CARTOONING!
THIS MIX OF NATURE AND FANTASY PROVED IDEAL FOR THE SUPER HERO GENRE!
CAPTAIN AMERICA COMICS #1 HIT THE STANDS ON DECEMBER 20, 1940, AND PROMPTLY SOLD OUT. SOON, CIRCULATION CLIMBED TO NEAR ONE MILLION COPIES -- DUE, IN NO SMALL PART, TO SIMON & KIRBY'S DYNAMIC LAYOUTS -- WHICH THEY EXPANDED INTO "SPLASH PAGES" (GIANT ONE-PAGE PANELS) ... AND EVEN TWO-PAGE PANORAMIC SPREADS!
BUT CAP'S SUCCESS HAD TO ALSO BE ATTRIBUTED TO THE SUPER HERO GENRE'S NEWLY PROVEN ABILITY TO ADDRESS READERS' CONTEMPORARY CONCERNS:

"WE WEREN'T AT WAR YET, BUT EVERYONE KNEW IT WAS COMING!!!
"THAT'S WHY CAPTAIN AMERICA WAS BORN -- AMERICA NEEDED A SUPERPATRIOT!"
WITH CAP'S SUCCESS, SUPER HEROES WERE INCREASINGLY DEPLOYED TO DO BATTLE WITH THE HATED AXIS POWERS OF GERMANY, ITALY, AND JAPAN ON THE COMICS PAGE!
IT'S NO COINCIDENCE WHAT'S COMMONLY KNOWN AS THE MEDIUM'S "GOLDEN AGE" COINCIDED WITH WORLD WAR II! DURING THIS TURBULENT AND VIOLENT TIME, SUPER HEROES THRIVED AND COMIC BOOK CIRCULATION TRIPLED!
(IT DIDN'T HURT THAT THE SUDDEN SPIKE IN THE DEFENSE INDUSTRY ENDED THE DEPRESSION, SO KIDS SUDDENLY HAD ALLOWANCE TO SPEND ON COMICS!)
Ryan Dunlavey 2008
BOMB Co.
NEWS
CANDY - COMIX
10¢
10¢
BOMB COMIX
INNOVATION:
SPLASHES & SPREADS

NOT EVERYBODY WAS THRILLED.

PICK OUT A LAMPPOST ON TIMES SQUARE, YOU !@$%! JEW!

WHEN HITLER COMES, WE'RE GONNA STRING YOU UP FROM IT!

~GULP!~

DEATH THREATS FROM NAZI SYMPATHIZERS PROMPTED NYC MAYOR FIORELLO LA GUARDIA TO INSTALL A POLICE DETAIL AROUND THE TIMELY OFFICES.

PHONE

NEVERTHELESS, SIMON FINALLY PERSUADED KIRBY TO LEAVE FOX AND JOIN HIM AT TIMELY. THEY WERE TWO OF THE FEW NON-GOODMAN RELATIVES EMPLOYED THERE.

THE YOUNGEST GOODMAN WAS MARTIN'S WIFE'S COUSIN, STANLEY LIEBER.

SOMETHING OF A HYPERACTIVE YOUTH, STANLEY WOULD DRIVE EVERYBODY CRAZY BY PLAYING HIS FLUTE IN THE OFFICE!

PROOFREADER, GOFER, ERASER OF PENCIL LINES FROM ART BOARDS AFTER THEY'D BEEN INKED...
...STANLEY WAS ALSO AN ASPIRING WRITER. SIMON ASSIGNED HIM TO PEN SOME OF THE BRIEF PROSE STORIES THAT QUALIFIED COMICS FOR A "MAGAZINE" POSTAL RATE.
UM ... IT ONLY HAS TO BE TWO PAGES LONG...

YOU WANT TO GO BY THE PEN NAME "STAN LEE," HUH?
THAT YOUR FIRST NAME SPLIT IN HALF OR THE FIRST HALVES OF YOUR FIRST AND LAST NAMES?
WHICHEVER SOUNDS BETTER, JOE!
by Stan Lee
IT SOUNDS CHINESE!

READERS WHO WANTED TO HELP SMASH THE ***NAZI MENACE*** COULD JOIN CAPTAIN AMERICA'S ***"SENTINELS OF LIBERTY"*** FAN CLUB.

THERE ARE ***STRANGE MOANS*** AND ***CREAKING NOISES*** COMING FROM MOM AND DAD'S ROOM!

MUST BE ***S.S. CODE!*** WE BETTER WARN ***CAP!***

THE LOW, LOW PRICE OF ONE, SHINY ***DIME*** LET KIDS ***"ENLIST NOW*** IN CAPTAIN AMERICA'S GREAT YOUNG ARMY OF ***SPY-FIGHTERS*** AND HELP FREE OUR COUNTRY OF ITS ***TRAITORS!"***

SIMON BECAME INCREASINGLY ***ANNOYED*** THAT HE AND KIRBY WEREN'T SEEING A ***PENNY*** FROM THOSE DIMES...

...MUCH LESS THE ***25% ROYALTY*** GOODMAN PROMISED S&K WHEN SIMON SOLD HIM CAP IN THE ***FIRST PLACE.***

AS YOU CAN ***SEE***, JOE, WITH SALARIES, OVERHEAD, OFFICE EXPENSES AND SUCH, WE HAVEN'T TURNED A ***PROFIT*** YET!

(THESE DAYS WE'D CALL THAT ***"HOLLYWOOD ACCOUNTING."***)

FED UP BY MID-1941, SIMON SECRETLY OFFERED S&K'S SERVICES TO ***NATIONAL***-- OR, AS IT WAS MORE COMMONLY KNOWN BY THEN, ***DC*** (THE INITIALS OF ONE OF ITS FIRST TITLES, *DETECTIVE COMICS*).

DONENFELD & CO. AGGRESSIVELY COURTED S&K. THEY FETED THEM AT A ***TIKI BAR*** WITH TRUE ***COMIC BOOK ROYALTY,*** SUPERMAN CO-CREATOR ***JERRY SIEGEL!***

I TRUST YOU'VE SEEN THE RECENT SPREAD ABOUT JOE SHUSTER AND ME IN THE SATURDAY EVENING POST... -SNIFF!-

SIEGEL & SHUSTER CONTINUED TO PRODUCE SUPERMAN COMICS FROM THEIR STUDIO IN *CLEVELAND*, WHERE THEY WERE *CELEBRITIES* AMONG THE LOCAL KIDS.
"AW, I *TOLD* YOU SUPERMAN DOESN'T LIVE HERE!"
"WELL, RIGHT NOW, HE'S ENGAGED ON ONE OF HIS MYSTERIOUS *MISSIONS*.
"BUT HE'S NOT FAR AWAY. HE OUGHT TO BE LANDING ON THE ROOF ANY *MINUTE!*"

SUPES STARRED IN A SMASH *RADIO SHOW*, HIS SYNDICATED COMIC STRIP RAN IN *230* PAPERS, HIS SOLO TITLE ALONE GROSSED *$950,000* A YEAR FOR D.C.
HE'S NOT *HERE* YET! -SIGH!-
THIS *SUCKS*.
LET'S GO THROW *ROCKS* AT *CARS!*

IN 1941, THE MAN OF STEEL BEGAN APPEARING IN A SERIES OF CARTOONS BEAUTIFULLY *ROTOSCOPED* BY MAX FLEISCHER FROM HIS NEW MIAMI STUDIOS.

THE SATURDAY EVENING POST PEGGED SIEGEL AND SHUSTER'S ANNUAL INCOME AT *$150,000*.

BUT...

...THE *POST ALSO* REPORTED, "THE *BUSINESSMEN* HAVE MADE AN EVEN BETTER THING OF SUPERMAN THAN HAVE HIS *AUTHORS*." IN THE ARTICLE, DONENFELD BOASTS HE MAKES OVER $500K *ANNUALLY* FROM SUPES *ALONE!*
THE SATURDAY EVENING POST
SUPERCHUMPS
JERRY... HAVE WE MADE A TERRIBLE, TERRIBLE *MISTAKE?*

SUPERMAN'S *MAINSTREAM SUCCESS* POINTED TOWARD COMIC BOOKS' GROWING *RESPECTABILITY*.
MISTER RESPECTABILITY, *WALT DISNEY*, EVEN ALLOWED HIS CREATIONS TO APPEAR IN FUNNY-BOOK FORM, ENTERING INTO A CONTRACT WITH GEORGE T. DELACORTE'S *DELL COMICS*.

WALT DISNEY'S COMICS & STORIES BEGAN IN OCTOBER 1940 AND -- PREDICTABLY -- ACHIEVED THE *HIGHEST CIRCULATION* OF ANY COMIC BOOK TITLE IN *HISTORY*.

SIMON & KIRBY CRAVED SOME OF THAT BIG, FAT SIEGEL & SHUSTER MONEY!
WE'RE STILL UNDER CONTRACT TO GOODMAN, SO WE'LL HAVE TO DEVELOP FEATURES FOR DC ON THE SLY!
THIS SEEMS VAGUELY FAMILIAR...
AS SOON AS DC AGREED TO PAY THEM $500 A WEEK, THE BOYS BEGAN WORKING ON NEW CONCEPTS IN A HOTEL ROOM DURING THEIR TIMELY LUNCH HOUR.

AFTER A FEW FALSE STARTS, S&K DELIVERED DC A HIT IN THE FORM OF BOY COMMANDOS. THIS NAKED WISH FULFILLMENT OF AN ALL-KID ALLIED FIGHTING UNIT SOLD ONE MILLION COPIES PER ISSUE AND WAS THE LAST BIG SUCCESS STORY OF THE GOLDEN AGE.
LOCK AND LOAD.
KA-CHIK!

BEFORE THAT, HOWEVER, S&K HAD TO DEAL WITH THEIR OWN BOY COMMANDO, WHO SOON FIGURED OUT:
"YOU GUYS MUST BE WORKING ON SOMETHING OF YOUR OWN!
"COME ON, I'M YOUR MAN! YOU GUYS NEED ME!"

SWORN TO STRICTEST SECRECY, STANLEY BEGAN GOFERING FOR THE CLANDESTINE S&K OPERATION AS WELL.

SOON ENOUGH, HOWEVER:
"YOU GUYS ARE SNEAKING BEHIND OUR BACKS, WORKING FOR SOMEONE ELSE! MARTIN IS FURIOUS!"
"YOU'LL FINISH THE (LATEST) ISSUE (OF CAPTAIN AMERICA)! THEN YOU'RE FIRED!"

C'MON, JACK, WE DON'T KNOW IT WAS STAN. THIS IS A SMALL INDUSTRY. LOTS OF PEOPLE COULD'VE RATTED ON US--
"THE NEXT TIME I SEE THAT LITTLE SON-OF-A-***** I'M GONNA KILL HIM!!"

BY *THAT* TIME, HOWEVER, ***WAR*** HAD FINALLY COME TO THE UNITED STATES... AND THE CREATORS OF *BOY COMMANDOS* WERE GOING INTO THE FIGHT ***THEMSELVES!***

Our Artists at War!

PERHAPS UNSURPRISINGLY, THE NAZIS WERE NOT BIG FANS OF AMERICAN COMICS.
IN 1940, THE SS NEWSPAPER DAS SCHWARZE KORPS DENOUNCED "THE INVENTIVE ISRAELITE" JERRY SIEGEL, DECLARING "THE DARING DEEDS OF SUPERMAN ARE THOSE OF A COLORADO BEETLE"...
...THEREBY COMPARING THE MAN OF STEEL TO AN INSIDIOUS CROP-DESTROYING PEST THAT THIRD REICH PROPAGANDA CLAIMED THE ALLIES HAD AIRDROPPED ONTO GERMAN FIELDS.
NAZI RAID

AFTER PEARL HARBOR, DC EDITORS CHOSE NOT TO HAVE SUPERMAN FIGHT THE WAR IN COMICS STORIES SO AS TO NOT CHEAPEN AMERICAN TROOPS' REAL-LIFE HEROICS.
COMIC CREATORS DIDN'T HAVE THE SAME RECOURSE. THEY WERE THE IDEAL DRAFTABLE AGE. FORTUNATELY FOR MANY, THE ARMED FORCES REALIZED THAT THEIR ARTISTIC SKILLS COULD BE PUT TO BETTER USE STATESIDE.
JOE SIMON SPENT THE WAR IN THE "COMBAT ART CORPS" DOWN THE STREET FROM THE U.S. CAPITOL, WHERE PAINTINGS, COMMERCIAL ART, AND, LATER, COMICS WERE PRODUCED FOR PR AND RECRUITMENT PURPOSES.

STAN LEE FOUND HIMSELF ASSIGNED TO THE ARMY'S TRAINING FILM DIVISION, WHERE HE SERVED WITH SUCH LUMINARIES AS DIRECTOR FRANK CAPRA AND GREAT NEW YORKER CARTOONIST CHARLES ADDAMS.
LEE WROTE SHORT FILMS, POSTERS AND PAMPHLETS ON SUCH THRILLING TOPICS AS ARMY FINANCE AND VENEREAL DISEASE.

"VD? Not me!"

WILL EISNER WOUND UP AT THE ORDNANCE DEPARTMENT'S ABERDEEN PROVING GROUND IN MARYLAND.
EISNER'S WEEKLY NEWSPAPER COMIC BOOK THE SPIRIT WAS A POPULAR FEATURE IN THE NEARBY BALTIMORE SUN; THE BRASS QUICKLY RECOGNIZED WILL AND MADE HIM ART DIRECTOR OF THE SERVICE MAGAZINE ARMY MOTORS.
POTATOES

ARMY MOTORS WAS A KEY PART OF ORDNANCE'S ON-GOING EFFORTS TO INURE THE CONCEPT OF PREVENTIVE MAINTENANCE INTO THE GI -- THE IDEA THAT KEEPING ONE'S WEAPONS AND EQUIPMENT IN GOOD CONDITION BEFORE THEY BROKE WAS MOST EFFICIENT AND SAFEST.
1
Manually unfasten and vertically depress lower extremity-covering clothing; THEN
2
Place cover into second, or ascendant, position; THEN
3
Turn body so face and genital area face away from stool-receiving device; THEN
4
Affix gluteus maximus to aperture so sphincter is directly over water basin; THEN
BUT, PRE-EISNER, IT WAS, LIKE MOST ARMY PUBLICATIONS, ANTISEPTIC, JARGON-RIDDEN AND BORING.

EISNER CONVINCED HIS SUPERIORS TO LET HIM USE COMICS TO TEACH PREVENTIVE MAINTENANCE WITHHUMOR AND PLAIN LANGUAGE, THUS IMPROVING SOLDIERS' COMPREHENSION AND RETENTION OF THE MATERIAL.
UP UNTIL THIS POINT, THE MILITARY HAD DEEMED COMICS FIT ONLY FOR PROPAGANDA-- SUCH AS "HOW TO SPOT A JAP," WHICH THE ARMY COMMISSIONED FROM TERRY AND THE PIRATES CARTOONIST MILTON CANIFF.
"How to Spot a Jap"
Evil thoughts
Baby-eating teeth
Freedom-hating finger-nails

PREDICTABLY, EISNER RAN UP AGAINST THE HIGHER-UPS' RESISTANCE TO ANYTHING THAT DEVIATED FROM PREVIOUSLY ESTABLISHED PROCEDURE.
WHAT IS THIS POPPYCOCK? ACCIDENT PREVENTION IS SERIOUS BUSINESS! YOU CAN'T USE SILLY DRAWINGS TO PROMOTE IT!
AND EVEN WORSE -- IN YOUR STRIPS YOU MOCK SUPERIOR OFFICERS BY INSINUATING WE DON'T KNOW WHAT WE'RE TALKING ABOUT!!!
ARMY MO

AS IF VOLUNTEERING TO PROVE WILL'S POINT, THE ADJUTANT GENERAL IN CHARGE OF PRODUCING ***TECHNICAL MATERIALS*** ARRANGED FOR THE ***UNIVERSITY OF CHICAGO*** TO RUN AN ***EFFICIENCY TEST*** PITTING STANDARD MANUALS AGAINST EISNER'S ***COMICS***.

THE ***COMICS*** WON ***HANDILY!***

with comics

without comics

AS BIOGRAPHER BOB ANDELMAN WRITES, "THE RESULTS ***REINFORCED*** WHAT EISNER BELIEVED TO BE ***CHARACTERISTIC*** OF THE COMIC STRIP:

"THE ***EASE*** WITH WHICH ***IMAGES*** DEMONSTRATED ***PROCESS***."

(THIS IS THE MAN, AFTER ALL, WHO, NEARLY FOUR DECADES LATER, WOULD COIN THE PHRASE "***SEQUENTIAL*** ART.")

ALSO, UNLIKE EVEN ***PHOTOS***, WHICH ARE CONSTRAINED BY WHAT IS ***PHYSICALLY PHOTOGRAPHABLE***, THE FLEXIBILITY OF COMICS' ***DRAWN*** IMAGES ALLOWED EISNER TO DEMONSTRATE A TECHNICALLY ***COMPLEX*** TASK --LIKE REMOVING ***VOLUTE SPRINGS*** FROM A ***TANK*** -- FROM THE POINT OF VIEW OF THE ***REPAIRMAN***.

COMIC ART DRAWS THE READER ***INTO*** THE SEQUENCE, MAKES HER A ***PART*** OF IT, STEP BY STEP!

ARMY MOTORS (AND ITS SUCCESSOR, ***PS: THE PREVENTIVE MAINTENANCE MONTHLY***) PROVED SUCH A SUCCESS WITH OFFICER AND GRUNT ALIKE THAT EISNER CONTINUED TO BE INVOLVED IN ITS ART DIRECTION WELL AFTER THE WAR -- UNTIL ***1971***, IN FACT!

SO IF ***WILL EISNER*** WAS THE CARTOONIST WHO MOST HELPED THE ***PENTAGON...***

...THE CARTOONIST MOST HELPED **BY** THE PENTAGON WAS UNDOUBTEDLY ***WALT DISNEY***.
WAIT-!
AFTER THE TRIUMPH OF *SNOW WHITE*, DISNEY HAD PRODUCED MOSTLY ***FLOPS***, INCLUDING *PINOCCHIO* (1940) AND *BAMBI* (1942).

IN 1941, THE STUDIO HAD SUFFERED THROUGH A DEBILITATING ***LABOR STRIKE*** EVEN MORE ***RANCOROUS*** THAN THE ONE AT FLEISCHER IN '37.
WALT DENOUNCED ORGANIZERS AS ***COMMUNISTS*** AND TRIED TO HAVE THE FBI ***ARREST*** THEM.
AS WITH FLEISCHER, THE ***GOVERNMENT*** HAD TO MEDIATE A RESOLUTION. LAYOFFS FOLLOWED, AND THE STUDIO ***SHUT DOWN***, SAVE FOR PRODUCTION ON ITS NEXT FEATURE (*DUMBO*) AND THE SYNDICATED MICKEY MOUSE ***COMIC STRIP***.
"***THERE*** HE IS--
"--THE MAN WHO BELIEVES IN ***BROTHER-HOOD*** FOR EVERYBODY BUT ***HIMSELF!***"
ARE WE MEN OR MICE?
NO STRINGS ON ME!
NO WISE QUACKS

MANY ANIMATORS, TURNED OFF BY THE POST-STRIKE ATMOPSHERE, LEFT ***VOLUNTARILY***, INCLUDING ARTIST ***WALT KELLY***.
DISNEY HIMSELF RECOMMENDED KELLY TO ***DELL COMICS***; THERE WALT CREATED A TRUE ***RARITY*** -- AN ORIGINAL ***COMIC BOOK*** FEATURE THAT BECAME A MORE POPULAR ***NEWSPAPER STRIP -- POGO THE POSSUM***, WHICH FIRST APPEARED IN DELL'S *ANIMAL COMICS*.
SWAMP

DESPERATE TO TURN A PROFIT BY THE TIME THE U.S. ENTERERD WWII, WALT SECURED CONTRACTS FOR A VARIETY OF ANIMATED INDUSTRIAL, TRAINING AND PROPAGANDA FILMS FROM THE ARMED SERVICES AND THE FEDERAL GOVERNMENT.
BY THE END OF 1942, ***SEVENTY-FIVE PERCENT*** OF THE STUDIO'S OUTPUT WAS FOR THE FEDS! THE ***WAR*** WAS THE ONLY THING KEEPING DISNEY ***AFLOAT!***
(HIS INAUGURAL GOVERNMENT EFFORT, "THE NEW SPIRIT," FEATURED ***ANIMATED DESK OBJECTS*** HELPING DONALD DUCK PAY HIS FEDERAL ***INCOME TAXES***.)
★1040

THE WAR DEPARTMENT CLASSIFIED DISNEY STUDIOS A ***STRATEGIC DEFENSE INDUSTRY***, REQUIRING ALL EMPLOYEES TO BE ***FINGER-PRINTED*** AND CARRY ORANGE ***ID BADGES***.
THE HEIGHTENED SECURITY INADVERTENTLY REFLECTED WALT'S OWN ***BUNKER MENTALITY***. LIKE MAX FLEISCHER, HE TOOK THE STRIKE QUITE ***PERSONALLY***. HIS RELATIONSHIP WITH HIS ANIMATORS ***SOURED***.

HIS PERFECTIONISM CURDLED INTO PERMANENT ***DISSATISFACTION*** WITH STAFF PERFORMANCE.
HE WOULD CRUELLY BERATE AND ***RIDICULE*** THOSE WHO DISPLEASED HIM AT THE ***SLIGHTEST*** PROVOCATION.
"YOU'D GO TO A MEETING AND TRY TO BE AS ***INVISIBLE*** AS POSSIBLE," RECALLS ANIMATOR WARD KIMBALL.

ONE STUDIO WRITER WAS SO ***TERRIFIED*** OF WALT SHE WOULD ***THROW UP*** AFTER EVERY PRESENTATION SHE GAVE TO HIM!
EMPLOYEES ***AVOIDED*** CO-WORKERS KNOWN TO HAVE FALLEN OUT OF FAVOR WITH WALT AS IF THEY WERE ***LEPERS***.
BLEEEEAAAALGGH!!

DISNEY HAD A PENCHANT FOR CREEPING AROUND THE STUDIO AT ***NIGHT***, EXAMINING ARTISTS' WORK AFTER HOURS.
WHEN AN ANIMATOR FOUND A ***CHESTERFIELD*** BUTT IN HIS ASHTRAY IN THE MORNING, HE KNEW THE BOSS HAD ***INSPECTED*** HIS WORK.

WALT GREW TO ***DESPISE*** THE PROPAGANDA THE GOVERNMENT HIRED HIM TO MAKE; IN FACT, HE WAS LOSING INTEREST IN ***MOVIEMAKING*** ALTOGETHER.
INCREASINGLY, HIS THOUGHTS WERE DOMINATED BY THE CREATION OF A ***THREE-DIMENSIONAL*** WORLD, NOT A FILM OR EVEN A STORY, BUT A CARTOON MADE ***REAL***, IN CONCRETE AND STEEL...
...A ***FANTASYLAND*** OVER WHICH WALT DISNEY WOULD HAVE ***TOTAL CONTROL***.

MORE INFORMALLY, WALT ASSIGNED FIVE ARTISTS TO DESIGN MILITARY INSIGNIAS -- "NOSE ART" FOR WARPLANES AND SHIPS -- AFTER A NAVAL OPERATIONS LIEUTENANT WROTE AND ASKED HIM TO CREATE ONE FOR HIS "MOSQUITO BOAT."
DISNEY'S TEAM TURNED OUT MORE THAN TWELVE HUNDRED INSIGNIAS GRATIS THROUGHOUT THE WAR.
"BOMBY"

OUT IN RANGOON, IN WHAT IS NOW MYANMAR, THE SECOND ("PANDA") SQUADRON OF THE FAMED "FLYING TIGERS" HAD THEIR INSIGNIAS DESIGNED BY ONE OF THEIR OWN.
BERT CHRISTMAN BECAME SO ENTRANCED BY FLYING AFTER DRAWING A PILOT NEWSPAPER STRIP (THE ASSOCIATED PRESS'S SCORCHY SMITH) THAT HE ENLISTED AS A NAVAL AVIATION CADET!

INCREDIBLY, CHRISTMAN CONTINUED TO FREELANCE FOR DC COMICS WHILE IN THE SERVICE!
HE WROTE AND DREW "THREE ACES," AN AVIATION BACK-UP FEATURE FOR "SUPERMAN" IN ACTION COMICS...
...AND, WITH WRITER GARDNER FOX, CREATED "THE SANDMAN!"

ON JANUARY 23, 1942, THE JAPANESE ATTACKED RANGOON. CHRISTMAN'S FIGHTER WAS HIT IN THE ENGINE, FORCING HIM TO BAIL OUT.

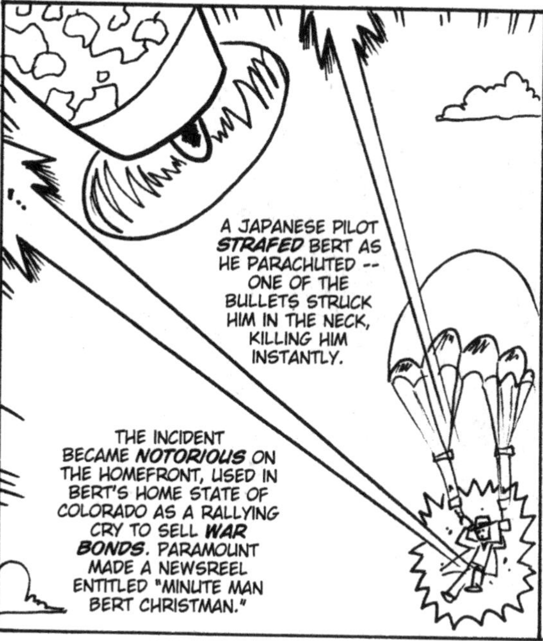
A JAPANESE PILOT STRAFED BERT AS HE PARACHUTED -- ONE OF THE BULLETS STRUCK HIM IN THE NECK, KILLING HIM INSTANTLY.
THE INCIDENT BECAME NOTORIOUS ON THE HOMEFRONT, USED IN BERT'S HOME STATE OF COLORADO AS A RALLYING CRY TO SELL WAR BONDS. PARAMOUNT MADE A NEWSREEL ENTITLED "MINUTE MAN BERT CHRISTMAN."

WHILE IN THE EUROPEAN THEATER, JACK KIRBY, DISPLAYING HIS LIFELONG INABILITY TO PLAY THE SYSTEM, ANY SYSTEM, DIDN'T GET A CUSHY ARMY ART JOB...
...HE GOT SHIPPED TO THE BEACHES OF NORMANDY RIGHT AFTER D-DAY WITH PATTON'S THIRD ARMY.
(A PASSWORD USED FOR NAVAL D-DAY BRIEFINGS WAS "MICKEY MOUSE.")

THIRD ARMY PURSUED THE NAZI RETREAT ACROSS FRANCE TO METZ, NEAR THE GERMAN BORDER, WHERE HITLER'S ARMY DUG IN AND FORCED A BLOODY STALEMATE.
PRIVATE FIRST CLASS KIRBY REPORTING FOR DUTY, SIR!
NOT JACK KIRBY, THE ARTIST?
ROSS

KIRBY WAS USED TO BEING RECOGNIZED AND ADMIRED IN THE SERVICE; COMICS WERE AMONG GI'S PREFERRED LEISURE READING, OUTSELLING "STRAIGHT" MAGAZINES TEN-TO-ONE AT ARMY POST EXCHANGES.
"YES, SIR. I DREW CAPTAIN AMERICA--"
"AND BOY COMMANDOS!"
ROSS

"SO YOU CAN DRAW?"
"YES, SIR. OF COURSE I CAN DRAW."
ROSS
"I WAS THINKING, 'GREAT, SOME OFFICER WANTS ME TO DRAW HIS PORTRAIT,'" KIRBY REMEMBERED.

"GOOD. I AM MAKING YOU A SCOUT. YOU GO INTO THESE TOWNS THAT WE DON'T HAVE AND SEE IF THERE IS ANYBODY THERE.
"DRAW MAPS AND PICTURES OF WHAT YOU SEE AND COME BACK AND TELL US IF YOU FIND ANYTHING."

"IF SOMEBODY WANTS TO KILL YOU, THEY MAKE YOU A SCOUT," KIRBY SAID. "NICE GUYS DON'T GET SCOUT DUTY."
BWHOOM!
HALT, AMERIKANER! HALT!
BUDDA! BUDDA! BUDDA!
HE LATER SAID IT WAS THE ONLY TIME IN HIS LIFE HE REGRETTED BECOMING AN ARTIST!

all you need is Love

AFTER WWII, THE SUPER HERO GENRE QUICKLY FELL INTO *DISFAVOR*.
PEOPLE WERE SICK OF *FIGHTING*, EVEN IN *FANTASY*.
WILL FIGHT CRIME FOR FOOD

TO GIVE JUST *ONE* EXAMPLE OF HOW THE MIGHTY FELL, THE CIRCULATION OF ONE OF THE *PREMIERE* SUPER HEROES, FAWCETT'S *CAPTAIN MARVEL*, PLUMMETED BY A GUT-WRENCHING *2.5 MILLION COPIES* BETWEEN 1945 AND 1947.

ONE OF THE *FIRST* PUBLISHERS TO ANTICIPATE THE FAILURE OF THE HERO TREND WAS *MLJ MAGAZINES*, FOUNDED BY THREE DISTRIBUTION VETERANS--

M
L
J

-- *M*AURICE COYNE, *L*OUIS SILBERKLEIT, AND *J*OHN GOLDWATER.

FIRST EMPLOYING THE SERVICES OF HARRY "A" CHESLER'S SHOP, THEY BEGAN PRODUCING SUPER HERO TITLES IN *1939*.

BUT MLJ DIDN'T FIND ITS ***NICHE*** UNTIL GOLDWATER HIT UPON THE IDEA TO BASE A SERIES ON THE MERCILESSLY WHOLESOME SCREEN PERSONA OF ***MICKEY ROONEY***, WHO SHOT TO STARDOM PLAYING *"AMERICA'S FAVORITE TEENAGER, ANDY HARDY"* IN SIXTEEN FILMS FROM 1937 TO 1958.

BUY WAR BONDS
1940

Fab
1970

SOYLENT GREEN
people feeding people!
2140

BROUGHT TO LIFE BY CARTOONIST ***BOB MONTANA***, *"ARCHIE ANDREWS, AMERICA'S TOP TEENAGER"* BEGAN AS A BACK-UP IN *PEP COMICS* IN 1941... AND HAS BEEN A FIXTURE IN SUPERMARKET CHECK-OUT LINES EVER ***SINCE!***
IN 1944, ARCHIE BECAME *PEP'S* ***LEAD*** FEATURE. SEEING THE WRITING ON THE WALL, MLJ ***RETIRED*** ALL THEIR SUPER HEROES IN 1947.
BY THEN THE COMPANY HAD EVEN RENAMED ITSELF ***"ARCHIE COMICS."***

SEVERAL PUBLISHERS ATTEMPTED TO ***APE*** ARCHIE'S SUCCESS. THE BALLYHOOED ***SIMON & KIRBY*** TEAM WAS HIRED TO PRODUCE A RIVERDALE WANNABE IN 1947.
HMMM... WHAT IF THE ***ROMANCE*** IN THESE STORIES WAS PLAYED ***STRAIGHT*** RATHER THAN AS A ***GAG*** TO ATTRACT AN ***OLDER*** READERSHIP?
MY DATE
THOUGH S&K'S *MY DATE* LASTED A SCANT ***FOUR ISSUES***, IT DID GIVE JOE SIMON A MUCH ***BETTER*** IDEA.

LIKE SO MANY RETURNING VETERANS, SIMON & KIRBY HAD LIT OUT FOR THE ***SUBURBS***, BUYING HOMES ACROSS THE STREET FROM EACH OTHER IN ***LONG ISLAND.***

CAUGHT IN THE ANTI-HERO ***BACKLASH***, THE UNDISPUTED ***MASTERS*** OF ADVENTURE COMICS RECEIVED FREELANCE WORK ***SPORADICALLY*** AT BEST.

SO IN THEIR NOW-COPIOUS ***SPARE TIME***, S&K MOCKED UP A SAMPLE OF THE FIRST TRUE ***ROMANCE COMIC***, *YOUNG ROMANCE*, BASED ON THE PROSE "TRUE LOVE CONFESSIONAL" MAGAZINES OF THE DAY.

JUST DOWN THE LINE ON THE ***LONG ISLAND RAIL ROAD*** FROM S&K LIVED MAURICE ROSENFELD, THE BUSINESS MANAGER FOR ***CRESTWOOD*** (AKA ***PRIZE***), A SMALL PUBLISHER PRIMIARLY KNOWN FOR PRINTING DICK BRIEFER'S HUMOROUS ***FRANKENSTEIN*** COMICS. THE THREE MEN WOULD OFTEN TAKE THE TRAIN TO AND FROM MANHATTAN TOGETHER.

ARMED WITH THEIR MOCK-UP, THE ARTISTS SOLD ROSENFELD ON *YOUNG ROMANCE* FOR ***50%*** OF THE PROFITS.

young
Love

YOUNG ROMANCE #1 DEBUTED IN SEPTEMBER 1947, ALONG WITH THE BIRTH OF SIMON'S FIRST CHILD, JON.

ON THE WAY TO THE HOSPITAL, HE AND KIRBY STOPPED OFF AT A CANDY STORE TO PICK UP SOME GIFTS, WHERE THEY OVERHEARD:

"I HOPE THEY PUT OUT MORE OF THESE!"

YOUNG ROMANCE BLEW THROUGH ITS INITIAL PRINT RUN OF 500,000 COPIES AT AN ***UNHEARD-OF*** SELL-THROUGH RATE OF ***92%***.

COMIX!
LOVE

YOUNG ROMANCE WENT OUT OF ITS WAY TO MAKE ITSELF LOOK ***SEAMIER*** THAN IT ACTUALLY WAS, DECLARING ON ITS COVER THAT IT WAS *"DESIGNED FOR THE MORE **ADULT** READERS OF COMICS."*

S&K NEMESIS ***MARTIN GOODMAN*** COMPLAINED TO THEIR DISTRIBUTOR THAT THAT ASSERTION "BORDERS ON ***PORNOGRAPHY***."

LOVE

STILL, AS SURELY AS WATER FLOWS ***DOWNHILL***, ROMANCE COMICS FROM RIVAL PUBLISHERS SOON ***FLOODED*** THE STANDS.

WITH ***99*** TITLES BY 1949, ROMANCE REMAINS THE ***FASTEST-GROWING GENRE*** IN COMICS HISTORY, SURPASSING EVEN THE SUPER HEROES!

OF COURSE, GOODMAN'S ***ATLAS*** COMICS, THE SUCCESSOR TO TIMELY, ***LED*** THE COPYCATS, CRANKING OUT NO LESS THAN ***THIRTY*** SEPARATE ROMANCE TITLES. (***VICTOR FOX*** WAS A DISTANT SECOND WITH ***EIGHTEEN*** TITLES.)

CAPED LOVE
BROKEBACK LOVE
CREEPY ALIEN LOVE

THOUGH THROUGH OUR ALLEGEDLY MORE "ENLIGHTENED" ***MODERN*** EYES, ROMANCE COMICS MAY BE SEEN AS SIMPLY REINSCRIBING THE MORE ***PATRIARCHAL*** ASPECTS OF AMERICAN SOCIETY (AS 99.9% OF THEM WERE WRITTEN ***AND*** DRAWN BY ***MEN***)...
OH, JOHN...
...I'M SO ***HAPPY*** YOU ***ALLOWED*** ME TO DROP MY CAREER TO COME POP OUT ***BABIES*** FOR YOU UNTIL YOU THROW ME ASIDE FOR YOUR ***SECRETARY*** IN TWO DECADES!

ME ***TOO***, SUGAR PLUM!
NOW SHUT YOUR YAP AND GO FIX ME A ***SANDWICH!***
CLICK!

...THEY ALMOST ALWAYS ENCOURAGED MARRYING FOR ***LOVE*** MORE THAN ANY OTHER CONSIDERATION...

...AND TRIED TO STEER HEROINES AWAY FROM THE ***WRONG*** KIND OF MAN, THE TEMPLATE FOR WHOM REMAINS BASICALLY THE SAME IN ***OUR*** DAY...

Mr. Right
MR. WRONG
Working-Class Joe
WELL-HEELED SHARPIE
Wants 2.5 Kids
WANTS IN YOUR PANTS
1-beer-a-day guy
DRUNK RIGHT NOW

...AND -- PARTICULARLY IN THE S&K STORIES -- ENCOURAGED MORE... ***UNUSUAL*** LOVE CHOICES.

FOR EXAMPLE, ***YOUNG ROMANCE*** WAS ONE OF THE FIRST COMICS TO OPENLY ATTACK ***ANTI-SEMITISM*** IN AN S&K TALE ENTITLED *"DIFFERENT"* (*YR #30*).

ROMANCE COMICS ALSO OFFERED ***RELATIONSHIP ADVICE*** TO THEIR CUPID-TORMENTED READERSHIP IN THEIR ***LETTER COLUMNS.***

Dear Editor, at first Joey said he liked me, but now he won't even accept the notes I pass to him in class. What should I do?

Signed, Lovelorn in Lansing

OF COURSE, COMICS PUBLISHERS WERE TOO ***CHEAP*** TO ACTUALLY HIRE ***FEMALE ADVICE COLUMNISTS.***

Dear Lovelorn, I remember the day I left behind the lilac-scented fancies of my girlish years and stepped through the threshold of womanhood...

BURRRRRAP!

SIMON & KIRBY CONTINUED TO OVERSEE *YOUNG ROMANCE*, THE FIRST AND MOST ***POPULAR*** OF THE GENRE, WITH A CIRCULATION OF OVER ***ONE MILLION*** COPIES PER ISSUE!

(FREELANCERS WOULD ***PRANK*** THE BOSSES BY SLIPPING IN LURIDLY ***PORNOGRAPHIC*** PAGES ALONG WITH THE SCRIPTED ALLOTMENT.)

THE COMIC BOOK INDUSTRY HAD ***SURVIVED*** THE TWILIGHT OF THE SUPER HEROES -- THOUGH ***THAT*** GENRE CONTINUED TOO, IN THE FORM OF POPULAR CHARACTERS LIKE SUPERMAN AND BATMAN.

INDUSTRY STUDIES SHOWED THAT IN 1947, A STUNNING ***95%*** OF AMERICAN BOYS AND 91% OF ***GIRLS*** BETWEEN THE AGES OF 6 AND 11 WERE HABITUAL COMICS READERS...

...ALONG WITH ***87%*** OF TEENAGED MEN AND 81% OF TEEN WOMEN; AND A STILL-IMPRESSIVE ***41%*** OF MEN AGED 18-30 AND -- ***BEFORE*** ROMANCE COMICS -- ***28%*** OF WOMEN THE SAME AGE READ COMICS REGULARLY.

THERE WERE DISNEY AND ARCHIE COMICS FOR THE ***KIDS*** -- SUPER HERO, WESTERN, SCI-FI AND OTHER ***ADVENTURE*** COMICS FOR YOUNG ADULTS -- CRIME AND SUSPENSE COMICS FOR ***MEN*** -- ***LOVE*** COMICS FOR ***WOMEN!***

IN FACT, ***ONE OUT OF THREE*** PERIODICALS SOLD IN 1947 ***WAS A*** COMIC-- THAT'S 180 ***MILLION*** A ***YEAR!***

COMICS WERE FOR ***EVERYONE!***
SO EVERYONE LIVED ***HAPPILY EVER AFTER***, RIGHT?

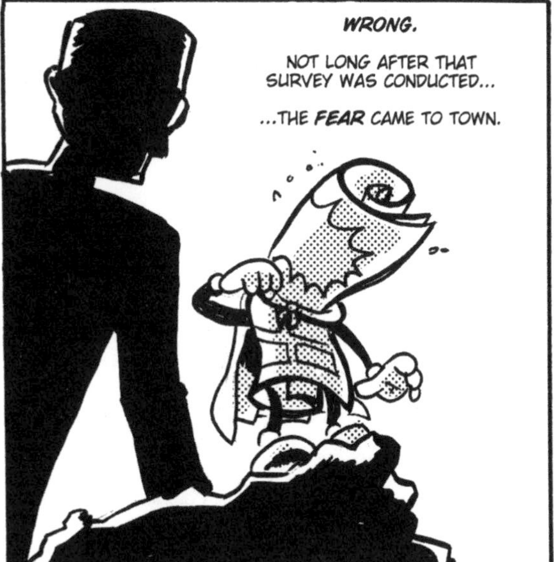
WRONG.
NOT LONG AFTER THAT SURVEY WAS CONDUCTED...
...THE ***FEAR*** CAME TO TOWN.

CRIME

OH MAN, DOES IT PAY!

WHY HELLO THERE, KIDDIES! IT'S BEEN A WHILE!

ARE YOU READY FOR ANOTHER FALSEHOOD-FREE FABLE OF FOOLISH FELONY?

WHAT'S THAT? SOME OF THE YOUNGER READERS WANT TO KNOW WHO I AM? WHAT MY NOM DE CRIME IS, AS THE FRENCHIES SAY?

WHY, THE FROGS GOT IT RIGHT EXACTLY! AND AS FOR WHAT I'M DOING HERE...

...WELL, I HAVE THE UNNERVING HABIT OF TURNING UP IN THE UNLIKELIEST OF PLACES... HE HE HO HO...

"TO TAKE JUST ONE FER-INSTANCE: ARMANDO'S HI-DE-HO CLUB IN NYC'S EAST 50'S, AROUND 1942..."
S-SAY, MISTER! I-I GOT A GIRL UPSTAIRS, IN MY ROOM!
Y-YOU WANNA GO... "VISIT" HER? WON'T COST YOU A CENT...
...SO'S LONG AS I CAN WATCH!

ER... I DON'T KNOW...
C'MON, CHARLEY! DON'T PRETEND YOU DON'T WANT TO!
CRIME
THIS IS ME YOU'RE TALKING TO! I KNOW YOU:
CHARLES BIRO! OCCUPATION: COMIC BOOK ARTIST!

"YOU STARTED OUT AT WHAT BECAME ARCHIE COMICS--MLJ, IN THE WESTERN UNION BUILDING ON LAFAYETTE!"
"DON'T YOU REMEMBER HOW YOU KNOCKED OUT A PIECE OF GLASS BETWEEN THE STUDIO AND THE DELIVERY GIRLS' LOCKER ROOM?"
"I DO!"

NAW... I'LL PASS, PAL!
IN FACT... IT'S HIGH TIME I CALLED IT A NIGHT!
EXIT
CRIME
OH HO HO... HE'LL BE BACK!
I KNOW A STAR PUPIL WHEN I SEE ONE!

OLEO
BIRO WAS STUNNED TO READ IN THE PAPER THE FOLLOWING MORNING THAT THE WOULD-BE VOYEUR GOT BUSTED NOT LONG AFTER HE LEFT THE BAR!
THE WEIRDO WAS HEIR TO A VAST MARGARINE FORTUNE WHO HAD KEPT "HIS" GIRL A PRISONER IN HIS ROOM!

BIRO AND FELLOW MLJ VETERAN, ROOMMATE, AND FREQUENT DRINKING BUDDY BOB WOOD EDITED LEV GLEASON'S COMIC BOOK LINE TOGETHER...
...CRANKING OUT A COMPETENT SUPER HERO AND ADVENTURE LINE STARRING DAREDEVIL, A MUTE VIGILANTE RAISED BY ABORIGINES.*
HAPPY B-DAY D.D.!
* YES, REALLY.

GLEASON HIMSELF WAS A POLITICALLY CONSCIOUS LEFTY WHO WOULD BE PURSUED BY THE HOUSE UN-AMERICAN ACTIVITIES COMMITTEE FOR PRINTING PRO-SOVIET PROPAGANDA ALONG WITH HIS COMIC BOOKS!
TRUE TO HIS POLITICS, GLEASON SHARED PROFITS WITH HIS EDITORS...

...SO BIRO & WOOD HAD AMPLE MOTIVATION TO KEEP THEIR EYES PEELED FOR WINNING COMICS CONCEPTS!
BOB! LET'S DO A COMIC ABOUT REAL-LIFE CRIMINALS LIKE THIS MARGARINE KOOK!
THE POLICE BLOTTER WILL GIVE US STORIES WAY CRAZIER THAN ANYTHING WE COULD DREAM UP!

HEAVILY-ILLUSTRATED "POLICE GAZETTES" HAD BEEN REGALING THE CURIOUS WITH BLOODY TALES OF CRIMINAL DEPRAVITY SINCE THE 1840s.

SWARTHY FOOTPAD: "Thy muttonchops **offend** me, sirrah! I shalt bust a **cap** in thy ass!
ARYAN GENTLEMAN: "Egad! I have soiled my **pantaloons**!"

BIRO & WOOD WERE THE FIRST TO ATTEMPT THE GENRE IN ***COMICS*** FORM. THEY NAMED THEIR NEW TITLE AFTER A SERIES OF MGM ANTI-CRIME ***DOCUMENTARY SHORTS*** FROM THE 1930s...

CRIME DOES NOT PAY

10¢

...BUT NO ONE SLAPPED DOWN HIS HARD-EARNED DIME FOR *CRIME DOES NOT PAY* EXPECTING A ***CIVICS LESSON***!

NO, *CDNP*'S APPEAL LAY IN THE VICARIOUS THRILL OF WATCHING REAL-LIFE OUTLAWS MERCILESSLY ***GUN DOWN*** THEIR ENEMIES, ALTERNATELY ***LOCK LIPS*** WITH AND ***SLAP AROUND*** BIG-BREASTED FLOOZIES, AND RECKLESSLY ***WALLOW*** IN EVERY MANNER OF ANTI-SOCIAL BEHAVIOR!

LET'S SEE HOW WELL YOU SQUEAL WITH ***NO MOUTH,*** CHIPPIE!!

FSSSSSS!!

AIIEEEEE!!

THOUGH EVERY STORY ENDED WITH THE CROOK GETTING HIS ***COMEUPPANCE*** AT THE HANDS OF THE ***LAW***, THE PERFUNCTORY ***HAND-WRINGING*** WAS USUALLY JUST OCCASION FOR EVEN ***MORE*** GORE AND VIOLENCE.

STILL, GIVEN THE SHEER NUMBER OF READER LETTERS BIRO & WOOD PRINTED FROM PEOPLE WHO CLAIMED TO STICK TO THE STRAIGHT AND NARROW PATH AFTER CONSUMING CDNP...
STOP IT, GUYS!! THE JOB'S OVER!!
DID YOU KNOW WE CAN GO TO PRISON FOR THIS?!
CRIME
...THEY CLEARLY WANTED TO KEEP UP APPEARANCES!

(OF COURSE, THEY DIDN'T PLAY UP THE FACT THAT READERS RECEIVED TWO DOLLARS FOR EVERY PUBLISHED TESTIMONIAL!)
SPORTING GOODS
$2
OPEN
I KNOW... I'LL TELL CRIME DOES NOT PAY THEY SAVED ME FROM BECOMIN' A RAPIST!

WITH ITS NOV. '42 ISSUE, CDNP DEBUTED AN EMCEE, "MR. CRIME" --INSPIRED BY COMIC STRIP SPOKESPERSON "MR. COFFEE NERVES" (HE PEDDLED POSTUM, A CAFFEINE SUBSTITUTE)-- TO SARCASTICALLY COMMENT ON FELONS' FOLLY!
CRIME
BOOT!
MR. COFFEE NERVES
BEAT IT, JAVA BOY!

CRIME DOES NOT PAY SOLD OKAY -- AT FIRST.
THROUGH 1943, ITS CIRCULATION WAS A MODEST 323,000 COPIES.
323K?!? "MODEST?!?"
TODAY'S CREATORS
SEX-MEN #82
WOLVERBEAN: "GRRR!"
GRRR!

THEN...THE WAR ENDED AND BATTLE-HARDENED VETS LOST INTEREST IN SUPER HEROES AND THEIR PHONY, FANTASTICAL VIOLENCE!
SUPER PANTS 10¢
HMMM... THIS ISN'T DOING IT FOR ME ANYMORE FOR SOME REASON...
THEY CRAVED SOMETHING A LITTLE MORE... REALISTIC.

SALES OF CDNP SHOT UP TO ONE MILLION COPIES BY 1948!
HE HE HO HO...GOOD WORK, BOYS! I KNEW YOU'D MAKE GREAT PUPILS!
(THOUGH GLEASON CLAIMED, WITH PASS-AROUNDS, THAT FIGURE WAS ACTUALLY 6 MILLON ON THE COVER!)

OTHER PUBLISHERS TOOK NOTICE AND TRANSFORMED MANY NON-CRIME TITLES INTO CRIME COMICS!
Fairy Tale PARADE 10¢
HAND OVER THE TARTS YOU TART!
FROM 1947 TO 1954-- THE ERA FILM NOIR DOMINATED HOLLYWOOD-- 150 NEW CRIME TITLES HIT THE STANDS!

INEVITABLY, THE INTENSE ***COMPETITION*** DROVE PUBLISHERS TO OUT-***GORE*** AND OUT-***SEX*** EACH OTHER.

ONE INDUSTRY LEGEND HAS A PRINTER OF CRIME COMICS RUNNING OUT OF ***RED INK!***

IT DIDN'T TAKE LONG FOR THE AUTHORITIES TO ***FREAK OUT.***

AND ***STAY*** OUT! YOUSE GIVIN' CHI-TOWN A ***BAD NAME!***

Chicago 1MILE

Shove!

BAD SIGN: THE MAYOR OF CHICAGO, CAPITAL OF ***GANGSTERDOM,*** ***BANNED*** *CDNP* IN OCTOBER 1947!

STORIES OF *CDNP*-INSPIRED ***COPYCAT CRIMES*** BEGAN CROPPING UP ALL OVER NORTH AMERICA...SOME BY PERPS AS YOUNG AS ***TEN!***

UH...

...THE ***COMIC*** MADE ME DO IT?

CRIME DOES NOT PAY!

OVER ***FIFTY*** U.S. CITIES ATTEMPTED TO REGULATE THE SALE OF CRIME COMICS--CANADA MADE THEM ***ILLEGAL!***

GLEASON SCRAMBLED TO STEM THE TIDE OF CRITICISM BY INSTALLING AN IN-HOUSE ***CODE***... SLAPPING ***DISCLAIMERS*** ALL OVER THE COVER...

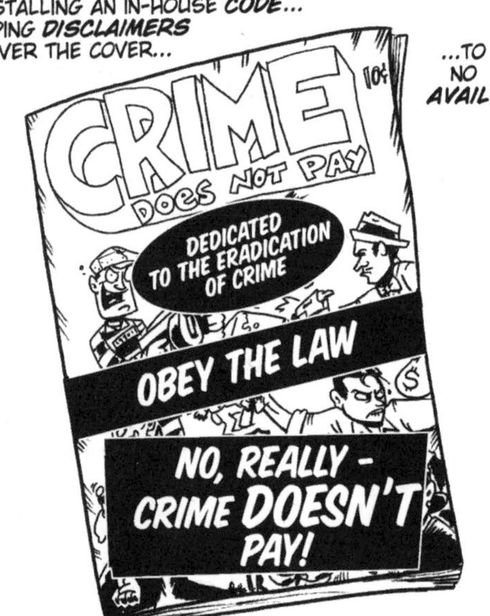
CRIME
DOES NOT PAY
10¢
DEDICATED TO THE ERADICATION OF CRIME
OBEY THE LAW
NO, REALLY - CRIME DOESN'T PAY!

...TO NO ***AVAIL!***

PUBLIC OUTCRY CLIMAXED IN THE COMICS CODE OF 1954, WHICH EMASCULATED THE CRIME COMICS, IMPOSING STRICT LIMITS ON VIOLENCE, SEX, AND THE REALISTIC DEPICTION OF CRIMINAL BEHAVIOR (AMONG MANY OTHER THINGS).
YOU'LL NEVER TAKE ME ALIVE CENSORS! UGH...

BIRO & WOOD ATTEMPTED TO SOLDIER ON UNDER THE CODE, BUT THE NEW, CLEANED-UP VERSION OF CDNP DIDN'T HAVE QUITE THE SAME APPEAL...
CAN YOU BELIEVE WOOLWORTH'S WANTED $5.99 FOR THIS PIECE O' JUNK? I GOT ME A FIVE-FINGER DISCOUNT!
NO, LEFTY! YOU HAVE TO RETURN IT! SHOP-LIFTING IS AGAINST THE LAW!
APPROVED BY THE COMICS CODE AUTHORITY
A NEW YORK STATE BAN ON THE USE OF THE WORD "CRIME" IN TITLES SOLD TO MINORS PROVED THE FATAL BLOW.

CRIME DOES NOT PAY CEASED PAYING WITH ITS JULY 1955 ISSUE.
CHARLES BIRO LEFT COMICS ENTIRELY AND BEGAN STORYBOARDING TV ADS.

AS FOR BOB WOOD... WELL... ONE NIGHT IN AUGUST 1958...
WHAT HAPPENED TO YOU, PAL? YOU KILL SOMEBODY OR SOMETHING?
YES...I KILLED A WOMAN WHO WAS GIVING ME A BAD TIME IN ROOM 91 AT THE IRVING HOTEL.
WHY DON'T YOU CALL A NEWSPAPER, MAKE YOURSELF A FEW BUCKS?

INSTEAD, THE CABBIE CALLED THE COPS--THEY DISCOVERED WOOD HAD BEATEN HIS LOVER TO DEATH WITH AN IRON AFTER A JOINT ELEVEN-DAY BENDER!
THE TABLOIDS ATE IT UP--THE CO-EDITOR OF CRIME DOES NOT PAY SENT TO SING-SING FOR MANSLAUGHTER!

NEW YORK
ATLANTIC CITY EXIT
"HE HE HO HO... ONCE OL' WOODY GOT SPRUNG, HE TRIED TO GET CARTOONING WORK, BUT IT WAS THE PRISON CROWD HE FELL BACK IN WITH... FELL INTO DEBT..."
"...AND SOMEBODY COLLECTED! THEY FOUND HIS BODY ON THE NEW JERSEY TURNPIKE. IT DIDN'T MAKE THE PAPERS THIS TIME!"

BETCHA DIDN'T SEE THAT ONE COMING, EH, KIDDIES? I TOLD YOU TO EXPECT THE UNEXPECTED WITH ME!
CRIME
THE MORAL OF OUR SORRY STORY--OR MAYBE YOU COULD CALL IT THE PUNCH LINE...
...IS THAT WHILE CRIME MAY PAY...
...GETTING CAUGHT WILL REALLY COST YOU! HA HA HA HA!!

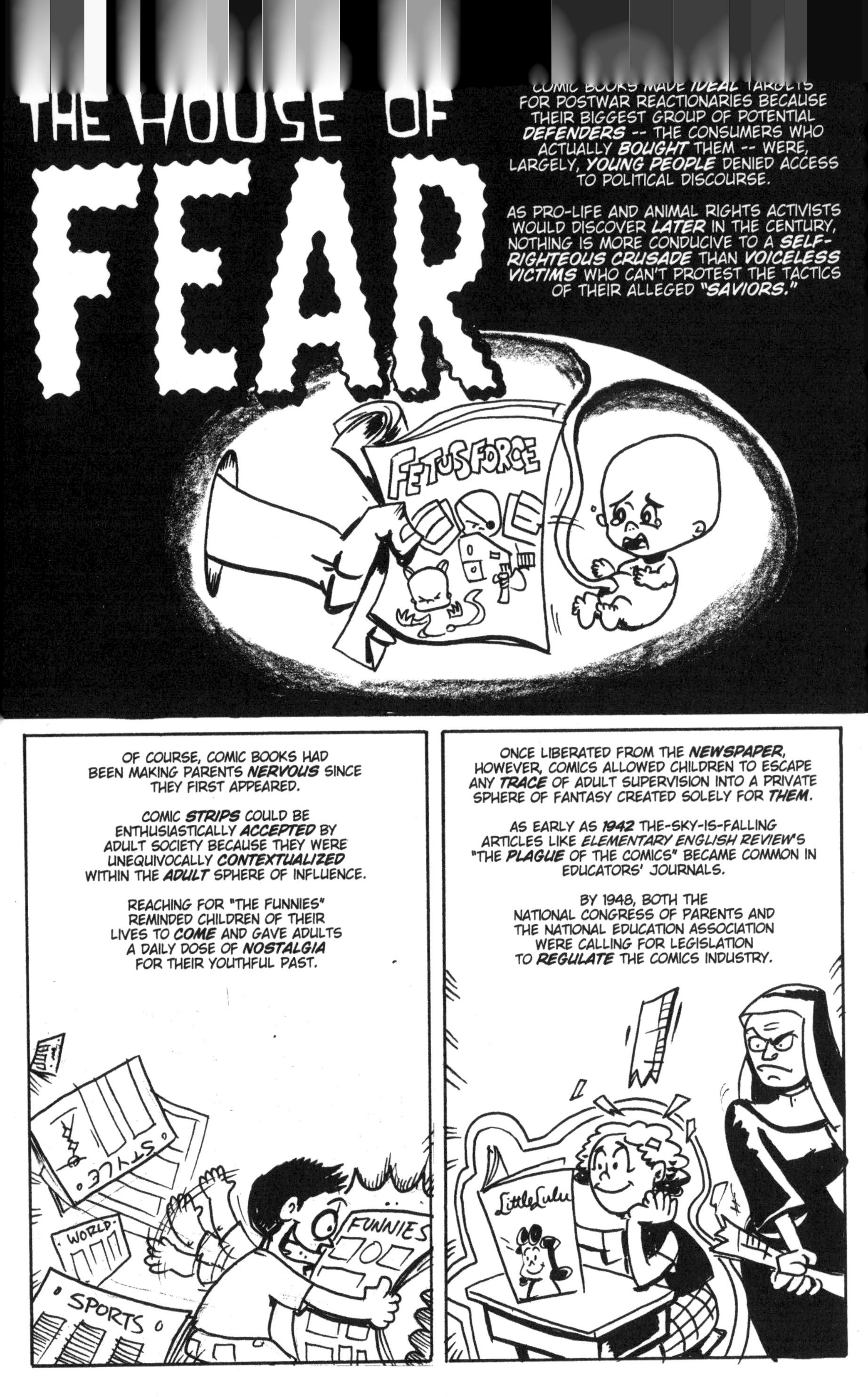

THE HOUSE OF FEAR

COMIC BOOKS MADE ***IDEAL*** TARGETS FOR POSTWAR REACTIONARIES BECAUSE THEIR BIGGEST GROUP OF POTENTIAL ***DEFENDERS*** -- THE CONSUMERS WHO ACTUALLY ***BOUGHT*** THEM -- WERE, LARGELY, ***YOUNG PEOPLE*** DENIED ACCESS TO POLITICAL DISCOURSE.

AS PRO-LIFE AND ANIMAL RIGHTS ACTIVISTS WOULD DISCOVER ***LATER*** IN THE CENTURY, NOTHING IS MORE CONDUCIVE TO A ***SELF-RIGHTEOUS CRUSADE*** THAN ***VOICELESS VICTIMS*** WHO CAN'T PROTEST THE TACTICS OF THEIR ALLEGED ***"SAVIORS."***

OF COURSE, COMIC BOOKS HAD BEEN MAKING PARENTS ***NERVOUS*** SINCE THEY FIRST APPEARED.

COMIC ***STRIPS*** COULD BE ENTHUSIASTICALLY ***ACCEPTED*** BY ADULT SOCIETY BECAUSE THEY WERE UNEQUIVOCALLY ***CONTEXTUALIZED*** WITHIN THE ***ADULT*** SPHERE OF INFLUENCE.

REACHING FOR "THE FUNNIES" REMINDED CHILDREN OF THEIR LIVES TO ***COME*** AND GAVE ADULTS A DAILY DOSE OF ***NOSTALGIA*** FOR THEIR YOUTHFUL PAST.

STYLE
WORLD
FUNNIES
SPORTS

ONCE LIBERATED FROM THE ***NEWSPAPER***, HOWEVER, COMICS ALLOWED CHILDREN TO ESCAPE ANY ***TRACE*** OF ADULT SUPERVISION INTO A PRIVATE SPHERE OF FANTASY CREATED SOLELY FOR ***THEM***.

AS EARLY AS ***1942*** THE-SKY-IS-FALLING ARTICLES LIKE ***ELEMENTARY ENGLISH REVIEW'S*** "THE ***PLAGUE*** OF THE COMICS" BECAME COMMON IN EDUCATORS' JOURNALS.

BY 1948, BOTH THE NATIONAL CONGRESS OF PARENTS AND THE NATIONAL EDUCATION ASSOCIATION WERE CALLING FOR LEGISLATION TO ***REGULATE*** THE COMICS INDUSTRY.

Little Lulu

ONE OF COMICS' EARLIEST CRITICS WAS THE CONSULTING PSYCHOLOGIST FOR FAMILY CIRCLE MAGAZINE, WILLIAM MOULTON MARSTON, WORLD-RENOWNED INVENTOR OF THE LIE DETECTOR.
"IT SEEMED TO ME, FROM A PSYCHOLOGICAL ANGLE... COMICS' WORST OFFENSE WAS THEIR BLOOD-CURDLING MASCULINITY.
"A MALE HERO, AT BEST, LACKS THE QUALITIES OF MATERNAL LOVE AND TENDERNESS WHICH ARE AS ESSENTIAL TO THE CHILD AS THE BREATH OF LIFE."

MARSTON'S CRITICISMS CAME TO THE ATTENTION OF ONE MAXWELL C. GAINES.
REMEMBER HIM? HE PIONEERED DIRECT RETAIL OF FAMOUS FUNNIES AND GOT SUPERMAN PUBLISHED.
HE HAD FORMED A SISTER COMPANY WITH NATIONAL, "ALL-AMERICAN COMICS," THAT DEVELOPED POPULAR DC HEROES LIKE FLASH AND GREEN LANTERN.

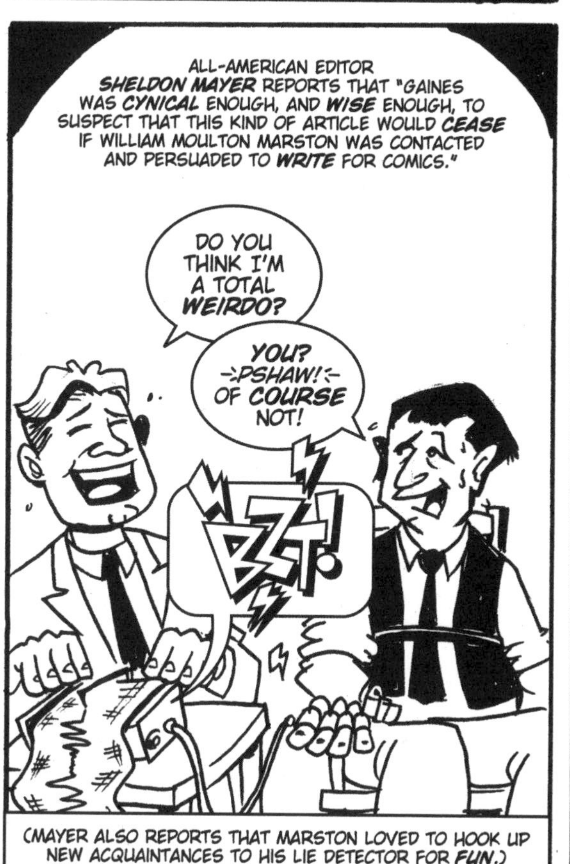

ALL-AMERICAN EDITOR SHELDON MAYER REPORTS THAT "GAINES WAS CYNICAL ENOUGH, AND WISE ENOUGH, TO SUSPECT THAT THIS KIND OF ARTICLE WOULD CEASE IF WILLIAM MOULTON MARSTON WAS CONTACTED AND PERSUADED TO WRITE FOR COMICS."
DO YOU THINK I'M A TOTAL WEIRDO?
YOU? -PSHAW!- OF COURSE NOT!
BZZT!
(MAYER ALSO REPORTS THAT MARSTON LOVED TO HOOK UP NEW ACQUAINTANCES TO HIS LIE DETECTOR FOR FUN.)

GAINES, AT THE TIME, PROBABLY HAD NO IDEA WHO HE WAS GETTING INTO BED WITH ... METAPHORICALLY SPEAKING. MARSTON LIVED IN A MENAGE A TROIS WITH HIS WIFE ELIZABETH AND HIS LOVER, JOURNALIST OLIVE BYRNE.
HE HAD MET OLIVE WHEN SHE WAS A GRADUATE STUDENT, AND THEY WERE BOTH (COUGH) "STUDYING" A SORORITY HAZING RITUAL CALLED A "BABY PARTY," IN WHICH PLEDGES DRESSED LIKE INFANTS, THEN WERE TIED UP AND PADDLED.
"WHEN WOMEN RULE, THERE WON'T BE ANY MORE (WAR) BECAUSE THE GIRLS WON'T WANT TO WASTE TIME KILLING MEN!
"THEY'D RATHER HAVE THEM ALIVE; IT'S MORE FUN FROM A FEMININE POINT OF VIEW!"

"TELL ME ANYBODY'S PREFERENCE IN STORY STRIPS, AND I'LL TELL YOU HIS SUBCONSCIOUS DESIRES!
"THESE... HIGHLY IMAGINATIVE PICTURE STORIES SATISFY LONGINGS THAT ORDINARY DAILY LIFE THWARTS AND DENIES.
"SUPERMAN AND THE ARMY OF MALE COMICS CHARACTERS WHO RESEMBLE HIM SATISFY THE SIMPLE DESIRE TO BE STRONGER AND MORE POWERFUL THAN ANYBODY ELSE."
BUT I SHALL ATTEMPT THE PROCESS IN REVERSE!
I WILL CREATE "PSYCHOLOGICAL PROPAGANDA FOR THE NEW TYPE OF WOMAN...
"...WHO SHOULD, I BELIEVE, RULE THE WORLD! THERE ISN'T LOVE ENOUGH IN THE MALE ORGANISM TO RUN THIS PLANET PEACEFULLY!"
TAPPING INTO HIS LIFELONG INTEREST IN GREEK AND ROMAN MYTHOLOGY, MARSTON INVENTED A PRINCESS OF THE ALL-FEMALE WARRIOR AMAZONS WHO WIELDED A TRUTH-COMPELLING MAGIC LASSO.
CONTRARY TO POPULAR BELIEF, "SUPREMA, THE WONDER WOMAN," AS MARSTON CALLED THE FIRST FEMALE SUPER HERO, WAS FULLY INTENDED FOR A MALE AUDIENCE.
"GIVE (MEN) AN ALLURING WOMAN STRONGER THAN THEMSELVES TO SUBMIT TO, AND THEY'LL BE PROUD TO BECOME HER WILLING SLAVES!"
WONDER WOMAN (SHELDON MAYER GOT MARSTON TO DROP THE "SUPREMA"), WRITTEN BY MARSTON (UNDER THE PSUEDONYM "CHARLES MOULTON"), DRAWN BY VETERAN ILLUSTRATOR HARRY PETER, FIRST APPEARED IN THE JANUARY 1942 ISSUE OF ALL STAR COMICS, AND WAS AN INSTANT SUCCESS.
AS MARSTON PREDICTED, DC SURVEYS SHOWED HER READERSHIP WAS 90% MALE! (GIRLS ACTUALLY PREFERRED TO READ SUPERMAN.)
SUPREMA
The WONDER WOMAN

THOUGH, FOR A PROTO-FEMINIST, MARSTON SURE LIKED TO HAVE HIS HEROINE GET TIED UP. A LOT. IN CHAINS, ROPE, FETTERS, HANDCUFFS... WHATEVER WAS HANDY.
ONE POSTHUMOUSLY PUBLISHED WW STORY (MARSTON DIED OF CANCER IN 1947) CONTAINED NO LESS THAN SEVENTY-FIVE PANELS OF BONDAGE!

ADMITS MAYER, "I SUSPECT IT PROBABLY SOLD MORE COMIC BOOKS THAN I REALIZED, BUT EVERY TIME I CAME ACROSS ONE OF THOSE TRICKS, I WOULD TRY TO CLEAN IT UP."
UM ... MAYBE THE VILLAINS COULD TRY TO, I DON'T KNOW... SHOOT WONDER WOMAN INSTEAD?
FOR ONCE?
-PSHAW!- "WOMEN ENJOY SUBMISSION!"

POOR SHELDON. NOT ONLY DID HE HAVE TO PUT UP WITH WONDER WOMAN'S LOOPY CREATOR, BUT ALSO GAINES' GOOFBALL SON, BILL, WHO GOFERED AROUND HIS DAD'S OFFICES DURING SUMMERS AND SCHOOL VACATIONS.
"CALLING ALL CARS! CALLING ALL CARS!"
BILL! SIT DOWN!

ONCE, MAYER WAS STARTLED BY A STRANGE SHAPE POPPING UP AT THE EDGE OF HIS DRAWING BOARD!

HE ACTED INSTINCTUALLY!
WHAKK!!

MAYER REPORTS HE HAD NEVER SEEN SO MUCH BLOOD IN HIS LIFE!

HE NEEDN'T HAVE WORRIED ABOUT ACCIDENTALLY INJURING THE BOSS'S SON...
"WHERE'S BILL?"
"I SENT HIM HOME."
"WHY THE HELL DID YOU DO THAT?"
"BECAUSE IF I DIDN'T, I WAS AFRAID I MIGHT DO HIM A PHYSICAL INJURY."
"WELL WHY DON'T YOU DO HIM A PHYSICAL INJURY? IT MIGHT DO HIM SOME GOOD."

...BECAUSE MAX HELD BILL IN NIGH-TOTAL CONTEMPT.
ONCE, WHEN BILL LAGGED TOO LONG AT LUNCH, MAX GAVE HIM A VICIOUS KICK -- RIGHT IN FRONT OF THE REST OF THE STAFF!

THANKS TO THE SUCCESS OF "WONDER WOMAN" AND OTHER FEATURES, MAX SOLD ALL-AMERICAN TO DC FOR HALF A MILLION DOLLARS IN 1945.
"I DON'T CARE HOW LONG IT TOOK MOSES TO CROSS THE DESERT!
"I WANT IT IN THREE PANELS!!"
HE USED THE MONEY TO START HIS OWN COMPANY, "EC," "EDUCATIONAL COMICS," WHICH PUBLISHED PICTURE STORIES FROM THE BIBLE TO HIS USUAL COST-CONSCIOUS STANDARDS.

EC STRUGGLED ALONG FOR A COUPLE YEARS, PRODUCING SIMILARLY WHOLESOME -- AND POOR-SELLING -- FARE.
THEN, TRAGICALLY, MAX AND A FRIEND WERE KILLED IN A BOAT COLLISION ON NEW YORK'S LAKE PLACID IN 1947.
OOPS.

AND, JUST LIKE THAT, WILLIAM M. "BILL" GAINES INHERITED THE FAMILY BUSINESS.
BILL WAS GOING TO BECOME A HIGH SCHOOL CHEMISTRY TEACHER. HE HAD NO INTEREST OR DESIRE TO RUN A COMIC BOOK COMPANY. HE WANTED TO SELL EC.
BUT HIS MOTHER INSISTED HE MAKE A GO OF IT, AS IT WAS THE ONLY THING THEY HAD LEFT OF HIS FATHER.

SHELDON MAYER SOON FOUND HIMSELF AWAKENED AT 3 AM.
BILL...?
"HOW THE HELL CAN I RUN A BUSINESS WHEN I COULDN'T EVEN MAKE IT AS THE OLD MAN'S STOCKROOM BOY?"
•NEVER SHOW ANYBODY STABBED OR SHOT
• SHOW NO TORTURE SCENES
•NEVER SHOW A HYPODERMIC NEEDLE.
• DON'T CHOP THE LIMBS OFF ANYBODY.
•NEVER SHOW A COFFIN, ESPECIALLY WITH ANYBODY IN IT.
HERE, LET ME GIVE YOU SOMETHING...
...THE EDITORIAL GUIDELINES YOUR FATHER FOLLOWED.
THEY SERVED ME WELL OVER THE YEARS-- I'M SURE THEY'LL DO THE SAME FOR YOU.
DAD'S RULES, EH...?
SO, FASTER THAN YOU CAN SAY "UNRESOLVED ISSUES"...
...BILL BEGAN PRODUCING COMICS THAT DIDN'T JUST BREAK MAX AND MAYER'S RULES...
...THEY CHOPPED THEM INTO BLOODY CHUNKS WITH AN AXE!
HORROR
EC
TALES FROM THE CRYPT
1950 SAW THE LAUNCH OF WHAT BILL DUBBED THE "NEW TREND IN COMIC BOOKS" FROM EC ... NOW RENAMED ENTERTAINING COMICS.

THE TYPICAL TALE FROM THE CRYPT INVOLVES AN ABUSIVE JACKASS...
HOW MANY TIMES HAVE I TOLD YOU, TIMMY?
KEEP THE PENCILS SHARP! ALWAYS KEEP THE PENCILS SHARP!
I'LL BEAT MY RULES INTO YOU UNTIL YOU LEARN THEM! C'MERE!

...RECEIVING HIS OR HER SUPERNATURAL COMEUPPANCE IN A SPECTACULARLY GORY ...AND IRONIC FASHION!
KEEP THE PENCILS SHARP... YES, WE MUST ALWAYS KEEP THE PENCILS SHARP... HEE!
AARGH!! THIS IS HIGHLY IMPLAUSIBLE... YET POETICALLY APPROPRIATE! AARGH!
NOTE: ACTUAL STORY IDEA SUBMITTED BY A TFTC READER!

(UNRESOLVED ISSUES, ANYONE?)
BILL! IT WAS AN ACCIDENT! I SWEAR!!!
NONE OF THIS MAYHEM TOOK ITSELF ALL THAT SERIOUSLY, BEFITTING THE PRANKSTER NATURE OF BILL GAINES HIMSELF.
LONG-TIME MAD ARTIST MORT DRUCKER RECALLS THAT, ONE SUMMER IN THE EARLY 1950s, "A YOUNG MAN HAD SECURED A JOB IN THE MAIL ROOM OF THE (EC) OFFICES...

"...BILL HAD DECIDED TO HAVE FUN WITH THIS YOUNG MAN AND HAD ONE OF THE STAFF MEMBERS INFORM HIM THAT BILL GAINES HAD AN EVIL TWIN BROTHER, AND TO TRY TO STAY OUT OF HIS WAY AS MUCH AS POSSIBLE."
I'M OFF TO LUNCH!
US MAIL

DON'T JUST STAND THERE, YOU BAG OF GUTS!
FETCH ME A BOURBON AND SOME CHILD PORNOGRAPHY!
"BILL PULLED OFF THE CHARADE THAT ENTIRE SUMMER...
"... AND TO THIS DAY THAT YOUNG MAN IS PROBABLY TELLING HIS GRANDCHILDREN OF THE SCARY AND CHILLING EVENTS OF THAT SUMMER JOB..."

GAINES WOULD LATER CALL THE "HORROR YEARS" THE ***BEST*** OF HIS LIFE.
EC, WHICH HAD BEEN ***$100K*** IN DEBT WHEN BILL TOOK OVER, WAS SOON ***THRIVING!*** "THE NEW TREND" WAS A HUGE SUCCESS THAT SPAWNED DOZENS OF IMITATORS!
BILL HAD ***SURPASSED*** HIS FATHER AT MAX'S OWN GAME -- DOING JUST WHAT ***HE*** WANTED!

THOUGH KNOWN FOR THE CLEVER PLOTS AND IRONIC ***HUMOR*** OF THE ***WRITING***, WHAT REALLY MADE THE "NEW TREND" STAND OUT WAS THE EYE-POPPING ***ARTWORK***.
IN THOSE DAYS, MANY COMIC BOOK PUBLISHERS PRESSURED ARTISTS TO DRAW IN A ***"HOUSE STYLE"*** SPECIFIC TO ***THAT*** COMPANY.

THIS NOT ONLY GRANTED ***CONSISTENCY*** TO THE COMPANY'S LINE...
...IT ALSO RENDERED ARTISTS IMMINENTLY ***REPLACEABLE*** IF THEY FLAKED OUT ... OR GOT TOO ***UPPITY***.

INNOVATION: STYLE AS STAR!

BUT GAINES' EDITOR, ***AL FELDSTEIN***, AN EXCELLENT ARTIST IN HIS OWN RIGHT (AND LATER AN ACCOMPLISHED ***PAINTER***), ENCOURAGED EACH EC PENCILLER TO DEVELOP HIS ***OWN*** INDIVIDUALISTIC STYLE, WHICH THE COMPANY THEN ***PUBLICIZED***...

...SO EC "FAN-ADDICTS" COULD ARGUE OVER WHETHER THEY PREFERRED THE WINDSWEPT, DECREPIT ***HORROR*** STORIES OF A ***GRAHAM "GHASTLY" INGELS***...

...OR THE BRUTAL REALISM ***HARVEY KURTZMAN*** BROUGHT TO HIS ***WAR*** BOOKS, *TWO-FISTED TALES* AND *FRONTLINE COMBAT*...

...OR THE SPECTACULAR ***TECHNOLOGY*** AND VOLUPTUOUS ***SPACE MAIDENS*** FEATURED IN *WEIRD SCIENCE* AND OTHER EC SCIENCE FICTION TITLES BY ***WALLY WOOD***.

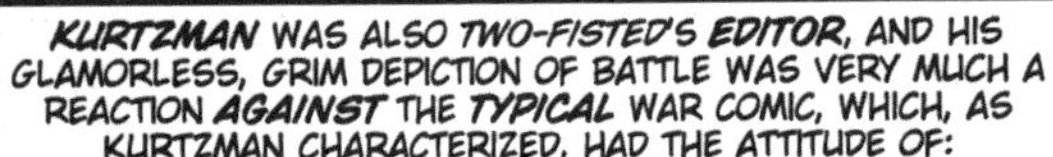
KURTZMAN WAS ALSO TWO-FISTED'S EDITOR, AND HIS GLAMORLESS, GRIM DEPICTION OF BATTLE WAS VERY MUCH A REACTION AGAINST THE TYPICAL WAR COMIC, WHICH, AS KURTZMAN CHARACTERIZED, HAD THE ATTITUDE OF:

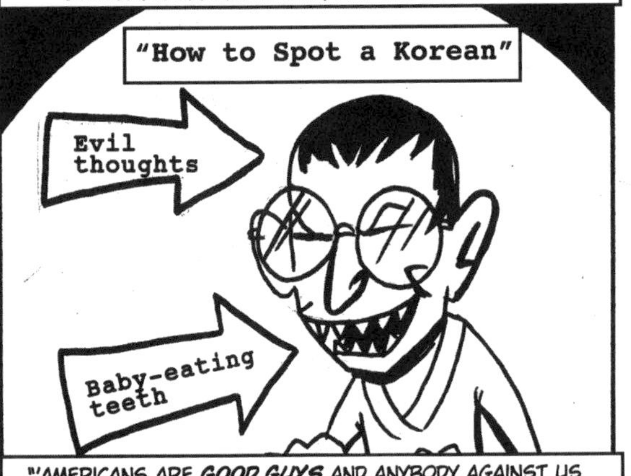
"How to Spot a Korean"
Evil thoughts
Baby-eating teeth
"'AMERICANS ARE GOOD GUYS AND ANYBODY AGAINST US IS THE BAD GUYS. WE'RE HUMAN. THEY'RE NOT. AND GOD IS ALWAYS ON OUR SIDE.' THIS TRASH HAD NOTHING TO DO WITH THE REALITY OF LIFE."

THE KOREAN WAR HAD JUST BEGUN, MAKING KURTZMAN, A VETERAN HIMSELF, FEEL HIS RESPONSIBILITY THAT MUCH MORE KEENLY:
"IF I WAS GOING TO TELL KIDS ANYTHING ABOUT WAR ... A-B-C LOGIC LED ME TO RESEARCH ACTUAL WAR AND TELL KIDS ABOUT WHAT WAS TRUE ABOUT WAR."
MEDIC
"NO, JACK, THE GAUZE PAD GOES TO THE RIGHT OF THE SULPHA..."
OH, FOR...

"THE AVERAGE COMIC-BOOK GUY WOULD LOOK AT ME AS IF I WERE NUTS.
"HE'D GO INTO A ROOM, HE'D BAT OUT A STORY, AND HE'D GET PAID; WHEREAS WITH ME...
"...I'D MAKE AN APPOINTMENT WITH THE AIR FORCE!
"I WASN'T MAKING ANY MONEY WITH THE WAR BOOKS. THERE WAS TOO MUCH RESEARCH AND LAYING OUT AND AUTHENTICITY INVOLVED..."

"...AND I THINK I WAS AVERAGING TWO WEEKS PER STORY, AS OPPOSED TO AL FELDSTEIN, WHO WOULD WRITE A STORY A DAY, OR A MINUTE, OR A SECOND."

PERHAPS IT WAS KURTZMAN'S CONSTANT COMPETITION WITH FELDSTEIN THAT MADE BILL TAKE HARVEY'S CONSTANT CRITICISM OF EC'S BREAD-AND-BUTTER, THE GORE-DRENCHED HORROR COMICS, WITH A GRAIN OF SALT.
HOW CAN YOU LET KIDS READ THIS STUFF?!?
LIGHTEN UP, HARV! NO ONE TAKES IT SERIOUSLY!
BABY EATING CORPSES

GAINES WAS WRONG. THE LEGISLATIVE OUTCRY AGAINST CRIME COMICS HAD BROUGHT A TIDAL WAVE OF FUNNYBOOK CRITICISM TO A HEAD.
EARLY IN 1954, THE HARTFORD COURANT ATTACKED HORROR COMICS (SINGLING OUT TALES FROM THE CRYPT) IN A FOUR-PART EDITORIAL ASSAULT ENTITLED "DEPRAVITY FOR CHILDREN." THEY GOT A FLOOD OF POSITIVE MAIL IN RESPONSE!

FORENSIC PSYCHIATRIST DR. FREDRIC WERTHAM SOON FOLLOWED WITH HIS BESTSELLER, SEDUCTION OF THE INNOCENT, WHICH ARGUED:
"IT IS MY OPINION, WITHOUT ANY REASONABLE DOUBT...
"...THAT COMIC BOOKS ARE AN IMPORTANT CONTRIBUTING FACTOR IN MANY CASES OF JUVENILE DELINQUENCY."

WHILE MAX GAINES MIGHT HAVE FIGURED OUT A CLEVER WAY TO CO-OPT WERTHAM'S AGENDA, JUST AS HE HAD WITH MARSTON...
YOU KNOW WHAT, FRED? -HIC!- YOU'RE THE BEST.
NO, MAX, YOU'RE THE BEST. -HIC!- YOU'RE WICKED AWESOME, DUDE!! -SOB!-

...BILL WAS NOT HIS FATHER. IN FACT, ALL HIS SUCCESS IN LIFE HAD BEEN ACHIEVED BY DOING THE OPPOSITE OF EVERYTHING MAX DID!
SO WHEN THE SENATE JUDICIARY COMMITTEE ANNOUNCED IT WOULD HOLD HEARINGS TO DETERMINE THE ACCURACY OF WERTHAM'S FINDINGS, ALL OTHER COMICS PUBLISHERS RAN AND HID...

...BUT GAINES DEMANDED TO BE HEARD! WERTHAM WAS JUST ANOTHER BULLY FOR BILL TO OVERCOME! THE DEFIANT PUBLISHER WOULD FORCE A CONFRONTATION WITH WERTHAM'S ANTI-COMICS FORCES...
...WITH NEITHER MAN REALIZING THAT THE BATTLE WOULD NEARLY DESTROY THEM BOTH!

THIS ISN'T A SENATE HEARING! THIS IS...

MADNESS

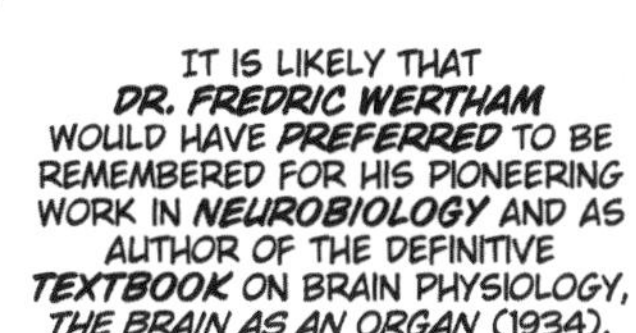

IT IS LIKELY THAT DR. FREDRIC WERTHAM WOULD HAVE PREFERRED TO BE REMEMBERED FOR HIS PIONEERING WORK IN NEUROBIOLOGY AND AS AUTHOR OF THE DEFINITIVE TEXTBOOK ON BRAIN PHYSIOLOGY, THE BRAIN AS AN ORGAN (1934).

OR FOR REINTERPRETING THE LOWENFELD MOSAIC TEST IN SUCH A WAY THAT THE AMERICAN JOURNAL OF PSYCHIATRY WOULD PROCLAIM:
"NO CHILD SHOULD BE DIAGNOSED AS SUFFERING FROM SCHIZOPHRENIA WITHOUT (WERTHAM'S) SCHIZOPHRENIC MOSAIC DESIGN."

OR AS THE AUTHOR OF PSYCHOLOGICAL STUDIES THAT CONCLUDED SEGREGATED SCHOOLS WERE DETRIMENTAL TO CHILDREN'S MENTAL HEALTH...
...WHICH PROVED PIVOTAL IN WINNING THE BROWN V. BOARD OF EDUCATION OF TOPEKA SUPREME COURT CASE IN 1954.

OR AS AN EARLY EXPERT WITNESS URGING JURIES TO CONSIDER THE SOCIAL BACKGROUND OF MENTALLY ILL DEFENDANTS...
...AS IN HIS ULTIMATELY FUTILE DEFENSE OF ALBERT FISH, THE INFAMOUS "VAMPIRE OF BROOKLYN," EXECUTED IN 1936 FOR CHOKING, DISMEMBERING AND EATING A TEN YEAR OLD GIRL.

DR. FREDRIC WERTHAM WAS AND IS ALL THESE THINGS AND MORE, BUT WHEN ONE SPENDS SO MUCH PUBLIC TIME AND ENERGY ENDEAVORING TO DEPRIVE MILLIONS OF CHILDREN OF THEIR FAVORITE PASTIME...
...IT IS PERHAPS NAIVE TO EXPECT A BALANCED NOTICE FROM HISTORY, WHICH WILL BE WRITTEN BY THOSE CHILDREN AS ADULTS WITH LONG MEMORIES AND GRUDGES TO SETTLE.
IN 1946, WERTHAM FOUNDED THE MULTIRACIALLY-STAFFED LAFARGUE CLINIC IN HARLEM. AS ONE OF THE ONLY PLACES IN AMERICA THE POOR, BLACK AND WHITE, COULD RECEIVE FREE OR LOW-COST PSYCHIATRIC CARE, LAFARGUE RECEIVED NUMEROUS REFERRALS OF JUVENILE OFFENDERS FROM NEW YORK CITY'S COURT SYSTEM.
WHILE ASSEMBLING DETAILED CASE HISTORIES ON THESE SO-CALLED "DELINQUENTS", WERTHAM WAS STRUCK AT HOW OBSESSED THEY WERE WITH COMICS, PARTICULARLY VIOLENT CRIME COMICS LIKE BIRO & WOOD'S CRIME DOES NOT PAY.
(OF COURSE, SINCE STUDIES SHOW 84% AND 92% OF ALL CHILDREN OF THAT ERA WERE COMICS-CRAZY, THE SIGNIFICANCE OF THAT OBSERVATION SEEMS RATHER QUESTIONABLE...)
AN AFICIONADO OF THE MARX-INFLUENCED FRANKFURT SCHOOL OF CRITICAL THEORY ESPOUSED BY HIS CLOSE PERSONAL FRIEND THEODOR ADORNO...
...WERTHAM SAW AN OBVIOUS CLASS BIAS IN WHICH RICH KIDS GOT OFF ON PSYCHIATRIC DEFENSES WHILE POOR KIDS, THOUGHT OF AS GENETICALLY, INTRINSICALLY, HOPELESSLY "ABNORMAL" GOT THE CHAIR.
MOMMY DIDN'T WUV ME ENOUGH! THAT'S WHY I STABBED MY BUTLER 385 TIMES!
AAAAAAAAAAAAAWWW...
INSISTING POLICY-MAKERS FOCUS ON SOCIAL CAUSES OF KIDDIE CRIME, WERTHAM ZEROED IN ON THE COMIC BOOK PUBLISHERS -- TO HIM, NOTHING MORE THAN EXPLOITATIVE CAPITALISTS CALLOUSLY FOISTING VIOLENT, PRURIENT IMAGES ONTO IMPRESSIONABLE MINDS, PLACING PROFITS OVER VULNERABLE CUSTOMERS:
"IT IS OBVIOUSLY EASIER TO SENTENCE A CHILD TO LIFE IMPRISONMENT THAN TO CURB A HUNDRED-MILLION-DOLLAR BUSINESS!"*
* WELL, MORE LIKE $41 MILLION IN 1950, BUT, AS WE'LL SEE, FACTS AREN'T EXACTLY THE GOOD DOCTOR'S STRONG SUIT...

BUT WERTHAM, LIKE MOST CENSORS, PROBABLY ALSO SUFFERED FROM A CONSERVATIVE REACTION AGAINST THE THREAT OF THE NEW.
THE GOL-DURNED INTERWEB WILL BE THE END OF US ALL!!!
SINCE THE BEGINNING OF HISTORY, EVERY TIME A NEW MEDIA HAS ARISEN IT HAS ALSO BEEN ACCOMPANIED BY CRIES THAT IT IS WORSE THAN ANYTHING THAT CAME BEFORE IT.
.COM
FOR EXAMPLE, ROBERT WARSHOW, AN EDITOR AT THE INFLUENTIAL COMMENTARY, WROTE AN ESSAY IN 1954 REFLECTING ON HIS DISCOMFORT WITH HIS 11 YEAR-OLD SON'S MEMBERSHIP IN EC COMICS' "FAN-ADDICT" CLUB.
EC
FAN-ADDICT
COMICS' "UTTER LACK OF MODULATION," WARSHOW WRITES, "YIELDS TOO READILY TO THE CHILD'S DESIRE TO RECEIVE HIS SATISFACTIONS IMMEDIATELY..."
HORROR
"...THUS TENDING TO SUBVERT THE CHIEF ELEMENTS IN THE PROCESS OF GROWING UP, WHICH IS TO LEARN TO WAIT."
OF COURSE, WARSHOW LOVED COMIC STRIPS, PENNING PRAISE OF THAT PERPETUAL PEN & INK DARLING OF THE INTELLIGENTSIA, GEORGE HERRIMAN'S KRAZY KAT...
...BUT SINCE HE WAS BORN IN 1917, WARSHOW WOULD HAVE GROWN UP READING NEWSPAPER STRIPS. THE CENSOR NEVER FINDS FAULT IN THE EPHEMERA AND NOVELTY FROM HIS OWN CHILDHOOD. (AFTER ALL, HE GREW UP JUST FINE, DIDN'T HE?)
POW!
ZIP!
THOUGH WARSHOW STRUGGLED WITH HISTORICAL ALIENATION FROM THE MEDIUM, HE STILL DISAPPROVED OF WERTHAM'S CONCLUSIONS:
I GOT NOTHIN'!
"DR. WERTHAM IS LARGELY ABLE TO IGNORE THE DISTINCTION BETWEEN 'BAD' AND 'GOOD' (COMICS) BECAUSE MOST (ADULTS) FIND IT HARD TO CONCEIVE OF WHAT A 'GOOD' COMIC BOOK MIGHT BE."
MAD
THOUGH WARSHOW DID ADMIT HE READ HIS SON'S COPIES OF EC'S SATIRE COMIC, MAD, "WITH A KIND OF IRRITATED PLEASURE."

MAD GREW DIRECTLY OUT OF EC WAR EDITOR ***HARVEY KURTZMAN'S*** FRUSTRATION THAT HORROR, CRIME AND SF EDITOR ***AL FELDSTEIN*** WORKED SO MUCH ***FASTER*** -- AND THEREFORE MADE SO MUCH MORE ***MONEY*** -- THAN HE.

TO PLACATE HIM, GAINES OFFERED:
"I'LL TELL YOU WHAT, HARVEY. I KNOW YOU'RE A HUMORIST. WHY DON'T YOU PUT OUT A HUMOR MAGAZINE.
"JUST SLIP IT IN BETWEEN YOUR TWO WAR BOOKS AND YOUR INCOME WILL GO UP FIFTY PERCENT!"

IN ITS FIRST ISSUE, ***"EC'S MAD MAG"*** BETRAYED THE GRIEVANCES OF ITS EDITOR BY PRIMARILY POKING FUN AT ***FELDSTEIN'S*** GENRE TITLES AND THEIR OFTEN-STRAINED ***"TWIST"*** ENDINGS.

ALMOST ***IMMEDIATELY***, HOWEVER, *MAD* ***EXPANDED*** ITS RANGE OF ATTACK TO INCLUDE ANY AND ***EVERY*** ASPECT OF POP CULTURE IT COULD GET ITS HANDS ON: OTHER COMICS, STRIPS, CARTOONS, MOVIES, RADIO, TV!

TALES FROM THE CRIB
FO' SHNIZZLE
666
PIMP

WARSHOW NOTED THAT MAD WAS, IN ITS OWN WAY, JUST AS VIOLENT AS EC'S HORROR AND CRIME BOOKS: "THE TENDENCY OF THE HUMOR ...IS TO REDUCE ALL CULTURE TO INDISCRIMINATE ANARCHY."
KIDS LOVE ANARCHY! BY 1953, MAD SALES HAD EXPLODED!
RIP

MAD WAS SO SUCCESSFUL THAT FELDSTEIN CONVINCED GAINES TO BEGIN A SECOND HUMOR COMIC, PANIC... WITH HIMSELF AS EDITOR. "I WAS PRETTY BITTER ABOUT IT," KURTZMAN WOULD RECALL.
PANIC
PANIC
MAD

IRONICALLY -- BUT NOT ***SURPRISINGLY***, PERHAPS, GIVEN THE NATURE OF THE ***FIFTIES*** -- IT WOULD NOT BE EC'S CRIME OR HORROR TITLES THAT LANDED THEM IN HOT WATER WITH THE LAW, BUT A SATIRICALLY-ILLUSTRATED VERSION OF ***"THE NIGHT BEFORE CHRISTMAS"*** IN *PANIC #1.*

PANIC

NOT LONG AFTER THE ISSUE HIT THE STANDS IN DECEMBER 1953, THE STATE OF MASSACHUSETTS ***BANNED*** IT, DECLARING IT ***"DESECRATED CHRISTMAS"*** AND DEMEANED SANTA CLAUS IN A ***PAGAN*** FASHION!

BRING ME THE HEAD OF THIS ***GAINES*** PUNK! ***NOBODY*** DISSES THE ***CLAUS!***

FURIOUS, GAINES DECLARED EC WOULD NO LONGER OFFER ITS *PICTURE STORIES FROM THE BIBLE* LINE IN MASSACHUSETTS...

(...NEGLECTING TO ADD THE COMPANY HADN'T PUBLISHED A ***NEW*** ISSUE IN ***FIVE YEARS...***)

NOBODY WAS ***LAUGHING***, THOUGH, WHEN NYC COPS BURST INTO THE EC OFFICES, DEMANDED RECEPTIONIST SHIRLEY NORRIS SELL THEM *PANIC #1* --

-- THEN ***BUSTED*** HER FOR PEDDLING ***"OBSCENE MATERIALS!"***

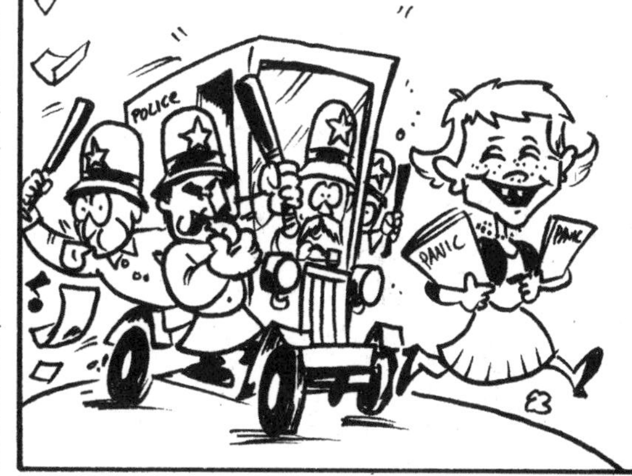
POLICE
PANIC
PANIC

MEANWHILE, DR. FREDRIC WERTHAM HAD ***TWICE*** ASSISTED IN PASSAGE OF LEGISLATION ***REGULATING*** THE SALE OF COMICS TO MINORS IN NEW YORK STATE...

...ONLY TO SEE ***BOTH*** BILLS VETOED BY GOV. THOMAS DEWEY (YES, ***THAT*** ONE) ON ***FIRST AMENDMENT GROUNDS!***

DEWEY DEFEATS WERTHAM

HAVING FAILED WITH THE ***POLITICIANS***, WERTHAM DECIDED TO TAKE HIS CASE DIRECTLY TO THE ***PUBLIC***. HE COLLECTED AND EXPANDED HIS EXTENSIVE ANTI-COMICS WRITINGS INTO A BOOK HE WANTED TO CALL *ALL OUR INNOCENTS...*
"IF YOU OPEN THE DOOR TO ***ANYTHING***, THE ***FILTH*** WILL POUR IN!"
...BUT HIS PUBLISHER PERSUADED HIM TO CHANGE THE TITLE TO EVOKE 19TH CENTURY ANTI-***DIME NOVEL*** CRUSADER ***ANTHONY COMSTOCK***'S 1883 SCREED *TRAPS FOR THE YOUNG:*
DUKE OF DEATH

SEDUCTION

COMICS ARE RACIST!
(FREQUENTLY TRUE...)
COMICS DESENSITIZE CHILDREN TO GORE AND VIOLENCE!
GROSS
BABY EATING CORPSES
DELISH!
(THE OLDEST PRO-CENSORSHIP ARGUMENT IN THE BOOK.)
COMICS GIVE GIRLS UNREALISTIC BODY IMAGES!
(AND ALL OTHER FORMS OF MEDIA DON'T?)

COMICS TEACH KIDS HOW TO COMMIT CRIMES!
COMIX
(DOES STICKING UP A LIQUOR STORE REALLY REQUIRE VOCATIONAL TRAINING?)

SUPER HEROES ARE FASCIST!
(THEIR JEWISH CREATORS MUST HAVE APPRECIATED THAT.)

COMICS PROMOTE ILLITERACY AND DISCOURAGE THE READING OF "REAL" BOOKS!
GAK!
WAR AND PEACE
(NUMEROUS STUDIES PROVE THIS FALSE.)

ALL COMIC BOOKS ARE REALLY CRIME COMIC BOOKS!
(UH ... WHAT?)

OF THE INNOCENT

...IN WHICH WERTHAM UNLEASHED A *DIZZYING* ARRAY OF CHARGES AT THE MEDIUM!

COMICS PROMOTE *HOMOSEXUAL BEHAVIOR!*
(ONLY IF YOU *LOOK* REAL HARD.)

COMIC ART CONTAINS *SUBLIMINAL SEXUAL MESSAGES!*
(ONLY IF YOU LOOK *HARDER.*)

COMICS ARE FILLED WITH ADS FOR PRODUCTS *UNHEALTHY* TO CHILDREN!
NEW
JUNIOR GARROTTE!
50¢
BE MOM'S FAVORIT —PERMANENTLY!
ITEM 211.....$.50
(THAT'S ACTUALLY TRUE.)
LIFE LIKE DUNLAVEY
HUGE 5½ FT!

COMICS ARE BAD FOR CHILDREN'S *EYES!*
(PERHAPS, IF THIS CHILD IS A 59 YEAR-OLD *FORENSIC PSYCHIATRIST.*)

COMICS REVEL IN *BONDAGE* AND *S&M* IMAGERY!
(ONLY IF YOU LOOK REAL...ER...
OKAY, HE MIGHT *HAVE* SOMETHING THERE...)

WONDER WOMAN IS A *LESBIAN!*
(NOT THAT THERE'S ANYTHING WRONG WITH THAT!)
INDIGO GIRLS

COMICS TEACH THAT STRENGTH IS *POWER,* AND THAT PROBLEMS CAN ONLY BE SOLVED THROUGH *FIGHTING!*
(*GREAT!* THEY'RE PREPPING OUR KIDS FOR THE *REAL WORLD!*)

A BOOK OF THE MONTH CLUB SELECTION, ILLUSTRATED WITH THE MOST LURID COMIC PANELS WERTHAM COULD REPRINT, SOTI WAS AN INSTANT BESTSELLER.
GASP! CHOKE!
BABY EATING CORPSES

NOT EVERYONE BOUGHT WERTHAM'S THESIS. COMMENTARY'S WARSHOW DISMISSED SEDUCTION AS "A CRIME COMIC BOOK FOR PARENTS":
"THERE IS THE SAME SIMPLE CONCEPTION OF MOTIVES, THE SAME SENSE OF OVER-HANGING DOOM, THE SAME MELODRAMATIC EMPHASIS ON PATHOLOGY, THE SAME DIRECT AND IMMEDIATE RELATION BETWEEN CAUSE AND EFFECT."
CRIME

AT THE SAME TIME, THE U.S. SENATE SUBCOMMITTEE CHARGED WITH INVESTIGATING THE NATION'S ALLEGED RISE IN JUVENILE DELINQUENCY WAS HOLDING HEARINGS AROUND THE COUNTRY.
THE CHAIR, ROBERT C. HENDRICKSON (R-NJ), ANNOUNCED THAT WHEN THE SENATORS ARRIVED IN NEW YORK THEY WOULD TAKE UP THE SUBJECT OF COMIC BOOKS.
A

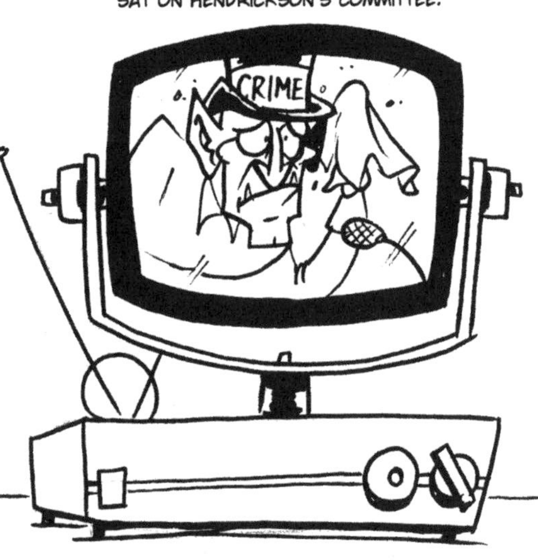
THE COMICS HEARINGS WOULD BE TELEVISED, IMMEDIATELY INVITING COMPARISONS TO THE SENATE'S ORGANIZED CRIME PROBE THAT BECAME A TV SENSATION IN 1951.
SENATOR ESTES KEFAUVER (D-TENN), THE CHAIR OF THOSE HEARINGS, ROCKETED TO NATIONAL CELEBRITY IN THE ANTI-MAFIA HULLABALLOO. HE ALSO SAT ON HENDRICKSON'S COMMITTEE.
CRIME

REACTING TO THE NEWS WITH FURY, WILLIAM M. GAINES CREATED A MOCK EC HOUSE AD -- "ARE YOU A RED DUPE?" -- THAT DECLARED, "THE GROUP MOST ANXIOUS TO DESTROY COMICS ARE THE COMMUNISTS!"
ARE YOU A RED DUPE?
I RESENT THE IMPLICATION THAT I AM SOME KIND OF A LEFT-WING THUG!
WHEN I AM SO CLEARLY A RIGHT-WING THUG!
HE SENT A COPY TO HENDRICKSON'S D.C. OFFICE. UNAMUSED, THE LEGISLATOR DENOUNCED GAINES ON THE SENATE FLOOR FOR TRYING TO INTIMIDATE HIM.

THOUGH NOT ORIGINALLY CALLED TO TESTIFY, GAINES REQUESTED, AND WAS GRANTED, THE RIGHT TO SPEAK. THE SUBCOMMITTEE SCHEDULED HIM TO APPEAR ON THE AFTERNOON OF APRIL 24, 1954, RIGHT AFTER WERTHAM.
"HITLER WAS A BEGINNER COMPARED TO THE COMIC BOOK INDUSTRY. THEY GET THE CHILDREN MUCH YOUNGER!"
HE HAD STAYED UP ALL NIGHT PREPARING HIS STATEMENT AND WAS CRASHING OFF DIET PILLS HE WAS TAKING.

THANKS IN NO SMALL PART TO "ARE YOU A RED DUPE?", THE SENATORS GREETED GAINES WITH OPEN HOSTILITY. KEFAUVER POUNCED WHEN GAINES TESTIFIED THAT THE ONLY LIMIT HE PLACED ON HIS COMICS WAS "GOOD TASTE."
CRIME SUSPENSE STORIES
"HERE IS YOUR MAY ISSUE.
"THIS SEEMS TO BE A MAN WITH A BLOODY AX HOLDING A WOMAN'S HEAD UP WHICH HAS BEEN SEVERED FROM HER BODY.
"DO YOU THINK THAT'S IN GOOD TASTE?"

"YES, SIR, I DO-- FOR THE COVER OF A HORROR COMIC.
"A COVER IN A BAD TASTE, FOR EXAMPLE, MIGHT BE DEFINED AS HOLDING THE HEAD A LITTLE HIGHER SO THAT THE BLOOD COULD BE SEEN DRIPPING FROM IT...
"...AND MOVING THE BODY OVER A LITTLE FURTHER SO THAT THE NECK OF THE BODY COULD BE SEEN TO BE BLOODY."
AS AESTHETICALLY DEFENSIBLE AS HIS ARGUMENTS MAY HAVE BEEN...

...TO PARENTS, GAINES' RESPONSES MADE PUBLISHERS LOOK AS DISINTERESTED IN CHILDREN'S WELFARE AS WERTHAM CLAIMED!
MURMUR
MURMUR
FROM A PUBLIC RELATIONS STANDPOINT, GAINES' TESTIMONY WAS AN UTTER DISASTER.

EVERYONE WATCHING ON TV *KNEW* IT, TOO, INCLUDING *JOE SIMON* AND *JACK KIRBY*, WHO SAW THE HEARINGS TOGETHER.
"STUPID. STUPID, STUPID!"
OY!
"NO HARM IN HORROR, COMICS ISSUER SAYS" SCREAMED THE *NEW YORK TIMES'* FRONT PAGE THE FOLLOWING MORNING.

THE PUBLIC BACKLASH WAS SWIFT AND DEVASTATING. CATHOLIC SCHOOLS, BOY AND GIRL SCOUT TROOPS, AND VARIOUS OTHER CIVIC ORGANIZATIONS SPONSORED *"BOOK SWAPS"* IN WHICH KIDS WERE GIVEN FREE *PROSE BOOKS* IN EXCHANGE FOR TURNING OVER THEIR COMIC BOOKS.
IN *REAL* LITERATURE, YOU WON'T BE EXPOSED TO SEX OR VIOLENCE OR BAD LANGUAGE AT *ALL*!
ULYSSES
JOYCE

A PRIZE WAS GIVEN TO THE CHILD WHO TURNED IN THE MOST COMICS (TYPICALLY *100+*), AND THE CONFISCATED BOOKS WOULD THEN BE THROWN ON A *PUBLIC BONFIRE*.
COMIC BOOK CREATORS FOUND THEMSELVES SNUBBED AT PARTIES AND DENOUNCED BY NEIGHBORS.
"IT WAS LIKE THE *PLAGUE*," REMEMBERS ARTIST CARMINE INFANTINO. "IF YOU SAID YOU DREW COMIC BOOKS, IT WAS LIKE SAYING YOU WERE A *CHILD MOLESTER*."
COMIX
COMIX
COMIX
COMIX
POW

GAINES FOUND THE ONLY *PERK* WAS *SYMPATHETIC* TREATMENT AT THE *LITTLE ITALY* RESTAURANTS NEAR EC'S LAFAYETTE STREET OFFICES.
I KNOW-A EXACTLY HOW YOU *FEEL*, DON GAINES-O...
FINALLY, BILL CIRCULATED A LETTER TO FELLOW PUBLISHERS RECOMMENDING THE CREATION OF AN *INDUSTRY ORGANIZATION* TO RESTORE PUBLIC CONFIDENCE IN THE MEDIUM.

ON AUGUST 17, 1954, THIRTY-EIGHT PUBLISHERS, WHOLESALERS AND PRINTERS MET TO DISCUSS GAINES' PLAN IN MANHATTAN'S *BILTMORE HOTEL*.
ARCHIE PUBLISHER *JOHN GOLDWATER* WAS ELECTED PRESIDENT OF THE NEW *COMICS MAGAZINE ASSOCIATION OF AMERICA* (CMAA), WHICH PROUDLY PROCLAIMED:
A

"TAKEN TOGETHER (THE CMAA'S NEW) PROVISIONS CONSTITUTE THE MOST SEVERE SET OF PRINCIPLES FOR ANY COMMUNICATIONS MEDIA IN USE TODAY, RESTRICTING THE USE OF MANY TYPES OF MATERIAL PERMITTED BY THE MOTION PICTURE CODE AND THE CODES FOR THE TELEVISION AND RADIO INDUSTRIES."
APPROVED BY THE COMICS CODE AUTHORITY
CRIME
IN ADDITION TO PREDICTABLE BANS ON DEPICTIONS OF SEX, DRUGS AND VIOLENCE, THE CMAA CONTENT CODE ALSO PROHIBITED THE USE OF THE WORDS "CRIME," "HORROR" AND "TERROR" IN TITLES...
BUT THIS WHOLE !@#$%! THING WAS MY IDEA!!!
THAT'S PAYBACK FOR YA, TUBBY!
...EFFETIVELY KILLING EC'S "NEW TREND" LINE, WHICH HAD ALL THOSE WORDS IN ITS TITLES!
MANY IN THE EC CAMP BELIEVED GOLDWATER HAD IT IN FOR BILL BECAUSE OF THE MAD PARODY OF ARCHIE THAT DEPICTED THE RIVERDALE GANG AS MERCILESS JUVIES.
BLUNTLY TOLD BY HIS DISTRIBUTORS THEY WOULD NOT CARRY ANY EC TITLE WITHOUT THE CMAA SEAL OF APPROVAL, GAINES ATTEMPTED A "NEW DIRECTION" OF TAMER, CODE-APPROVED TITLES, BUT THEY STRUGGLED MISERABLY.
PUBLISHERS FREQUENTLY FOUND THE CENSORS' REQUESTED CHANGES ARBITRARY AND BIZARRE.
ATLAS EDITOR STAN LEE TELLS OF BEING BAFFLED WHEN THE CODE OFFICE REJECTED AN ISSUE OF KID COLT, OUTLAW FOR BEING "TOO VIOLENT"...
...WHEN HE ASKED WHY, HE WAS TOLD IT WAS BECAUSE TOO MUCH SMOKE CAME OUT OF THE HERO'S SIX-GUN WHEN HE FIRED IT.
IN ORDER TO QUALIFY FOR THE SEAL, COMICS STORIES HAD TO FIRST BE SENT TO THE CMAA OFFICES, WHERE A CRACK SQUAD OF RETIRED SCHOOLTEACHERS WOULD RUTHLESSLY INSPECT THEM FOR ANYTHING OBJECTIONABLE.
COMIX

FOR GAINES, THE LAST STRAW CAME IN 1956, WHEN A CODE CENSOR OBJECTED TO SWEAT ON THE BROW OF AN AFRICAN-AMERICAN ASTRONAUT IN THE LATEST ISSUE OF INCREDIBLE SCIENCE FICTION...
THEY WANT ME TO CUT WHAT?!
(WHITE MAN SWEAT APPROVED BY THE COMICS CODE AUTHORITY)
...JUSTIFYING ITS REMOVAL UNDER THE CODE'S "RIDICULE OR ATTACK ON ANY RELIGIOUS OR RACIAL GROUP" PROHIBITION.

CONVINCED HE'D NEVER GET A FAIR SHAKE FROM THE CMAA, GAINES CANCELLED EC'S MEMBERSHIP.
MERRY CHRISTM
YOU'RE
YOU'RE FIRED
YOU'RE FIRED
HE WAS CERTAIN HE'D HAVE TO LAY OFF THE ENTIRE EC STAFF RIGHT AFTER CHRISTMAS.

BUT:
BILL, UNLESS YOU LET ME TURN MAD INTO A GLOSSY MAGAZINE, I QUIT!

LIKE SO MANY OTHER ARTISTS, KURTZMAN FELT THAT "COMICS WERE A BASTARD FORM. I WANTED TO GET INTO THE WORLD OF SLICKS. THAT WAS PUBLISHING."
WHEN PAGEANT MAGAZINE, ONE SUCH "SLICK," WOOED THE FAMED CREATOR OF MAD TO BECOME ITS ASSISTANT EDITOR, KURTZMAN DELIVERED HIS ULTIMATUM TO GAINES.
$$$!

GAINES REALIZED THAT AS A MAGAZINE, MAD WOULD FALL OUTSIDE THE JURISDICTION OF THE COMICS CODE.
HARVEY, YOU'RE A GENUIS!
I...AM?

BEFITTING HIS NEW AMBITIONS, KURTZMAN SECURED ADDITIONAL MATERIAL FOR THE MAGAZINE VERSION OF MAD FROM SOME OF THE GREATEST COMEDIANS OF THE 1950s, INCLUDING ERNIE KOVACS, IRA WALLACH, AND STAN FREBURG.
MAD, SANS-C.M.A.A. SEAL, WENT ON TO INFLUENCE GENERATIONS OF COMEDY WRITERS AND STAND-UPS.

IN MAD'S PAGES KURTZMAN ATTACKED THE COMMERCIALIST DOGMA OF U.S. CULTURE IN THE SAME WAY HE ATTACKED NATIONALIST JINGOISM IN HIS WAR COMICS! HIS WAS THE PARODIC VOICE OF OPPOSITION!
MAD
PHILOSOPHER OF MEDIA MARSHALL MCLUHAN WROTE, "TODAY THE TEN-YEAR-OLD CLUTCHES HIS OR HER MAD IN THE SAME WAY THAT THE RUSSIAN BEATNIK TREASURES AN OLD PRESLEY TAPE OBTAINED FROM A GI BROADCAST!"
UNFORTUNATELY, RELATIONS BETWEEN GAINES AND KURTZMAN DETERIORATED ALONG WITH MAD MAGAZINE'S SUCCESS.
KURTZMAN WANTED TO PAY HIS ARTISTS MORE MONEY, BUT FRUGAL GAINES REFUSED...
MAD
...AND KURTZMAN'S PERFECTIONISM FRUSTRATED GAINES, FOR IT MEANT HIS "BIMONTHLY" MAGAZINE CAME OUT FOUR TIMES A YEAR.
WHEN PLAYBOY FOUNDER HUGH HEFNER INVITED HARVEY TO CREATE A HUMOR MAGAZINE FOR HIM, KURTZMAN TOLD GAINES THAT UNLESS HE GOT A 51% SHARE OF EC HE WOULD DEFECT.
GUESS WHAT HAPPENED?
THE HEFNER/KURTZMAN PROJECT, THE GLOSSY TRUMP, WAS WIDELY PRAISED-- BUT IT FALED TO TURN A PROFIT BECAUSE OF HIGH PRODUCTION COST AND FOLDED AFTER A MERE TWO ISSUES.
GAINES, WHO PERSONALLY OPENED ALL OF MAD'S MAIL, GREW ENRAGED EVERY TIME A CONFUSED READER SENT A SUBSCRIPTION REQUEST FOR TRUMP TO HIS OFFICES.
Dear Publishers of Trump...
NEVERTHELESS, THANKS TO MAD, GAINES MANAGED TO GET THE BETTER OF HIS ENEMIES AT THE COMICS CODE.
"LIVING WELL IS THE BEST REVENGE," AS THEY SAY.

GAINES WAS ONE OF THE ***LUCKY*** ONES.

THOUGH THE ENTRENCHED ***CHILDREN'S*** PUBLISHERS (DELL, DC, HARVEY, ARCHIE, ETC.) SURVIVED AND IN SOME CASES ***THRIVED*** UNDER THE CODE'S CONTENT RESTRICTIONS, THE CMAA ***EMASCULATED*** COMICS' ABILITY TO APPEAL TO READERS WHO HAD REACHED PUBERTY AND BEYOND. ANYONE INTERESTED IN PRODUCING MORE ***ADULT*** MATERIAL WAS ESSENTIALLY RUN OUT OF BUSINESS.

THE INDUSTRY STIGMATIZED ITSELF AS MERE ***"KIDDIE FARE"*** FOR DECADES!

(HERE WE CALL THIS THE ***"LOGAN'S RUN*** EFFECT.")

ADULT
COMICS

THIS LACK OF DIVERSITY CAME AT THE ***WORST*** POSSIBLE TIME, AS ***TELEVISION*** WAS BECOMING WIDESPREAD IN THE U.S. IF AMERICANS ***WANTED*** ANTISEPTIC IMAGERY, ALL THEY HAD TO DO WAS TURN ON THEIR ***SET***.

BETWEEN COMPETITION FROM TV, THE ELIMINATION OF NON-CODE-APPROVED PRODUCT, AND SPOOKED DISTRIBUTORS REFUSING TO CARRY ***ANY*** COMICS AT ALL, SEAL OR NO, THE NUMBER OF TITLES PUBLISHED DROPPED WELL OVER ***50%*** FROM 1954 TO 1956.

THE DISASTROUS ***DOMINO EFFECT*** CONTINUED UP AND DOWN THE SUPPLY CHAIN: WHEN EC COMICS WENT DOWN, ITS DISTRIBUTOR, ***LEADER NEWS***, WENT ***BANKRUPT***...
...TAKING WITH IT ***MAINLINE***, THE PUBLISHER FOUNDED BY ***JOE SIMON*** AND ***JACK KIRBY***. THE ARTISTIC DUO, WHICH HAD WORKED TOGETHER FOR ***FIFTEEN YEARS***, CHOSE TO GO THEIR ***SEPARATE WAYS*** AFTER THAT.

IN THE END, ONLY TWO PUBLISHERS, GILBERTON (***CLASSICS ILLUSTRATED***) AND THE DISNEY-ALLIED ***DELL COMICS***, REFUSED TO JOIN THE CMAA. DELL CLAIMED ITS OWN ***IN-HOUSE*** CODE WAS ACTUALLY ***STRICTER*** THAN THE AUTHORITY'S.
APPROVED BY THE COMICS CODE
CA

AND NO DISTRIBUTOR DARED REFUSE TO CARRY THE ALMIGHTY ***MOUSE*** FOR SOMETHING AS FRIVOLOUS AS LACK OF A ***COMICS CODE SEAL.***

MEANWHILE, PUBLICATION OF THE HENDRICKSON COMMITTEE'S FINAL REPORT WAS DELAYED UNTIL EARLY SPRING, 1955...
-PSST!- PSSST! HEY, BUDDY...
WANNA READ A SENATE SUBCOMMITTEE REPORT?
...SINCE THE GOVERNMENT PRINTING OFFICE PROTESTED THE GORY, SOTI-STYLE COMICS PANELS IT REPRINTED WERE "UNSUITABLE FOR REPRODUCTION IN A SENATE DOCUMENT."
REPORT
THOUGH IT URGED SELF REGULATION TO REIN IN THE INDUSTRY'S MORE IRRESPONSIBLE ELEMENTS (I.E. GAINES), THE REPORT CONCLUDED THAT:
"COMIC-BOOK READING IS NOT THE CAUSE OF EMOTIONAL MALADJUSTMENT IN CHILDREN!"
COMICS ARE CLEARED! COMICS ARE CLEARED! YAAAAAAAAY!!
THE PUNCH LINE TO THIS WHOLE STORY, OF COURSE, IS THAT NO ONE HATED THE COMICS CODE MORE...
THIS HYPOCRITICAL PAP IS EVEN WORSE THAN IT WAS BEFORE!!
...THAN DR. FREDRIC WERTHAM.
AUTHORITY
THE GOOD DOCTOR (RIGHTLY) POINTED OUT THAT CODE-SANITIZED COMICS STORIES NOW SIMPLY OMITTED THE CONSEQUENCES OF CRIME AND VIOLENCE...
OW.
...THEREBY PRESENTING AN EVEN MORE DISTORTED VIEW OF REALITY THAN PRE-CODE MATERIAL.
BUT NOW WERTHAM'S PLEAS FELL ON DEAF EARS.
FOR IT WAS CLEAR TO ALL REASONABLE OBSERVERS FROM THE SHEER VOLUME OF PUBLISHERS THAT WENT OUT OF BUSINESS IN THE WAKE OF THE PSYCHIATRIST'S PURGES...
...THAT THE COMIC BOOK IN AMERICA WAS FINISHED.
HARRY "A CHESLER
QUALITY
HILLMAN
VICTOR FOX
NOVELTY
EC
LEV GLEASON
EASTERN COLOR

FANBASE Presents...
THOUGH EC, SANS MAD, DIED WITH THE BIRTH OF THE CMAA, THE 20,000 MEMBERS OF ITS OFFICIAL "FAN-ADDICT" CLUB KEPT ITS MEMORY ALIVE...
...TRADING AND SELLING OLD COMICS, SWAPPING MEMORIES, AND SHARING THEIR OWN EC-STYLE STRIPS THROUGH HOMEMADE FANZINES LIKE POTRZEBIE, HOOHAH, ECHHH...
...AND FOO, A GENTLE MAD PASTICHE WRITTEN AND DRAWN BY THE CRUMB BROTHERS, CHARLES AND ROBERT, OF DOVER, DELAWARE.
CRIME SUSPENSTORIES
WEIRD FANTASY
TWO-FISTED TALES
THE CRUMBS TRIED TO SELL FOO AT THEIR SCHOOL AND DOOR-TO-DOOR AT THE LOCAL AIR FORCE BASE WITHOUT MUCH SUCCESS IN 1958.
FOO
FOO
FOO!
FOO
THE BROTHERS BEGAN CREATING FAN COMICS AT AN EARLY AGE. CHARLES FIRST BECAME OBSESSED WITH DELL'S DISNEY-LICENSED PRODUCT AND, ROBERT REMEMBERS, "FORCED ME TO DRAW COMICS! IF I DIDN'T DRAW COMICS, I WAS A USELESS HUMAN BEING.
"I DREW YEARS AND YEARS OF BROMBO THE PANDA COMICS THAT WERE REALLY UNINSPIRED, BUT I HAD TO TURN THEM OUT ON A MONTHLY SCHEDULE (BECAUSE OF CHARLES)."
CHARLES' MANY OBSESSIONS HELPED HIM ESCAPE THE BOYS' ABUSIVE, DOMINEERING EX-MARINE FATHER.
HE STARTED DRESSING LIKE LONG JOHN SILVER AFTER SEEING DISNEY'S FIRST LIVE-ACTION EFFORT, TREASURE ISLAND (1950), ON ABC'S WALT-HOSTED DISNEYLAND.

(IT WAS REALLY **TELEVISION** THAT TRANSFORMED DISNEY STUDIOS INTO THE **MEGAGIANT** IT IS TODAY. WALT'S THREE-DECADE-DEEP ARCHIVE OF **FAMILY-FRIENDLY** FARE GAVE THE FLEDGLING ABC NETWORK ITS ***IDENTITY***.
(IT INCREASED THE SPREAD AND REACH OF THE DISNEY BRAND; AND **WALT** HIMSELF, AS THE HOST, BECAME THE MOST ***RECOGNIZED*** *AUTEUR* IN THE WORLD IN ***ANY*** MEDIUM.)

FROM DISNEY AND DELL ***ROBERT*** CRUMB GRADUATED TO *MAD* AND THE WORK OF ***HARVEY KURTZMAN***, STARTING WITH *HUMBUG*, HARV'S POST-*TRUMP* (AND EQUALLY ***TROUBLED***) SATIRE EFFORT.
Hey Kids COMICS!
Hey Kids COMICS!
COMICS
HUMBUG
THE END OF THE WORLD IS

ROBERT BECAME AN OBSSESIVE KURTZMAN ***COLLECTOR***: "I ***LIVED***, BREATHED AND ***ATE*** THE PAGES OF HIS MAGAZINES!"
BUT WHEN HE AND CHARLES FAILED TO EXCITE THEIR NEIGHBORHOOD OVER THEIR OWN EFFORT, *FOO*, THEY ***BURNED*** THE UNSOLD PRINT RUN.
FOO

STILL:
"THE ***REAL*** IMPORTANCE OF *FOO* WAS THAT IT CONNECTED CHARLES AND ME WITH THE NATIONAL ***FANZINE NETWORK***," ROBERT ATTESTS.
"THESE COMICS ***FANS*** WERE IMPRESSED WITH *FOO*. WE RECEIVED OUR FIRST ***VALIDATION*** FROM THE WORLD, THAT MAYBE IT WAS WORTHWHILE DOING THESE COMICS AND THAT WE MIGHT BE ***GOOD*** AT IT. IT GAVE US REASON TO ***HOPE*** WE MIGHT HAVE A CAREER IN THAT WORLD."
Dear Foo,
Keep up the great work!
Love,
E.C. Fan Addict #3094

THAT FAN ***NETWORK***, WHICH FIRST NURTURED THE ARTIST WHO WOULD HAVE THE GREATEST IMPACT ON THE MEDIUM SINCE ***SIEGEL & SHUSTER***, SPRANG FROM A TRADITION BEGUN A GENERATION ***BEFORE*** BY HUGO GERNSBACK...

INCOMING TRANSMISSION!!! FROM ***JULIUS SCHWARTZ***, 817 CALDWELL AVE., BRONX, NY RE: "PERILS OF THE PIRATE PLANET" IN OUR DECEMBER ISSUE!!!

...WHO PRINTED THE ***FULL ADDRESSES*** OF THE AUTHORS OF THE ***LETTERS TO THE EDITOR*** IN HIS SCI-FI PULPS, ALLOWING FANS TO THEN CORRESPOND WITH ***EACH OTHER***.

AMONG THE FIRST GENERATION OF GERNSBACK FANS WAS JULIUS "JULIE" SCHWARTZ, WHO MET FELLOW BRONX ROCKET JUNKIE MORT WEISINGER THROUGH THE READERS' COLUMN OF AMAZING STORIES. TOGETHER, THEY FOUNDED THE TIME TRAVELLER, "SCIENCE FICTION'S ONLY FAN MAGAZINE."
PAST
THE FIRST ISSUE DEBUTED JANUARY 9, 1932 WITH ARTICLES ON SF HISTORY, INTERVIEWS AND AUTHOR BIOS BY SCHWARTZ, WEISINGER AND THEIR FRIEND, FUTURE FAMOUS MONSTERS OF FILMLAND CREATOR FORREST J. ACKERMAN.
FUTURE

THROUGH HIS 'ZINE, JULIE BECAME A LITERARY AGENT FOR PULP AUTHORS LIKE ROBERT BLOCH AND H.P. LOVECRAFT.
YOU WANT TO BUY AT THE MOUNTAINS OF MADNESS. YOU WILL PAY FOUR CENTS A WORD FOR IT...
I WANT TO BUY...
XXX

SCHWARTZ WOUND UP AT MAX GAINES' ALL-AMERICAN COMICS AND STAYED WITH THE COMPANY AFTER DC BOUGHT GAINES OUT.
HE GOT MANY OF HIS SF BUDDIES AND EX-CLIENTS TO WRITE FOR DC, DESPITE SCI-FI FANDOM'S GENERAL CONTEMPT FOR THE COMICS MEDIUM.
NERD!
ALL-STAR

THANKS TO SCHWARTZ, DC BECAME A LEADER IN SCIENCE FICTION COMICS WHEN HE BROUGHT OUT TWO TITLES TO COMPETE WITH EC'S SF FARE: STRANGE ADVENTURES (1950) AND MYSTERY IN SPACE (1951).
DC
MONKEYS IN SPACE!
(STRANGE ADVENTURES BEGAN THE NOW-LEGENDARY 1950s DC TREND OF FEATURING GORILLAS ON INNUMERABLE COVERS, SINCE THEY ALLEGEDLY SOLD BETTER THAN NON-GORILLA COVERS.)

NEXT SCHWARTZ HIT ON THE IDEA OF REVAMPING ALL-AMERICAN'S SUPER HEROES -- CANCELLED EN MASSE AFTER THE WAR -- ALONG SF LINES.
FWEEEEEEET!!
HELMETS ON, BOYS! I'M PUTTIN' YOU BACK IN!

"I POINTED OUT THAT THE AVERAGE COMIC BOOK READER STARTED READING THEM AT THE AGE OF EIGHT AND GAVE THEM UP AT THE AGE OF TWELVE," SCHWARTZ WRITES IN HIS AUTOBIOGRAPHY.
"AND SINCE MORE THAN FOUR YEARS HAD ALREADY PASSED (SINCE THE HEROES WERE CANCELLED), THERE WAS A WHOLE NEW AUDIENCE OUT THERE WHO REALLY DIDN'T KNOW THE FLASH HAD FLOPPED, AND MAYBE THEY MIGHT GIVE IT A TRY."
FLASH
FLASH
FLASH
FLASH
AND SO SUPER-SPEEDSTER THE FLASH GOT A "REALISM MAKEOVER" IN THE DC TRY-OUT ANTHOLOGY, SHOWCASE.
AND, PERHAPS INADVERTENTLY, BY REINVENTING THE HEROES IN WAYS MORE SOPHISTICATED TO MODERN EYES, HE WAS RETAINING SOME OLDER READERS WHO MIGHT HAVE OTHERWISE STOPPED READING HERO COMICS.

EMBOLDENED BY THE NEW FLASH'S SUCCESS, SCHWARTZ'S NEXT ALL-AMERICAN MAKEOVER WAS GREEN LANTERN, DESIGNED BY VETERAN ARTIST GIL KANE.
KANE BASED THE LOOK OF THE NEW HERO, HAL JORDAN, ON HIS ONE-TIME NEXT-DOOR NEIGHBOR AND CREATION-OF-ISRAEL EXODUS MOVIE STAR PAUL NEWMAN.
IN BRIGHTEST MITZVAH, IN DARKEST CHUMITZ, NO NO-GOODNIK SHALL ESCAPE MY SIGHT!
LET GONIFS WHO WORSHIP MISHUGGENAH'S MIGHT... FEH! GET FARKLEMPT AT MY POWER...GREEN MENORAH'S LIGHT!
AND THE ALIEN OOMPAH-LOOMPAHS WHO GRANT JORDAN HIS POWER WERE MODELED ON ISRAEL'S FIRST PRIME MINISTER, DAVID BEN-GURION.

SUPER HERO CREATORS HAVE BEEN FOLLOWING SCHWARTZ'S TEMPLATE FOR TEACHING OLD TIGHTS NEW TRICKS EVER ***SINCE...***

THE EVOLUTION OF THE SUPER HERO

GOLDEN AGE:
WHAT THE--?
THE MYSTIC CAPE THAT MYSTERIOUS WIZARD GAVE ME HAS MYSTICALLY GIVEN ME THE MYSTIC POWERS OF THE FLAMING CAPE!
I MUST NOW USE THESE STRANGE AND WOND'ROUS POWERS TO SAVE WANDA WHITEBREAD FROM THAT ORIENTAL MASTERMIND, DOCTOR JAPANAZI!
AW-HAW-HAW!! SO SOLLY, OCCIDENTAL SWINE!!
SAVE ME, FLAMING CAPE!
FC

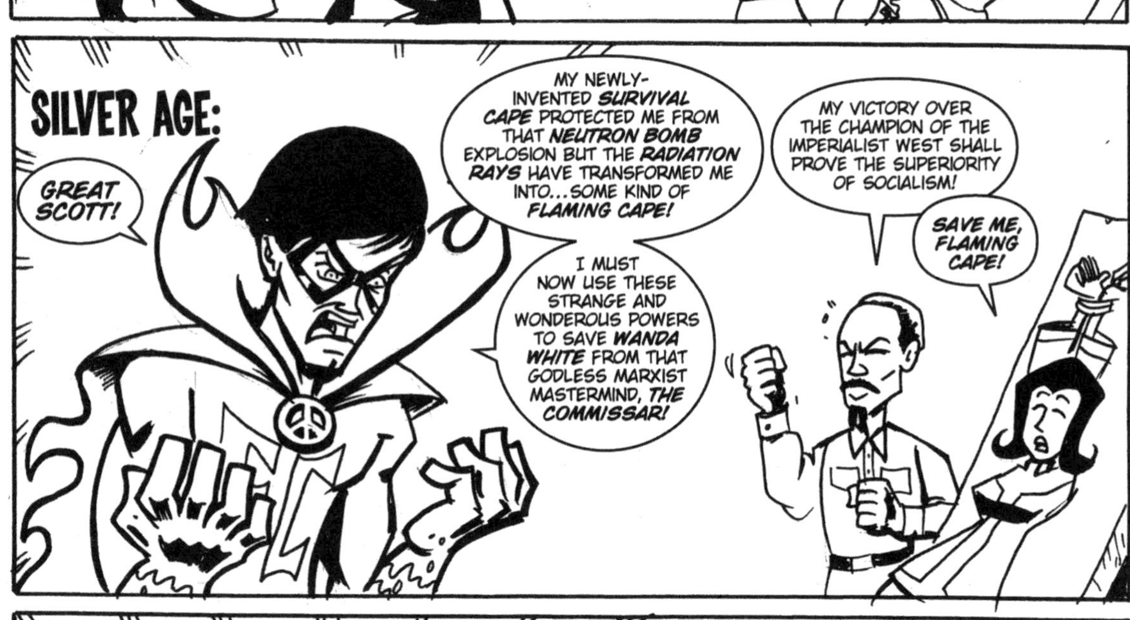
SILVER AGE:
GREAT SCOTT!
MY NEWLY-INVENTED SURVIVAL CAPE PROTECTED ME FROM THAT NEUTRON BOMB EXPLOSION BUT THE RADIATION RAYS HAVE TRANSFORMED ME INTO...SOME KIND OF FLAMING CAPE!
I MUST NOW USE THESE STRANGE AND WONDEROUS POWERS TO SAVE WANDA WHITE FROM THAT GODLESS MARXIST MASTERMIND, THE COMMISSAR!
MY VICTORY OVER THE CHAMPION OF THE IMPERIALIST WEST SHALL PROVE THE SUPERIORITY OF SOCIALISM!
SAVE ME, FLAMING CAPE!

MODERN AGE:
Holy Christ Rape!
While I was trapped in that virtual reality simulation, the nanomachines that top-secret military agency injected into me have ionized the air molecules around me into super-hot plasma!
Now I can seriously eff-up those terrorists and save President White...
...while Twittering about it on Facebook!
Too late, a-hole!
I stuffed her inside this refrigerator!
MILK EGGS
Ryan Dunlavey 2009

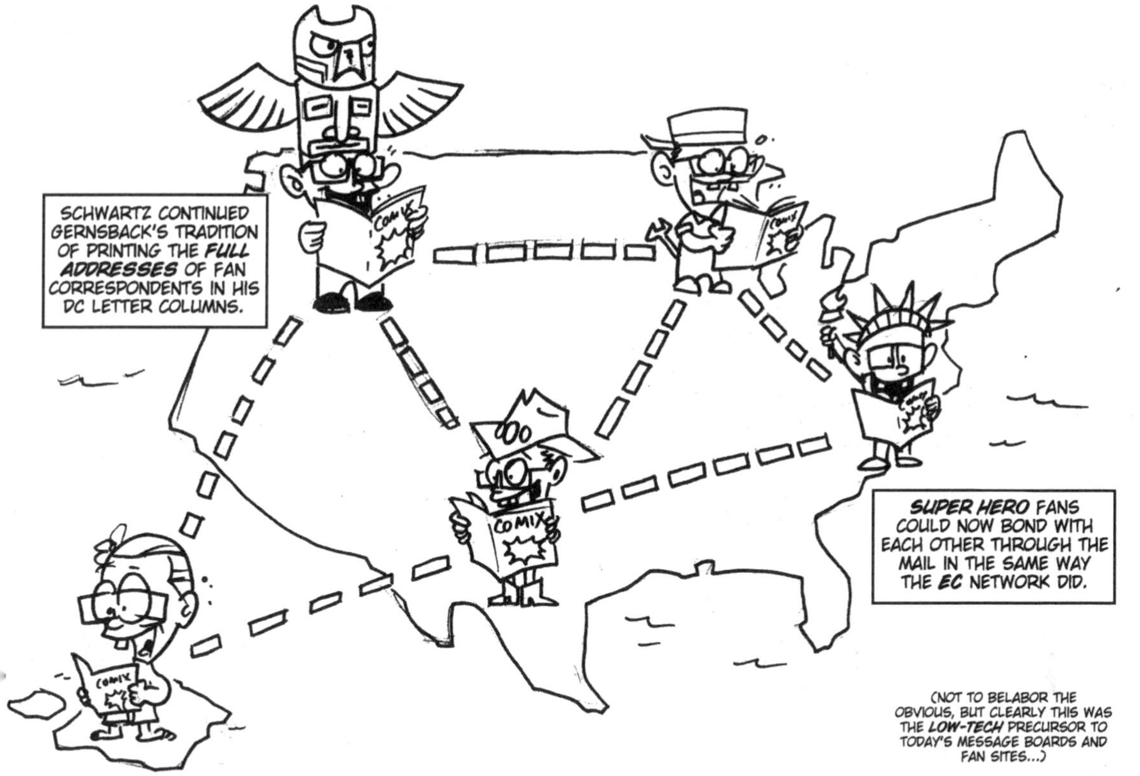

SCHWARTZ CONTINUED GERNSBACK'S TRADITION OF PRINTING THE ***FULL ADDRESSES*** OF FAN CORRESPONDENTS IN HIS DC LETTER COLUMNS.

COMIX

SUPER HERO FANS COULD NOW BOND WITH EACH OTHER THROUGH THE MAIL IN THE SAME WAY THE ***EC*** NETWORK DID.

(NOT TO BELABOR THE OBVIOUS, BUT CLEARLY THIS WAS THE ***LOW-TECH*** PRECURSOR TO TODAY'S MESSAGE BOARDS AND FAN SITES...)

PRE-SCHWARTZ, DC HAD NOT BEEN SO ADEPT AT ***FAN RELATIONS.***
WHEN YOUNG READER ***ROY THOMAS*** WROTE IN TO REQUEST BACK ISSUES, THE COMPANY TOLD HIM IT COULD NOT SANCTION SELLING ***OLD COMICS*** BECAUSE THEY MIGHT ***"SPREAD DISEASE!"***
ACTION COMICS 10¢

ONCE AN ADULT LOCKED INTO THE ***FAN NETWORK,*** THOMAS AND ANOTHER READER, DETROIT PROFESSOR ***JERRY BAILS,*** CONSPIRED TO MAKE ***"THE ATOM"*** THE NEXT ALL-AMERICAN HERO SLATED FOR RESURRECTION...
TARGET:

...GOING SO FAR AS TO SUBMIT THEIR ***OWN PLAN*** TO SCHWARTZ. BY A "FANTASTIC COINCIDENCE" (OR SO JULIE SAID), DC WAS WORKING ON A SIMILAR REVAMP OF THE MIGHTY MITE ***THEMSELVES***, WHICH APPEARED IN ***SHOWCASE*** #34 (OCT. 1961).
S-SO ***TINY***--YET WTH THE STRENGTH OF ***MANY!***

EMBOLDENED BY THE ENCOURAGEMENT HE RECEIVED FROM SCHWARTZ, BAILS, WITH THE ASSISTANCE OF THOMAS AND OTHERS, FOUNDED THE INFLUENTIAL HERO FANZINE ***ALTER-EGO*** IN MARCH 1961.
BURSTING WITH RETROSPECTIVES ABOUT OLD STORIES AS WELL AS ORIGINAL FAN FICTION AND ARTICLES ABOUT THIS CURRENT "SILVER AGE" OF COMICS, ***AE*** HERALDED THE COMING OF A NEW CREATURE IN U.S. POP CULTURE--
FAN MAN
OPINIONS
WORST! ISSUE! EVER!
--THE PROFESSIONAL COMICS FAN!

MEANWHILE, IN SPACE...

NO HEARTS BEAT AS FAST AS THOSE OF SCIENCE FICTION FANDOM (EXCEPT MAYBE THE PENTAGON'S) WHEN THE SOVIET UNION SUCCESSFULLY LAUNCHED ITS SPUTNIK SATELLITE ON OCTOBER 4, 1957.
THE RESULTING COLD WAR SPACE RACE BROUGHT THE GENERAL PUBLIC'S ATTENTION SOLIDLY TOWARD THE STARS ... AND THE SCIENCE FICTION GENRE GAINED UNPRECEDENTED POPULAR CACHE!

JULIE SCHWARTZ WAS NOT THE ONLY SF EDITOR AT DC.
JACK SCHIFF HELMED SPECULATIVE TITLES LIKE TALES OF THE UNEXPECTED AND MY GREATEST ADVENTURE.
IN JANUARY 1958 THE GEORGE MATTHEW ADAMS SERVICE, A SMALL NEWSPAPER SYNDICATE, CONTRACTED SCHIFF TO COME UP WITH AN SF COMIC STRIP TO CAPITALIZE ON THE SPACE CRAZE.
TAKE US TO YOUR SYNDICATE, EARTH SCUM!

GIVEN HIS BOSSES' BLESSING TO PICK FROM THE COMPANY'S FREELANCERS FOR THIS NEW VENTURE, SCHIFF SETTLED ON JACK KIRBY, WHO HAD RETURNED TO DC AFTER SPLITTING WITH SIMON POST-WERTHAM.
KIRBY'S LIFELONG LOVE OF SF MADE HIM THE NATURAL CHOICE.

HOW EXCITING THIS OPPORTUNITY MUST HAVE BEEN FOR A LIFELONG COMIC BOOK ARTIST LIKE JACK KIRBY!
LIKE ALL HIS GENERATION, HE YEARNED FOR THE STABILITY, THE PRESTIGE AND THE INCOME THAT CAME WITH A SYNDICATED STRIP!
TO JACK KIRBY
Ka-Ching!
$$$
Syndicate

SCRIPTED BY DAVE WOOD (BROTHER TO CRIME DOES NOT PAY'S BOB), KIRBY'S STRIP, SKY MASTERS OF THE SPACE FORCE, DEBUTED ON THE FUNNIES PAGE ON SEPTEMBER 8, 1958.
ACTING AS AGENT, SCHIFF EXPECTED 4% FROM THE CREATORS' PROCEEDS.
YOU'RE SUED!
WITHIN THREE MONTHS, SCHIFF SLAPPED A LAWSUIT ON KIRBY FOR FAILING TO PAY HIM HIS SHARE!
AT TRIAL, KIRBY CLAIMED THE EDITOR MADE HIM SIGN THEIR AGREEMENT UNDER DURESS...
"SIGN IT!"
...THAT SCHIFF INSINUATED HE WOULD GREATLY REDUCE KIRBY'S DC ASSIGNMENTS IF THE ARTIST DIDN'T COMPLY!
DC
BUT KIRBY LOST THE LAWSUIT AND AS A RESULT OF BAD BLOOD COULD NO LONGER WORK FOR DC.
SKY MASTERS WAS CANCELLED BY 1960 AND NOW, BEREFT OF OTHER WORK, HE FELT HE HAD NO OTHER CHOICE BUT TO RETURN...
C'MON, JACK, WE DON'T KNOW IT WAS STAN. THIS IS A SMALL INDUSTRY. LOTS OF PEOPLE COULD'VE RATTED ON US--
"THE NEXT TIME I SEE THAT LITTLE SON-OF-A-BITCH, I'M GONNA KILL HIM!!"
...TO THE ONE PLACE HE SWORE HE'D NEVER RETURN TO!
JACK! YOU'RE BACK! C'MERE AND GIVE YOUR OL' BUDDY STAN A HUG!
HI, STANLEY...
...SIGH!
TIMELY, AKA ATLAS, AKA MARVEL COMICS!

Tales to Marvel (at)

AFTER LEAVING THE SERVICE, ***STAN LEE*** BECAME THE EDITOR-IN-CHIEF OF HIS COUSIN-IN-LAW ***MARTIN GOODMAN***'S COMICS COMPANY, WHICH AROUND 1951 BEGAN CALLING ITSELF ***ATLAS***.

1948
LOVE
STAN LEE
STANLEY! WHY ARE WE CRANKING OUT ALL THIS SUPER HERO CRAP? THOSE TRAITORS SIMON & KIRBY ARE MAKING A KILLING WITH ROMANCE!
I WANT LOVE, LOVE, LOVE!
HEROIC HEROES

1951
DETH
STAN LEE
STANLEY! WHY ARE WE CRANKING OUT ALL THIS ROMANCE CRAP? THAT PUNK GAINES IS MAKING A KILLING WITH HORROR!
I WANT GORE, GORE, GORE!
LOVELY LOVE

WHATEVER THE ***NAME***, GOODMAN'S COMPANY CONTINUED ITS OVERALL PHILOSOPHY OF COPYING *AD NAUSEUM* WHATEVER THE MOST POPULAR ***TREND*** HAPPENED TO BE AT THE TIME.

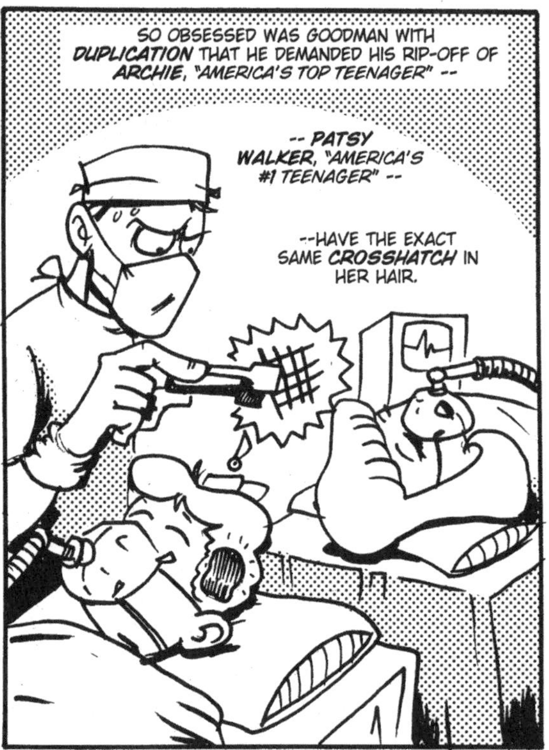

SO OBSESSED WAS GOODMAN WITH DUPLICATION THAT HE DEMANDED HIS RIP-OFF OF ARCHIE, "AMERICA'S TOP TEENAGER" --
-- PATSY WALKER, "AMERICA'S #1 TEENAGER" --
--HAVE THE EXACT SAME CROSSHATCH IN HER HAIR.

1955
STANLEY! WHY ARE WE CRANKING OUT ALL THIS HORROR CRAP? THE COMICS CODE IS CRACKING DOWN! WE GOTTA GET WHOLESOME!
I WANT COWBOYS, COWBOYS, COWBOYS!
HORRIFIC HORROR

THE ATLAS MOTTO COULD HAVE BEEN *"QUANTITY BEFORE QUALITY."* THEY CRANKED OUT A WHOPPING ***15.2 MILLION*** FUNNYBOOKS IN 1952 ALONE -- TWICE AS MUCH AS ANY OTHER PUBLISHER BUT ***DELL*** (AT 10 MIL).

IN THE WAKE OF THE WERTHAM PURGE, GOODMAN TRANSFERRED DISTRIBUTION OF HIS COMICS TO THE INDUSTRY LEADER, AMERICAN NEWS CORPORATION...
...RIGHT BEFORE THE FEDS TRUST-BUSTED IT FOR ALSO OWNING AMERICA'S LARGEST CHAIN OF NEWSVENDORS, UNION NEWS.
WHEN ANC CEASED OPERATIONS, IT LEFT NEARLY HALF OF AMERICA'S COMIC BOOK PUBLISHERS WITHOUT ANY WAY TO GET TO MARKET... INCLUDING ATLAS.
AM. NEWS CORP
DEPT OF JUSTICE
LEE WROTE, "IT WAS LIKE WE HAD BEEN THE LAST ONES TO BOOK PASSAGE ON THE TITANIC!"

IN 1957 GOODMAN ORDERED LEE TO FIRE THE ENTIRE ATLAS STAFF EXCEPT HIMSELF.
FACE FRONT, TRUE BELIEVERS!
I'VE GOT SOME GOOD BULLPEN BULLETINS AND I'VE GOT SOME BAD BULLPEN BULLETINS.
THE GOOD BULLETIN...
...IS THAT MARTIN IS GOING ON VACATION TO FLORIDA... -HEH!-

GOODMAN CONVINCED HIS OLD BOSSES AT THE DC-OWNED INDEPENDENT NEWS TO PICK UP DISTRIBUTION OF HIS LINE.
DC HOBBLED ITS COMPETITOR BY LIMITING ATLAS TO A PALTRY SIXTEEN TITLES, A MIX OF ROMANCE, WESTERN, WAR AND TEEN HUMOR...
DC
MARVEL
... EDITED AND WRITTEN BY STAN, AND DRAWN BY FREELANCE ARTISTS WHO WORKED FROM HOME.

1958
"GOJIRA"
STANLEY! WHY ARE WE CRANKING OUT ALL THIS WESTERN CRAP? THE JAPS ARE MAKING A KILLING WITH GODZILLA!
I WANT MONSTERS, MONSTERS, MONSTERS!
WESTERN OF THE WEST

METAA!!
THE THING THAT WALKED LIKE A MAN THAT WALKED LIKE A THING THAT WALKED LIKE A MAN!

WAIT... *HOW* DO I WALK?

RUN!!! HIS DECONSTRUCTED SIGNIFIER CHALLENGES MY CONCEPTS OF REINSCRIBED HEGEMONY!!

AAAHHH!!! MY GENDERED SUBJECT CAN'T SURVIVE THIS POSTSTRUCTURALIST THREAT!

AROUND THE TIME KOOKY, *KAIJU*-STYLE MONSTERS BECAME THE COMPANY'S NEW STAPLE, IT KIND-OF SORT-OF STARTED CALLING ITSELF ***"MARVEL"*** COMICS.

MARVEL'S MOST IMPRESSIVE MONSTER STRIPS WERE DRAWN BY NEWLY RETURNED PRODIGAL ***JACK KIRBY*** AND A LARGELY UNKNOWN YOUNGSTER NAMED ***STEVE DITKO***.

BUT ONE DAY DC'S ***JACK LIEBOWITZ*** TOLD MARTIN GOODMAN THAT ***HIS*** BEST-SELLING TITLE WAS THE JULIE SCHWARTZ-EDITED ***JUSTICE LEAGUE OF AMERICA***:

"INSTEAD OF HAVING IT BASED AROUND A *SINGLE* SUPER HERO, WE HAVE A WHOLE *TEAM* OF SUPER HEROES WORKING TOGETHER AGAINST A GIVEN MENACE OR VILLAIN IN A BOOKLENGTH ADVEN-TURE, AND THE KIDS *LOVE* IT.
"QUITE A *NOVEL* IDEA...AND PRETTY MUCH EVERY ISSUE IS A *SELLOUT!"*
GUESS WHAT HAPPENED NEXT?
1961
JUSTICE LEAGUE OF AMERICA
STANLEY! WHY ARE WE CRANKING OUT ALL THIS *MONSTER* CRAP?
I WANT *SUPER HEROES, SUPER HEROES, SUPER HEROES!*
AMAZING ADULT FANTASY

NAY! I SAY THEE...NO MORE!!
THOOOM!
LO, THERE MUST COME... A RECKONING!

MY JAUNDICED JOURNEY THROUGH THE BACKWATER BURG OF COMICSVILLE WAS ONLY SUPPOSED TO BE A TEMPORARY LAYOVER--
--INSTEAD IT'S GOBBLED UP TWENTY YEARS OF MY LIFE!
I HAVE OTHER KINDS OF WRITING EXPERIENCE! JOKE BOOKS! ARTICLES! VD PAMPHLETS!

FORBUSH KNOWS I'VE TRIED TO PLEASE MARTIN OVER THE YEARS, BUT THIS? SUPER HEROES? AGAIN?
'TIS TOO MUCH! I SHALL MARCH INTO MARTIN'S OFFICE AND HAND IN MY RESPLENDENT RESIGNATION THEN SALLY FORTH TO A LAND WHERE WRITERS ARE TRULY RESPECTED--
--LA!
HOLLYWOOD

VERILY, JOAN*, I DOTH HAD IT!!
WAIT, STAN-- IF YOU'RE GOING TO QUIT ANYWAY, WHY NOT DO THE SUPER HERO TEAM MARTIN WANTS YOU TO -- BUT PUT SOME BLOODY EFFORT INTO IT FOR ONCE?
WHY NOT DO A COMIC YOU'D LIKE TO READ?
* ALL EVIL-TWINIACS SHOULD RECOGNIZE STAN'S ENGLISH MODEL WIFE, WHOM HE MARRIED IN THE SPASTIC STAN-MAN #145 (AKA DEC. 5, 1947) --"RIGHT SAID" FRED

WISER WORDS MY WINSOME WIFE HATH NEVER SAID!!!
MY PLAGARISTIC PUBLISHER WILL HAVE THE COSTUMED CREW HE CRAVES!
BUT WE'RE PLAYIN' BY STAN'S RULES NOW!!

STAN PRODUCED THIS LATEST TITLE, *THE FANTASTIC FOUR,* IN MUCH THE SAME WAY HE PRODUCED HIS MONSTER BOOKS. AS HE EXPLAINS, "I WROTE AN ***OUTLINE*** CONTAINING THE BASIC DESCRIPTION OF THE NEW CHARACTERS AND THE SOMEWHAT OFFBEAT STORY LINE AND GAVE IT TO MY MOST TRUSTED AND DEPENDABLE ARTIST, THE INCREDIBLY TALENTED ***JACK KIRBY***."

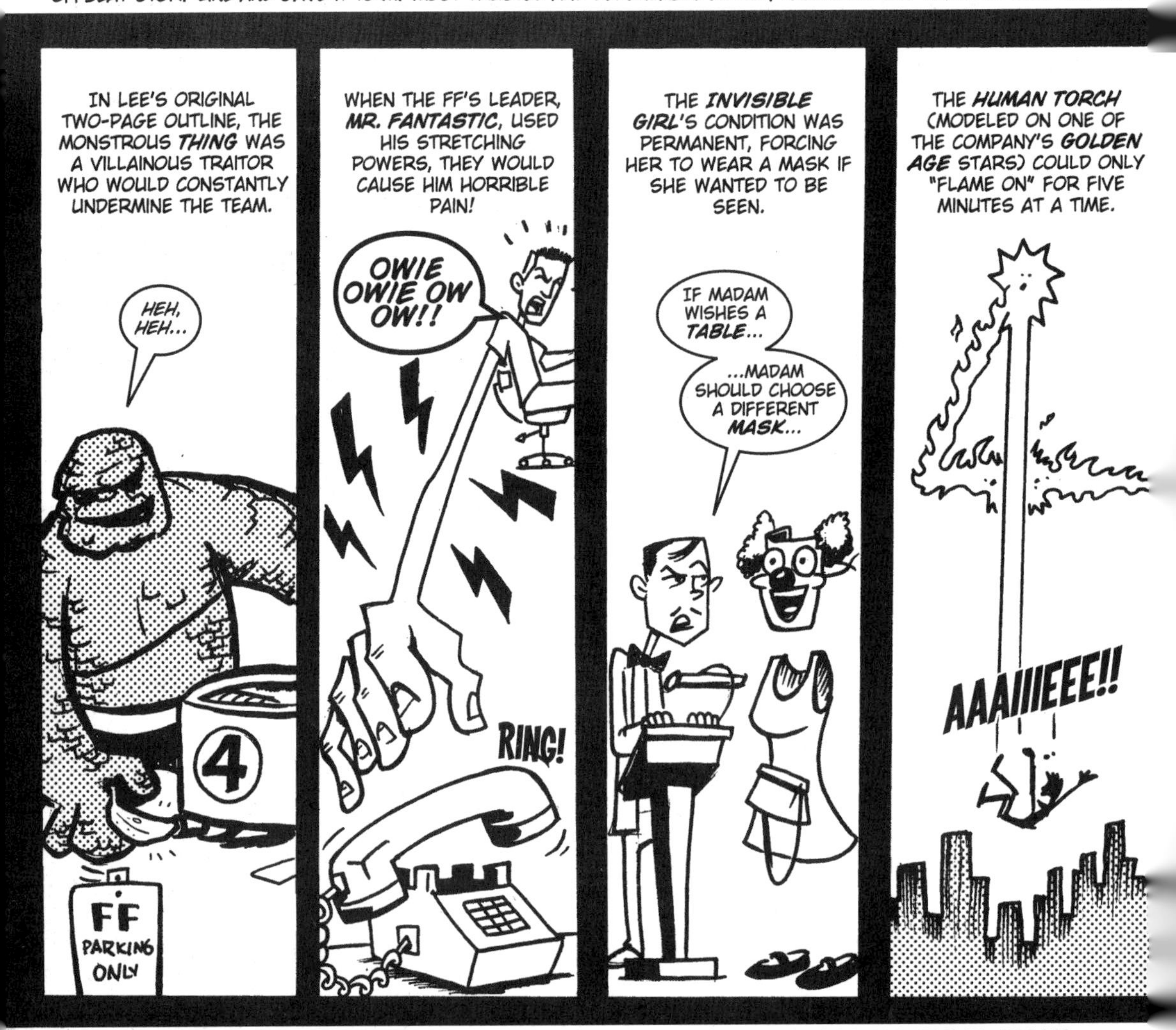

IN LEE'S ORIGINAL TWO-PAGE OUTLINE, THE MONSTROUS ***THING*** WAS A VILLAINOUS TRAITOR WHO WOULD CONSTANTLY UNDERMINE THE TEAM.

HEH, HEH...

4

FF PARKING ONLY

WHEN THE FF'S LEADER, ***MR. FANTASTIC***, USED HIS STRETCHING POWERS, THEY WOULD CAUSE HIM HORRIBLE PAIN!

OWIE OWIE OW OW!!

RING!

THE ***INVISIBLE GIRL***'S CONDITION WAS PERMANENT, FORCING HER TO WEAR A MASK IF SHE WANTED TO BE SEEN.

IF MADAM WISHES A ***TABLE***...

...MADAM SHOULD CHOOSE A DIFFERENT ***MASK***...

THE ***HUMAN TORCH*** (MODELED ON ONE OF THE COMPANY'S ***GOLDEN AGE*** STARS) COULD ONLY "FLAME ON" FOR FIVE MINUTES AT A TIME.

AAAIIIEEE!!

THE FACT THAT THE ***PUBLISHED*** VERSION OF THE STRIP DEVIATED SO FAR FROM THE ORIGINAL OUTLINE MAY HAVE SOMETHING TO DO WITH LEE'S ***UNIQUE*** WAY OF WORKING WITH HIS ARTISTS. LEE TOLD THE 1975 SAN DIEGO COMIC CON THAT HE DEVELOPED THIS PROCESS BECAUSE:

"I'D BE WRITING A STORY FOR KIRBY, AND STEVE DITKO WOULD WALK IN AND SAY,
'HEY, I NEED SOME WORK NOW.'
'I CAN'T GIVE IT TO YOU NOW, STEVE, I'M FINISHING KIRBY'S.'
"BUT WE COULDN'T AFFORD TO KEEP STEVE WAITING, BECAUSE TIME IS MONEY, SO I'D HAVE TO SAY:

"'LOOK, STEVE, I CAN'T WRITE A SCRIPT FOR YOU NOW, BUT HERE'S THE PLOT WE'LL USE FOR THE NEXT (ISSUE).'
"'GO HOME AND DRAW ANYTHING YOU WANT, AS LONG AS IT'S SOMETHING LIKE THIS, AND I'LL PUT THE (DIALOGUE) IN LATER.'"

"BECAUSE ANY ARTIST WHO REALLY *BELONGS* IN THIS FIELD -- AND OF COURSE OUR ARTISTS *DO* -- IS A STORYTELLER *HIMSELF*.

"SO IF HE JUST KNOWS WHAT THE *GENERAL* PLOT IS, THE *IDEA* IS: LET HIM GO HOME, LET HIM DRAW THE THINGS THAT HE THINKS ARE THE MOST *INTERESTING*.

"JUST IMAGINE HOW MUCH *EASIER* IT IS TO LOOK AT A DRAWING AND SUIT THE DIALOGUE PERFECTLY TO THE *EXPRESSION* OF THE CHARACTER'S FACE--TO WHAT THE DRAWING *REPRESENTS*--THAN TO TRY AND WRITE PERFECT DIALOGUE WHEN YOU'RE LOOKING AT A *BLANK* SHEET OF PAPER, TRYING TO *IMAGINE* WHAT THE DRAWING WILL BE LIKE."
?
!!

IN EMPLOYING WHAT HE SAYS "STARTED OUT AS *A LAZY MAN'S DEVICE*," LEE PERFORMED HIS AUTHORIAL DUTIES ONLY AT THE *INCEPTION* AND *FINALIZATION* OF A COMIC BOOK STORY, LEAVING THE *EXECUTION* -- THE ACTUAL *TELLING* OF THE STORY -- TO HIS ARTISTIC COLLABORATORS.

MANY ARTISTS, LIKE GIL KANE, FOUND THIS *"MARVEL METHOD"* EXTREMELY *LIBERATING*, CALLING IT "THE BEST THING IN TERMS OF WRITING AND DRAWING AND EFFECTING A *BALANCE*."

?
!!
STEP 1: INCEPTION!
STEP 2: EXCECUTION!
STEP 3: FINALIZATION!

KANE SAID, "I THINK WITHOUT QUESTION THAT THE (RESULTING) WRITING IS INFINITELY MORE *SPONTANEOUS*, MORE VARIED, MORE *EFFECTIVE* THAN IT EVER COULD BE..."
FRED
IS WATCHING YOU
SCRIPT
JU DRAW WHAT FEDERICO WRITE, ART MONKEY!
YESSUH MASSAH SUH!!
"...IF THE WRITER JUST SITS DOWN AND TYPES OUT 'PANEL ONE, SCENE ONE' AND DICTATES THE THING RIGHT FROM THE START. AND THE ARTIST IS MERELY AN *INSTRUMENT*."

LEE HAD WORKED THIS WAY FOR ***YEARS***, AND NOBODY COMPLAINED...
...PROBABLY BECAUSE, UNTIL THE PUBLICATION OF *FANTASTIC FOUR #1* IN NOVEMBER 1961, NO ONE PAID MUCH ATTENTION TO WHAT ATLAS/MARVEL PUBLISHED.
ATLAS
NEWS

BUT THE FF HIT ***BIG*** WITH READERS, AND THE LEE/KIRBY/DITKO BRAIN TRUST SOON BEGAN CRANKING OUT *THE HULK, SPIDER-MAN, THOR, THE X-MEN, DR. STRANGE*... AN ENTIRE ***UNIVERSE*** OF CLEVER SUPER HERO CHARACTERS!

FROM A ***READER'S*** PERSPECTIVE, THE ONE CONSTANT, THE ONE NAME THAT WAS ON ***EVERY*** MARVEL COMIC, WHETHER THE ARTIST WAS KIRBY, DITKO, OR ANOTHER FREELANCER, WAS THAT OF WRITER/EDITOR ***STAN LEE*** HIMSELF.
FACE FRONT, TRUE BELIEVERS!!
THE SELF-CONSCIOUS, TONGUE-IN-CHEEK HUMOR OF LEE'S DIALOGUE GROUNDED MARVEL'S SUPER HEROICS IN THE ***REAL WORLD.***

AND THAT SAME VOICE SPOKE DIRECTLY ***TO*** THE READER IN THE FORM OF EDITORIAL ASIDES WITHIN THE COMICS AND IN THE LETTER COLUMNS, IMMERSING THE MARVEL READER IN A ***SEAMLESS NARRATIVE EXPERIENCE***, WITH ***LEE*** AS THE PRIMARY FILTER.
(LEE SETTLED ON THE MOTTO OF NEW YORK STATE-- ***"EVER UPWARD"*** IN LATIN-- AS HIS PERSONAL CATCHPHRASE.)
EXCELSIOR!
COPYCAT!
EXCELSIOR

MARVEL'S SPIKE IN POPULARITY COINCIDED ALMOST PRECISELY WITH THE AMERICAN ELITE'S EMBRACE OF LOWBROW CULTURE EMBODIED IN THE ***POP ART*** MOVEMENT.

the AMAZING SPIDER-MAN
MARVEL POP ART PRODUCTIONS 12¢

INDEED, BRIEFLY IN 1965, LEE STOPPED CALLING HIS TITLES "COMICS" ON THE COVERS, BRANDING THEM INSTEAD ***"POP ART PRODUCTIONS."***

THE NEUROTIC, SELF-DEPRICATING MARVEL SUPER HEROES GARNERED ***HUGE FOLLOWINGS*** ON COLLEGE CAMPUSES.

"WE THINK OF MARVEL COMICS AS THE TWENTIETH-CENTURY MYTHOLOGY AND YOU AS THIS GENERATION'S HOMER!"
A LEE LECTURE AT BARD COLLEGE DREW A BIGGER AUDIENCE THAN FORMER PRESIDENT EISENHOWER.

THIS WAS THE SAME PERIOD IN WHICH AMERICA DISCOVERED THE SCHOOL OF FRENCH ***FILM*** CRITICISM KNOWN AS *"AUTEUR THEORY"*...

...WHICH POINTED TO A MOVIE'S ***DIRECTOR*** AS ITS PRIMARY *"AUTHOR,"* CITING FILMMAKERS LIKE ***ALFRED HITCHCOCK*** AS FILMMAKERS WITH A ***DISTINCTIVE*** VOICE.

AN UNSPOKEN ASSUMPTION IN *AUTEUR* THEORY IS THAT A FILM ***HAD*** TO HAVE AN "AUTHOR" IN ORDER TO ***BE*** ART...

...THAT IS TO SAY, A PERSONAL, ***INDIVIDUAL*** ENTITY MUST DRIVE ITS CREATION, LIKE A PAINTING OR A NOVEL...

ART
COMIX
PRODUCT
JUGGS

...WHILE ***COLLABORATIONS***, OR, GOD HELP US, ***CORPORATE*** PRODUCT, ***CANNOT*** BE ART AND ARE...

...SOMETHING ***LESSER.***

TO A PUBLIC UNFAMILIAR WITH THE INNER WORKINGS OF THE "MARVEL METHOD," STAN LEE WAS UNEQUIVOCALLY THE AUTEUR OF MARVEL COMICS.
IN ADDITION TO HIS NAME BEING ON EVERY BOOK, HE ALSO "GAVE GREAT COPY" TO THE MAINSTEAM MEDIA, AS THEY SAY.
THE CUMULATIVE EFFECT OF ALL THIS PRO-LEE HYPE WAS INEVITABLE:
"AS A YOUNG CHILD, I ASSUMED THE NAME STAN LEE WAS BEING FOISTED ON ME SO MUCH BECAUSE HE MUST HAVE DRAWN IT TOO, RIGHT?" REMEMBERS ACCLAIMED PAINTER AND COMICS ARTIST ALEX ROSS.
EXCELSIOR!
"WHEN YOU SEE A MARVEL COMIC AS A KID, YOU ASSUME IT SAYS STAN LEE BECAUSE HE DID IT ALL."
SPIDER-MAN
SGT FURY
X-MEN
FANTASTIC FOUR
DOCTOR STRANGE
AVENGERS
LEE'S FELLOW AUTEURS, EUROPEAN FILMMAKERS, HERALDED HIS GENIUS. HIROSHIMA, MON AMOUR DIRECTOR ALAIN RESNAIS ASKED TO COLLABORATE WITH LEE ON SCREENPLAYS! FEDERICO FELLINI VISITED THE MARVEL OFFICES!
"I LIKE VERY MUCH YOUR COMICS!"
THE IDEA THAT THERE COULD BE MORE THAN ONE "AUTHOR" -- THAT PERHAPS THERE COULDN'T BE A SINGLE "CREATOR" WHEN THE "MARVEL METHOD" WAS USED -- NEVER CAME UP.
IT DIDN'T TAKE LONG FOR TENSIONS BETWEEN LEE AND HIS PRIMARY ARTISTIC "CO-AUTHORS" TO REACH THE BREAKING POINT.

JACK KIRBY WAS *INFURIATED* BY THE NAKED BIAS OF A 1966 *NEW YORK HERALD TRIBUNE* ARTICLE WRITTEN BY A REPORTER WHO HAD SAT IN ON ONE OF HE AND LEE'S *FANTASTIC FOUR* "MARVEL METHOD" PLOTTING SESSIONS:
"Lee arrives at his plots in sort of **ESP sessions** with the artists.
"Here he is in action at his weekly Friday morning summit meeting with Jack 'King' Kirby, a veteran comic book artist, a man who created many of the visions of your childhood and mine:

"The King is a middle-aged man with baggy eyes and a baggy Robert Hall-ish suit. He is sucking a huge green cigar and if you stood next to him on the subway you would peg him for the assistant foreman in a girdle factory.

"'The Silver Surfer has been somewhere out in space since he helped the FF stop Galactus from destroying Earth. Why don't we bring him back?'
"'Ummh.'
"'Suppose Alicia, the Thing's blind girlfriend, is in some kind of trouble. And the Silver Surfer comes to help her!'"

GIL KANE WOULD GO TO LUNCH WITH KIRBY DURING THIS PERIOD AND REPORTS HOW ANGRY HE COULD GET OVER LEE.
ESP?!? *ESP?!?!*
"THAT GUY DOESN'T KNOW! I'M GONNA BLOW!"
TRIBUNE
"YOU'D HAVE TO ALMOST *TIE* HIM INTO HIS SEAT -- HE WOULD JUST BE *RAGING!* ... BUT HE *NEVER* CONFRONTED STAN, *EVER*."

BUT SPIDER-MAN CO-CREATOR STEVE DITKO WAS A DIFFERENT STORY.
HE WAS AN ADMIRER OF PHILOSOPHER AND NOVELIST AYN RAND.
THE CENTRAL TENET OF HER SCHOOL OF THOUGHT, OBJECTIVISM, IS "A = A."
THAT IS TO SAY, THE WORLD IS AS IT IS, UNINFLUENCED BY HUMAN PERCEPTIONS OR PREJUDICES.
A
A

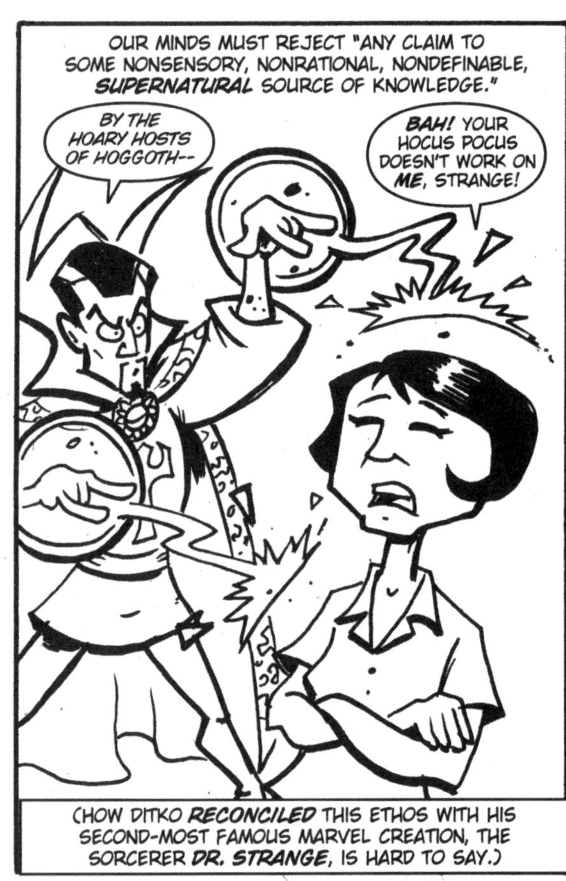
OUR MINDS MUST REJECT "ANY CLAIM TO SOME NONSENSORY, NONRATIONAL, NONDEFINABLE, SUPERNATURAL SOURCE OF KNOWLEDGE."
BY THE HOARY HOSTS OF HOGGOTH--
BAH! YOUR HOCUS POCUS DOESN'T WORK ON ME, STRANGE!
(HOW DITKO RECONCILED THIS ETHOS WITH HIS SECOND-MOST FAMOUS MARVEL CREATION, THE SORCERER DR. STRANGE, IS HARD TO SAY.)

RAND WROTE THAT TO ENJOY THE FRUITS OF ONE'S REASON -- ONE'S OWN PRODUCTIVE ACHIEVEMENT -- IS THE MORAL PURPOSE OF MAN'S LIFE.
SHE SAID THE ONLY MORAL POLITICAL SYSTEM IS LAISSEZ-FAIRE CAPITALISM, FOR HERE PEOPLE ACT AS EQUAL TRADERS, BY FREE EXCHANGE, ACCURATELY REFLECTING THEIR RELATIVE POSITIONS IN LIFE.

DITKO GREW TO BELIEVE THAT THE CREDITS IN HIS MARVEL COMICS INACCURATELY REFLECTED THE RELATIONSHIPS THEREIN! HE WROTE YEARS LATER THAT IN THE "MARVEL METHOD" LEE WOULD DEVELOP:
"'TITLE,' 'CONCEPT,' 'CHARACTERS.' THEY ARE ALL ABSTRACTIONS. THERE ARE NO SPECIFICS, NO SENSORY EVIDENCE, NO REAL, CONCRETE IDENTITIES. THEY ARE JUST WORDS AND SOUNDS."
NO, NO, NO...

"THERE CAN BE NO CREATION *VERSUS* EXECUTION.
A CREATION WITHOUT AN EXECUTION IS A CONTRADICTION.
EXECUTING *IS* CREATING.
"A CREATION WITHOUT AN EXECUTION IS LEE'S *DEAD IDEA*, DORMANT AND EXISTING ONLY IN ITS *'DREAMED UP'* STATE."
I'M SORRY, YOUR IDEA IS... **STILLBORN**.
OH, THE HUMANITY! >SOB!<
THE SPIDER MAN

FROM *DITKO'S* POINT OF VIEW, "THE MARVEL (METHOD) COMIC STORY IDEA, SYNOPSIS, WRITER/ARTIST METHOD, IS LIKE SOMEONE *WANTING* A BUILDING.
"HE HAS SOME IDEAS BUT THEY *REMAIN* IDEAS, ABSTRACT FRAGMENTS, PIECES LOOSELY IDENTIFIED, UNCONNECTED THINGS...

"...UNTIL THE *ARCHITECT* (THE ARTIST) SUPPLIES ALL THE NECESSARY DETAILS, WORKMANSHIP AND EXECUTION TO MAKE THE IDEA INTO A COMPLETE, CONCRETE AND EXISTING, *(SIC)* NOT IN A 'DREAMED UP' STATE BUT *EXISTING IN REALITY*."

DITKO DID NOT WANT TO *REMOVE* LEE FROM THE CREDITS; RATHER, HE DEMANDED A MORE *ACCURATE* DESCRIPTION OF WHAT WAS *ACTUALLY* GOING ON IN THE CREATIVE PROCESS.
EDITOR/DIALOGUIST OR "SCRIPTER" (STEPS 1 & 3)
PLOTTER/ ARTIST (STEP 2)
DITKO HAD BEEN THE SOLE PLOTTER ON *AMAZING SPIDER-MAN* SINCE ISSUE #18 (NOV. '64), WITH LEE ONLY PROVIDING *DIALOGUE* WHEN THE FINISHED ART PAGES ARRIVED AT THE MARVEL OFFICES.
HE RECEIVED HIS LONG-DESIRED "PLOTTED AND DRAWN BY" CREDIT IN *AMAZING SPIDER-MAN* #26 (JULY '65).
?
!!

BUT THE DISPUTE HAD TAKEN ITS TOLL ON THE MEN'S RELATIONSHIP.
EXIT
THEY STOPPED SPEAKING TO EACH OTHER. DITKO MADE SURE TO DROP OFF PAGES FOR DIALOGUING ONLY WHEN HE KNEW LEE WOULD BE OUT.

THE LAST STRAW FOR DITKO CAME WHEN HE DISCOVERED HE WOULDN'T RECEIVE A DIME FROM THE MERCHANDISE AND CARTOON DEALS MARTIN GOODMAN HAD ENTERED INTO WITH HIS SPIDER-MAN CHARACTERS!
AS YOU CAN SEE, STEVE, WITH SALARIES, OVERHEAD, OFFICE EXPENSES AND SUCH, WE HAVEN'T TURNED A PROFIT YET!

THE LOOTERS ARE UNFAIRLY EXPLOITING THE FRUITS OF YOUR REASON!
AFTER TURNING IN ASM #38 (JULY '66), DITKO QUIT MARVEL, NEVER TO RETURN TO HIS MOST FAMOUS CREATION.
BUT YOU'RE STILL MY FAVORITE, JACK, YOU ADORABLE PLOTTER YOU!
(IS IT A COINCIDENCE THAT LEE'S WRITER CREDIT WAS THEN DROPPED IN FANTASTIC FOUR #56 (NOV. '66), REPLACED BY THE FAR VAGUER "BY STAN LEE AND JACK KIRBY?")

IN CONTRAST TO DITKO, KIRBY HAD SPENT MOST OF HIS LIFE AVOIDING DIRECT CHALLENGES TO AUTHORITY.
HE DID LITTLE TO PUBLICLY CONTRADICT THE WIDESPREAD BELIEF THAT LEE WAS THE PRIMARY CREATOR OF SUCH CHARACTERS AS GALACTUS AND THE SILVER SURFER...
...WHEN INDUSTRY LEGEND HAS IT THAT KIRBY RECEIVED LITTLE MORE EDITORIAL DIRECTION FROM LEE THAN IN THAT ISSUE, THE FF SHOULD "MEET GOD!"

BUT BEHIND THE SCENES, KIRBY WAS QUIETLY PLOTTING HIS *FLIGHT* FROM MARVEL...
BOOM!
QUICKLY, JACK! USE THE *BOOM TUBE!*
...CREATING A NEW UNIVERSE OF GODS AND HEROES THAT HE WOULD WRITE AND DRAW ENTIRELY *BY HIMSELF.*

IN 1970, KIRBY DEFECTED FROM MARVEL TO DC FOR THE *SECOND* TIME IN HIS CAREER, BRINGING WITH HIM THE *"FOURTH WORLD"* OF TITLES HE HAD CREATED: *NEW GODS, MR. MIRACLE* AND *THE FOREVER PEOPLE.*
BOOM!
THE SUDDEN MOVE *STUNNED* THE COMICS INDUSTRY AND SENT MARVEL INTO A *PANIC!*

ANOTHER MARVEL ARTIST, *JOHN BUSCEMA*, REMEMBERS, "I'LL NEVER FORGET WHEN I WALKED INTO STAN'S OFFICE AND HEARD THAT JACK LEFT.

"I THOUGHT THEY WERE GOING TO *CLOSE UP!*

"AS FAR AS I WAS CONCERNED, JACK WAS THE *BACKBONE* OF MARVEL."

MARVEL

AN ANONYMOUS WISE GUY IN THE MARVEL BULLPEN PROVIDED HIS OWN INTERPRETATION OF KIRBY'S DEPARTURE.

TOUGH TIMES WERE AHEAD FOR THE NEWSSTAND COMICS INDUSTRY... AND MARVEL WOULD HAVE TO FACE THEM *WITHOUT* THE SERVICES OF ITS MOST POPULAR ARTIST!

I QUIT!

POP

IN THE 1940s, OHIO STATE UNIVERSITY ART PROFESSOR ***HOYT L. SHERMAN*** USED A ***UNIQUE*** METHOD TO DEVELOP HIS STUDENTS' POWERS OF ***PERCEPTION***.

HE WOULD FLASH AN IMAGE BRIEFLY ONTO A SCREEN IN A DARKENED CLASSROOM.

THE STUDENT WOULD THEN HAVE TO ***DRAW*** THE IMAGE COMPLETELY FROM ***MEMORY***. IN THE ***"FLASH ROOM,"*** SHERMAN ARGUED...

...THE ARTIST COULD DEVELOP HIS POWERS OF OBSERVATION AS A PURELY MECHANICAL FUNCTION OF OPTICS, DEVOID OF THE IMPOSITION OF MEANING.

ONE OF HIS STUDENTS EXPLAINED, "YOU'D GET A VERY STRONG ***AFTERIMAGE***, A TOTAL IMPRESSION, AND THEN YOU'D DRAW IT IN THE DARK--

"THE POINT BEING THAT YOU'D HAVE TO ***SENSE*** WHERE THE ***PARTS*** WERE IN RELATION TO THE ***WHOLE***.

"IT WAS A MIXTURE OF SCIENCE AND AESTHETICS, AND IT BECAME THE CENTER OF WHAT I WAS INTERESTED IN.
"I'D ALWAYS WANTED TO KNOW THE DIFFERENCE BETWEEN A MARK THAT WAS ART AND ONE THAT WASN'T.

"SHERMAN WAS HARD TO UNDERSTAND, BUT HE TAUGHT THAT THE KEY TO EVERYTHING LAY IN WHAT HE CALLED ***PERCEPTUAL UNITY***."

THAT STUDENT'S NAME WAS ROY LICHTENSTEIN.

AFTER COLLEGE, LICHTENSTEIN TAUGHT AROUND THE COUNTRY AND BECAME A MINOR ABSTRACT EXPRESSIONIST, IN THE STYLE THAT DOMINATED POSTWAR AMERICAN PANTING.
HAW! YOU CALL DIS CRUD "ART?!"
MY SIX YEAR-OLD COULD DO DAT!
BEER
Cy Twombly
Leda & the Swan
1962
IN 1960, LICHTENSTEIN ACCEPTED A PROFESSORSHIP AT RUTGERS IN NEW JERSEY.
STILL SEARCHING FOR HIS ARTISTIC NICHE, HE BEGAN DOODLING MICKEY MOUSE AND BUBBLE GUM CARTOONS TO AMUSE HIS YOUNG SONS.
MAYBE HE COULD, MY MOUTH-BREATHING FRIEND...
MAYBE HE COULD...
COLLEAGUES ENCOURAGED HIM TO CONCENTRATE ON HIS COMIC STRIP DRAWINGS.
"I THINK I STARTED OUT MORE AS AN OBSERVER THAN AS A PAINTER," HE SAYS, "BUT, WHEN I DID ONE, ABOUT HALFWAY THROUGH THE PAINTING I GOT INTERESTED IN IT AS A PAINTING."
COMIC BOOK COMICS
OUR ARTISTS AT WAR!
HE BRANCHED OUT FROM STRIPS AND COMMERCIAL ART TO LOOK THROUGH COMIC BOOKS--MOSTLY WAR AND ROMANCE TITLES--FOR INSPIRATION.
HE FOUND INDIVIDUAL PANELS FROM COMICS (ROMANCE ARTISTS RUSS HEATH AND MIKE SEKOWSKY AND WAR PENCILLER IRV NOVICK WERE AMONG HIS FAVORITES)...
THIS I CAN WORK WITH...
...THEN COPIED THE PANEL IN A FREEHAND SKETCH...
...WHICH HE WOULD THEN PROJECT ONTO THE WALL AND TRACE, IN THE PROCESS PURPOSEFULLY SIMPLIFYING THE DRAWING, BREAKING IT DOWN TO ITS ESSENCE, TRYING TO REMOVE THE ORIGINAL ARTIST'S STYLE AND PERSONALITY...
...INSISTING THAT SUCH AN "AFTERIMAGE" WAS AN IMPROVEMENT UPON THE ORIGINAL AND A WHOLLY UNIQUE PIECE OF ART.

LICHTENSTEIN BROUGHT HIS "COMIC STRIP PAINTINGS" TO LEGENDARY NEW YORK DEALER ***LEO CASTELLI***, OF WHOM ***WILLEM DE KOONING*** ONCE SAID COULD SELL ***ANYTHING*** AS ART, EVEN ***BEER CANS***.

SOLD!

CASTELLI IMMEDIATELY SAW THE ***COMMERCIAL*** POTENTIAL OF THIS NEW DIRECTION.

IN A BIZARRE COINCIDENCE, JUST A FEW WEEKS LATER, A RELATIVELY UNKNOWN DESIGNER NAMED ANDY WARHOL TURNED UP ON CASTELLI'S DOORSTEP, TRYING TO PUSH HIS OWN COMICS-INSPIRED PAINTINGS.
PFFT! BEEN THERE, DONE THAT!
B-BUT I THOUGHT I WAS SO UNIQUE!
PUFF!

CLEARLY SOMETHING WAS IN THE ***AIR*** -- A ZEITGEIST OF LATE 50s/EARLY 60s CULTURE THAT HERALDED THE BIRTH OF ***"POP"*** ART. THE TERM, DEPENDING ON WHO YOU ASK, CAME FROM THE WORD ***"POPULAR"***...

...OR THE ***TOOTSIE POP*** HELD BY THE BODYBUILDER IN ***THIS***, WHAT IS GENERALLY CONSIDERED TO BE THE ***FIRST*** TRUE WORK OF POP ART, BRITISH ARTIST RICHARD HAMILTON'S 1956 COLLAGE ***"JUST WHAT IS IT THAT MAKES TODAY'S HOMES SO DIFFERENT, SO APPEALING?"***

(NOTE ***JACK KIRBY'S*** COVER TO *YOUNG ROMANCE #26* ON THE WALL!)

HEY, LOOK! I COPIED A WHOLE BUNCH OF OTHER GUYS' STUFF!

I'M A GEN-YOO-WHINE ***POP ARTIST!*** -HYUK!-

AFTER SEEING LICHTENSTEIN'S WORK, WARHOL ABANDONED HIS COMIC STRIP PAINTINGS. HE ENVIED ROY'S PAINTED-ON (THROUGH A WIRE SCREEN) "BENDAY" DOTS.

WHY DIDN'T I THINK OF THAT?
NINETEENTH CENTURY ARTIST BENJAMIN DAY INVENTED THE DOTS UPON THE ADVENT OF "PROCESS" ENGRAVING TO CREATE GRADATIONS IN PRINTED ARTWORK.

BUT LICHTENSTEIN TURNED BACK THE CLOCK ON PRINTING HISTORY, USING PRIMARY COLORS AND SIMPLISTIC STYLES IN HIS BENDAY DOTS TO EMPHASIZE FLATNESS, BANALITY AND A LACK OF INDIVIDUALISM, JUST AS WARHOL'S FUTURE SILKSCREENS AND SCULPTURES UNDERSCORED THE BANALITY OF HIS SUBJECT MATTER -- ANTI-GLAMORIZING THE EVERYDAYNESS OF OBJECTS LIKE BRILLO PADS.
Brillo
STOP! WHAT ARE YOU DOING?!
WHA'?

THOUGH MANY ASSUMED LICHTENSTEIN'S USE OF TRITE ROMANCE AND WAR COMIC BOOK IMAGERY AND WARHOL'S OF CONSUMER PRODUCTS WAS INTENDED AS A CRITIQUE OF COMMERCIALIST CULTURE...
STOP
...THE POP ARTISTS VEHEMENTLY REJECTED SUCH A READING! THEY YEARNED TO REFLECT SOCIETY, NOT CRITICIZE IT! THE WORLD WAS THEIR MUSEUM, AND THEY WANTED TO BE AS MILITANTLY SHALLOW AS IT!

"HOW CAN YOU LIKE BAD ART?"
"HOW CAN YOU LIKE EXPLOITATION?"
"HOW CAN YOU LIKE THE COMPLETE MECHANIZATION OF WORK?"
"I HAVE TO ANSWER THAT I ACCEPT IT AS BEING THERE, IN THE WORLD."
ROY!

BUT THE MASS CULTURE POP ART TRIED TO EMULATE BECAME, AS THE MOVEMENT REACHED THE HEIGHT OF ITS INFLUENCE IN THE MID-60s, MORE AND MORE LIKE POP...
ROY!

..."EMPHASIZING STYLE" TO "SLIGHT CONTENT," IN THE WORDS OF SUSAN SONTAG'S 1964 ESSAY "NOTES ON CAMP"...
...MIRRORING THE HIPSTER'S IRONIC CONSUMPTION OF "SQUARE" CULTURE IN ORDER TO MOCK IT...
HA, HA! IT'S JUST SO STUPID!
...SUCH AS HUGH HEFNER'S FAMOUS SCREENINGS OF CHEESY OLD MOVIE SERIALS LIKE BATMAN & ROBIN (1949) IN THE PLAYBOY MANSION.

CREATED AT THE BEGINNING OF THE SUPERMAN FAD (1939) BY WRITER BILL FINGER AND ARTIST BOB KANE, BATMAN IS ARGUABLY NOT A "SUPER" HERO AT ALL...
...BUT RATHER THE MOST SUCCESSFUL PULP AVENGER IN THE SCARLET PIMPERNEL-ZORRO-SHADOW MODE, WITH NO SUPERNATURAL ABILITIES, JUST A SPOOKY OUTFIT, ATHLETICISM AND RICH TWIT ALTER-EGO.

BY THE 1950s, UNDER THE GUIDANCE OF SF-HAPPY EDITOR JACK SCHIFF, BATS STRAYED FAR FROM HIS URBAN ROOTS, ROUTINELY BATTLING DINOSAURS AND FLYING SAUCERS.
SALES DROPPED THROUGHOUT THE DECADE AS THE DARK KNIGHT INCREASINGLY BECAME A CAMP PARODY OF HIMSELF...

...AN IMPRESSION NOT HELPED BY WERTHAM'S ASSERTION, IN SEDUCTION OF THE INNOCENT, THAT BATMAN AND HIS SIDEKICK ROBIN EMBODIED "A WISH DREAM OF TWO HOMOSEXUALS LIVING TOGETHER."

ABC MARKET-RESEARCHED VARIOUS COMICS FRANCHISES FOR *TV ADAPTATION*...

...BATS CAME IN *THIRD*, BEHIND CHESTER GOULD'S COMIC STRIP DETECTIVE *DICK TRACY*, WHICH THE CHICAGO TRIBUNE SYNDICATE ALREADY HAD UNDER DEVELOPMENT AT *NBC*...

...AND *SUPERMAN*, WHOSE RIGHTS WERE TIED UP WITH THE *BROADWAY MUSICAL IT'S A BIRD, IT'S A PLANE, IT'S SUPERMAN*, A CAMP/POP TREATMENT OF THE MAN OF STEEL...

...THAT FEATURED A *SHOWSTOPPER* IN WHICH THE CAST SANG FROM INSIDE A COMIC BOOK PAGE-STYLE *PANEL FRAMEWORK.*

MEANWHILE...

DESPITE BEING DECLARED "THE BEST MUSICAL OF THE SEASON" BY THE *NEW YORK TIMES* AND GREAT SONGS BY THE *BYE, BYE BIRDIE* LYRICIST/COMPOSER TEAM OF CHARLES STROUSE AND LEE ADAMS, *IT'S A BIRD! FLOPPED*, CLOSING AFTER A MERE 128 PERFORMANCES.

ABC ASSIGNED *BATMAN'S* DEVELOPMENT TO VETERAN TV PRODUCER *WILLIAM DOZIER*. BEFORE FLYING TO NEW YORK TO DISCUSS THE SHOW WITH EXECUTIVES, DOZIER STOPPED BY LA SECOND-HAND STORES AND BOUGHT A BUNCH OF OLD BAT-COMICS TO READ ON THE PLANE.
BATMAN
DETECTIVE
"AT FIRST, I THOUGHT THE COMICS WERE *CRAZY*," HE SAID. "I REALLY THOUGHT (ABC) WAS *CRAZY*, IF THEY THOUGHT THEY WERE GOING TO PUT *THIS* ON TELEVISION.
"I FELT A BIT LIKE AN *IDIOT*" WHEN AN EXEC FROM AD AGENCY *YOUNG & RUBICAM* CAUGHT HIM READING *BATS* ON THE FLIGHT.
GUESS YOU MUST GET SICK OF READING *SCRIPTS* ALL THE TIME!
BATMAN
NO, I'M NOT-- A, UH, *CHILD* OR *IMBECILE* MUST HAVE LEFT IT IN THE SEAT POCKET IN FRONT OF ME... *HEH!*

BUT THEN DOZIER HAD "THE SIMPLE IDEA OF OVERDOING IT, OF MAKING IT SO SQUARE AND SO SERIOUS THAT ADULTS WOULD FIND IT AMUSING."
POW!
HE PITCHED THIS CONCEPT TO THE NETWORK, WHICH LOVED IT, INCLUDING HIS FLOURISH OF TRANSPOSING BRIGHT, POP ART-STYLE SOUND EFFECTS OVER THE FIGHT SCENES...

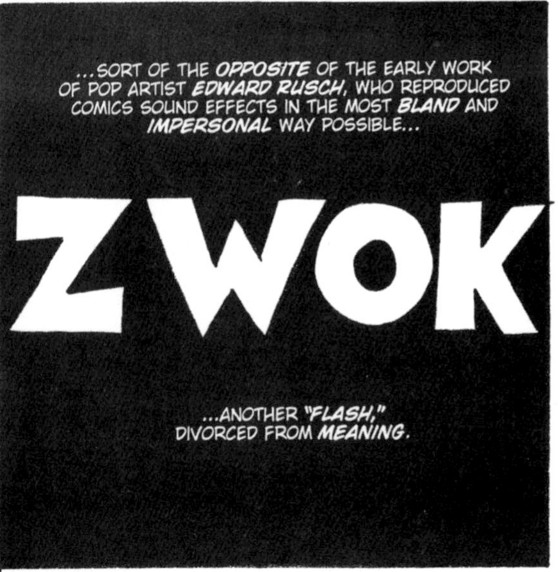
...SORT OF THE OPPOSITE OF THE EARLY WORK OF POP ARTIST EDWARD RUSCH, WHO REPRODUCED COMICS SOUND EFFECTS IN THE MOST BLAND AND IMPERSONAL WAY POSSIBLE...
ZWOK
...ANOTHER "FLASH," DIVORCED FROM MEANING.

ABC'S BATMAN WOULD BE "FLASH" MORE LITERALLY, WITH SELF-CONSCIOUSLY ARTIFICIAL SETS SPLASHED WITH BRIGHT, LICHTENSTEIN-ESQUE PRIMARIES-- NOTHING AS LOUD AND AS VIBRANT HAD EVER BEEN SEEN ON AMERICAN TV BEFORE!
BAT JOHN
BAT MIRROR
BAT TOILET PAPER
BAT SINK
BAT PLUNGER
BAT PORN
(A LOT OF MONEY WENT INTO THOSE SETS, CAUSING EACH EPISODE TO RUN AN AVERAGE $1 MILLION OVER BUDGET-- THIS ULTIMATELY DOOMED BATMAN AFTER THREE SEASONS.)

TO PLAY THE CAPED CRUSADER, DOZIER HIRED AN ACTOR FROM A NESTLE'S COMMERCIAL HE LIKED, ADAM WEST, WHO IMMEDIATELY UNDERSTOOD THE DIRECTION OF THE SHOW.
FASCINATING...
TO RESEARCH THE ROLE, WEST READ CARTOONIST AND EISNER SHOP VETERAN JULES FEIFFER'S BOOK THE GREAT COMIC BOOK HEROES...
THE GREAT COMIC BOOK HEROES

...ITSELF A REFLECTION OF THE 1960'S WAVE OF NOSTALGIA FOR THE GOLDEN AGE OF COMICS (WHICH DIDN'T HURT THE POP ART CRAZE).
NOW-ADULT COLLECTORS WERE PAYING BIG BUCKS FOR THE FUNNYBOOKS OF THEIR FORMATIVE YEARS...
...INSPIRING "IF-MY-MOM-HADN'T-THROWN-OUT-MY-COMICS-I'D-BE-A-MILLIONAIRE" LAMENTS FROM THOUSANDS...
FAMOUS FUNN
ACTION COMICS

ABC ARRANGED A PREMIERE PARTY FOR *BATMAN* ON THE NIGHT OF JANUARY 12, 1966, AT TRENDY ***HARLOW'S*** IN MANHATTAN. THE NETWORK INVITED OVER ***500*** LUMINARIES, INCLUDING LICHTENSTEIN, WARHOL, AND OTHER POP ARTISTS.

THE SHOW WAS AN INSTANT ***SENSATION***, DRAWING A STUNNING ***55%*** RATING AND QUICKLY RACKING UP MORE THAN $3 BILLION IN MERCHANDISING.

POW!
OH-HO-HO! IT'S SO STUPID!

WEST AND HIS CO-STAR, BURT "ROBIN" WARD, BECAME ***SUPERSTARS***, ALONG WITH ALL THE NUBILE ***PERKS*** THAT WENT WITH FAME IN THE ***SWINGING 60s.***

THOUGH WEST AND HIS PAL, FELLOW CAST MEMBER FRANK "RIDDLER" GORSHIN, GOT TOSSED OUT OF THEIR FIRST AND ONLY HOLLYWOOD ***ORGY*** FOR OVERDOING THE BAT-SCHTICK.

RIDDLE ME THIS, BATMAN:
WHAT HAS ONE EYE, A TURTLE-NECK, AND IS REALLY HAPPY TO BE HERE?
WHY, YOU PERVERTED PUZZLER...!

ABC MARKET RESEARCH SUGGESTED DOZIER WAS WHOLLY CORRECT IN HIS ASSESSMENT OF THE SHOW'S AUDIENCE.

SURVEYS SHOWED KIDS UNDER THE AGE OF ***FIFTEEN*** LOVED *BATMAN* -- BUT ***TEENAGERS*** FROM 16 TO 18 LOST INTEREST. ONCE THEY HIT ***19***, THOUGH, PEOPLE BECAME ***FANS*** AGAIN!

COOL!
MEH!
HILARIOUS!

ADOLESCENTS' LACK OF APPRECIATION FOR *BATMAN* CAN BE AT LEAST PARTLY ATTRIBUTED TO A REALIZATION THAT ***THEIR*** CULTURE WAS BEING ***MOCKED*** BY IT.

AS WEST WOULD LATER WRITE:

"I ***LOATHED*** THE WORD ***'CAMP.'***

"IT ***DEMEANED*** OUR EFFORTS BY SUGGESTING THAT WHAT WE WERE WORKING ***HARD*** TO ACHIEVE WAS SO ***EASY*** OR CORNY OR ***BAD*** THAT ***ANYONE*** COULD DO IT."

WEST

BUT OF COURSE, THAT WAS, MORE OR LESS, ***EXACTLY*** WHAT THE POP ARTISTS WERE SAYING.

PERHAPS THEY ACTUALLY BELIEVED THEIR OWN HYPE -- THAT THEY WERE ASSAILING THE CONCEPTION THAT ARTISTS WERE SOMEHOW ABOVE REGULAR SOCIETY -- NO, NO, THEY WERE JUST REGULAR JOES!
(WARHOL DID NAME HIS STUDIO "THE FACTORY," AFTER ALL...)
IN
OUT
BUT THIS IS A CHIMERA.
JUST "ANYONE" CANNOT MAKE "ART."

CORPORATE PRODUCT LIKE BRILLO PADS AND COMICS CAN BE "HIGH ART" ONLY WHEN APPROPRIATED BY THOSE DEEMED OFFICIAL "ARTISTS" BY DEALERS LIKE CASTELLI, THROUGH WHOSE SOLE POWER SUCH OBJECTS MAY BE DECLARED "UNIQUE" WORKS TO BE SOLD LIKE SNAKE OIL TO WEALTHY PATRONS.
YOU ARE A RICH TWIT

THERE IS NO "WORLD MUSEUM" -- THE POP ARTISTS' FINANCIAL SUCCESS WAS A REFLECTION OF NOTHING MORE THAN THE "UNREAL" ART WORLD ITSELF!
LICHTENSTEIN'S MECHANISTIC PASTICHES RAKED IN BIG BUCKS WHILE THE COMIC BOOK ARTISTS HE SWIPED FROM TOILED IN OBSCURITY!
$5000
12¢

AND ABC'S BATMAN, BIRTHED FROM POP, DEFINED AN ENTIRE MEDIUM AS CAMPY TRASH FOR THE MILLIONS WHO WATCHED IT.
GGGRRRRRR!!
HOLY PULITZER BATMAN!
MAUS

POP ART LOVED COMICS, BUT IT WAS THE LOVE A VILLAGE HAS FOR ITS IDIOT, THE CONDESCENDING AFFECTION OF A SLUMMING ELITE.
IT WOULD BE UP TO THE CREATORS AND LOVERS OF THE MEDIUM TO ULTIMATELY PROVE POP WRONG.

THOUGH INDEPENDENT COMICS **GREW UP** ON THE STREETS OF **SAN FRANCISCO**, THEY WERE BORN IN **AUSTIN** AND CARRIED **WEST** BY THOSE **PIONEERS** THE HIPPIES AFFECTIONATELY DUBBED...

THE TEXAS MAFIA!

IN THE EARLY 1960s, THE STAFF OF THE TEXAS RANGER, THE HUMOR MAGAZINE FOR THE UNIVERSITY OF TEXAS AT AUSTIN, LIVED IN A FORMER FRAT HOUSE.
THOSE FILTHY HIPPIES ARE MAKING A MOCKERY OF EVERYTHING LAMBDA SIGMA DELTA STOOD FOR!
THEY WERE AS KNOWN FOR THE QUALITY OF THEIR PARTIES AS THE QUALITY OF THEIR MAGAZINE.
TEXAS

GOD NOSE, A RANGER STRIP ABOUT A PEACE-LOVING SINUS DEITY, WAS CREATED BY HOUSEMATE JACK JACKSON.
THOUGH JACKSON GREW UP WORSHIPPING EC'S JACK DAVIS, HE STUDIED ACCOUNTING AT TEXAS A&I SO HE WOULDN'T HAVE TO RETURN TO WORK HIS UNCLE'S FARM IN STOCKDALE.
!
SHOP!

JACKSON WORKED FOR TEXAS'S SALES TAX AUTHORITY. THE PRINTER IN THE BASEMENT OF THE STATE CAPITOL OFFERED TO PRINT A COMPILATION OF GOD NOSE FOR HIM ON THE SLY IN 1964.
"I CAN'T SAY THAT HE REALLY THOUGHT IT WAS A GREAT BOOK," JACKSON REPORTS, "BUT HE OBVIOUSLY REALIZED HE WAS PUTTING ONE OVER ON THE BIGWIGS."
YEE-HAW!
GOD NOSE
GOD NOSE

TO PRESERVE HIS STRAIGHT JOB, JACKSON PUBLISHED UNDER THE NICKNAME "JAXON" (AFTER THE BEER) BESTOWED ON HIM BY RANGER EDITOR GILBERT SHELTON.
GOD NOSE, GENERALLY CONSIDERED TO BE THE FIRST-EVER UNDERGROUND COMIC, SOLD OUT OF ITS 1,000-COPY PRINT RUN ON THE STREETS OF AUSTIN IN A MATTER OF WEEKS!
?
GOD NOSE

AFTER USING HIS *GOD NOSE* EARNINGS TO MOTORCYCLE THROUGH ***EUROPE,*** JAXON HEEDED THE SIREN-SONG OF THE ***COUNTER-CULTURE*** AND LIT OUT FOR ***HAIGHT-ASHBURY*** IN 1966.

SUMMER of LOVE
UNFUNNY DRUG HUMOR
UNSUSTAINABLE UTOPIAN FANTASIES
BABY BOOMER B.S.
URBAN BLIGHT
SMUG SELF-RIGHTEOUSNESS
UNDERAGE SEX
TOO MUCH PATCHOULI

ONE OF THE SF SCENE'S ***"TRIBAL LEADERS"*** WAS PROMOTER ***CHET HELMS***, HIMSELF A LONGHORN ALUM WHO GOT UT DROPOUT ***JANIS JOPLIN*** TO HEADLINE A ***BAND*** HE MANAGED, ***BIG BROTHER AND THE HOLDING COMPANY.***

THE ***AUSTIN*** CONNECTION LANDED JAXON A JOB WITH HELMS, ***AKA "FAMILY DOG,"*** KEEPING THE BOOKS OF THE PSYCHEDELIC ***POSTER PRINTING*** PART OF HIS OPERATION.

THE GUY WE HAVE **NOW** ISN'T REALLY **WORKING OUT...**
I CAN **HEAR** THE NUMBERS **TALKING** TO ME, MAN...

INTENDED TO ***PROMOTE*** CONCERTS AND "BE-INS," THE POSTERS BECAME A LUCRATIVE BUSINESS UNTO ***THEMSELVES,*** SELLING SO WELL IN HEAD SHOPS AROUND THE COUNTRY THEY ACTUALLY ***UNDERWROTE*** HELMS' SHOWS AT THE ***AVALON BALLROOM.***

JAXON WAS SOON JOINED BY EX-AUSTIN HOUSEMATE ***GILBERT SHELTON,*** WHO HAD TURNED HIS HERO PARODY *WONDER WART-HOG* INTO A POPULAR STRIP IN INDY PAPERS ACROSS AMERICA.

THE ARMY DECLARED GILBERT ***"MEDICALLY UNFIT"*** FOR VIETNAM AFTER HE GAVE THEM A BLOW-BY-BLOW RECITATION OF HIS ***DRUG USE.***

zZZ z
...PEYOTE, **GRASS**, LSD, GRASS, PSILOCYBIN, **GRASS...**

HELMS' SUCCESS INSPIRED JAXON, SHELTON AND TWO OTHER AUSTIN TRANSPLANTS, ***DAVE MORIARTY*** AND ***FRED TODD***, TO PLUNK DOWN $75 EACH FOR A ***PRINTING PRESS*** IN 1969 AND FORM THEIR ***OWN*** COMPANY...

...***RIP OFF PRESS***, WHICH BECAME THE MOST ***IMPORTANT*** OF THE EARLY INDY PUBLISHERS, PRODUCING SHELTON'S *FABULOUS FURRY FREAK BROTHERS* AND JACKSON'S *COMANCHE MOON*, AMONG MANY OTHER IMPORTANT COMIX...

...BUT THEY WERE EQUALLY KNOWN FOR THEIR ***PARTIES.*** INEVITABLY, JACKSON REMEMBERS, "THERE WOULD BE THREE OR FOUR HUNDRED ***TEXANS.*** IT WAS LIKE A LITTLE BIT OF ***TEXAS*** TRANSPLANTED TO THE ***WEST COAST.***

"THE ***TEXAS MAFIA***, AS WE WERE CALLED, WERE REALLY A ***NOTICEABLE GROUP.*** WE HAD OUR FINGERS IN ***EVERYTHING."***

THERE GOES THE **NEIGHBORHOOD**, MAN...

FEED
YOUR
HEAD

MEANWHILE, IN CLEVELAND...
SHY, NEUROTIC, MISANTHROPIC COMICS FAN ROBERT CRUMB HAD GROWN INTO A SHY, NEUROTIC, MISANTHROPIC STAFF ARTIST FOR THE AMERICAN GREETINGS CARD COMPANY.
-SIGH-

HELP!

CRUMB MADE A ***BRIEF*** ATTEMPT TO BREAK INTO THE ***COMICS*** WORLD, TRAVELING TO NEW YORK TO BECOME ASSISTANT EDITOR OF HIS IDOL ***HARVEY KURTZMAN***'S LATEST SATIRE MAGAZINE, *HELP!*

HE ARRIVED JUST IN TIME TO SEE ALL THE FURNITURE GET HAULED OUT OF THE OFFICE!

HELP!'S PUBLISHER, JIM WARREN OF *FAMOUS MONSTERS OF FILMLAND* MAGAZINE, CANCELLED IT WITH THE SEPT. 1965 ISSUE.

CRUMB WOULD HAVE JOINED QUITE AN ACCIDENTAL ASSEMBLAGE OF FUTURE CELEBRITIES IF HAD HE JOINED THE STAFF OF HELP!
CARTOONIST AND ANIMATOR TERRY GILLIAM PRECEDED CRUMB AS ASSISTANT EDITOR.
AND MS. MAGAZINE FOUNDER GLORIA STEINEM WAS THE MAGAZINE'S EDITORIAL ASSISTANT!
BRITISH COMIC ACTOR JOHN CLEESE MODELED FOR ONE OF ITS PHOTO COMICS. HE AND GILLIAM WOULD FORM ONE-THIRD OF MONTY PYTHON AFTER MEETING AT HELP!
BUT NOW MAROONED IN NEW YORK, CRUMB STRUGGLED AS A FREELANCE ARTIST. HE LIVED WITH HIS WIFE IN A RUNDOWN LOWER EAST SIDE APARTMENT "IN A DISMAL MARRIED ROUTINE...THE ONLY THING WE HAD IN COMMON WAS OUR DESPERATION."
LIKE WE GOT ANYTHING ELSE BETTER TO DO...
DANA CRUMB OBTAINED THROUGH HER PSYCHIATRIST THE NOT-YET-ILLEGAL HALLUCINOGENIC, LSD.
"WHILE ON LSD, I REALIZED THAT MY MIND WAS A GARBAGE RECEPTACLE OF MASS MEDIA IMAGES AND INPUT," CRUMB REPORTS.
"I SPENT MY WHOLE CHILDHOOD ABSORBING SO MUCH CRAP THAT MY PERSONALITY AND MIND ARE SATURATED WITH IT.
"ALMOST EVERY TIME I TOOK LSD, AT SOME POINT I'D FIND MYSELF ON MY HANDS AND KNEES, PUKING MY GUTS OUT AND ASKING:"
"WHAT THE HELL DOES IT ALL MEAN?!"
(ONE COULD ARGUE DRUGS DID CHEMICALLY FOR CRUMB WHAT MAD HAD DONE FOR HIS WHOLE GENERATION, THANKS TO ITS MOCKING RECONFIGURATION OF POPULAR CULTURE.)
HELP!
(IN FACT, BECAUSE KURTZMAN'S HELP! FIRST PUBLISHED SO MANY COUNTERCULTURE ARTISTS (INCLUDING CRUMB), IT'S BEEN CALLED THE "FIRST UNDERGROUND COMIC!")

IT WAS OBVIOUS TO CRUMB FROM THE PSYCHEDELIC POSTERS COMING OUT OF SAN FRANCISCO PROMOTING "FAMILY DOG'S" CONCERTS THAT ARTISTS RICK GRIFFIN AND VICTOR MOSCOSO WERE EXPERIMENTING WITH THE DRUG, TOO!
DOC! I CAN SEE THE CRIMSON BANDS OF CYTTORAK...
(THE DOG'S FIRST SHOW IN OCTOBER 1965 FEATURED JEFFERSON AIRPLANE AND WAS CALLED "A TRIBUTE TO DR. STRANGE!")

THAT NOVEMBER, CRUMB TOOK BAD "BROWN ACID" THAT LEFT HIM "CRAZY AND HELPLESS" FOR SIX MONTHS.
HE TRIED TO LEAVE HIS WIFE, BUT SHE SAT ON HIM AND TRIED TO FEED HIM CHICKEN SOUP LACED WITH SLEEPING PILLS.

DURING THIS "FUZZY PERIOD" HE FILLED HIS SKETCHBOOKS WITH NEARLY ALL THE CHARACTERS THAT WOULD LATER MAKE HIM FAMOUS: MR. NATURAL, FLAKY FOONT, ANGEL-FOOD MCSPADE, "KEEP ON TRUCKIN'"...
"I WAS RELIEVED WHEN IT WAS FINALLY OVER, BUT I ALSO IMMEDIATELY MISSED THE EGOLESS STATE OF THAT STRANGE INTERLUDE.
"PSYCHEDELIC DRUGS BROKE ME OUT OF MY SOCIAL PROGRAMMING."

NEVERTHELESS, HE RETURNED TO HIS SOUL-CRUSHING JOB IN CLEVELAND.
I GUESS THIS IS ALL I CAN EXPECT OUT OF LIFE... MAYBE IT'S ALL I DESERVE!
AMERICAN GREETINGS TAUGHT HIM HOW TO DRAW "CUTE." HE PENNED CARTOONS FOR THE EMPLOYEE NEWSLETTER, DEVELOPING HIS DISNEY-ESQUE FRITZ THE CAT CHARACTER.

BUT IN JANUARY 1967 HE LEARNED TWO CLEVELAND DRINKING BUDDIES WERE DRIVING TO SAN FRANCISCO *THAT NIGHT*.

"HEY, GOT ROOM FOR ONE MORE?"

"YEAH, SURE! COME WITH US!"

ALL HE HAD WITH HIM WAS WHAT HE WORE TO THE BAR AND WHATEVER MONEY WAS IN HIS POCKET.

HAIGHT

ASHBURY

CRUMB LANDED IN THE HAIGHT-ASHBURY DISTRICT AT THE ***HEART*** OF THE HIPPIES' "SUMMER OF LOVE."

"I USED TO COME UP EVERY DAY AND TRY AND BE ***ONE*** OF THEM. MY MAIN MOTIVATION WAS, GET SOME OF THAT ***FREE LOVE ACTION***, BUT I WASN'T TOO ***GOOD*** AT IT.

YOU A ***NARC***, MAN?

"IT WASN'T THE RIGHT ***COSTUME***. I REMEMBER ***JANIS JOPLIN**** GIVING ME THIS PIECE OF ADVICE:
"CRUMB, WHAT'S THE MATTER WITH YOU? DON'T YOU LIKE GIRLS?
"***OF COURSE*** I LIKE GIRLS. WHAT DO YOU THINK?"
"JUST LET YOUR HAIR GROW LONG, GET ONE OF THOSE SATIN, BILLOWY SHIRTS, VELVET JACKETS, AND BELL BOTTOMS AND PLATFORM SHOES. YOU'LL DO ALL RIGHT, YOU'LL DO OKAY."

LIVING ON ***WELFARE***, REGULARLY TAKING ***LSD***, CRUMB SOLD COMIC STRIPS DERIVED FROM HIS ***"BROWN ACID"*** SKETCHBOOKS TO ***UNDERGROUND NEWSPAPERS.***

ADVANCES IN OFFSET PRINTING TECHNOLOGY HAD ENABLED THE PRODUCTION OF TABLOID PAPERS AT A FRACTION OF THE PREVIOUS COST.

SINCE 1965, MOST MAJOR CITIES BOASTED COUNTER-CULTURE RAGS LEADING THE CHARGE AGAINST THE ***VIETNAM WAR*** AND PROMOTING OTHER LEFTY CAUSES...

...*THE EAST VILLAGE OTHER* IN NEW YORK, *THE SAN FRANCISCO ORACLE*, THE *LA FREE PRESS*, *YARROWSTALKS* IN PHILADELPHIA...
MALT SH
FREE JUGHEAD!
RIVERDALE REVOLUTION

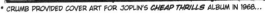

* CRUMB PROVIDED COVER ART FOR JOPLIN'S ***CHEAP THRILLS*** ALBUM IN 1968...

DON DONAHUE, AN ASPIRING ALTERNATIVE PUBLISHER, HAD SEEN CRUMB'S CARTOONS IN *YARROW-STALKS* AND BEEN BLOWN AWAY.
ROBERT... *CRUMB?*
THAT'S *ME!*
"I THOUGHT HE MUST BE AN *OLD MAN,*" DONAHUE SAID, "BECAUSE THAT'S THE WAY (*HIS CARTOONS*) LOOKED. MAYBE HE'D BEEN DRAWING COMIC BOOKS BACK IN THE 20S OR 30S AND HE WENT *BERSERK* OR SOMETHING!"
HE WAS *STUNNED* TO DISCOVER THE ARTIST WAS BARELY *TWENTY-FIVE.*

CRUMB HAD COMPLETED AN ENTIRE COMIC *BOOK*'S WORTH OF MATERIAL. DONAHUE OFFERED TO PUBLISH *ZAP COMIX* THROUGH HIS COMPANY, APEX NOVELTIES.
ONCE COPIES OF *ZAP* ROLLED OFF THE PRESSES, CRUMB, JOINED IN 'FRISCO BY HIS VERY PREGNANT *WIFE*, HAWKED THEM ON THE STREET OUT OF A *BABY CARRIAGE!*

BUT THE BULK OF *ZAP COMIX* FOUND ITS WAY INTO THE HIPPIE SUPPLY CHAIN--COMPANIES LIKE *THIRD WORLD DISTRIBUTION* ON HAIGHT THAT KEPT "HEAD SHOPS" IN BONGS, ROLLING PAPERS...
...AND NOW, *COMICS!*
COMIX

UNLIKE "STRAIGHT" COMICS CREATORS, WHO HAD TO FEND FOR THEMSELVES ON GENERIC *NEWSSTANDS*, CRUMB ENJOYED A SPECIALIZED DISTRIBUTION NETWORK THAT *MAINLINED* HIS PRODUCT *DIRECTLY* TO THOSE MOST INTERESTED IN IT!
I'M GETTING *HIGH*--ON *COMIX!*
ZAP!

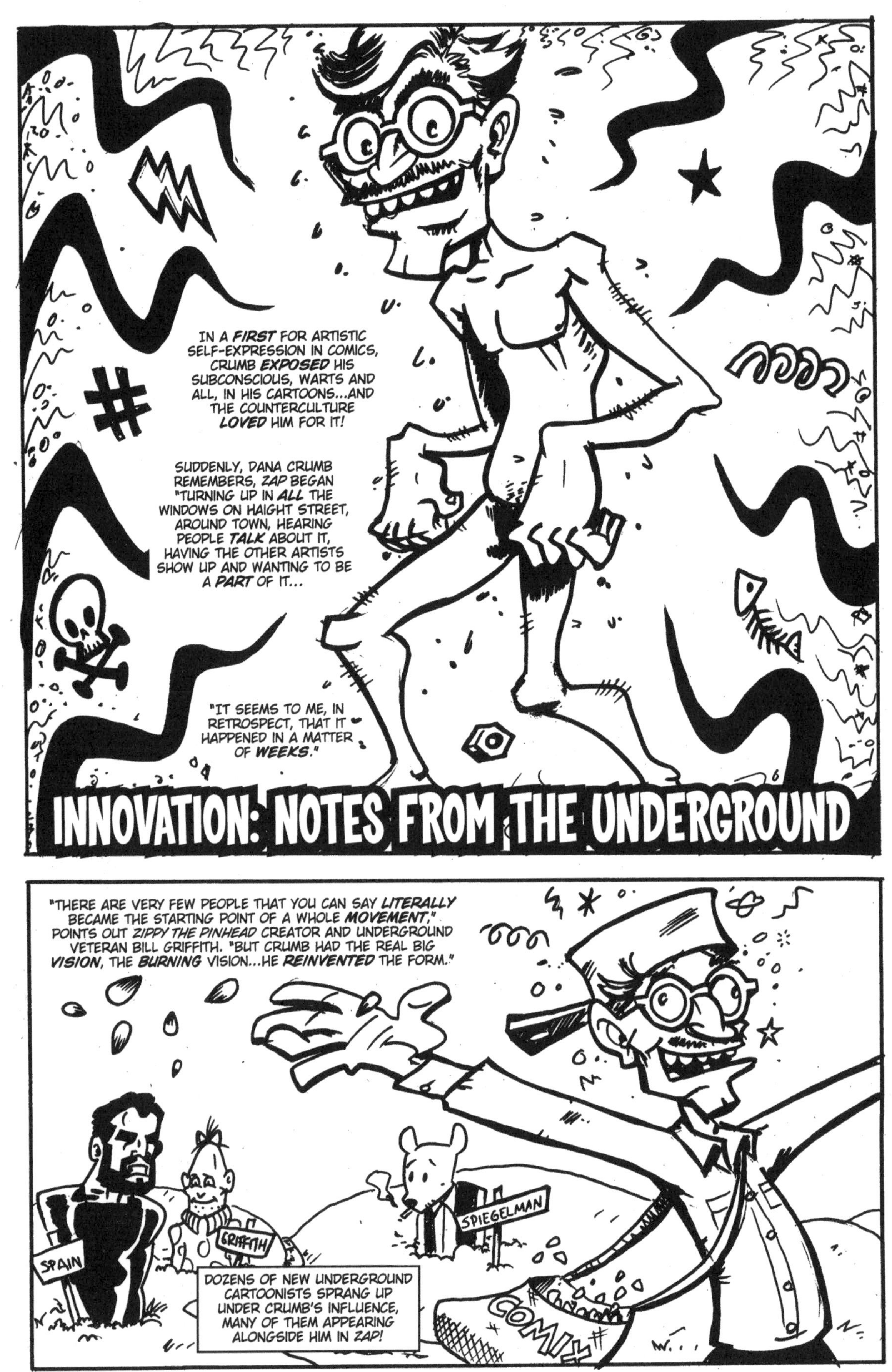
IN A FIRST FOR ARTISTIC SELF-EXPRESSION IN COMICS, CRUMB EXPOSED HIS SUBCONSCIOUS, WARTS AND ALL, IN HIS CARTOONS...AND THE COUNTERCULTURE LOVED HIM FOR IT!
SUDDENLY, DANA CRUMB REMEMBERS, ZAP BEGAN "TURNING UP IN ALL THE WINDOWS ON HAIGHT STREET, AROUND TOWN, HEARING PEOPLE TALK ABOUT IT, HAVING THE OTHER ARTISTS SHOW UP AND WANTING TO BE A PART OF IT...
"IT SEEMS TO ME, IN RETROSPECT, THAT IT HAPPENED IN A MATTER OF WEEKS."
INNOVATION: NOTES FROM THE UNDERGROUND
"THERE ARE VERY FEW PEOPLE THAT YOU CAN SAY LITERALLY BECAME THE STARTING POINT OF A WHOLE MOVEMENT," POINTS OUT ZIPPY THE PINHEAD CREATOR AND UNDERGROUND VETERAN BILL GRIFFITH. "BUT CRUMB HAD THE REAL BIG VISION, THE BURNING VISION...HE REINVENTED THE FORM."
SPAIN
GRIFFITH
SPIEGELMAN
DOZENS OF NEW UNDERGROUND CARTOONISTS SPRANG UP UNDER CRUMB'S INFLUENCE, MANY OF THEM APPEARING ALONGSIDE HIM IN ZAP!
COMIX

ONE STRIP FROM *ZAP* IN PARTICULAR, THE NONSENSICALLY OPTIMISTIC ***"KEEP ON TRUCKIN',"*** BECAME SOMETHING OF A ***HERALDRY CREST*** FOR EASY-GOING HIPPIES...

HEY HEY HEY...
METHADONE
LOVE TRUCKIN!

...APPEARING ON POSTERS, PATCHES, T-SHIRTS, CIGARETTE PAPERS, BATH MATS, BEACH TOWELS, MUD FLAPS, BUMPER STICKERS (*WE COULD GO ON*)... ***NONE*** OF WHICH MADE CRUMB A ***DIME!***

CRUMB AND OTHER CARTOONISTS COULD TRAVEL THE COUNTRY, CRASH WITH THE LOCAL LEFTY NEWSPAPERS AND EARN THEIR KEEP BY ***DRAWING*** FOR THEM.
HE WATCHED THE DISASTROUS 1968 ***DEMOCRATIC NATIONAL CONVENTION*** IN CHICAGO FROM A HILL WITH ARTIST JAY LYNCH: "WE WERE WATCHING ***MASSES*** OF HUMANITY BEING ***GASSED.***"

DESPITE (OR ***BECAUSE*** OF) HIS LEGENDARY STATUS IN THE COUNTER-CULTURE, THE HIPPIES BEGAN TO ***GRATE*** ON CRUMB; HE GREW INCREASINGLY CONTEMPTUOUS OF THEIR ATTITUDE OF:
"I'M ***BEAUTIFUL.*** I'M ***SPIRITUAL.*** I'VE ***LOST*** MY EGO AND YOU ***HAVEN'T.***"
BIBLE
"IT WAS LIKE MEETING SOME SMUG ***CHRISTIAN,*** WHO SAYS, '***I'M*** SAVED AND ***YOU'RE*** GOING TO GO TO HELL, UNLESS YOU, ***TOO,*** ARE SAVED.' IT WAS ***THAT*** KIND OF ATTITUDE."

OF COURSE, THIS COULD HAVE JUST BEEN CRUMB'S ENDEMIC ***SELF-LOATHING*** ASSERTING ITSELF.
"I WOULDN'T BELONG TO ANY CLUB THAT WOULD HAVE ***ME*** AS A MEMBER," AS GROUCHO MARX ONCE SAID...

THOUGH THE INEXHAUSTIBLE PARADE OF ***HUCKSTERS*** AND ***HANGERS-ON*** THAT GRAVITATED TOWARD CRUMB'S FAME ANNOYED HIM, HE GAINED INSPIRATION FROM THE ***CARTOONISTS*** ALSO DRAWN INTO HIS ORBIT...

...PARTICULARLY ***S. CLAY WILSON***, A FORMER ***ARMY MEDIC*** WHOSE WORK EXPLORED THE ARTIST'S FASCINATION WITH CASTRATION, MUTILATION, AND EVERY CONCEIVABLE FORM OF ***UGLY SEXUAL VIOLENCE***.

"I WAS JUST COMPLETELY ***BLITZKRIEGED*** BY THE GUY!"

CRUMB REALIZED THAT WILSON HAD BLOWN THROUGH ALL THE BARRIERS OF ***SELF-CENSORSHIP*** THAT HE STILL IMPOSED ON HIS OWN WORK.

CRUMB INVITED WILSON TO CONTRIBUTE TO *ZAP* AND BEGAN DEPICTING HIS OWN DOMINEERING SEX FANTASIES IN HIS COMIX...

...BLOWING THROUGH EVERY CONCEIVABLE ***TABOO*** ON PRINCIPLE, EVEN EXPLORING ***RACIST*** AND ***SEXIST*** IMAGERY IN SELF-CONSCIOUSLY ***OFFENSIVE*** STRIPS.

MANY OF THE LEFTIES AND LIBERALS WHO HAD EMBRACED CRUMB TURNED ON HIM.
HEH, HEH... SUCCESS!
"I GOT TOO MUCH LOVE," CRUMB CLAIMED. "I HAD TO MAKE THEM BACK OFF BY SHOWING THEM THIS OTHER SIDE OF MYSELF -- A REAL WEIRDNESS. AND THEY DID INDEED BACK OFF. MY POPULARITY WENT DOWN QUITE A BIT..."

NEVERTHELESS, AS CRUMB WENT, SO DID THE UNDERGROUND.
SEX SOON BECAME AS ESSENTIAL TO COMIX AS POTHEAD SURREALISM.
SNATCH COMICS
$
WITH PURITANICAL PREDICTABILITY, THE SUDDENLY-RACIER UNDERGROUNDS SOON FOUND THEMSELVES RUNNING INTO TROUBLE WITH THE LAW.

ZAP #4
BERKELEY POLICE RAIDED NEW ZAP PUBLISHER PRINT MINT OVER A CRUMB STORY, "JOE BLOW", ABOUT A WHOLESOME NUCLEAR FAMILY GLEEFULLY GANG-BANGING EACH OTHER.
BUT THE OWNER HAD BEEN TIPPED OFF, AND HID THE ENTIRE PRINT RUN IN HIS GARAGE!
BERKELEY COPS ALSO BUSTED A GALLERY EXHIBITION OF "THE NEW COMIX", ARRESTED THE OWNERS AND IMPOUNDED EVERY UNDERGROUND COMIC THEY COULD GET THEIR HANDS ON.
(THOUGH PROSECUTORS HAD TO DROP THE CHARGES BECAUSE ALL THE COMIX MYSTERIOUSLY DISAPPEARED FROM THE POLICE EVIDENCE ROOM... HMMMM...)
SNATCH COMIX
"THERE WAS A SHAKY PERIOD THERE IN 70-71," UNDERGROUND ARTIST AND PAINTER ROBERT WILLIAMS REMEMBERS.
"THERE WAS A CHANCE THERE THAT THE COUNTRY COULD HAVE SWUNG TO THE RIGHT. WE KNOW FOR A FACT THAT THEY WERE RECONDITIONING (JAPANESE) INTERNMENT CAMPS IN EASTERN AND SOUTHERN CALIFORNIA.
"EITHER WE WERE GOING TO GET FORCED INTO THE ARMY, OR WE'D GET THROWN INTO AN INTERNMENT CAMP...FOR THREE OR FOUR YEARS IT WAS A SCARY SITUATION."
IT WASN'T JUST HIPPIE PARANOIA. WHEN ARTIST SKIP WILLIAMSON TRIED TO PRINT A BENEFIT COMIC TO HELP THE DEFENSE OF ABBIE HOFFMAN AND THE CHICAGO SEVEN, MYSTERIOUS MEN IN SUITS VISITED HIS PRINTER!
"WE CAN'T STOP YOU FROM PRINTING THIS, BUT IF YOU DO, WE'LL PUT YOU OUT OF BUSINESS."
REBEL COMIX
INK

NONE OF THIS PUT MUCH OF A DENT IN THE UNDERGROUND'S POPULARITY, WHICH REACHED ITS ZENITH IN THE EARLY '70S.
"EVENTUALLY WE WILL OWN AND OPERATE EVERY PHASE IN THE CREATION, PRODUCTION AND DISTRIBUTION OF OUR BOOKS...
"...AND WILL BE DEPENDENT UPON NO OUTSIDE FORCE THAT WOULD PRESUME TO CONTROL OR CONTAIN OUR ENERGY!"
PIONEERING UNDERGROUND'ER JACK "JAXON" JACKSON PREDICTED THE STRUGGLING "STRAIGHT" COMICS INDUSTRY WOULD SOON COLLAPSE, LEAVING ONLY COMIX BEHIND!

AS PER THEIR USUAL MODUS OPERANDI, MAINSTREAM COMICS TRIED ATTEMPTED TO APE THE UNDERGROUNDS' SUCCESS... WITH MIXED RESULTS.
STAN LEE TAPPED UNDERGROUND PUBLISHER DENIS KITCHEN TO PRODUCE A COUPLE ISSUES OF A NEWSSTAND COMIX BOOK FOR MARVEL, BUT IT BOMBED.
FACE FRONT, TRUE BELIEVERS!
NARC! CHEESE IT!
COMIX BOOK

STILL, SOME OF THIS "VITALITY AND FREEDOM" STUFF WAS RUBBING OFF ON CORPORATE COMICS.
IN 1969, WRITER DENNIS O'NEIL AND ARTIST NEAL ADAMS BEGAN A SOCIALLY-CONSCIOUS SUPER HERO COMIC, GREEN LANTERN-GREEN ARROW, IN WHICH THE COSTUMED CRUSADERS BATTLED AGAINST ISSUES RIPPED FROM THE DAY'S HEADLINES (WITH DISAPPOINTING COMMERCIAL RESULTS).
MY POWER RING IS USELESS... AGAINST RACISM! -SOB!-
GREEN LANT
DON'T YOU FIND IT A BIT CONDESCENDING TO ASSUME THAT THE ONLY WAY SUPER HERO FANS WILL ENGAGE IN REAL ISSUES IS IF YOU COUCH THEM IN SPANDEX, SCI-FI CLICHES?
CONDESCENDING... AND TRUE!

IN 1971, MARVEL'S LEE DEFIED THE COMICS CODE AUTHORITY BY PUBLISHING A THREE-ISSUE RUN OF AMAZING SPIDER-MAN WITHOUT ITS SEAL BECAUSE THE CENSORS REFUSED TO APPROVE A STORY THAT DEPICTED THE DANGERS OF DRUG USE...AS PART OF A REQUEST BY THE U.S. DEPARTMENT OF HEALTH!
THIS FIRST INSTANCE OF A MAJOR COMPANY* DEFYING THE COMICS CODE SIGNALED THE BEGINNING OF THE END OF THE AUTHORITY'S POWER AFTER SIXTEEN YEARS OF DOMINATION!
* OBVIOUSLY UNDERGROUND COMIX, WHICH HAD AN INDEPENDENT, NON-NEWSSTAND DISTRIBUTION SYSTEM, IGNORED THE CODE PROCESS ENTIRELY.
APPROVED BY THE COMICS CODE
CA
!!

AS FOR CRUMB, HE HAD BY THIS TIME WITHDRAWN FROM THE MOVEMENT HE ORIGINATED, HAVING LOST INTEREST IN ZAP BY THE EARLY SEVENTIES.
THOUGH HE CONTINUED TO PRODUCE COMIX, HE DID SO FROM THE ANONYMITY OF A FARM HE HAD BOUGHT WITH THE MONEY HE MADE OFF THE FRITZ THE CAT ANIMATED FILM.
"I NEVER HAD ANY DESIRE TO BE 'AMERICA'S BEST LOVED UNDERGROUND CARTOONIST!'
"THAT WAS SUPPOSED TO BE A JOKE, NOT MY LIFE!"

IN THE SPRING OF 1970, ANIMATOR RALPH BAKSHI AND PRODUCER STEVE KRANTZ ASKED A RELUCTANT CRUMB TO SELL THEM THE RIGHTS TO A FRITZ CARTOON FEATURE.
"I COULDN'T COPE WITH THEIR AGGRESSIVENESS... (KRANTZ) WAS THE BUTCHER. AND I WAS THE MEAT!"
CRUMB FEARED FROM THE OUTSET THAT THE PROJECT WOULD BE AN EMBARRASSMENT; BUT HIS FIRST WIFE AND LAWYERS PERSUADED HIM TO PLAY BALL.

THE BIG CLAIM TO FAME OF BASHKI'S FRITZ THE CAT FILM WHEN IT OPENED IN 1972 WAS THAT IT WAS THE FIRST X-RATED CARTOON.
OMG!!
ABANDONING CRUMB'S ORIGINAL COMICS WITHIN THE FIRST TWENTY MINUTES OR SO, THE FILM WAS A PSYCHEDELIC MESS OF RACISM, RAPE, NAZISM, TORTURE, AND VIOLENCE.

THE MOVIE'S OPENING IDENTIFIED ITS SETTING AS "THE 1960s, HAPPY TIMES, HEAVY TIMES," AS IF THE SUMMER OF LOVE HAD ALREADY RECEDED INTO THE DISTANT PAST.
INDEED, THE END TO THE VIETNAM WAR IN 1973 REMOVED THE SINGLE BIGGEST UNIFYING ISSUE OF THE COUNTER-CULTURE.
HAIGHT
ASHBUR
THE HIPPIE COALITION SPLINTERED INTO VARIOUS RADICAL FACTIONS, ORGANIZED CRIME TOOK OVER THE DRUG TRADE FOR GOOD, AND THE CULTURE WARS OF THE DECADE WOULD SOON BEGIN IN EARNEST.

THE FORTUNES OF UNDERGROUND COMIX **WANED** WITH THE DREAMS OF THE '60S. ANTI-**DRUG PARAPHERNALIA** LAWS PUT THE **HEAD SHOPS**, THE UNDERGROUND'S PRIMARY RETAILERS, **OUT OF BUSINESS**.
THE OWNERS OF **RIP-OFF PRESS** WERE FORCED TO BURN THEIR OWN COMICS FOR **HEAT!**
FABULOUS FURRY FREAK BROTH
REAK

CRUMB SAW THE INDUSTRY'S WOUNDS AS LARGELY **SELF-INFLICTED**, HOWEVER:

U.G.

"THOSE 'UG' PUBLISHERS... WOULD PUBLISH **ANYTHING** THAT FAINTLY RESEMBLED AN UNDERGROUND COMIC, **GLUTTING** THE MARKET WITH A MULTITUDE OF UNREADABLE, INCOHERENT BOOKS...

"THEY BEHAVED LIKE ANY **OTHER** BUSINESS IN THE THROES OF A **TREND**... PUMP IT FOR ALL IT'S WORTH 'TIL THE BUBBLE **BURSTS!**"

ROBERT CRUMB HAD GONE FROM BEING A SHY, REPRESSED, MISANTHROPIC COMICS FAN TO A SHY, REPRESSED, MISANTHROPIC ***LIVING ARTISTIC LEGEND!***

CRUMB PURGED HIMSELF OF FRITZ THE CAT BY HAVING THE CHARACTER'S OSTRICH GIRLFRIEND ***STAB HIM TO DEATH*** WITH AN ICE PICK IN A 1972 COMIC.

FRITZ

HAW, HAW! GOOD RIDDANCE!

BUT SINCE THE FRITZ FILM HAD GROSSED $100 MILLION AT THE BOX OFFICE, THE PRODUCERS RESPONDED ...

NOW SHOWING

NINE LIVES OF FRITZ CAT

...WITH THE 1974 ***SEQUEL***, THE ***NINE LIVES*** OF FRITZ THE CAT...

"YOU CAN'T WIN!!"

MOUSE PIRATES

THE CARTOONISTS COMPRISING THE SOON-TO-BE-***INFAMOUS*** AIR PIRATES COLLECTIVE FIRST MET AT THE 1970 ***SKY RIVER ROCK FESTIVAL & LIGHTER THAN AIR FAIR*** ON A FARM IN WASHINGTON STATE THAT FEATURED ***TEN DAYS*** OF MUSIC AND *"FREE LOVE."*

MANAGEMENT REMINDS YOU NOT TO "***RAPE OUR SISTERS...***"*

REFRESHMENTS

HOT DOGS 15¢
SOUP 20¢ / LSD $1
MESCALINE 35¢
MARIJUANA $8-10 LID

* *ACTUAL ANNOUNCEMENT!*

EVEN WITHIN THE UNDERGROUND COMIX SCENE, THE AIR PIRATES WERE MISFITS WHO DIDN'T MESH WELL WITH THE OTHER FACTIONS.
BOBBY LONDON, YOUNGEST OF THE PIRATES, QUIT WORKING FOR THE NEW YORK RAT AND SEED IN CHICAGO BECAUSE HE REFUSED TO DRAW COMMUNIST PROPAGANDA.
"I CONSIDERED MYSELF TO BE A CARTOONIST... (NOT) A PAIR OF HANDS FOR THE COUNTER-CULTURE!"

THE PIRATES' ELDER STATESMAN AND RINGLEADER, DAN O'NEILL, WAS THE ONLY ESTABLISHED CARTOONIST AMONG THE BUNCH, HAVING DRAWN A NEWSPAPER STRIP FOR THE SAN FRANCISCO CHRONICLE, ODD BODKINS, SINCE 1964.
IN A BIZARRE SCHEME TO WREST CONTROL OF THE STRIP'S COPYRIGHT, DAN WORKED 28 WALT DISNEY CHARACTERS INTO BODKINS, HOPING THE CHRONICLE WOULD GIVE THE STRIP TO HIM RATHER THAN FACE THE ENSUING LAWSUIT.
(INSTEAD, THEY JUST FIRED HIM.)

O'NEILL AND LONDON, ALONG WITH ARTISTS GARY HALLGREN, SHERRY FLENNIKEN AND TED RICHARDS, SET UP A STUDIO IN A SAN FRANCISCO FIREHOUSE USED BY FRANCIS FORD COPPOLA TO STORE PROPS FROM GEORGE LUCAS' FIRST FILM, THX-1138.
O'NEILL CLAIMED HIS LAWYER TOLD HIM THAT THE COPYRIGHT TO MICKEY MOUSE HAD LAPSED. HE PROPOSED THE COLLECTIVE SEIZE CONTROL OF DISNEY'S CHARACTERS BY PRODUCING THEIR OWN VERSIONS OF THEM.
SOAP

WHOEVER THIS ALLEGED LAWYER WAS, HE WAS A TAD CONFUSED.
GAWRSH, IT ALL MAKES PERFECT SENSE TO ME! HYUH-YUH!
FANTASYLAND LAW SCHOOL
IN 1956 DISNEY RENEWED ITS COPYRIGHT TO STEAMBOAT WILLIE, THE FIRST MICKEY SHORT, UNTIL 1984.

REGARDLESS OF THE SCHEME'S SHAKY LEGAL PREMISE, LONDON OBJECTED TO IT ON MORAL GROUNDS -- HE DIDN'T FEEL RIGHT USING CHARACTERS CREATED BY OTHER PEOPLE.
TO OTHER PIRATES LIKE FLENNIKEN, HOWEVER, THEY WERE STRIKING A BLOW AGAINST A MOUSE- ER, MOUTH-PIECE "FOR THE MILITARY-INDUSTRIAL COMPLEX, AND THERE WAS THIS INCREDIBLE DISILLUSIONMENT WITH -- AND OUTRAGE AT -- '50S AMERICA, WHICH THE MOUSE REPRESENTED."

RICHARDS CLAIMED "DISNEY SUPPLANT(ED) HIMSELF AS A LIVING GRIMM BROTHER OR HANS CHRISTIAN ANDERSEN, WHEN THE FACT WAS THAT HE DIDN'T POSSESS THE REAL TALENT TO CREATE THOSE STORIES OR THE PHILOSOPHY AND TRADITION BEHIND THEM."
MOVE OVER, POOR MAN!
ANDERSEN
"I THOUGHT IT WAS A PISS-OFF THAT DISNEY HAD COPYRIGHTED ALL THAT STUFF AND CLAIMED IT AS HIS OWN, WITHOUT PUTTING IN THE LITERARY SWEAT TO ADD MORE TO IT. HE JUST COPIED IT."

O'NEILL DREAMED OF RUNNING AN UNDERGROUND PUBLISHER MORE LIKE A REAL BUSINESS, PRODUCING MONTHLY TITLES ON A RELIABLE SCHEDULE. USING DISNEY CHARACTERS WOULD GIVE THEM INSTANT LEGITIMACY AND SUSTAINED SOLVENCY.
WHEN IT CAME TO DISTRIBUTION, THE PIRATES' PLANS WERE LESS PRACTICAL, LIKE DROPPING THEIR COMICS FROM BLIMPS -- OR HIRING WINOS DRESSED LIKE COPS TO SELL THEM ON THE STREET.
ULTIMATELY, 20,000 COPIES OF AIR PIRATES FUNNIES #1 & 2 WERE PUBLISHED BY HELL COMICS (A PLAY ON DELL) IN THE SUMMER OF 1971.
THEIR MOTTO: "IF YOU'RE LOOKING FOR LAUGHS, GO TO HELL!"
AIR PIRATES
AIR PIRATES
IN THE PAGES OF AIR PIRATES, MICKEY, MINNIE, DONALD, PEGLEG PETE, GOOFY, HUEY, DUEY AND LOUIE (AMONG OTHER DISNEY CHARACTERS) CURSED, SMUGGLED DRUGS (ON THE COVER, NO LESS), MASTURBATED AND PERFORMED ORAL SEX ON EACH OTHER.
MUCH TO O'NEILL'S DISMAY, HOWEVER, THE DISNEY COMPANY DIDN'T EVEN NOTICE.
"WHY HAVE A FIGHT IF NO ONE COMES?"
FINALLY, O'NEILL MET THE SON OF DISNEY'S CHAIRMAN AT A PARTY. OPENLY GAY AND OWNER OF A BOOKSTORE IN SAN FRAN, THE MOUSE SCION WAS MORE THAN HAPPY TO SMUGGLE AIR PIRATES FUNNIES INTO THE NEXT BOARD MEETING... WHERE IT HAD THE DESIRED EFFECT.
ON OCTOBER 21, 1971, WALT DISNEY PRODUCTIONS FILED SUIT AGAINST THE AIR PIRATES, HELL COMICS, O'NEILL, RICHARDS, HALLGREN, AND LONDON...
AIR PIRATES
AIR PIRATES

...THOUGH O'NEILL CLAIMED IT TOOK DISNEY FOUR MONTHS TO LOCATE THE PIRATES AND SERVE THEM THE SUIT, DESPITE THE FACT THEIR "SECRET HIDEOUT" WAS LISTED IN THE SAN FRANCISCO YELLOW PAGES!
Air Pirates Secret Hideout
WHEN THE PROCESS SERVER DID SHOW UP, THE PIRATES PULLED A REVERSE SPARTACUS ON HIM.
"ARE YOU DAN O'NEILL?"
"NO, HE'S DAN O'NEILL!"
"NO, SHE'S DAN O'NEILL!"
"NO, HE'S--"
THE FIRST HEARING FELL ON MARCH 10, 1972. THE PIRATES DID THEIR BEST TO TURN IT INTO A CIRCUS, HOLDING A PRESS CONFERENCE PROUDLY PROCLAIMING THEIR GUILT.
O'NEILL SHOWED UP TO THE COURTHOUSE DRESSED LIKE AN OLD WEST GUNFIGHTER. WHEN HE TRIED TO DRAW HIS HOLSTERED BANANA, HE WAS RESTRAINED BY THE U.S. MARSHAL IN ATTENDANCE.
"THE LINE BELONGS TO US! IF IT ENDS UP A MOUSE, IT'S STILL A LINE!
"WE HAVE ABSOLUTE FREEDOM TO COPY ANYTHING AS LONG AS WE ADD TO IT!"
DISNEY'S CASE AGAINST THE PIRATES WAS PRETTY STRAIGHTFORWARD, ALLEGING THE DEFENDANTS HAD USED COPYRIGHTED CHARACTERS WITHOUT PERMISSION (CITING THE 1909 COPYRIGHT ACT, WHICH SAID ALL COPYRIGHTABLE COMPONENTS OF A COPYRIGHTED EXPRESSION ARE PROTECTED TOO)...
...AND THAT THE PIRATES HAD ALSO VIOLATED THEIR TRADEMARKS BY:
(A)
REPLICATING THEM TO THE POINT THAT THE CONSUMER WOULD BE MISLED INTO THINKING THEY WERE PURCHASING A DISNEY-AUTHORIZED PRODUCT, AND THAT
(B)
THE SEXUAL AND/OR CRIMINAL ACTS PERFORMED BY THE CHARACTERS IN AIR PIRATES FUNNIES DAMAGED DISNEY'S BUSINESS BY DISPARAGING THEIR BRAND.

THE PIRATES HAD SECURED THE *PRO BONO* SERVICES OF TWO COUNTER-CULTURE-FRIENDLY LAW FIRMS. THEIR DEFENSE WAS MULTIFOLD:

FIRST, THEY CLAIMED *AIR PIRATES FUNNIES* WAS FIRMLY IN THE WESTERN TRADITION OF ***PARODY AND SATIRE***, AND THUS PROTECTED BY *"FAIR USE"* LAWS.

THEY ALSO CLAIMED THAT NO CONSUMER WOULD MISTAKE THE PIRATES' MICKEY FOR DISNEY'S, FOR WHILE THEY ***LOOKED*** SIMILAR, THEY ***BEHAVED*** COMPLETELY DIFFERENTLY.

FOR THAT MATTER, SINCE, LIKE ALL UNDERGROUND COMIX, *APF* WAS SOLD NOT IN NEWSSTANDS BUT ***HEAD SHOPS***, A MARKET DISNEY SHUNNED, THE DEFENSE CONTENDED THE COMPANY WASN'T LOSING A DIME.

SPARE DRUGS?

UNDER THE ***FIRST AMENDMENT***, THE DEFENSE ARGUED, THE PIRATES HAD EVERY RIGHT TO TAKE A CRITICAL EYE TO DISNEY'S CHARACTERS, FOR THEY WERE ***INTERNATIONALLY RECOGNIZED*** SYMBOLS OF AMERICAN ***CULTURAL POWER***.

IN OTHER WORDS, LIKE ANY POLITICIAN OR SIGNIFICANT PUBLIC FIGURE, DISNEY WAS TOO INFLUENTIAL ***NOT*** TO BE CRITICIZED.

BY ADDING THEIR ***OWN*** IDEAS, THE AIR PIRATES HAD ALSO TRANSFORMED THE DISNEY ICONS INTO A ***DIFFERENT*** ARTISTIC EXPRESSION ***OUTSIDE*** THE COMPANY'S COPYRIGHT.

EACH PIRATE SUBMITTED A STATEMENT OF PURPOSE TO THE COURT. IN HIS, O'NEILL SAID HIS OBSESSION WITH DISNEY'S CHARACTERS WAS THE COMPANY'S ***OWN FAULT!***

THEY HAD INGRAINED THESE IMAGES IN HIM AS A ***CHILD*** AND IT WAS UNFAIR OF THEM TO PREVENT HIM FROM EXAMINING THEIR EFFECT AS AN ***ADULT***:

"MY PURPOSE IN USING THE MOUSE AS A CHARACTER IS NOT TO ***DESTROY*** THE DISNEY PRODUCT...
"...BUT TO ***DEAL*** WITH THE IMAGE IN THE AMERICAN CONSCIOUSNESS THAT THE DISNEY IMAGE ***IMPLANTED***."

IN RETROSPECT, AIR PIRATES LAWYER MICHAEL KENNEDY ADMITS, THE DEFENSE MAY HAVE GONE A LITTLE ***OVERBOARD***:
"IF (THE JUDGE) WASN'T A FAN OF DISNEY'S AT THE START, HE ***WAS*** BY THE END. WE MAY'VE DRIVEN HIM THERE BY BEING SO OBNOXIOUS AND THE WORK SO PROFANE. JONATHAN SWIFT, HE DID ***NOT*** THINK WE WERE."
BANG
JUDGE ALBERT C. WOLLENBERG SAID IF HE AGREED WITH THE AIR PIRATES' ARGUMENTS IT WOULD ***"OBLITERATE COPYRIGHT PROTECTION."*** ALSO, HE FOUND "SOME ***DIFFICULTY*** IN DISCOVERING THE SIGNIFICANT ***CONTENT*** OF THE ***IDEAS*** WHICH THE DEFENDANTS ARE EXPRESSING."
AT THE PLAINTIFF'S REQUEST, WOLLENBERG RENDERED A ***SUMMARY JUDGMENT*** (IN LIEU OF A TRIAL) THAT ENJOINED THE PIRATES FROM MAKING MORE DISNEY COMICS. HE ORDERED THE ARTISTS TO PAY THE MOUSE MORE THAN ***$200,000*** IN DAMAGES, ATTORNEY'S FEES, AND COSTS.
O'NEILL APPEALED ALL THE WAY TO THE U.S. SUPREME COURT, WHICH ***REFUSED*** TO HEAR THE CASE IN 1979.
IN DEFIANCE, HE PRODUCED A ***NEW*** COMIC SHOWING MICKEY AND MINNIE RETIRED ON A CALIFORNIA FARM AND CREDITING THE AIR PIRATES WITH GETTING THEM OFF BOOZE & DRUGS.
DISNEY DEMANDED WOLLENBERG DECLARE O'NEILL IN CONTEMPT OF COURT SO HE COULD BE PROSECUTED ***CRIMINALLY***, BUT THE JUDGE REFUSED.
THE COMPANY SPENT NEARLY ***TWO MILLION DOLLARS*** PURSUING THE AIR PIRATES, WITH NOTHING TO SHOW FOR IT BUT A WRITTEN PROMISE O'NEILL WOULD NEVER DRAW ***MICKEY MOUSE*** AGAIN. HE DECLARED ***VICTORY***:
"DOING SOMETHING STUPID ***ONCE*** IS JUST PLAIN ***STUPID.***
"DOING SOMETHING STUPID ***TWICE*** IS A ***PHILOSOPHY!***"
IRONICALLY, IF THE CASE HAD BEEN TRIED TODAY, THE OUTCOME MAY HAVE BEEN SUBSTANTIALLY ***DIFFERENT***.
IN 1994 THE SUPREME COURT RULED THAT A PROFANE PARODY OF THE SONG *"OH, PRETTY WOMAN"* BY 2 LIVE CREW DID ***NOT*** CONSTITUTE COPYRIGHT INFRINGEMENT.
EVEN THOUGH THE RAPPERS' *"PRETTY WOMAN"* SAMPLED WHOLE ***RIFFS*** FROM ROY ORBISON'S ORIGINAL...
...THE JUSTICES RULED ***UNANIMOUSLY*** THAT THEIR VERSION HAD TRANSFORMED IT INTO SOMETHING COMPLETELY DIFFERENT AND ***UNIQUE***...
...***EXACTLY*** WHAT THE AIR PIRATES HAD ARGUED ALL ALONG!

HEAVY METTLE

IN THE ***FRENCH***-SPEAKING WORLD, COMICS ARE CALLED *LA BANDE DESSINÉE* -- LITERALLY, ***"DRAWN STRIPS."*** AS THE TERM WOULD ***SUGGEST***, THE FIRST TRUE FRENCH "COMIC ***BOOK***"...

...WAS, LIKE *FAMOUS FUNNIES* IN THE U.S., A REPRINT OF ***NEWSPAPER*** COMICS.
Le Café
MICKEY

LE JOURNAL DE MICKEY DEBUTED IN 1934 AS AN EIGHT-PAGE, FULL-COLOR, WEEKLY MAGAZINE FEATURING THE ***TRANSLATED*** ADVENTURES OF DISNEY'S MOUSE AND OTHER STRIPS OWNED BY THE ***KING FEATURES*** SYNDICATE.

IMITATORS SOON COVERED THE CONTINENT, INCLUDING *SPIROU* IN BELGIUM AND *ROBBEDOES* IN FLEMISH HOLLAND...
HA HA HA! EUROPE IS ***MINE!***

--ALL LARGELY SHOWCASING REPRINTS OF COMICS FROM ***AMERICAN*** SYNDICATES.

WHEN THE ***THIRD REICH*** CONQUERED WESTERN EUROPE IN THE EARLY 1940s, HOWEVER, THE GERMANS PROPMPTLY ***CUT OFF*** ALL AMERICAN IMPORTS.
HEY!! FIND YOUR ***OWN*** MARKETS, KRAUT!!

NOW EUROPEANS HAD TO DEPEND WHOLLY ON ***HOMEGROWN*** TALENT.

THE CONTINENT'S MOST ***ENDURING*** COMICS HERO WAS CREATED BY ***GEORGES REMI***, A STAFF ARTIST FOR THE CATHOLIC NEWSPAPER *LE VINGTIÈME SIÈCLE* (*"20TH CENTURY"*) IN BRUSSELS, BELGIUM.

TINTIN WAS A FICTIONAL REPORTER FOR THE PAPER'S CHILDREN'S SUPPLEMENT (*LE PETITE VINGTIÈME*) WHO TRAVERSED THE GLOBE ON JOURNALISTIC ADVENTURES.

Follow the money... Kof!
Deep Throat needs a lozenge!

THE STRIP PREMIERED ON SEPTEMBER 23, 1929, UNDER REMI'S PENNAME ***HERGÉ*** (THE FRENCH PRONUNCIATION OF HIS INITIALS ***REVERSED***).

THANKS TO TINTIN'S SUCCESS, CIRCULATION OF *LE VINGTIÈME SIÈCLE* SKYROCKETED! HIS EXPLOITS WERE SOON TRANSLATED ALL OVER EUROPE.

AT THE END OF EACH SERIALIZED SOJOURN, AN ACTOR PLAYING TINTIN AND A DOG REPRESENTING HIS FAITHFUL TERRIER ***MILOU*** WOULD ARRIVE AT THE BRUSSELS TRAIN STATION TO BE DRIVEN THROUGH ADORING CROWDS!

WHEN THE NAZIS CONQUERED BELGIUM, THEY SHUT DOWN THE CATHOLIC PRESS, BUT INVITED HERGÉ TO CONTINUE *TINTIN* IN *LE SOIR*, THE COUNTRY'S BIGGEST NEWSPAPER.

HERGÉ ACCEPTED. HE HOPED TO HELP BELGIANS THROUGH THE TRAUMA OF WAR WITH THE COMFORT OF THE ***FAMILIAR***.

Le Soir

UNFORTUNATELY, *LE SOIR* BECAME A NAKED ***PROPAGANDA ORGAN*** FOR THE OCCUPYING FORCES! *TINTIN* RAN DAILY NEXT TO ***OUTRAGEOUS*** NAZI LIES!

BELGIANS CONTEMPTUOUSLY DUBBED THE PAPER *"LE SOIR VOLÉ"* ... "THE ***STOLEN*** *SOIR*!"

Le Soir

HITLER= AWESOME!

TINTIN

AFTER THE BRITISH ***LIBERATED*** BRUSSELS IN 1944, HERGÉ FOUND HIMSELF BRANDED A ***COLLABORATOR***!

GALERIE des TRAITRES

ZEMO

HERGÉ

ROBOT

MASTER MAN

SKULL

THOT

DETAINED ***FOUR TIMES*** BY A NEW BELGIAN REGIME HUNGRY FOR ***PAYBACK*** AGAINST GERMAN SYMPATHIZERS, HERGÉ SPENT A NIGHT IN A CELL CROWDED WITH SUSPECTED NAZIS.
BLACKLISTED SO HE COULDN'T GET A NEWSPAPER JOB, HERGÉ'S FUTURE--AND ***TINTIN'S***--SEEMED IN DOUBT.

FORTUNATELY, HERGÉ'S REPUTATION WAS RESCUED BY ENTREPRENEUR ***RAYMOND LEBLANC***, A VETERAN OF THE ***RESISTANCE*** WHO HAD, AS THE CARTOONIST ***INTENDED***, BEEN ***CHEERED*** BY THE WARTIME CONTINUATION OF *TINTIN* IN *LE SOIR*.
Ho, ho! Oh, Milou... What trouble will you get into next?

IGNORING THE WHISPERS, THE WAR HERO SECURED FOR HIS CARTOONIST HERO THE NECESSARY "GOOD CITIZENSHIP" PAPERS IN MAY 1946. LEBLANC COULD NOW MAKE HERGÉ ART DIRECTOR OF A NEW COMICS MAGAZINE THAT WOULD FEATURE THE CONTINUED EXPLOITS OF THE BOY REPORTER WITH WORK BY NEW BELGIAN CARTOONISTS.

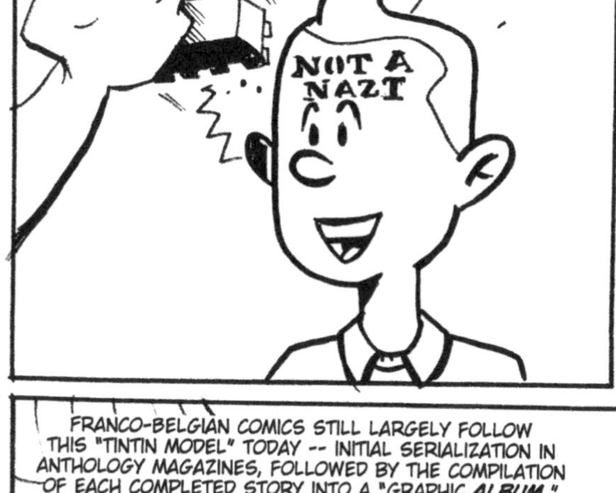
NOT A NAZI

TINTIN THE MAGAZINE DEBUTED SEPTEMBER 26, 1946, AND PICKED UP RIGHT WHERE HERGÉ LEFT OFF ALMOST EXACTLY TWO YEARS EARLIER IN LE SOIR WITH THE ADVENTURE OF THE SEVEN CRYSTAL BALLS.
LEBLANC ALSO SECURED A DEAL WITH BELGIUM'S LARGEST PUBLISHER, CASTERMAN, TO COLLECT EACH COMPLETED TINTIN SAGA INTO A SINGLE VOLUME TO BE SOLD IN THE BOOK MARKET.
TINTIN

FRANCO-BELGIAN COMICS STILL LARGELY FOLLOW THIS "TINTIN MODEL" TODAY -- INITIAL SERIALIZATION IN ANTHOLOGY MAGAZINES, FOLLOWED BY THE COMPILATION OF EACH COMPLETED STORY INTO A "GRAPHIC ALBUM."
IN FRANCE, THE MOST SUCCESSFUL AND INFLUENTIAL COMICS MAGAZINE WAS PILOTE (EST. 1959), WHICH PREMIERED SUCH MEGA-POPULAR STRIPS AS GOSCINNY & UDERZO'S ASTERIX AND CHARLIER & GIRAUD'S BLUEBERRY.
Désolé, il n'y a plus de place pour vous!

U.S. COMICS DID NOT RETURN IN ANY DOMINANT WAY TO FRANCE AFTER THE WAR ... WITH THE HELP OF CULTURAL PROTECTIONISM.
CRIME
USA
FRENCH COMMUNISTS SPONSORED A BILL IN 1949 BANNING VIOLENT PERIODICALS FOR YOUTH, AIMED IN PART AT GETTING RID OF AMERICAN PUBLICATIONS SUCH AS COMICS.

IN THE 1960s, IMPORTED MARVEL COMICS ALSO GOT INTO TROUBLE WITH AUTHORITIES OVER THE VIOLENCE ISSUE. WHILE FRANCE IS ARGUABLY MORE OPEN-MINDED THAN AMERICA IN GENERAL, THE NATION STILL HAD SOME "COMMUNITY STANDARDS" WHEN IT CAME TO COMICS' CONTENT...

...WHICH CHAFED CARTOONISTS LIKE BLUEBERRY CO-CREATOR JEAN "MOEBIUS" GIRAUD, WHO, PARTLY INSPIRED BY CRUMB AND THE AMERICAN UNDERGROUNDS...
...ABANDONED PILOTE IN 1974 WITH ARTISTS JEAN-PIERRE DIONNET AND PHILIPPE DRUILLET TO FOUND MÉTAL HURLANT MAGAZINE AS A HOME FOR DARKER, MORE ADULT MATERIAL.

THE FOLLOWING YEAR, THE EDITOR OF AMERICAN HUMOR MAGAZINE NATIONAL LAMPOON TRAVELED TO EUROPE LOOKING FOR CARTOONS AND CARTOONISTS FOR HIS MAG.
LAMPOON'S PARENT COMPANY, 21ST CENTURY COMMUNICATIONS, THOUGHT A TRANSLATED VERSION OF METAL HURLANT COULD SUCCEED IN THE U.S. MARKET.

AS JULIE SIMMONS, THE EDITOR OF HEAVY METAL (THE LAMPOON VERSION OF HURLANT), EXPLAINS:
"WHERE THE LAMPOON TOOK OVER MAD'S READERS ... HEAVY METAL (WOULD TAKE OVER THE READERS WHO STOPPED) READING DC AND MARVEL...
NATIONAL LAMPOON
MAD
HULK
HEAVY METAL
"THERE'S A CERTAIN MATURITY LEVEL WHERE YOU STOP READING MARVEL AND YOU'RE STILL INTO COMICS. HEAVY METAL'S GIVING YOU ANOTHER OUTLET."

HEAVY METAL STARTED OUT LARGELY WITH EUROPEAN WORKS IN TRANSLATION, BUT SOON RECRUITED MORE AND MORE TALENTED AMERICAN ARTISTS LIKE RICHARD CORBEN AND BERNIE WRIGHTSON UNTIL OVER HALF ITS CONTRIBUTORS CAME FROM THE U.S.
THE STORIES TENDED TO COMBINE GENRE EXPLOITATION (SCIENCE FICTION AND FANTASY) WITH THE HARDCORE SEX AND TRIPPY DRUG REFERENCES OF THE UNDERGROUNDS.
Je me suis envoyé en l'air sur votre fusée... Soupir!
ASTRO TURF

DURING THIS SAME PERIOD, U.S. COMICS LEGENDS WERE INCREASINGLY INVITED TO APPEAR AS GUESTS OF HONOR AT EUROPEAN COMIC ART FESTIVALS.
On ne le vaut pas! On ne le vaut pas!

THESE AMERICAN MASTERS COULD NOT HELP BUT CONTRAST THE RESPECT AFFORDED THEM IN EUROPE WITH THE CONTEMPT HEAPED ON THEM IN THEIR NATIVE LAND!
INCREASED EXPOSURE TO THE WORK AND ATTITUDES OF THE CONTINENT LED TO A GROWING CONSENSUS WITHIN THE U.S. COMICS COMMUNITY THAT THIS COUNTRY HAD LOST ITS WAY WITH REGARDS TO A MEDIUM WHICH HAD ORIGINATED HERE!
U SUK! HAW!

EUROPE AND AMERICA'S RADICALLY DIFFERENT CULTURAL ATTITUDES TOWARD COMICS ARE NOT THAT DIFFICULT TO EXPLAIN.
REMEMBER THAT THE NAZIS SHUT OFF ACCESS TO AMERICAN COMICS DURING THEIR GOLDEN AGE--THE SAME PERIOD IN WHICH SUPER HEROES TOOK OVER THE U.S. INDUSTRY IN A WAY THEY COULDN'T IN EUROPE!

SO EUROPEAN COMICS WERE NEVER DOMINATED BY A ***SINGLE*** GENRE, AND INSTEAD TEEMED WITH A WIDE ***VARIETY*** OF POPULAR FRANCHISES.

AND FRANCE'S RARE PAROXYSMS OF COMICS CENSORSHIP TENDED TO BE ***ANTI-AMERICAN*** IN NATURE. ERGO, THE FRENCH INDUSTRY DID NOT FEEL THE NEED TO ***CASTRATE*** ITSELF WITH A ***COMICS CODE***.

WHILE MAINLINE U.S. PRODUCERS WERE ***PROHIBITED*** FROM APPEALING TO OLDER AUDIENCES FOR NEARLY ***THREE DECADES***, EUROPEAN PUBLISHERS WERE FREE TO CULTIVATE MORE ***SOPHISTICATED*** MARKETS!

ADULT
COMICS

FRENCH CULTURE EMBRACED COMICS AS LE NEUVIÈME ART -- THE "NINTH ART" WORTHY TO SIT ALONGSIDE THE OTHER MAJOR FORMS.
NEVERTHELESS, MÉTAL HURLANT FOLDED IN 1987, WHILE THE AMERICAN HEAVY METAL IS STILL GOING STRONG AS OF THIS WRITING!
AMERICAN COMICS PUBLISHERS COULDN'T IGNORE HM'S SUCCESS IN THE MIDST OF A DYING 1970'S NEWSSTAND MARKET!
BY 1974, THE NUMBER OF MAINSTREAM U.S. COMICS PUBLISHERS HAD DWINDLED TO SIX: MARVEL, ARCHIE, CHARLTON, GOLD KEY (SUCCESSOR TO DELL), HARVEY AND DC...
...AND IN 1978 THE ONCE-MIGHTY DC WAS FORCED TO OVERHAUL ITS DISTRIBUTION SYSTEM, CANCELLING A MASSIVE THIRTY-ONE TITLES IN WHAT FANDOM DUBBED "THE DC IMPLOSION."
EQUALLY-STRUGGLING MARVEL WAS SAVED ONLY BY ACQUIRING THE COMICS RIGHTS TO AN AS YET-UNRELEASED SCIENCE-FANTASY FILM BY AMERICAN GRAFFITI DIRECTOR GEORGE LUCAS.
DC
STAR WARS #1 CAME OUT BEFORE THE MOVIE AND BECAME THE FIRST NEWSSTAND COMIC SINCE THE 1940s TO SELL MORE THAN ONE MILLION COPIES PER ISSUE.
THE POST-STAR WARS MANIA FOR ALL THINGS SCIENCE FICTION AND FANTASY CONTRIBUTED TO HEAVY METAL'S SUCCESS, AND EMBOLDENED MARVEL TO COMPETE WITH HM ON ITS OWN TURF.
1980 SAW THE DEBUT OF EPIC ILLUSTRATED, A GLOSSY MARVEL MAGAZINE FEATURING MORE ADULT GENRE STORIES -- AND THE EDITORS INSISTED THAT, UNLIKE MARVEL'S CORPORATE-OWNED SUPER HEROES, THE CREATORS WOULD OWN THEIR STORIES, JUST AS HM'S ARTISTS DID!
"IT TOOK A LITTLE CONVINCING OF THE LAWYERS UPSTAIRS," SAID EPIC EDITOR RICK MARSCHALL AT THE TIME, "BECAUSE THEY'RE JUST NOT USED TO MARVEL WORKING THAT WAY...
EXIT
"...BUT ONCE WE EXPLAINED THAT THIS IS THE WAY IT WORKS IN THE REAL WORLD, THERE WAS NO PROBLEM."

BUT THE ***REAL WORLD*** WAS ABOUT TO INVADE THE ***COMICS*** WORLD SOON ENOUGH -- FOR THE STRUGGLE BETWEEN ***"WORK FOR HIRE"*** AND ***CREATORS' RIGHTS*** BECAME THE ***NEXT*** GREAT INDUSTRY BATTLE!

THE
GRABBERS

COPYRIGHT, A CREATOR'S RIGHT TO EXCLUSIVE USE OF HER "ORIGINAL WORKS OF AUTHORSHIP," IS GUARANTEED BY THE UNITED STATES CONSTITUTION.
ARTICLE I, SECTION VIII, CLAUSE 8 READS:
"The Congress shall have power…to promote the progress of science and useful arts, by securing for limited times to authors and inventors the exclusive right to their respective writings and discoveries."

AND AS A SIGNATORY TO THE 1886 BERNE CONVENTION FOR THE PRODUCTION OF LITERARY & ARTISTIC WORKS, THE USA RECOGNIZES AUTHORS' COPYRIGHT AS AUTOMATIC--THAT IS, AS SOON AS YOU CREATE SOMETHING BY AFFIXING THAT EXPRESSION TO A SPECIFIC MEDIUM, YOU OWN IT--PERIOD!
(THOUGH ONLY BY REGISTERING YOUR COPYRIGHT AT THE LIBRARY OF CONGRESS CAN YOU SEEK STATUTORY DAMAGES AND ATTORNEY'S FEES IN COURT.)

ACCORDING TO THE COPYRIGHT ACT OF 1909, THOUGH, "AN EMPLOYER WHO HIRES ANOTHER TO CREATE A COPYRIGHTABLE WORK IS THE AUTHOR OF THE WORK…ABSENT AN AGREEMENT TO THE CONTRARY."
I GOTS MY RIGHTS, DON'T I? HAW!
IN OTHER WORDS, IF SOMEBODY ELSE PAID YOU TO CREATE IT, THEY OWN IT.
IN THE BIZ THIS IS KNOWN AS "WORK FOR HIRE."

WE'VE ALREADY SEEN JERRY SIEGEL AND JOE SHUSTER CREATE THE SUPERMAN STRIP AT THEIR OWN INSTANCE AND EXPENSE IN THE MID-1930S AND SUBMIT IT TO MULTIPLE PUBLISHERS BEFORE FINDING IT A HOME AT DC COMICS.

ON MARCH 1, 1938, DC HAD THE INEXPERIENCED CREATORS SIGN A CONTRACT ASSIGNING "EXCLUSIVE RIGHT(S)" TO SUPERMAN "TO HAVE AND HOLD FOREVER" FOR $130 -- $10 PER PAGE FOR THE FIRST 13-PAGE SUPES STORY IN ACTION #1.
DC
CONTRACT

DC THEN REGISTERED THE COPYRIGHT TO SUPERMAN IN ITS NAME, THEREBY DECLARING JOE AND JERRY "EMPLOYEES OF A WORK MADE FOR HIRE."
Aa Bb Cc
ACTION COMICS
DC

BUT THESE "EMPLOYEES" ACTED MORE LIKE INDEPENDENT CONTRACTORS, PRODUCING SUPERMAN FROM THEIR STUDIO IN CLEVELAND AND PAYING THEIR ASSISTANTS OUT OF POCKET.
AND WHILE THEY WERE FAR FROM STARVING, THE CREATORS OF SUPERMAN WERE MAKING CONSIDERABLY LESS THAN THE SUITS IN NEW YORK!
THE SATURDAY EVENING POST
SUPERCHUMPS

JERRY SIEGEL, A PRICKLY PERSONALITY AT THE BEST OF TIMES, GREW INCREASINGLY AGITATED BY THE MONEY SITUATION.
HIS CORRESPONDENCE WITH DC HEAD JACK LIEBOWITZ THROUGHOUT THE 1930s & '40s SEETHES WITH DEMANDS FOR HIGHER PAYCHECKS AND COMPLAINTS OF EDITORIAL MEDDLING.
LIEBOWITZ, IN TURN, CONTINUALLY BLASTS SIEGEL OVER THE QUALITY OF JOE'S ARTWORK AND JERRY'S SCRIPTS.

AFTER JERRY WAS ***DRAFTED*** (JOE'S POOR EYESIGHT KEPT HIM OUT OF THE WAR), DC DECIDED TO INTRODUCE A YOUNGER VERSION OF SUPERMAN, ***SUPERBOY***, IN 1944.

JERRY WAS ***FURIOUS***. DC HAD REJECTED A SIMILAR PROPOSAL ***HE*** HAD MADE YEARS BEFORE. EVEN THOUGH HIS STUDIO WAS CREATING MANY OF THE SUPERBOY STORIES, HE STILL FELT HE WASN'T BEING PROPERLY ***COMPENSATED*** FOR A WORK DERIVED FROM HIS ORIGINAL.

GET HIM DOWN FROM THERE!!

SIEGEL FOUND A SYMPATHETIC EAR WITH ANOTHER SOLDIER AT HIS POST: LAWYER ALFRED ***"ZUGGY"*** ZUGSMITH.

YOU'RE GETTING ***SCREWED***, KID! WE SHOULD SUE FOR THE RIGHTS TO SUPERBOY--AND GET SUPER***MAN*** BACK, TOO!

SIEGEL TOOK ACTION NOT LONG AFTER WAR'S END. BELIEVING ***BATMAN*** CREATOR ***BOB KANE***'S CONTRACT WOULD BE UP SOON, JERRY TRIED TO ENLIST HIM IN A ***JOINT SUIT*** AGAINST DC.

AS YOU KNOW, JER, I'M A STRONG BELIEVER IN ***CREATOR'S RIGHTS...***

(KANE TOOK ***SOLE CREDIT*** FOR BATMAN EVEN THOUGH SCRIPTER ***BILL FINGER*** CO-CREATED THE CHARACTER AND WROTE EVERY STORY. IT WAS FINGER, WITH ASSISTANT ARTIST ***JERRY ROBINSON***, WHO CREATED BATS' ARCHNEMESIS THE ***JOKER*** AND HIS SIDEKICK ***ROBIN***.)

KRAK!

...MINE! BWAH HAHA!!

KANE WENT BEHIND SIEGEL'S BACK AND WARNED LIEBOWITZ OF THE SUPERMAN DUO'S PLANS.

HE ALSO MANAGED TO RENEGOTIATE HIS ***OWN*** CONTRACT, EARNING A FAT NEW PAGE RATE AND A PERCENTAGE OF SUBSIDIARY RIGHTS TO BATMAN.

HE CLAIMED HIS ORIGINAL DC CONTRACT WAS ***INVALID***, BECAUSE HE HAD SIGNED IT AS A ***MINOR!***

ZUGGY FILED SUIT AGAINST DC IN APRIL 1947 FOR OWNERSHIP OF SUPERMAN AND SUPERBOY AND $5 MILLION IN DAMAGES.

BUT THE COURTS RULED IN THE COMPANY'S FAVOR ON SUPERMAN (THOUGH SIEGEL ACTUALLY ***WON*** ON SUPER***BOY***). LIEBOWITZ MADE SIEGEL AND SHUSTER A DEAL: ACCEPT $100,000 FOR ***ALL*** RIGHTS TO SUPERMAN ***AND*** SUPERBOY, THEN LEAVE DC BE.

THE PAIR RELUCTANTLY AGREED. NOT ONLY DID MOST OF THE MONEY GO TO PAY ZUGGY'S ***FEE***, THEY NOW MISSED OUT ON ALL ***FUTURE*** SUPES REVENUE... INCLUDING THE ***SWEETEST*** PLUM, ONE OF THE MOST POPULAR TELEVISION SHOWS OF ALL TIME, ***THE ADVENTURES OF SUPERMAN***, WHICH PREMIERED IN 1953.

PART OF THE PHILOSOPHY BEHIND COPYRIGHT IS THAT IT IS A FINANCIAL INCENTIVE FOR ARTISTS TO MAKE THE RESULTS OF THEIR CREATIVITY PUBLIC FOR THE BETTERMENT OF THE NATION...THE LOGIC BEING, OF COURSE, THAT IT'S HARDER TO CREATE ART IF YOU CAN'T MAKE A LIVING AT IT.
AH... DOWNLOADING FREE TORRENTS! A VICTIMLESS CRIME!
REMEMBER, THOUGH, THAT THE CONSTITUTION PROVIDES COPYRIGHTS FOR A "LIMITED TIME" ONLY.
AUTHORS MAY EXCLUSIVELY EXPLOIT THEIR WORKS OVER A CERTAIN PERIOD, BUT THEN THE WORK ENTERS THE PUBLIC DOMAIN, WHERE IT MAY BE USED BY ALL.
STOP!! YOU CAN'T MAKE A PORNO VERSION OF MOBY DICK!!
AU CONTRAIRE, HERMAN! PUBLISHED IN 1856. WE CAN MAKE A KARAOKE VERSION, IF WE WANT!
AND WILL!
THAT'S WHY THE COPYRIGHT TERM EXTENSION ACT OF 1998 CHAMPIONED BY REP. SONNY BONO (R-CA) PROVED SO CONTROVERSIAL. CRITICS CALLED IT THE "MICKEY MOUSE PROTECTION ACT" BECAUSE THE WALT DISNEY COMPANY LOBBIED SO SUCCESSFULLY TO PREVENT ITS CHARACTERS FROM SLIPPING INTO PUBLIC DOMAIN BY EXTENDING TERMS OF "CORPORATE AUTHORSHIP" TO 120 YEARS AFTER THEIR CREATION!
"I GOT YOU, BABE..."
BUT CREATIONS OF THE GOLDEN AGE OF COMICS ARE GOVERNED BY THE 1909 ACT, WHICH SAYS A COPYRIGHT HAS TO BE RENEWED EVERY TWENTY-EIGHT YEARS TO AVOID SLIPPING INTO THE PUBLIC DOMAIN.
WHEN SUPERMAN'S INITIAL COPYRIGHT REGISTRATION EXPIRED IN THE 1960s, SIEGEL & SHUSTER TOOK DC TO COURT AGAIN, SEEKING SOLE RIGHT OF RENEWAL BECAUSE THEY DID NOT CREATE THE STRIP AS "WORK MADE FOR HIRE."
GIMME, GIMME, GIMME!!
DC

LIKEWISE, JOE SIMON FILED A LAWSUIT IN FEDERAL COURT TO ENJOIN MARVEL COMICS FROM RENEWING THE COPYRIGHT TO CAPTAIN AMERICA IN (1941 + 28 =) 1969.
MWAH-HAH-HAH...
ZZZ

MARVEL GOT CAP BACK IN AN OUT-OF-COURT SETTLEMENT WITH SIMON. THEY ASKED JACK KIRBY, SIMON'S COLLABORATOR AND THEIR TOP ARTIST, TO SIGN A STATEMENT REAFFIRMING THE COMPANY'S OWNERSHIP. MARVEL TOLD HIM THEY WOULD PAY HIM AS MUCH AS THEY WERE PAYING SIMON IF HE DID SO.
KIRBY AGREED, NOT REALIZING THAT MOST OF THE MONEY WAS GOING TO SIMON'S LAWYER (THEN TO SIMON), SO HE ENDED UP GETTING CONSIDERABLY LESS THAN JOE...
...AND EVEN STILL, MARVEL HADN'T PAID BY THE TIME HE DEFECTED TO DC IN 1970.

IN 1972, MARTIN GOODMAN'S UMBRELLA COMPANY, MAGAZINE MANAGEMENT, SPUN MARVEL OFF INTO ITS OWN ENTITY. THEY ASKED KIRBY, NOW ONE OF DC'S TOP ARTISTS, TO SIGN A STATEMENT REAFFIRMING THEIR OWNERSHIP OF ALL THE CHARACTERS HE CREATED OR CO-CREATED, LIKE THE FANTASTIC FOUR, THE HULK, THOR, IRON MAN, AND X-MEN.
KIRBY SIGNED THE DOCUMENT ONLY ON THE CONDITION THAT MARVEL PAY WHAT THEY OWED HIM FROM THE SIMON SETTLEMENT, WHICH THEY DID IN JUNE OF 1972.
M

BY THIS POINT, THE MAINSTREAM COMIC BOOK FIELD HAD BECOME MORE TRADITIONALLY CORPORATE.
MOGUL STEVE ROSS BOUGHT DC IN 1967, THEN STRUGGLING MOVIE STUDIO WARNER BROTHERS IN 1969 AND MERGED THE COMPANIES TOGETHER.
WARNER COMMUNICATIONS CONVINCED SIEGEL TO DROP HIS SUIT AGAINST DC TO CLEAR THE WAY FOR DEVELOMENT OF A SUPERMAN MOVIE WITH A SCRIPT BY RED-HOT GODFATHER AUTHOR MARIO PUZO (WHO WROTE FOR MARTIN GOODMAN'S MEN'S MAGAZINES TO PAY HIS RENT WHILE FINISHING HIS MAFIA MAGNUM OPUS).
SUPERMAN
Luthor, I'm gonna make you an offer you can't refuse...

JERRY DROPPED HIS LAWSUIT ON THE PROMISE OF A WARNERS STIPEND FOR HE AND JOE THAT NEVER MATERIALIZED. SIEGEL NOW WORKED AS A MAIL CLERK FOR THE CALIFORNIA PUBLIC UTILITIES CORPORATION. SHUSTER, LEGALLY BLIND, LIVED IN A BROTHER'S CARE.

WHEN HE READ IN VARIETY THAT PUZO WAS GETTING THREE MILLION DOLLARS TO WRITE THE SUPERMAN SCREENPLAY WHILE HIS FAMILY SQUEAKED BY ON $7,000 A YEAR, SIEGEL SNAPPED.
HE TYPED UP A PRESS RELEASE CURSING THE FILM AND DETAILING THE VARIOUS INDIGNITIES HE AND JOE HAD ENDURED AT THE HANDS OF SUPERMAN'S VARIOUS CORPORATE MASTERS. HE MAILED THE SCREEDS TO ONE THOUSAND MEDIA OUTLETS.

RESPONSE WAS SLOW, BUT SIEGEL WAS EVENTUALLY ABLE TO TELL HIS STORY ON TOM SNYDER'S LATE NIGHT TOMORROW SHOW.
POLITICAL CARTOONIST JERRY ROBINSON HAPPENED TO CATCH THE PROGRAM WHILE WORKING. A FORMER PRESIDENT OF THE NATIONAL CARTOONISTS SOCIETY, HE WAS APPALLED BY SIEGEL AND SHUSTER'S PLIGHT AND RESOLVED TO HELP THEM...
THAT'S NOT FUNNY!

...PERHAPS IN PART BECAUSE HE HIMSELF HAD BEEN DENIED HIS DUE FOR CO-CREATING THE JOKER AND ROBIN WHEN HE WORKED AS AN ARTIST FOR BOB KANE!
ROBINSON JOINED FORCES WITH NEAL ADAMS, ONE OF DC'S MOST POPULAR ARTISTS AND A LONGTIME ADVOCATE FOR CREATORS' RIGHTS, AND GAINED THE SUPPORT OF THE NCS, THE SCREEN CARTOONISTS GUILD AND THE WRITERS GUILD OF AMERICA.
KRAK!

AFTER A FEW MONTHS OF TENSE NEGOTIATIONS WITH THE ROBINSON-ADAMS CAMP, WARNERS REACHED AN AGREEMENT WITH SIEGEL AND SHUSTER RIGHT BEFORE CHRISTMAS 1975.
THE WRITER AND ARTIST WHO CREATED SUPERMAN WOULD EACH RECEIVE A $20,000 STIPEND FOR LIFE AND "CREATED BY" CREDIT ON ALL PRINTED MATTER, TV AND MOVIES (BUT NOT TOYS).
A STRETCH LIMO BROUGHT THE DUO TO THE SUPERMAN: THE MOVIE PREMIERE THREE YEARS LATER.
HE WHO LAUGHS LAST, LAUGHS BEST!

THE COPYRIGHT ACT OF 1976

WENT INTO EFFECT JANUARY 1, 1978 AS THE FIRST MAJOR REVISION TO U.S. LAW SINCE 1909 AND CLARIFIED ***"WORK MADE FOR HIRE"*** AS:

"WORK FOR HIRE"
STORYCO™
STORY CO™
STORY Co.™
STORYCO™

(1) a work prepared by an employee within the scope of his or her employment; or

(2) a work specially ordered or commissioned for use as a contribution to a collective work if the parties expressly agree in a written instrument signed by them that the work shall be considered a work made for hire.

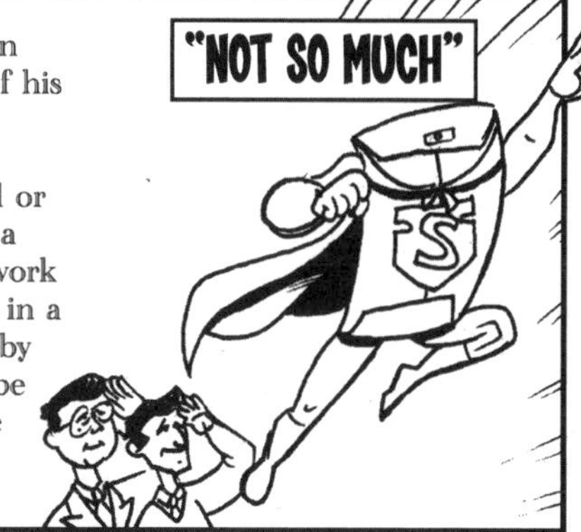
"NOT SO MUCH"

THE LONGER DEFINITION AMOUNTED TO A ***REVERSAL OF FORTUNE*** FOR THE BIG COMICS COMPANIES.

FOR FOUR DECADES THEY HAD ESTABLISHED A HIGHLY ***DUBIOUS*** *"WORK FOR HIRE"* RELATIONSHIP WITH CREATORS BY A VAGUE LEGEND ***STAMPED*** ON THE BACK OF FREELANCERS' PAYCHECKS ***AFTER*** SCRIPTS AND ART HAD ***ALREADY BEEN TURNED IN!***

(AND THE COMPANIES HAD SUBSEQUENTLY ***THROWN AWAY*** MOST OF THOSE CHECKS!)

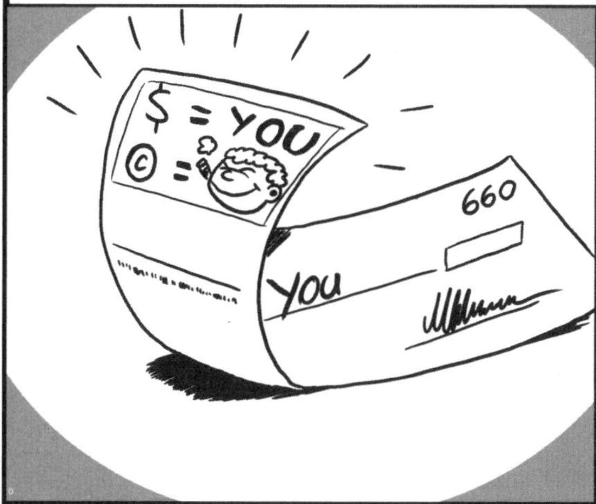
$ = YOU
© =
660
YOU

PUBLISHERS SCRAMBLED TO RETROACTIVELY ***CLARIFY*** THEIR BUSINESS RELATIONSHIPS WITH THEIR CREATORS. OTHERWISE, ARTISTS & WRITERS COULD CLAIM THEIR WORK WASN'T ***COMMISSIONED*** AS WORK FOR HIRE AND THUS ONLY ***THEY*** COULD RENEW THE COPYRIGHTS ONCE THE ORIGINAL TERMS EXPIRED!
UM... GUYS?
HEY, ONE LAST THING...
DC

MARVEL EXECS CONCOCTED WHAT ***SOMEBODY*** MUST HAVE THOUGHT WAS A ***CLEVER*** WAY TO SECURE THE NECESSARY DOCUMENTATION...
NOK, NOK...
...INVOLVING THE NEARLY ***37,000*** ORIGINAL ART BOARDS DATING BACK TO 1960 STACKED IN A CRUMBLING WAREHOUSE IN A W. 22ND STREET NEIGHBORHOOD ***SO*** BAD THE ATTENDANT REFUSED TO ANSWER THE DOOR WITHOUT A ***BUTCHER KNIFE*** IN HER HAND!

THE ORIGINAL ART BOARDS WERE WHAT MARVEL COMICS WERE *PRINTED* FROM. ONCE THEY SERVED THEIR MAIN FUNCTION, HOWEVER, THE COMPANY SEEMED TO BE AT A LOSS AS TO WHAT TO *DO* WITH THEM.
MANY CLASSIC ORIGINAL PAGES AND COVERS WERE SIMPLY GIVEN AWAY AS *PERKS* TO EXECUTIVES OF COMPANIES AND LICENSORS MARVEL DID BUSINESS WITH.
AMAZING FANTASY

STILL OTHERS WERE *STOLEN* BY UNSCRUPULOUS STAFFERS. WHEN THE 22ND ST WAREHOUSE WAS BROKEN INTO IN 1978, THE EDITOR-IN-CHIEF ORDERED SOME OF THE MOST VALUABLE ORIGINALS TO BE BROUGHT INTO THE MAIN MARVEL OFFICES IN A BOX...
AMAZING SPIDER MAN
ART
...WHICH WAS INEXPLICABLY *"STORED"* IN A BREAKROOM NEAR THE *FREIGHT ELEVATOR*. THE BOX AND ITS RICHES QUICKLY *VANISHED*.

HUNDREDS IF NOT *THOUSANDS* OF FILCHED PAGES FOUND THEIR WAY TO THE CONVENTION CIRCUIT, WHERE THEY SOLD FOR *BIG BUCKS--NONE* OF WHICH WENT TO THE ORIGINATING ARTISTS!
HEY! HEY, BUDDY! WANNA BUY AN ORIGINAL *KIRBY MARVEL PAGE?*
ARTSY FARTSY
JACK KIRBY REPORTED, "(THE DEALERS) HIDE THEM FROM US. BUT IF SOMEONE GOES OVER AND ASKS FOR A KIRBY PAGE, HE CAN EASILY GET IT."

MARVEL BEGAN RETURNING ART TO CREATORS AROUND 1976, BUT IN ORDER TO RECEIVE THEIR PAGES, ARTISTS WOULD FIRST HAVE TO SIGN A ONE-PAGE *RELEASE FORM* REAFFIRMING MARVEL'S OWNERSHIP TO THE *COPYRIGHT* OF THE PAGE AS "WORK FOR HIRE."
WHETHER OR NOT MARVEL HAD ANY RIGHT TO HOLD ONTO THE ART IN THE *FIRST PLACE*, HOWEVER, WAS LEGALLY *QUESTIONABLE*. COPYRIGHT PROTECTS THE SPECIFIC *EXPRESSION* OF AN IDEA, NOT THE *PHYSICAL FORM* THAT EXPRESSION TAKES.
"I DIDN'T SELL THEM *DRAWINGS*, I SOLD THEM *STORIES*.
"JUST LIKE AN AUTHOR WOULD OWN HIS (MANU-)SCRIPT IN *BOOK* PUBLISHING, AN ARTIST OWNS HIS ART IN *VISUAL* PUBLISHING."

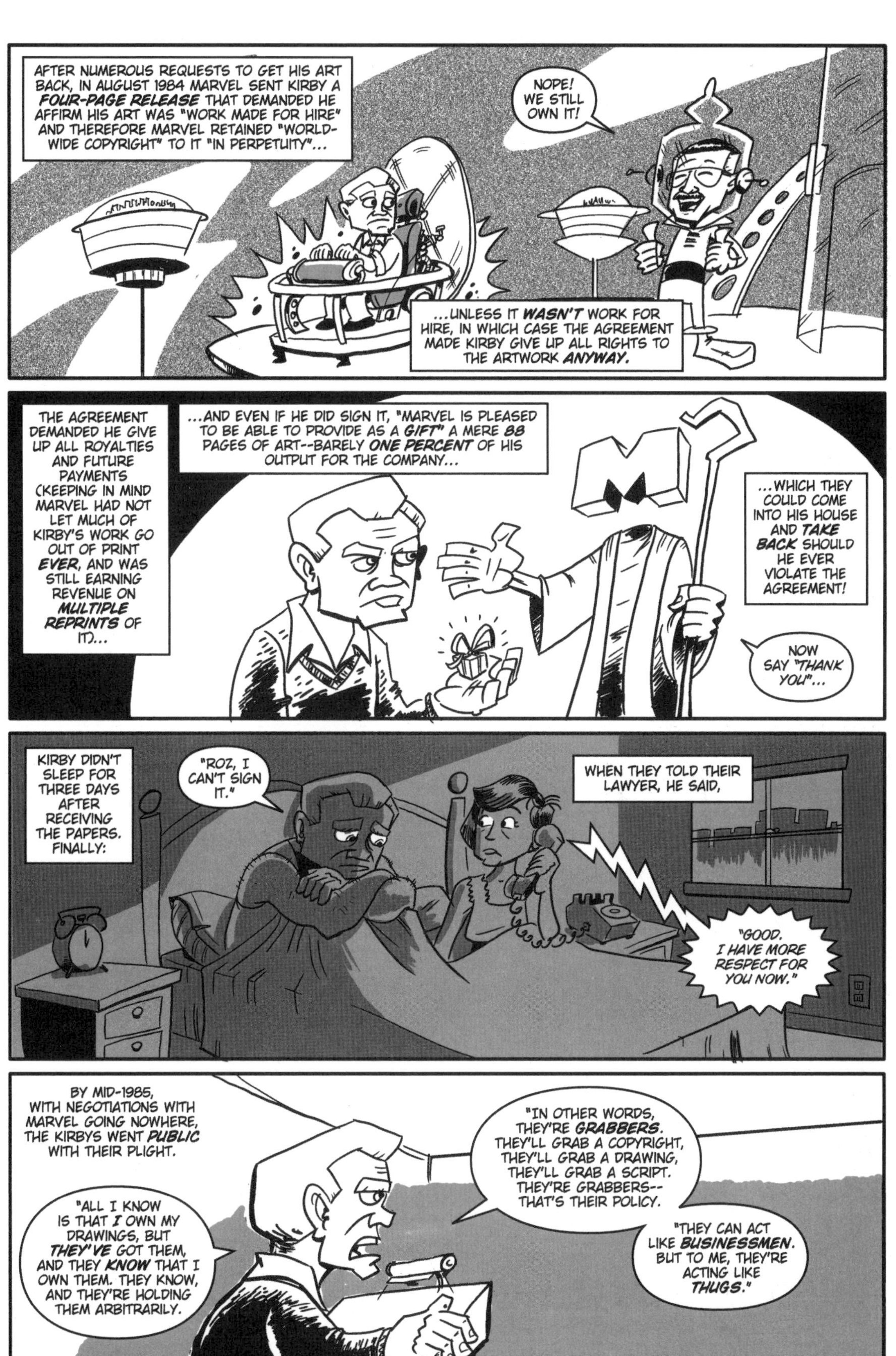
AFTER NUMEROUS REQUESTS TO GET HIS ART BACK, IN AUGUST 1984 MARVEL SENT KIRBY A FOUR-PAGE RELEASE THAT DEMANDED HE AFFIRM HIS ART WAS "WORK MADE FOR HIRE" AND THEREFORE MARVEL RETAINED "WORLD-WIDE COPYRIGHT" TO IT "IN PERPETUITY"...
NOPE! WE STILL OWN IT!
...UNLESS IT WASN'T WORK FOR HIRE, IN WHICH CASE THE AGREEMENT MADE KIRBY GIVE UP ALL RIGHTS TO THE ARTWORK ANYWAY.
THE AGREEMENT DEMANDED HE GIVE UP ALL ROYALTIES AND FUTURE PAYMENTS (KEEPING IN MIND MARVEL HAD NOT LET MUCH OF KIRBY'S WORK GO OUT OF PRINT EVER, AND WAS STILL EARNING REVENUE ON MULTIPLE REPRINTS OF IT)...
...AND EVEN IF HE DID SIGN IT, "MARVEL IS PLEASED TO BE ABLE TO PROVIDE AS A GIFT" A MERE 88 PAGES OF ART--BARELY ONE PERCENT OF HIS OUTPUT FOR THE COMPANY...
...WHICH THEY COULD COME INTO HIS HOUSE AND TAKE BACK SHOULD HE EVER VIOLATE THE AGREEMENT!
NOW SAY "THANK YOU"...
KIRBY DIDN'T SLEEP FOR THREE DAYS AFTER RECEIVING THE PAPERS. FINALLY:
"ROZ, I CAN'T SIGN IT."
WHEN THEY TOLD THEIR LAWYER, HE SAID,
"GOOD. I HAVE MORE RESPECT FOR YOU NOW."
BY MID-1985, WITH NEGOTIATIONS WITH MARVEL GOING NOWHERE, THE KIRBYS WENT PUBLIC WITH THEIR PLIGHT.
"ALL I KNOW IS THAT I OWN MY DRAWINGS, BUT THEY'VE GOT THEM, AND THEY KNOW THAT I OWN THEM. THEY KNOW, AND THEY'RE HOLDING THEM ARBITRARILY.
"IN OTHER WORDS, THEY'RE GRABBERS. THEY'LL GRAB A COPYRIGHT, THEY'LL GRAB A DRAWING, THEY'LL GRAB A SCRIPT. THEY'RE GRABBERS-- THAT'S THEIR POLICY.
"THEY CAN ACT LIKE BUSINESSMEN. BUT TO ME, THEY'RE ACTING LIKE THUGS."

KIRBY'S DILEMMA INSPIRED THE *"CREATORS' RIGHTS"* MOVEMENT OF THE 1980s, AT THE HEART OF WHICH WAS THE PRINCIPLE UNDERPINNING THE AMERICAN DREAM:

HARD WORK SHOULD BE JUSTLY REWARDED.

EVERYWHERE ***ELSE*** IN THE ARTS, PERFORMERS, FILMMAKERS, AUTHORS, AND NEWSPAPER CARTOONISTS WHO CREATE POPULAR PROPERTIES REAPED THE ***BENEFITS*** OF THEIR CREATIONS, EVEN WHEN THAT CREATIVE LABOR WAS ***WORK-FOR-HIRE.***

BUT NOT, HISTORICALLY, IN ***COMICS.***

JACK KIRBY, NOW ALMOST ***70 YEARS OLD,*** LIVED A MODEST, MIDDLE-CLASS EXISTENCE. THOUGH HE NEVER FELL AS DESTITUTE AS SIEGEL & SHUSTER, HE NEVER ***SUED HIS PUBLISHER,*** EITHER.

HE DID NOT RECEIVE A LIFE INSURANCE POLICY OR A RETIREMENT PLAN. HE DID NOT OWN ANY COPYRIGHTS, DID NOT RECEIVE "CREATED BY" CREDIT, NOR ROYALTIES FROM A COMPANY THAT HAD EARNED HUNDREDS OF MILLIONS OF DOLLARS OVER THE LAST QUARTER-CENTURY FROM HIS CREATIONS.

HE HAD ***TWICE***--IN 1969 AND 1972--SIGNED DOCUMENTS GIVING AWAY ***ALL RIGHTS*** TO MARVEL.

TO BE ASKED TO DO SO A ***THIRD*** TIME, IN ORDER TO GET BACK ART HE BELIEVED WAS THE ONLY THING THAT WAS ***HIS*** IN THE FIRST PLACE, THE ONLY LEGACY HE COULD GIVE TO HIS GRANDCHILDREN, WAS, FOR KIRBY, THE ***LAST STRAW.***

MARVEL TOOK A TREMENDOUS ***PUBLIC RELATIONS BEATING*** FOR ITS STANCE. DC DELIGHTED IN STICKING IT TO THEIR ARCHRIVAL BY TRUMPETING THE FACT THEY HAD ***ALREADY*** GREATLY LIBERALIZED (BY COMICS STANDARDS) THEIR PROFIT-SHARING AND ART RETURN PROGRAMS IN THE WAKE OF THE SIEGEL & SHUSTER STANDOFF.

WARNERS HAD PAID KIRBY FOR USING HIS ***NEW GODS*** CHARACTERS IN THE SATURDAY MORNING *SUPER FRIENDS* CARTOON AND TOY LINE, EVEN THOUGH THEY CONSIDERED KIRBY'S COMICS FOR THEM *"WORK FOR HIRE"* TOO.

ANTI-LIFE MEANS DARKSEID IS RICH, BEEYOTCH!

"THE PEOPLE AT DC ARE VERY PROUD OF SAYING THAT THEY HAVE PAID JACK KIRBY MORE MONEY FOR CREATING ***DARKSEID*** THAN HE WAS PAID FOR CREATING THE ENTIRE MARVEL UNIVERSE," REPORTED ONE OF KIRBY'S ALLIES, HIS FORMER ASSISTANT, WRITER AND HISTORIAN MARK EVANIER.

FINALLY, THE SUITS ***BLINKED.*** THEY SENT KIRBY A REVISED, ONE-PAGE RELEASE FORM THAT HE SIGNED ON MAY 16, 1987.

A FEW MONTHS LATER, HE RECEIVED 1,900 ART PAGES FROM MARVEL--MORE THAN 88, BUT STILL ONLY ABOUT ***ONE-FIFTH*** OF WHAT HE HAD DRAWN FOR THEM. THE REST, PRESUMABLY, HAD BEEN DESTROYED, GIFTED, OR STOLEN.

UNDER NEW MANAGEMENT, MARVEL WOULD JOIN DC IN LIBERALIZING ITS ROYALTY AND CHARACTER OWNERSHIP POLICIES.

BUT MANY CREATORS CONTINUED TO ASSERT THEIR RIGHTS UNDER THE 1976 COPYRIGHT ACT OVER PRE-1978 WORKS THEY DID NOT CONSIDER TO BE "FOR HIRE."

(UN-)OFFICIAL HANDBOOK TO THE LEGAL UNIVERSE

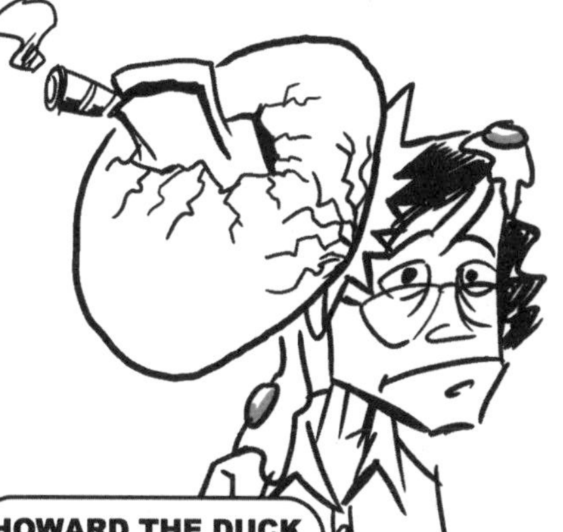

HOWARD THE DUCK
CREATOR: Steve Gerber (writer)
PUBLISHER: Marvel
FIRST APPEARED: ***Adventures Into Fear #19*** (December 1973)
COPYRIGHT DISPUTED: 1978
REASONS GIVEN: Gerber claimed his contract did not give Marvel "work for hire" rights to any ancillary characters he created in the comics he wrote for them.
OUTCOME: Out of court settlement for undisclosed terms, 1983. Marvel retains ownership.
HISTORY: The philosophy-spouting waterfowl, an unexpected hit in the 1970s, has the dubious distinction of being the first Marvel character to star in a major motion picture, from producer George Lucas in 1986, which went on to be one of the most infamous bombs in Hollywood history, grossing a mere $10 million against its $36 million price tag.

BLADE
CREATOR: Marv Wolfman (writer)
PUBLISHER: Marvel
FIRST APPEARED: ***Tomb of Dracula #10*** (July 1973)
COPYRIGHT DISPUTED: 1997
REASONS GIVEN: Like Gerber, Wolfman claimed his contract did not assign Marvel "work for hire" copyright to the characters he created while working for them.
OUTCOME: As Marvel was in bankruptcy at the time, the characters were treated as assets and Wolfman's case was heard in bankruptcy court. Judge Roderick McKelvie ruled in favor of Marvel in November 2000.
HISTORY: Wolfman's suit claimed ownership of 71 characters created during his tenure with Marvel, including Nova (which Wolfman had first sketched out in a fanzine long before coming to Marvel), but McKelvie ruled against all his claims.

JOSIE AND THE PUSSYCATS
CREATOR: Dan DeCarlo (writer/artist)
PUBLISHER: Archie
FIRST APPEARED: ***Archie's Gals 'n' Pals #23*** (Winter 1962-1963)
COPYRIGHT DISPUTED: 2000
REASONS GIVEN: DeCarlo first developed Josie, whom he named after his wife, for a comic strip in the 1950s, bringing it later to be published by Archie as a comic book. Like the other creators, he said he never intended for Archie Comics to own the characters outright as "work for hire."
OUTCOME: Federal District Court ruled in favor of Archie, and the Supreme Court turned down DeCarlo's appeal on December 11, 2001. Archie was less than thrilled with DeCarlo's actions and ended their 43-year relationship with the artist, one of their most important creators, as a result of the suit.
HISTORY: As in the case of Blade, DeCarlo may have been inspired to pursue his claims by the Pussycats appearing in a 2001 film based on their 1970-1 Saturday morning cartoon.* In terms of box office, however, the Josie movie was a bit closer to *Howard the Duck*: A big ole bomb.

** That's not to be meant as a knock on either Wolfman or DeCarlo. Lawyers' fees being what they are, going after a more lucrative movie property is one of the few ways a creator can attract counsel to his or her case.*

CAPTAIN AMERICA
CREATOR: Joe Simon (writer/artist)
PUBLISHER: Timely/Marvel
FIRST APPEARED: ***Captain America Comics #1*** (March 1941)
COPYRIGHT DISPUTED: 1999
REASONS GIVEN: Simon owns a character concept sketch he drew in 1940 to show Martin Goodman before he had been hired as Timely's editor. The sketch depicts Cap more or less as he appears now and notes he should have a sidekick "or he'll be talking to himself all the time." Simon contends this proves he did not create Cap at Marvel's instance and expense, and therefore cannot be considered "work for hire."

WAIT, WAIT--DIDN'T WE *DO* THIS ONE ALREADY?

WE DID, BUT UNDER THE 1976 ACT, ONCE A TERM REACHES ITS 56TH YEAR, CREATORS OF WORKS PRIOR TO JANUARY 1, 1978, CAN TERMINATE ANY PRIOR GRANT OF RIGHTS, REGARDLESS OF THE TERMS OF THE ASSIGNMENT!
SIMON JUST BEAT THE DECEMBER 20, 1999 DEADLINE TO NOTIFY MARVEL OF HIS INTENT TO RECLAIM CAP'S COPYRIGHT...AND THIS TIME THEY SUED HIM!
JERRY SIEGEL'S HEIRS (JOE DIED IN 1992, JERRY IN 1996) HAD TAKEN THE SAME ACTION AGAINST DC EIGHT MONTHS BEFORE.

WHILE MARVEL ULTIMATELY SETTLED WITH SIMON (AGAIN), ON MARCH 26, 2008, JUDGE STEPHEN G. LARSON OF THE CENTRAL DISTRICT OF CALIFORNIA RULED:
SJ
"ALL THE SUPERMAN MATERIAL CONTAINED IN ACTION COMICS #1 IS NOT A WORK-MADE-FOR-HIRE...
"...AND THEREFORE IS SUBJECT TO TERMINATION."

"AFTER SEVENTY YEARS, JEROME SIEGEL'S HEIRS REGAIN WHAT HE GRANTED SO LONG AGO -- THE COPYRIGHT IN THE SUPERMAN MATERIAL THAT WAS PUBLISHED IN ACTION COMICS VOL. 1."
THE FULL IMPLICATIONS OF THAT DECISION ARE STILL BEING WORKED OUT, BUT IT SEEMS TO BE IN THE HEIRS' BEST INTEREST TO WORK WITH THE COMPANY.
GIVEN THE SEVENTY-PLUS YEARS OF WORK VARIOUS DC STAFFERS AND FREELANCERS HAVE PUT INTO SUPERMAN, MANY OF THE ELEMENTS CONSIDERED CRUCIAL TO THE MYTHOS HAVE APPEARED SINCE ACTION #1 AND ARE INCONTROVERTIBLY OWNED BY DC.

SOME FANS, FAR MORE EMOTIONALLY INVESTED IN FICTIONAL HEROES THAN FLESH-AND-BLOOD CREATORS -- AND FEARING THAT DC MIGHT LOSE ALL RIGHTS TO SUPERMAN, THUS DISRUPTING THEIR SUPPLY OF PRECIOUS, PRECIOUS FAMILIARITY --
-- DENOUNCED THE HEIRS' EXERCISE OF THEIR LEGAL RIGHTS AS GREEDY AND SELF-SERVING.
TO WHICH WE CAN ONLY REPLY:
YES! OF COURSE! GOOD FOR THEM!
TURNABOUT IS FAIR PLAY!
M
DC

IT RHYMES WITH TRAFFIC HOVEL

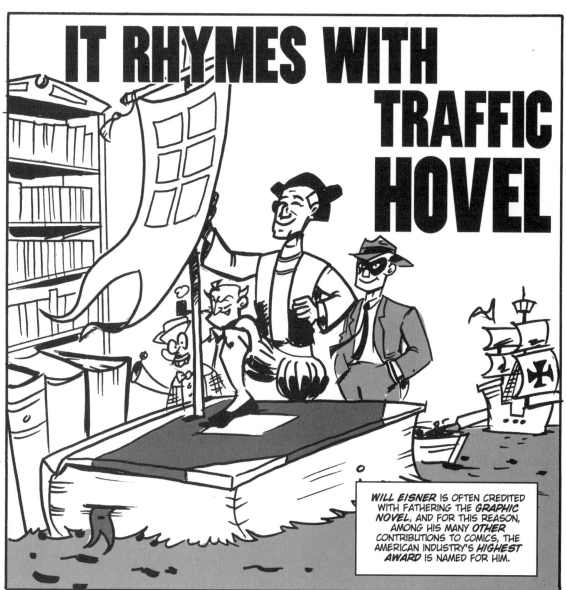

WILL EISNER IS OFTEN CREDITED WITH FATHERING THE ***GRAPHIC NOVEL***, AND FOR THIS REASON, AMONG HIS MANY ***OTHER*** CONTRIBUTIONS TO COMICS, THE AMERICAN INDUSTRY'S ***HIGHEST AWARD*** IS NAMED FOR HIM.

MANY BELIEVE, HOWEVER, THAT THE HONOR OF THE GRAPHIC NOVEL'S CREATION -- INDEED, OF CREATING THE COMIC STRIP ITSELF -- BELONGS MORE RIGHTLY TO SWITZERLAND'S RODOLPHE TÖPFFER (1799-1846).
BAH! AMERICANS-- ALWAYS HOGGING CREDIT FOR EVERYTHING!

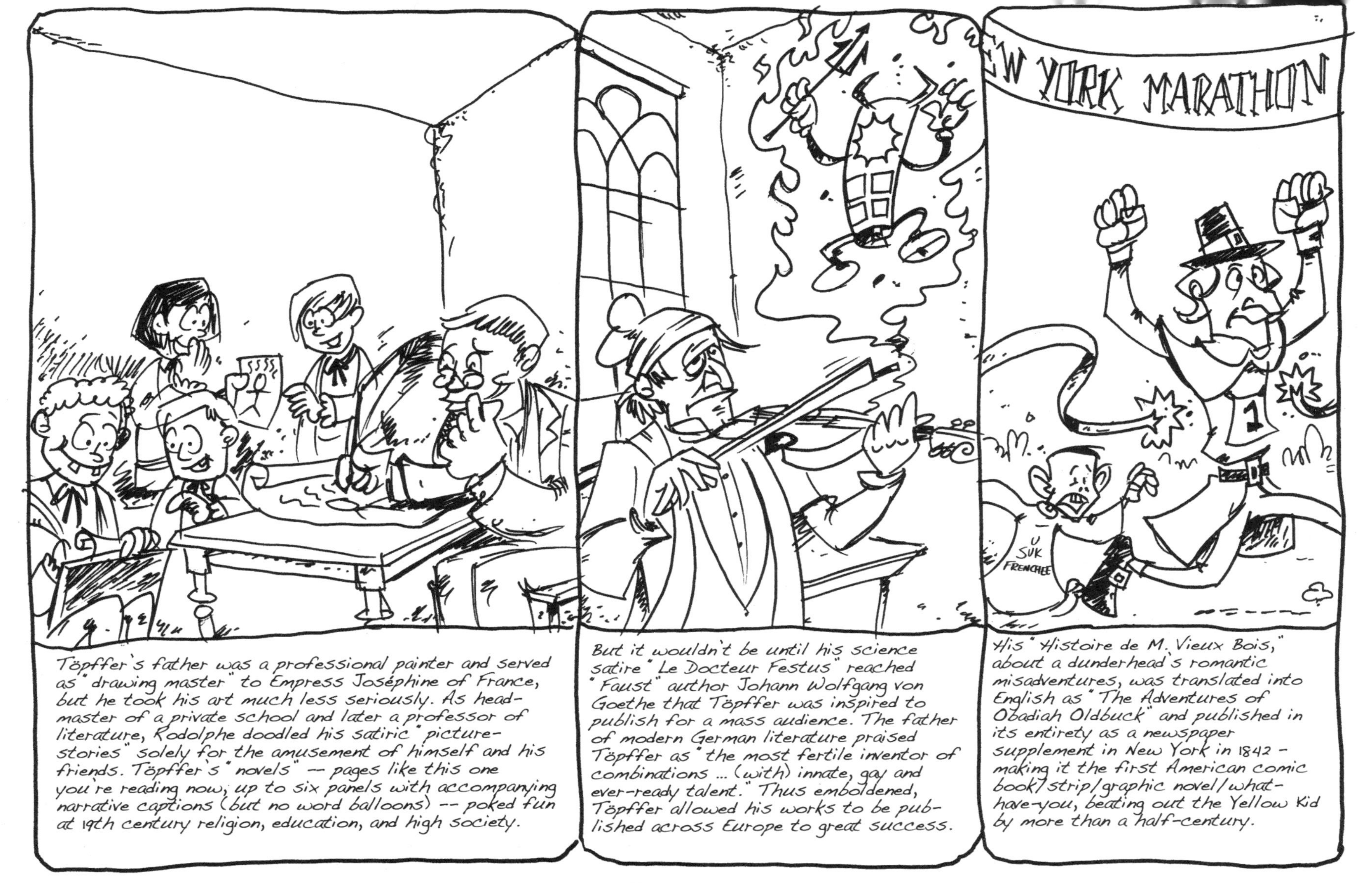
Töpffer's father was a professional painter and served as "drawing master" to Empress Joséphine of France, but he took his art much less seriously. As head-master of a private school and later a professor of literature, Rodolphe doodled his satiric "picture-stories" solely for the amusement of himself and his friends. Töpffer's "novels" -- pages like this one you're reading now, up to six panels with accompanying narrative captions (but no word balloons) -- poked fun at 19th century religion, education, and high society.
But it wouldn't be until his science satire "Le Docteur Festus" reached "Faust" author Johann Wolfgang von Goethe that Töpffer was inspired to publish for a mass audience. The father of modern German literature praised Töpffer as "the most fertile inventor of combinations ... (with) innate, gay and ever-ready talent." Thus emboldened, Töpffer allowed his works to be published across Europe to great success.
EW YORK MARATHON
U SUK FRENCHEE
His "Histoire de M. Vieux Bois," about a dunderhead's romantic misadventures, was translated into English as "The Adventures of Obadiah Oldbuck" and published in its entirety as a newspaper supplement in New York in 1842 - making it the first American comic book/strip/graphic novel/what-have-you, beating out the Yellow Kid by more than a half-century.

EVER ***SELF-DEPRECATING***, TÖPFFER WROTE AN ANONYMOUS ***BAD REVIEW*** OF HIS FIRST PUBLISHED WORK, *HISTOIRE DE M. JABOT* (1833), THAT HIGHLIGHTS THE CHALLENGES FACED BY COMICS CREATORS OF ***ANY*** ERA:

"IF (THE CREATOR) IS AN ***ARTIST***, HIS DRAWING IS ***FEEBLE***, BUT HE HAS A CERTAIN PRACTICE IN ***WRITING***;

"THE ***DRAWINGS***, WITHOUT THIS TEXT, WOULD ONLY BE ***OBSCURE*** IN MEANING;

"THE ***TEXT*** WITHOUT THE DRAWINGS WOULD MEAN ***NOTHING***.

"IF (THE CREATOR) IS A ***LITERARY*** TYPE, HIS WRITING IS ***MEDIOCRE***, BUT HE DOES HAVE, ON THE OTHER HAND, IN THE MATTER OF ***DRAWING***, A PRETTY ***AMATEUR*** TALENT.

"THE ***WHOLE*** CONSTITUTES A SORT OF ***NOVEL***, ALL THE MORE ***ORIGINAL*** IN THAT IT DOES NOT RESEMBLE A NOVEL MORE THAN ANYTHING ***ELSE***."

TÖPFFER INTENDED HIS SATIRES TO AMUSE A SOPHISTICATED ***ELITE***.

EUROPE'S ***NEXT*** GENERATION OF PICTURE STORY-TELLERS, HOWEVER, FOUND INSPIRATION IN THE STARK ***CLASS STRUGGLES*** OF THE EARLY 20TH CENTURY.

FLEMISH ILLUSTRATOR FRANS MASEREEL PERFECTED HIS BLOCKY BLACK-AND-WHITE NEWSPAPER SPOT ART STYLE USING ***WOODCUTS*** TO CREATE A WORDLESS ***"NOVEL"*** OF ONE PANEL PER PAGE, *25 IMAGES DE LA PASSION D'UN HOMME*, IN 1918.

HIS MOST FAMOUS WORK, ***MON LIVRE D'HEURES*** (BETTER KNOWN IN ENGLISH AS ***PASSIONATE JOURNEY***), FOLLOWED NEXT YEAR, THE 167-WOODCUT ACCOUNT OF A YOUNG MAN'S REBELLION AGAINST CONVENTIONAL SOCIETY AND NATURE ITSELF.

AMERICAN ART STUDENT LYND WARD DISCOVERED MASEREEL'S "PICTORIAL NARRATIVES" (WARD'S WORDS) WHILE STUDYING PRINTMAKING IN LEIPZIG.
INSPIRED, HE CREATED A WOODCUT ALLEGORY OF HIS OWN, ABOUT A NEOPHYTE ARTIST WHO MAKES A SUPERNATURAL BARGAIN FOR SUCCESS, BUT AT TERRIBLE PERSONAL COST.
WHY THE POPULARITY OF THE OLDEST PRINT MEDIUM FOR SUCH A MODERN FORMAT? WARD PROPOSES:

"THE ***WOODBLOCK***, WHETHER CUT WITH A KNIFE OR ENGRAVED, DEVELOPS ITS IMAGE BY BRINGING DETAILS OUT OF ***DARKNESS*** INTO THE ***LIGHT***.

"THIS SEEMS TO GIVE IT AN ***ADVANTAGE*** OVER WAYS OF WORKING THAT START WITH AN EMPTY ***WHITE*** AREA.

"IN A SENSE, WHAT IS HAPPENING IS ALREADY THERE ***IN*** THE DARKNESS, AND CUTTING THE BLOCK INVOLVES LETTING ONLY ENOUGH LIGHT INTO THE FIELD OF VISION TO ***REVEAL*** WHAT IS GOING ON.

"IN ADDITION, THE INTERPLAY BETWEEN ***CUTTING TOOL*** AND THE ***RELUCTANT WOOD*** IMPOSES A DEGREE OF ***ARBITRARINESS*** OF RENDERING ON A VARIETY OF SUBJECTS, WHICH SEEMS TO BIND ***UNIT TO UNIT*** MORE EFFECTIVELY THAN IS TRUE OF OTHER TECHNIQUES."

GODS' MAN, WARD'S WORDLESS ***"NOVEL IN WOODCUTS,"*** WAS PUBLISHED IN OCTOBER 1929 -- FOUR YEARS BEFORE *FAMOUS FUNNIES* AND THE WEEK THE STOCK MARKET ***CRASHED*** -- TO SURPRISE ***SUCCESS***, SELLING ***20,000 COPIES*** OVER THE NEXT FOUR YEARS.

THE GENERATION THAT HAD GROWN UP WATCHING ***SILENT MOVIES*** HAD NO TROUBLE READING SILENT ***COMICS***.

GODS' MAN RECEIVED THE SINCEREST COMPLIMENT OF SUCCESS -- A ***PARODY***, FROM NO LESS A TALENT THAN NEWSPAPER GAG MAESTRO ***MILT GROSS***.

HE DONE HER WRONG: THE GREAT AMERICAN NOVEL (AND NOT A WORD IN IT!), CAME OUT IN 1930 AND DREW FROM WARD'S BOOK AS WELL AS SILENT COMEDY TROPES TO WEAVE A SLAPSTICK TALE OF A YUKON STRONGMAN RESCUING HIS TRUE LOVE FROM A NEW YORK SWINDLER.

THE ADVENT OF THE COMIC ***BOOK*** LATER IN THE '30S DIDN'T ***END*** COMICS' ATTEMPTS TO BE ***"NOVELISTIC"***... THE ***FORM*** THEY TOOK JUST ***MUTATED*** TO MATCH NEW MARKETPLACES AND DEMOGRAPHICS.

YET THE COMICS SERIES THAT SWORE UP AND DOWN IT WAS THE MOST ***"LITERARY"*** WAS ***PUBLIC ENEMY NUMBER ONE*** ON GOLDEN AGE TEACHERS' FOUR-COLOR ***HATE LIST...***

I'D LIKE TO REGALE THE CLASS IF I MAY, MRS. HODGKISS, WITH MY BOOK REPORT ON GOETHE'S *FAUST*...
WAIT A...
...DID YOU READ THE ***BOOK***, OR THE *CLASSICS ILLUSTRATED* VERSION?!

CLASSICS ILLUSTRATED WAS FOUNDED IN 1941* BY ALBERT LEWIS KANTER, A RUSSIAN IMMIGRANT WHO HAD PREVIOUSLY CREATED A ***TOY TELEGRAPH***.

HMMM...MY *THREE MUSKETEERS* IN ***MORSE CODE*** ISN'T REALLY COMING ACROSS...
I KNOW! I'LL TRY ***COMICS!***

THEIR COMIC BOOK ADAPTATIONS OF CLASSIC WORKS OF LITERATURE LIKE *ROBINSON CRUSOE, MACBETH,* AND *GULLIVER'S TRAVELS* PROVED ***SO*** IMMENSELY POPULAR...

* *ORIGINALLY CLASSICS* ***COMICS***; *THE NAME CHANGED IN* ***1947***, *PROBABLY TO AVOID ADULTS' GROWING OUTCRY AGAINST ALL THINGS COMICS-Y.*

...THAT THEY WENT THROUGH MULTIPLE *REPRINTINGS* (*UNHEARD OF* FOR COMICS IN THOSE DAYS) AND ALLOWED KIDS IN *TWO DOZEN* COUNTRIES TO CHEAT ON BOOK REPORTS IN *NINE LANGUAGES!*
ME GUSTA REGALAR A SU CLASE, SRA. HODGKISS, MI REPORTE DE LIBRO SOBRE *FAUST* DE GOETHE...
ESPERA UN...

WHEN THE INDUSTRY BEGAN REGULATING ITSELF WITH THE 1955 ***COMICS CODE AUTHORITY***, *CLASSICS ILLUSTRATED* ***REFUSED*** TO CARRY THE CCA SEAL, CLAIMING THEY HELD THEMSELVES TO ***HIGHER*** LITERARY STANDARDS THAN THE CODE DEMANDED ANYWAY!

YOU WOULDN'T DARE *CENSOR* THE BARD OF *AVON*, WOULD YOU?
NAW, SO LONG AS YOU DON'T HAVE THE *MURDER*, INCEST, TORTURE AND *WITCHCRAFT* THE CODE PROHIBITS!
APPROVED BY THE COMICS CODE A AUTHORITY
HAMLET
Macbeth
TITUS
UM... NO, OF *COURSE* NOT, DON'T BE *SILLY*... *HEH!*

"IN A WORLD OF ***BAD*** COMICS, WE WERE THE ***BEST,***" SNIFFED *CLASSICS* EDITOR AND WRITER MEYER KAPLIN.

"WE WERE THE ***CLEANEST***, WE WERE THE MOST ***RESEARCHED***, AND, WITHIN THE LIMITATIONS OF OUR PAGE LENGTH, AS ***FAITHFUL*** TO THE ORIGINAL AS HUMANLY POSSIBLE."

THOUGH REDUCING 400- AND 500-PAGE PROSE NOVELS TO, ON AVERAGE, ***48 PAGES*** OF COMIC BOOK MEANT A CERTAIN AMOUNT OF MATERIAL HAD TO BE... ***TRUNCATED...***

HOMER'S
THE ODYSSEY
(IN ONE PANEL)
HONEY, I'M HOME!
WELL *THAT* WAS QUICK...

ALL KIDDING ASIDE, *CLASSICS ILLUSTRATED* CAN BE CREDITED WITH AWAKENING A LOVE OF LITERATURE IN ***MILLIONS*** OF KIDS.

CIRCULATION PEAKED IN 1960, WHEN THE AVERAGE ADAPTATION ENJOYED A PRINT RUN OF ***262,000 COPIES***.

BUT NEW TITLES STOPPED APPEARING IN ***1962***, DONE IN BY COMPETITION FROM *CLIFF'S NOTES*, WHICH DEBUTED IN 1958.

I'M SO MUCH MORE "LITERARCILY" THAN THOSE STUPID *COMICS*, RIGHT?
CLIFF
THAT *IS* HOW YOU SAY THAT, RIGHT...?
NOOOOOO!!

SPORADIC ATTEMPTS TO MARKET ORIGINAL LONG-FORM GRAPHIC FICTION DURING THE COMIC BOOK'S HEYDAY MET WITH *FAILURE*.
SOLDIERS-TURNED-UNDERGRADS ARNOLD DRAKE AND LESLIE WALLER REALIZED OTHER COMICS-LOVING VETERANS WERE ENTERING COLLEGE UNDER THE *GI BILL*, "LEAPING FROM *BATMAN* TO *BEOWULF*," AS DRAKE PUT IT.
"WHY NOT (BUILD) A *BRIDGE* BETWEEN COMIC BOOKS AND *BOOK-BOOKS*, STORIES ILLUSTRATED AS COMICS BUT WITH MORE MATURE PLOTS, CHARACTERS AND DIALOGUE? WE CALLED THEM '*PICTURE NOVELS*.'"
COLLEGE
BEOWULF
I JUST *GOTTA* GET ME SOMMA *THIS* ACTION!

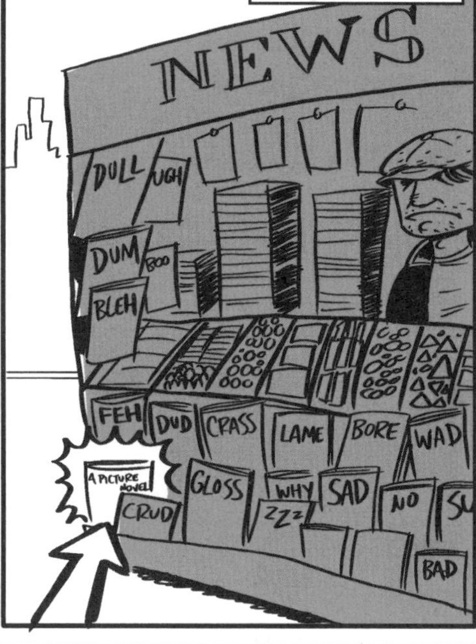
DRAKE & WALLER CONVINCED ST. JOHN PUBLICATIONS TO BRING OUT THEIR FIRST PICTURE NOVEL, *IT RHYMES WITH LUST*, ESSENTIALLY A 120-PAGE *ROMANCE COMIC*, IN *1950*.
DESPITE WONDERFUL ARTWORK FROM ONE OF THE BEST EARLY *AFRICAN-AMERICAN* PENCILLERS, *MATT BAKER*, THE DIGEST-SIZED *LUST* GOT *LOST* ON NEWSSTANDS WITH THE OTHER COMICS.
NEWS
DULL
UGH
DUM
BOO
BLEH
FEH
DUD
CRASS
LAME
BORE
WAD
A PICTURE NOVEL
GLOSS
WHY
SAD
NO
CRUD
ZZZ
BAD

MASTER SUPER HERO ARTIST *GIL KANE* RAN AFOUL OF THE COMICS CODE WHEN HE PUBLISHED HIS OWN LONG-FORM ULTRAVIOLENT ESPIONAGE THRILLER, *HIS NAME IS ... SAVAGE!* IN 1968.
"I LOST *THREE* OF THE PRINTERS THAT I HAD BY HAVING PEOPLE MAKE PHONE CALLS AND SUGGEST THAT I WAS TURNING OUT A *PORNOGRAPHIC BOOK*, SOMETHING THAT WOULD BRING GREAT *DISREPUTATION* (SIC) TO THE ENTIRE FIELD."

AT THE SAME TIME, THE AMBITIOUS KANE SOLD TO *BANTAM* AN EIGHT-VOLUME SERIES OF MASS PAPERBACK SWORD AND SORCERY COMIC NOVELS, *BLACKMARK*.
THE COMPANY'S ENTHUSIASM FOR THE PROJECT MIGHT HAVE OWED TO KANE *UNDERBIDDING* FOR HIS SERVICES ON AN INSANE DEADLINE. KANE HAD TO PULL IN HIS FRIEND, *MAD* CREATOR *HARVEY KURTZMAN*, TO ASSIST ON LAYOUTS TO GET THE BOOK DONE IN TIME!
THOUGH KURTZMAN TOLD KANE THE COMPLETED BOOK WAS "THE *BEST THING* HE EVER SAW," THE FINAL PRODUCT *BAFFLED* BOOKSTORES. *BLACKMARK* DIED ON THE SHELVES AND NO FURTHER VOLUMES APPEARED.

KURTZMAN HAD SOME EXPERIENCE IN THE ***ORIGINAL PAPERBACK COMICS*** FIELD HIMSELF. IN 1959, BALLANTINE BOOKS, HAVING LOST PAPERBACK REPRINT RIGHTS TO *MAD*, COMMISSIONED HIM TO CREATE SATIRIC CARTOONS ***FOR*** THE BOOK MARKET.

HARVEY KURTZMAN'S JUNGLE BOOK CONTAINED FOUR HILARIOUS TALES THAT DID NOT SELL TERRIBLY WELL, BUT FURTHER CEMENTED HIS DESTINY AS THE ***GUIDING LIGHT*** OF THE COMIX COUNTER-CULTURE.

"I TOLD HARVEY THAT I THOUGHT ***HE*** WAS A MORE SIGNIFICANT FACTOR THAN ***POT*** AND ***LSD*** ON THE SHAPE OF THE '***60S***,'" SAYS WRITER/ARTIST ***ART SPIEGELMAN***, WHO DEVOURED *JUNGLE BOOK* WHEN HE WAS ELEVEN.

IN 1970, SPIEGELMAN, NOW 22 BUT ALREADY A ***VETERAN*** UNDERGROUND CARTOONIST, MET ***LYND WARD*** AT A GALLERY SHOWING OF THE ARTIST'S PRINTS IN BINGHAMTON, NEW YORK.

WARD, WHO HAD PUBLISHED ***SIX*** WOODCUT NOVELS DURING THE DEPRESSION, WAS SURPRISED SOMEONE AS YOUNG AS SPIEGELMAN ***ADMIRED*** HIS PICTORIAL NARRATIVES; SPIEGELMAN WAS SURPRISED WARD HAD NO EXPERIENCE WITH ***COMICS***, AS HIS MINISTER FATHER ***BANNED*** THEM FROM THE WARD HOME.

"TWO YEARS AFTER MEETING LYND WARD," SPIEGELMAN WROTE IN 2010, "WHEN I WAS BEGINNING TO SERIOUSLY EXPLORE THE LIMITS AND POSSIBILITIES OF COMICS, I DREW A FOUR-PAGE COMICS STORY ABOUT MY ***MOTHER'S SUICIDE*** CALLED '*PRISONER ON THE HELL PLANET*'.
"I WAS THEN TWENTY-FOUR YEARS OLD (THE SAME AGE AS ***WARD*** WHEN HE MADE *GODS' MAN*) AND THE SCRATCHBOARD DRAWINGS I DID WERE VERY ***INFLUENCED*** BY WARD'S ENGRAVINGS AND BY GERMAN EXPRESSIONIST WOODCUTS."

ANJA SPIEGELMAN, LIKE HER HUSBAND ***VLADEK***, WERE POLISH-JEWISH ***AUSCHWITZ SURVIVORS***. THE SAME YEAR SPIEGELMAN DREW "MAUS," A THREE-PAGE STORY FOR THE UNDERGROUND *FUNNY AMINALS* (SIC), NARRATING HIS FATHER'S CONCENTRATION CAMP EXPERIENCES WITH JEWS DEPICTED AS ***MICE*** AND THE NAZIS AS ***CATS***.

"(A FILMMAKER FRIEND) POINTED OUT THAT THE MIC WERE LIKE NEGROES IN A LO OF THE (OLD) CARTOONS ... I STARTED THINKING ABOUT THE MOUSE AS TH ***OPPRESSED*** AND THE CAT AS THE ***OPPRESSOR***."

THIS SUBVERSION OF HOARY OLD ***CARTOON TROPES*** CAME ***NATURALLY*** TO A ***KURTZMAN ACOLYTE*** LIKE ***SPIEGELMAN!***

MEANWHILE, AFTER RETIRING HIS SIGNATURE NEWSPAPER COMIC BOOK *THE SPIRIT* IN 1952, **WILL EISNER** HAD CONTINUED HIS INSTRUCTIONAL COMICS FOR THE U.S. MILITARY. HE TOURED HOTSPOTS LIKE THE **KOREAN DMZ** AND **SAIGON**, WHERE HE GOT **GLOWING REVIEWS** FROM SOLDIERS THEMSELVES!
WHEN EISNER GOT OUT OF THE COMMERCIAL ART BUSINESS IN 1972, HIS WIFE ANN ENCOURAGED HIM TO TAKE THE NEXT BIG LEAP AND CREATE A COMIC AIMED AT **ADULTS**, WITH ADULT THEMES.
"YOU THE GUY WHO DOES THOSE **PICTURES?**"
"YEAH..."
"MAN, YOU SAVED MY @$$, YOU KNOW THAT?"

HIS INSPIRATION CAME IN THE FORM OF DARKEST **TRAGEDY**.
IN 1969, EISNER'S TEENAGE DAUGHTER **ALICE** HAD SUCCUMBED TO **LEUKEMIA**.
THE ARTIST POURED HIS GRIEF AND RAGE INTO A SHORT COMICS STORY, "*A CONTRACT WITH GOD*," ABOUT A DEPRESSION-ERA JEW WHO REJECTS HIS FAITH WHEN HIS DAUGHTER DIES UNEXPECTEDLY.

EISNER COMBINED THAT TALE WITH THREE OTHERS ABOUT 1930s JEWS IN HIS NATIVE BRONX, CALLING THE COLLECTION *A CONTRACT WITH GOD AND OTHER TENEMENT STORIES*.
HE FELT WEIGHTY MATERIAL SUCH AS THIS DEMANDED TO BE PUBLISHED AND DISTRIBUTED BY A **NON-COMICS** PUBLISHER, BUT STRUGGLED OVER A WAY TO **MARKET** THE UNIQUE PROJECT.
IT'S... A... UH... "GRAPHIC" ...ER... AH... "NOVEL!"
YEAH, THAT'S THE TICKET!
"OH, THAT SOUNDS INTERESTING; I'VE NEVER **HEARD** OF THAT BEFORE."

THIS **"GRAPHIC NOVEL,"** AS THE COVER OF ITS 1978 PAPERBACK EDITION CALLED IT, WAS RACKED IN **BOOKSTORES** AS ITS AUTHOR INTENDED --
BUT CONFUSED CLERKS DIDN'T KNOW WHETHER TO SHELVE *CONTRACT* IN THE "RELIGION" OR "HUMOR" SECTIONS... AS OPPOSED TO **"FICTION,"** WHERE IT RIGHTLY BELONGED!
THIS "COMIC" HAS **NAKED LADIES** AND **BAD WORDS** IN IT! WHAT IS IT DOING NEXT TO MY PRECIOUS, PRECIOUS **GARFIELD?!**
HUMOR
A CONTRACT GOD
MISTER SIMMONS! HAAAALP!!
OY!
Garfie

EISNER HIMSELF NEVER CLAIMED TO HAVE COINED THE TERM "GRAPHIC NOVEL" AND INDEED THERE WERE USAGES PRIOR TO CONTRACT.
IN 1976, HEAVY METAL VETERAN RICHARD CORBEN CAME OUT WITH BLOODSTAR, AN ADAPTION OF THE ROBERT E. HOWARD SHORT STORY "THE VALLEY OF THE WORM" THAT WAS DESCRIBED AS A "GRAPHIC NOVEL" ON ITS DUST JACKET...
...AND THE PHRASE ALSO APPEARED THE SAME YEAR ON THE TITLE PAGE OF A COLLECTION OF UNDERGROUND CARTOONIST GEORGE "MOONDOG" METZGER'S STRIPS, BEYOND TIME & AGAIN.

BUT UNLIKE TÖPFFER'S BOOKS, CONTRACT HAD WORD BALLOONS...
STAB!

...AND UNLIKE WARD, MOSS & MASREEL, IT HAD WORDS.
!@#$
Aa

UNLIKE LUST & SAVAGE, IT APPEARED IN BOOKSTORES, NOT NEWSSTANDS...
BOOKS
...AND UNLIKE JUNGLE BOOK, BLACKMARK, BLOODSTAR & BEYOND, IT STOOD SQUARELY IN A LITERARY GENRE.

SO, PARTLY OWING TO HIS PREEMINENT REPUTATION IN THE FIELD AND CONTRACT'S OWN QUALITY, WHEN EISNER USED THE TERM "GRAPHIC NOVEL"...
(...TO DESCRIBE A COLLECTION OF UNRELATED SHORT STORIES...)
...IT STUCK!
PSHAW! SEMANTICS!

AT THE SAME TIME, ART SPIEGELMAN CHOSE TO *EXPAND* HIS SHORT STORIES ABOUT HIS PARENTS AND BEGAN INTERVIEWING HIS FATHER IN QUEENS ABOUT THE HOLOCAUST.
SPIEGELMAN SERIALIZED *MAUS* IN THE AVANT-GARDE COMICS MAGAZINE HE EDITED WITH WIFE FRANÇOISE MOULY, *RAW*. WHEN THE FIRST COLLECTED VOLUME CAME OUT IN 1986, IT WAS AN INSTANT CRITICAL AND COMMERCIAL ***SUCCESS***. SPIEGELMAN:

"WHAT HAPPENED IN *MAUS* WAS THE ABSOLUTE ***SHOCK*** OF AN ***OXYMORON***: THE HOLOCAUST IS ABSOLUTELY THE ***LAST*** PLACE ONE WOULD LOOK FOR SOMETHING TO BE MADE IN THE FORM OF ***COMICS***, WHICH ONE ASSOCIATES WITH ESSENTIALLY TRIVIAL, SIMPLIFIED MATTER.
HEY! YOU GOT YOUR ***COMICS*** IN MY HOLOCAUST!
YOU GOT YOUR ***HOLOCAUST*** INTO MY ***COMICS!***
BUMP
JUDE

"SO THESE TWO PARTICULAR THINGS CAME TOGETHER AND IGNITED AN ***EXPLOSION*** THAT I WAS ABLE TO HARNESS."
"ONE THING THAT'S ***IRRITATING*** IS THAT I NEVER THOUGHT OF (*MAUS*) AS A '***GRAPHIC NOVEL;***' IT WASN'T A PHRASE IN MY HEAD.
MMMMMM...
JUDE

"I WAS AWARE OF WHAT WILL EISNER HAD DONE WITH *A CONTRACT WITH GOD*, BUT FELT NO MORE CONNECTED TO ***IT*** THAN TO GIL KANE'S *BLACKMARK* OR EVEN HARVEY KURTZMAN'S *JUNGLE BOOK* (WHICH WAS SOMETHING I ***LOVED***).
"I WAS TRYING TO MAKE SOMETHING ***DIFFERENT***, A STRUCTURED LONG WORK WITH A BEGINNING, MIDDLE, AND END...
"I WANTED IT TO HAVE THE DENSITY TO WITH-STAND, EVEN ***DEMAND***, REREADING...I WAS MAKING A ***LONG COMIC BOOK*** BUT I KNEW I DIDN'T WANT IT TO ***LOOK*** LIKE A COMIC BOOK. SO, I GUESS IT MEETS THE PARAMETERS OF WHAT IS NOW CALLED A GRAPHIC NOVEL."

AS PROOF COMICS COULD STRIVE FOR ***AND*** ACHIEVE LITERARY GREATNESS -- NOT AS ***ADAPTATIONS***, BUT ON THEIR ***OWN*** MERITS -- ***MAUS*** WON A ***PULITZER PRIZE*** IN 1992. RATHER THAN CARRYING AN ESTABLISHED CATEGORY, THE JUDGES GAVE THE WORK A "***SPECIAL*** AWARD," BECAUSE THEY FOUND IT...
NEWS
"...HARD TO CLASSIFY..."
*YEAH, YEAH, YEAH... JUST **HAND IT OVER** ALREADY...*

1986 AD

THE **UNITED KINGDOM** HAS AS PROUD A COMICS TRADITION AS AMERICA OR FRANCE, DATING BACK AT LEAST TO **1825**, WHEN ***THE LOOKING GLASS***, THE FIRST WEEKLY JOURNAL OF CARICATURES AND OTHER HUMOROUS DRAWINGS, APPEARED IN **GLASGOW**.

WORLD WAR II BROUGHT AMERICAN COMICS TO BRITAIN AS THE FAVORED READING MATERIAL OF THE THOUSANDS OF GI'S STATIONED THERE.
OH-HO-HO! JOLLY GOOD FUN, WOT?
WHEN THE YANK SOLDIERS LEFT, THE YANK FUNNYBOOKS STAYED... TO THE DISMAY OF MANY.
Archie

THE HUE AND CRY AGAINST "AMERICAN-TYPE COMICS" STARTED IN THE LATE '40s THANKS TO BRITONS LIKE PETER MAUGER.
THAT YOUNG LAD IS ACTUALLY... GASP! CHOKE! ...ENJOYING READING!
CLEARLY, SOMETHING'S NOT QUITE CRICKET!
BLACK MAGIC
MAUGER SAW A TEN-YEAR-OLD READING A U.S. COMIC: "I BECAME AWARE AFTER ABOUT AN HOUR THAT THE BOY'S CONCENTRATION HADN'T LAPSED AT ALL.

"I GOT FASCINATED BY THIS BECAUSE, BEING A TEACHER, I THOUGHT THIS WAS MOST UNUSUAL.
"SO I ASKED HIM IF I COULD HAVE A LOOK. HE SAID CERTAINLY, AND HE HANDED OVER SOME COMICS...
BABY-EATING CORPSES!
"...AND I WAS ABSOLUTELY HORRIFIED BY THEM."

IF BRITISH COMICS CRITICISM SOUNDS ***FAMILIAR*** -- TOO VIOLENT, TOO SEXY, INSPIRING COPYCAT CRIMES, SUPER HEROES ARE FASCIST, ***ETC., ETC.*** ...

U.S.A.

...IT'S BECAUSE THEY ECHO FREDRIC (*SEDUCTION OF THE INNOCENT*) WERTHAM'S SIMULTANEOUS LINE OF ATTACK IN AMERICA.

U.K.

IT MAKES SENSE THAT THE ANTI-COMICS MOVEMENT IN THE UK WOULD FIND AFFINITY WITH WERTHAM'S FRANKFURT SCHOOL-INFLUENCED THEORIES...

...BECAUSE THE BRITISH OUTCRY WAS SPEARHEADED LARGELY BY MEMBERS OF THE ***COMMUNIST PARTY*** LIKE PETER MAUGER!
HAH, HAH! BRITISH BUTTINSKIS DON'T SUSPECT A THING!
THE COMMUNIST INFORMATION BUREAU (*COMINFORM*) IN MOSCOW ENCOURAGED LOCAL PARTIES TO DENOUNCE U.S. INFLUENCE ON THEIR CULTURES UNDER THE RUBRIC OF *"NATIONAL INDEPENDENCE"*.

BY DECLARING THAT *"AMERICAN-STYLE"* COMICS THREATENED THE ***BRITISH*** WAY OF LIFE, CRITICS ADDED ***XENOPHOBIA*** TO WERTHAM'S LIST OF UGLY TACTICS. MAUGER WROTE:
"IT IS BY APPEALING TO THE BEST INSTINCTS OF ORDINARY DECENT PEOPLE THAT WE CAN STOP THIS ***AMERICAN*** VULGARIZATION, THIS DEGRADATION, THIS PERVERSION OF ***OUR*** YOUNG PEOPLE."
USA #1

BUT THE POWERFUL COLD WAR ALLIANCE BETWEEN THE U.S. AND THE UK RENDERED SUCH A BLATANTLY ANTI-AMERICAN STANCE POLITICALLY UNTENABLE.

BRITISH COMMUNISTS DIDN'T GET MUCH TRACTION FOR THEIR CAMPAIGN UNTIL THE ***NATIONAL UNION OF TEACHERS*** GOT INVOLVED AND BEGAN REFERRING TO THE SCOURGE AS *"HORROR"* OR *"CRIME-AND-HORROR"* COMICS INSTEAD.

UNLIKE THE WERTHAM PURGES IN THE U.S., THE BRITISH ANTI-COMICS CAMPAIGN ACTUALLY SUCCEEDED IN PRODUCING LEGISLATION.
IN 1955 PARLIAMENT PASSED THE CHILDREN AND YOUNG PERSONS (HARMFUL PUBLICATIONS) ACT, WHICH MADE SELLING CRIME OR HORROR COMICS THAT "WOULD TEND TO CORRUPT A CHILD OR YOUNG PERSON INTO WHOSE HANDS IT MIGHT FALL" PUNISHABLE BY UP TO £100 AND/OR FOUR MONTHS IN JAIL.
EVIL COMICS

THOUGH THE ONLY TIME IT WAS ENFORCED IN THE NEXT THREE DECADES SEEMS TO HAVE BEEN IN 1970, WHEN L. MILLER & CO. WAS FINED £25 FOR REPRINTING AMERICAN HORROR COMICS.
B-BUT--I RETIRED FROM CRYPT-KEEPING IN '55!
TELL IT TO THE JUDGE, YOU!
OI, WHO'S 'AT, LUV?

L. MILLER BEGAN REPRINTING AMERICA'S FAWCETT COMICS FOR THE BRITISH MARKET IN THE MID-1940S.
"IS THERE A NICOTINE STAIN ON HIS INDEX FINGER? A DIME NOVEL HIDDEN IN THE CORNCRIB? IS HE STARTING TO MEMORIZE JOKES FROM CAP'N BILLY'S WHIZ BANG?"
Capt Billy's Whiz Bang
FOUNDED IN 1919 BY WILFORD "CAP'N BILLY" FAWCETT, THE PUBLISHER'S FIRST MAGAZINE WAS A RISQUE COLLECTION OF MILITARY HUMOR IMMORTALIZED IN "TROUBLE" FROM THE MUSIC MAN.

FAWCETT JUMPED ON THE SUPER HERO BANDWAGON IN 1940 WITH WHIZ COMICS, STARRING CAPTAIN MARVEL, A/K/A NEWSBOY BILLY BATSON...
SHAZAM!
NOT YOU, GOMER. I LIKE LITTLE BOYS...
...BOTH NODS TO THE COMPANY'S INAUGURAL PUBLICATION.

THOUGH ALL SUPER HEROES ARE ARGUABLY SUPERMAN RIP-OFFS, CAP BECAME MORE POPULAR THAN SUPES, SELLING A STUNNING 14 MILLION COMICS IN 1944 ALONE. THE MAN OF STEEL'S PUBLISHER, DC, SENSED AN EXISTENTIAL THREAT AND SLAPPED A COPYRIGHT INFRINGEMENT LAWSUIT ON FAWCETT.

THE SUIT WENT TO TRIAL IN 1948. THOUGH THE LOWER COURT AGREED WITH DC THAT CAPTAIN MARVEL WAS AN UNLAWFUL COPY OF SUPERMAN...
...IT ALSO HELD THAT DC HAD FAILED TO PROPERLY REGISTER SOME OF SIEGEL & SHUSTER'S NEWSPAPER STRIPS, AND THEREFORE ABANDONED THE COPYRIGHT! THIS AMOUNTED TO A WIN FOR FAWCETT.

DC APPEALED, AND IN 1952 STORIED JUDGE LEARNED HAND OF THE U.S. SECOND CIRCUIT REVERSED THE ORIGINAL DECISION, SIDING WITH DC AND SENDING THE CASE BACK TO TRIAL COURT FOR A DETERMINATION OF DAMAGES.
BY THIS TIME, HOWEVER, SUPER HERO SALES WERE TANKING -- INCLUDING CAP'S -- AND WERTHAM'S WITCH-HUNT WAS GAINING SERIOUS STEAM.

MEANWHILE, FAWCETT HAD BEEN EXPERIMENTING WITH MASS-MARKET PAPERBACKS. MICKEY SPILLANE'S LURID MIKE HAMMER MYSTERY I, THE JURY SOLD OVER 2 MILLION COPIES IN THE NEW FORMAT!
DETERMINING FURTHER BATTLE WITH DC WOULD BE FUTILE, FAWCETT SETTLED THE CASE IN 1953 AND CANCELLED ITS ENTIRE COMICS LINE TO FOCUS ON PAPERBACK PROSE.
EVERYBODY WALKED AWAY HAPPY...

...EXCEPT L. MILLER & SON, FAWCETT'S BRITISH PUBLISHER! REPRINTS OF CAPTAIN MARVEL AND CAPTAIN MARVEL JR. WERE THEIR BEST-SELLING COMICS!
SORRY, LIMEY! I'M OUTTIE!
BOCA RATON
!@#$%?! BIG RED WANKER!!
CUT OFF FROM ITS SUPPLY OF U.S. MATERIAL, MILLER HIRED WRITER/ARTIST MICK ANGLO'S STUDIO TO CREATE BRITISH KNOCKOFFS.

AS OF FEBRUARY 3, 1954, CAPTAIN MARVEL IN THE UK BECAME MARVEL*MAN*, CAPTAIN MARVEL JUNIOR BECAME *KID* MARVELMAN, AND THE MAGIC WORD *"SHAZAM!"* BECAME *"KIMOTA!"* ("ATOMIC" MISSPELLED BACKWARDS...)

MARVELMAN

THIS IS JUST AS BIG A RIP-OFF AS ***WHIZ COMICS!*** YOU SHOULD GO AFTER ***THEM*** TOO!

EHHH...THEY'RE ALL THE WAY OVER IN ***ENGLAND...***

I'LL ***DO*** IT ***TOMORROW...***

DAILY PLANET

CANCELLATION PROVED JUST THE ***BEGINNING*** OF THE CAPTAIN'S PROBLEMS: WHEN THE CHARACTER'S ***TRADEMARK*** LAPSED, MARVEL ***COMICS*** RUSHED OUT THEIR OWN HERO BY THE ***SAME NAME*** IN 1967 TO REGISTER IT FOR THEMSELVES!

SHAZA--

NUH-UH-UH!

MARVEL'S REACH EXTENDED ACROSS THE *POND*, TOO. PATRIOTIC *ODHAMS PRESS*, PUBLISHERS OF *JOHN BULL* MAGAZINE, PRODUCED UK REPRINTS OF *FANTASTIC FOUR* AND *SPIDER-MAN*.
I *SAY*, FACE *FRONT*, TRUE BELIEVERS!
MARVEL
(APPARENTLY THE DAYS OF PREVENTING THE *AMERICAN* CORRUPTION OF *BRITISH* YOUTH WERE *OVER*.)
ODHAMS WEEKLIES *FANTASTIC* AND *SMASH!* THRILLED FANS LIKE YOUNG *ALAN MOORE* FROM WORKING CLASS *NORTHAMPTON* WITH THEIR REPRINTED MARVELS.
UNLIKE THEIR UK COUNTERPARTS, MOORE REMEMBERS, "TAKING PLACE AGAINST SOME ANONYMOUS NORTHERN BRITISH BACKDROP, (AMERICAN COMICS) TOOK PLACE IN CITIES LIKE *NEW YORK*, WHICH TO ME WERE AS EXOTIC AS *MARS*."
"I'D ALREADY BEEN ATTRACTED TO MYTHOLOGY, FAIRY STORIES, ANYTHING WHICH HAD PEOPLE THAT COULD *FLY* OR BECOME INVISIBLE OR COULD LIFT HUGE MOUNTAINS OR COULD PERFORM *ANY* OF THESE HEROIC ACTS FOR WHICH GODS AND HEROES ARE LARGELY *FAMOUS*.
"THIS BECAME A *PREOCCUPATION*."

MOORE WAS KICKED OUT OF SCHOOL AT 17 FOR BEING, AS HE TOLD THE BBC IN 2008, "ONE OF THE WORLD'S MOST ***INEPT*** LSD DEALERS":

"IF YOU'RE SAMPLING YOUR OWN PRODUCT, YOUR VIEW OF PRACTICAL REALITY WILL PROBABLY BECOME HORRIBLY DISTORTED AND YOU MAY END UP BELIEVING THAT YOU HAVE SUPERNATURAL POWERS AND ARE COMPLETELY IMMUNE TO ANY FORM OF RETALIATION OR PROSECUTION.

YOU LOOK LIKE YOU COULD USE A HIT, MATE...
"THIS IS ***NOT*** THE CASE."

MOORE TOOK VARIOUS JOBS TO MAKE ENDS MEET, INCLUDING REMOVING SHEEPSKINS FROM BLOODY VATS AT A TANNERY AND CLEANING HOTEL TOILETS.

AT THE SAME TIME HE WROTE AND DREW A COMIC STRIP FOR THE LOCAL PAPER AT £10 A WEEK, ***"MAXWELL THE MAGIC CAT."***

HE HAD BEEN HUGELY INFLUENCED BY THE WORK OF ***HARVEY KURTZMAN***-- PARTICULARLY A SAVAGE DECONSTRUCTION OF THE MAN OF STEEL HARV DID WITH ARTIST WALLY WOOD IN ***MAD***.
SUPERDUPERMAN

AS A CHILD, "I WANTED TO DO A SUPER HERO PARODY STORY THAT WAS AS FUNNY AS '***SUPERDUPERMAN***' BUT I THOUGHT IT WOULD BE BETTER IF I DID IT ABOUT AN ***ENGLISH*** SUPER HERO." HE CHOSE ***MARVELMAN***.

AS A YOUNG ADULT, HE BEGAN TO REALIZE SUCH A REIMAGINING OF A CLASSIC CHARACTER "COULD BE ... SOMETHING QUITE STARTLING AND ***POIGNANT***, TAKING A KIND OF VERY INNOCENT AND SORT OF SIMPLISTIC 1950s SUPER HERO AND DROPPING HIM IN A MUCH MORE COMPLEX, DARKER 1980s ENVIRONMENT."

BOLLOCKS... WHAT ***YEAR*** IS IT...?
HMM... MAYBE I CAN ***DO*** SOMETHING WITH THIS...
MM

MOORE DECIDED HE DIDN'T HAVE THE TALENT TO IMPROVE HIS DRAWING, SO HE CONCENTRATED INSTEAD ON ***WRITING***.

HE SOLD SEVERAL WELL-REGARDED SHORT STORIES TO UK COMICS MAGAZINES LIKE ***2000AD***, WHICH WAS INSPIRED BY A 1975 NEWSPAPER ARTICLE ABOUT GEORGE LUCAS' ***STAR WARS***, THEN FILMING IN ENGLAND.

SINCE ***TWELVE YEARS*** WAS THE STANDARD LIFESPAN FOR A SUCCESSFUL COMIC BOOK IN BRITAIN, THE NEW SCI-FI MAG WAS ENTITLED *2000 AD* "BECAUSE IT WOULD BE ***DEAD AND BURIED*** BY THEN," JOKED MANAGING EDITOR JOHN SANDERS.

BUT *2000AD*'S GRITTY, SATIRICAL FEATURES, TYPIFIED BY THE POST-APOCALYPTIC COP ***JUDGE DREDD***, CATAPULTED THE MAGAZINE TO ***INSTANT SUCCESS.***

2000 AD
BEST BEFORE:
DEC 31 1999

DEZ SKINN, FORMER EDITOR-IN-CHIEF OF MARVEL'S UK DIVISION, STARTED UP HIS OWN MAGAZINE, *WARRIOR*, IN 1982. HE WANTED TO ANCHOR THE NEW BOOK WITH A FAMILIAR CHARACTER, AND ATTEMPTED TO LICENSE ***MARVELMAN***, WHOSE TITLE HAD BEEN ***CANCELLED*** IN 1963.
ANGLO
BUT HE COULDN'T FIGURE OUT WHO TO ACQUIRE THE RIGHTS ***FROM***. L. MILLER & SON HAD LONG SINCE GONE OUT OF BUSINESS AND MICK ANGLO (AT THE TIME) SIMPLY GAVE SKINN HIS BLESSING TO ***"DO WHAT YOU LIKE."***
SO WHILE ALAN MOORE BROUGHT HIS MODERNIZATION OF MARVELMAN TO LIFE IN THE PAGES OF *WARRIOR* TO CONSIDERABLE CRITICAL ACCLAIM, HE MAY HAVE NEVER HAD THE ***LEGAL RIGHT*** TO DO SO!
CONFUSING MATTERS FURTHER, WHEN ***ECLIPSE COMICS*** BEGAN REPRINTING MOORE'S SERIES IN THE U.S., THE STRIP HAD TO BE RETITLED ***"MIRACLE***MAN" TO STAVE OFF A LEGAL CHALLENGE FROM MARVEL ***COMICS***.
U.S.A.
U.K.
BY THIS TIME MOORE'S WRITING HAD GARNERED NUMEROUS BRITISH COMICS AWARDS THAT IMPRESSED AMERICAN PUBLISHERS--IF NOT ***MOORE HIMSELF:***
"THE AMERICANS TEND TO THINK THAT EVERY AWARD IS AN ***OSCAR*** AND DIDN'T REALIZE THAT THE COMIC INDUSTRY AWARDS ARE ALL VOTED FOR BY THIRTY PEOPLE IN ***ANORAKS*** WITH DREADFUL SOCIAL LIVES."
IN 1983, DC COMICS EDITOR LEN WEIN HIRED MOORE TO REVITALIZE WEIN'S OWN CREATION, THE MONSTROUS ***SWAMP THING***.
THE DC BRASS SOON ENTRUSTED MOORE WITH AN ENTIRE ***LINE*** OF HEROES...

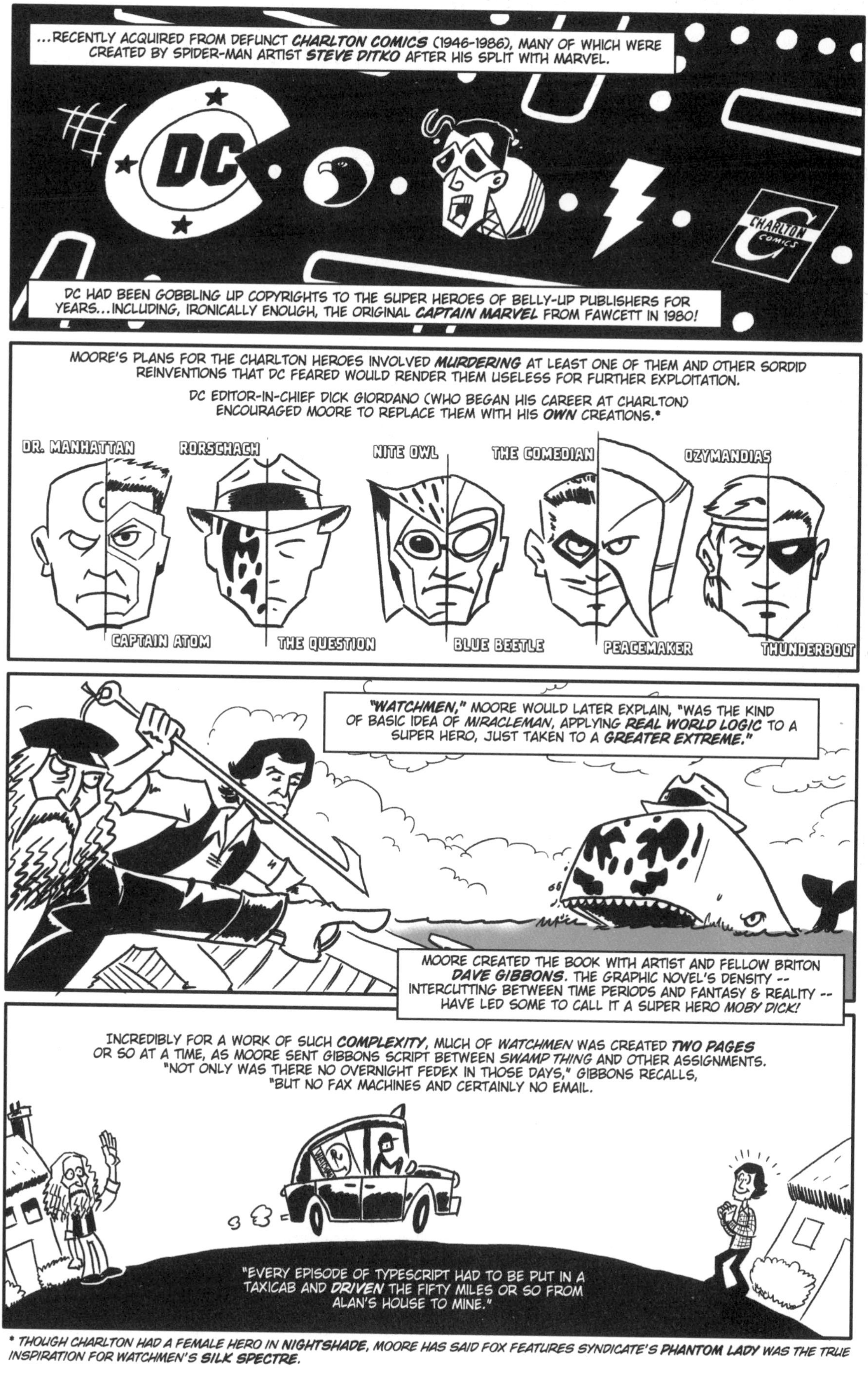

...RECENTLY ACQUIRED FROM DEFUNCT CHARLTON COMICS (1946-1986), MANY OF WHICH WERE CREATED BY SPIDER-MAN ARTIST STEVE DITKO AFTER HIS SPLIT WITH MARVEL.
DC
CHARLTON COMICS
DC HAD BEEN GOBBLING UP COPYRIGHTS TO THE SUPER HEROES OF BELLY-UP PUBLISHERS FOR YEARS...INCLUDING, IRONICALLY ENOUGH, THE ORIGINAL CAPTAIN MARVEL FROM FAWCETT IN 1980!

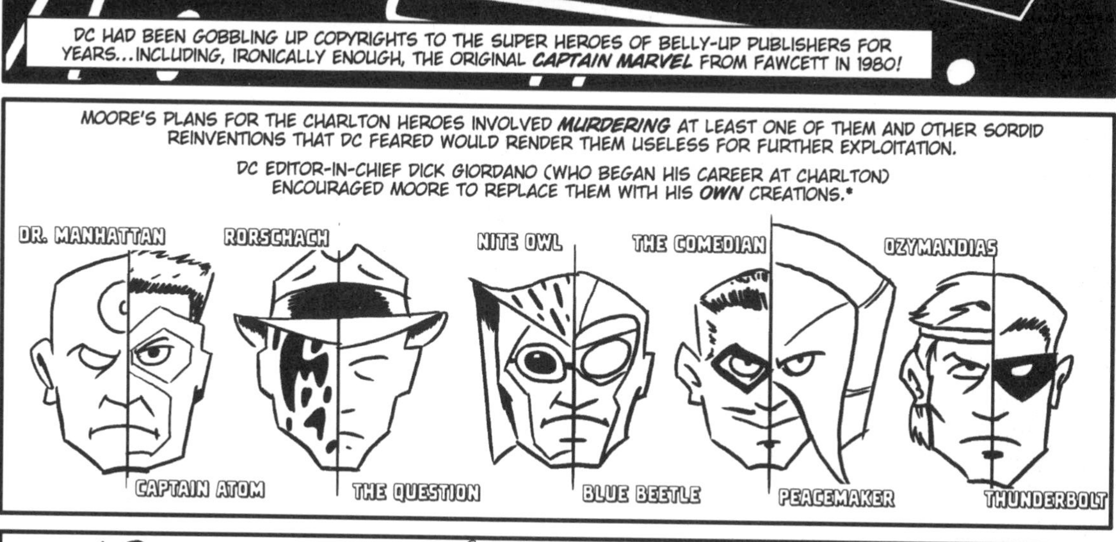
MOORE'S PLANS FOR THE CHARLTON HEROES INVOLVED MURDERING AT LEAST ONE OF THEM AND OTHER SORDID REINVENTIONS THAT DC FEARED WOULD RENDER THEM USELESS FOR FURTHER EXPLOITATION.
DC EDITOR-IN-CHIEF DICK GIORDANO (WHO BEGAN HIS CAREER AT CHARLTON) ENCOURAGED MOORE TO REPLACE THEM WITH HIS OWN CREATIONS.*
DR. MANHATTAN
CAPTAIN ATOM
RORSCHACH
THE QUESTION
NITE OWL
BLUE BEETLE
THE COMEDIAN
PEACEMAKER
OZYMANDIAS
THUNDERBOLT

"WATCHMEN," MOORE WOULD LATER EXPLAIN, "WAS THE KIND OF BASIC IDEA OF *MIRACLEMAN*, APPLYING ***REAL WORLD LOGIC*** TO A SUPER HERO, JUST TAKEN TO A ***GREATER EXTREME.***"

MOORE CREATED THE BOOK WITH ARTIST AND FELLOW BRITON ***DAVE GIBBONS***. THE GRAPHIC NOVEL'S DENSITY -- INTERCUTTING BETWEEN TIME PERIODS AND FANTASY & REALITY -- HAVE LED SOME TO CALL IT A SUPER HERO *MOBY DICK!*

INCREDIBLY FOR A WORK OF SUCH ***COMPLEXITY***, MUCH OF *WATCHMEN* WAS CREATED ***TWO PAGES*** OR SO AT A TIME, AS MOORE SENT GIBBONS SCRIPT BETWEEN *SWAMP THING* AND OTHER ASSIGNMENTS. "NOT ONLY WAS THERE NO OVERNIGHT FEDEX IN THOSE DAYS," GIBBONS RECALLS, "BUT NO FAX MACHINES AND CERTAINLY NO EMAIL.

"EVERY EPISODE OF TYPESCRIPT HAD TO BE PUT IN A TAXICAB AND ***DRIVEN*** THE FIFTY MILES OR SO FROM ALAN'S HOUSE TO MINE."

** THOUGH CHARLTON HAD A FEMALE HERO IN **NIGHTSHADE**, MOORE HAS SAID FOX FEATURES SYNDICATE'S **PHANTOM LADY** WAS THE TRUE INSPIRATION FOR WATCHMEN'S **SILK SPECTRE**.*

MOORE & GIBBONS' HARD WORK PAID OFF:
HUGO
WATCHMEN WAS LAUDED AS THE GREATEST SUPER HERO STORY EVER TOLD EVEN BEFORE THE FINAL OF ITS TWELVE ISSUES CAME OUT; INDEED, STILL THOUGHT OF AS THE ESSENTIAL LONG UNDERWEAR TALE, THE COLLECTED EDITION HAS BEEN A BESTSELLER SINCE IT FIRST ARRIVED ON BOOKSTORE SHELVES IN 1987.
IT BECAME THE FIRST NOVEL IN SEQUENTIAL ART FORMAT TO WIN SCIENCE FICTION'S COVETED HUGO AWARD THE FOLLOWING YEAR (IN THE "OTHER FORMS" CATEGORY).

MOORE & GIBBONS WERE FETED ON BOTH SIDES OF THE ATLANTIC; THOUGH, AS USUAL, COMICS REMAINED ONE STEP AHEAD OF MAINSTREAM PERCEPTIONS OF THEM.
UPON SHOWING UP FOR A SHOOT WITH THE FACE, THE UK'S LEADING STYLE MAGAZINE, THE DUO DISCOVERED THE PHOTOGRAPHER PLANNED TO STAGE THEM LIKE:
"BATMAN AND ROBIN! YOU BOTH HANG ON TO THE ROPE AND LEAN FORWARD, THEN WE TURN THE PRINT SIDEWAYS AND YOU'RE CLIMBING A WALL!"
(FORTUANTELY OUR HEROES SOUNDLY REJECTED THIS IDEA.)

WATCHMEN'S ASTOUNDING SUCCESS SPARKED TWO IMMEDIATE RESULTS:
A "BRITISH INVASION" OF WRITING & ARTISTIC TALENT FROM THE UK INDUSTRY BEGAN CREATING BOOKS FOR AMERICAN PUBLISHERS AT AN UNPRECEDENTED RATE.
ENGLISHMEN NEIL GAIMAN AND WARREN ELLIS, SCOTS GRANT MORRISON AND MARK MILLAR, AND GARTH ENNIS FROM NORTHERN IRELAND, AMONG OTHERS, BROUGHT FRESH NEW PERSPECTIVES TO GENRE COMICS.

GAIMAN HAS ARGUED THAT THE SIGNIFICANCE OF THE UK CREATORS' IMPACT CAME, IN PART, BECAUSE THEY HAD MANY *DIFFERENT* CULTURAL INFLUENCES AS OPPOSED TO THEIR U.S. COUNTERPARTS: "I THINK IN AMERICA, UNFORTUNATELY, COMICS HAVE BECOME VERY *INCESTUOUS*... IN THE MAINSTREAM, YOU'VE GOT PEOPLE WHO LEARNED TO WRITE FROM PEOPLE WHO LEARNED TO WRITE FROM PEOPLE WHO LEARNED TO WRITE BY COPYING *STAN LEE*.

"IT'S LIKE A *XEROX*: TAKE AN IMAGE, PHOTOCOPY IT, PHOTOCOPY THE PHOTOCOPY, THEN PHOTOCOPY THE PHOTOCOPY, AND SOONER OR LATER YOU *LOSE* THE IMAGE. I THINK PART OF THAT IS WHAT'S *WRONG* WITH AMERICAN COMICS.
"A LOT OF MAINSTREAM SUPER HERO COMICS ARE LIKE BAD FOURTH AND *FIFTH GENERATION* PHOTOCOPIES OF 1960s OR 1970s COMICS."
HERO MAN

THAT URGE TO ***EMULATE*** CONTRIBUTED TO WHAT MANY FEEL IS *WATCHMEN*'S ***LESS*** POSITIVE LEGACY.

GRAVITATING MORE TO THE NOVEL'S FRANK SEX, VIOLENCE AND ADULT LANGUAGE THAN ITS ***SOPHISTICATION***, CREATORS FLOODED THE MARKET WITH A WAVE OF *"DARK"* -- IF NOT TERRIBLY *"MATURE"* -- SUPER HERO COMICS IN THE LATE 1980s AND '90s.

YOU PUKES RAPED MY **DOG**... NOW YOU'RE GONNA **PAY!!**

AAHH!! CHEESE IT! IT'S... **CROTCHSHOT!**

HE ONLY SHOOTS CROTCHES!!

ONE PERSON WHO FELT THIS WAY WAS ALAN MOORE HIMSELF. HE TOLD WIRED MAGAZINE IN 2009 THAT WATCHMEN'S RECEPTION WAS:
"JUDGED AS MIRACULOUS AS A DOG RIDING A BICYCLE BACK IN THE 1980s. IT DOESN'T MATTER WHETHER HE'S RIDING IT PARTICULARLY WELL; IT MATTERS THAT HE'S RIDING IT AT ALL.
CROTCHSHOT

"I THINK THERE WERE A SURPRISING NUMBER OF PEOPLE OUT THERE WHO SECRETLY LONGED TO KEEP UP WITH THE ADVENTURES OF GREEN LANTERN BUT WHO FELT THEY WOULD HAVE BEEN SOCIALLY OSTRACIZED IF THEY HAD BEEN SEEN READING A COMIC BOOK IN A PUBLIC PLACE.
"COMIC BOOK"
WATCHMEN

"WITH THE ADVENT OF BOOKS LIKE WATCHMEN, I THINK THESE PEOPLE WERE GIVEN LICENSE BY THE TERM GRAPHIC NOVEL. EVERYBODY KNEW THAT COMICS WERE FOR CHILDREN AND FOR INTELLECTUALLY SUBNORMAL PEOPLE, WHEREAS GRAPHIC NOVEL SOUNDS LIKE A MUCH MORE SOPHISTICATED PROPOSITION.
"GRAPHIC NOVEL"
WATCHMEN

"AT THE TIME I THOUGHT THAT A BOOK LIKE WATCHMEN WOULD PERHAPS UNLOCK A LOT OF POTENTIAL CREATIVITY, THAT PERHAPS OTHER WRITERS AND ARTISTS IN THE INDUSTRY WOULD SEE IT AND WOULD THINK:
'THIS IS GREAT, THIS SHOWS WHAT COMICS CAN DO. WE CAN NOW TAKE OUR OWN IDEAS AND THANKS TO THE SUCCESS OF WATCHMEN WE'LL HAVE A BETTER CHANCE OF EDITORS GIVING US A SHOT AT THEM.'
"I WAS HOPING NAIVELY FOR A GREAT RASH OF INDIVIDUAL COMIC BOOKS THAT WERE EXPLORING DIFFERENT STORYTELLING IDEAS AND TRYING TO BREAK NEW GROUND.

"THAT ISN'T REALLY WHAT HAPPENED. INSTEAD IT SEEMED THAT THE EXISTENCE OF WATCHMEN HAD PRETTY MUCH DOOMED THE MAINSTREAM COMIC INDUSTRY TO ABOUT TWENTY YEARS OF VERY GRIM AND OFTEN PRETENTIOUS STORIES THAT SEEMED TO BE UNABLE TO GET AROUND THE MASSIVE PSYCHOLOGICAL STUMBLING BLOCK THAT WATCHMEN HAD TURNED OUT TO BE, ALTHOUGH THAT HAD NEVER BEEN MY INTENTION WITH THE WORK."
WOO, HOO!
WATCHMEN

MOORE IS BEING TOO HARSH ON HIMSELF... AND GIVING HIMSELF FAR TOO MUCH CREDIT.
AS BRILLIANT AS WATCHMEN IS, ITS UPDATING THE TROPES OF SUPER HERO COMICS IS PART OF A LONG TRADITION THAT STRETCHES BACK TO AT LEAST THE MID-1950s, WHEN JULIE SCHWARTZ MODERNIZED DC'S ALL-AMERICAN HEROES.

NOR WAS WATCHMEN CREATED IN A VACUUM. THE SAME YEAR ITS FIRST ISSUE APPEARED, 1986, ALSO SAW THE FIRST VOLUMES OF FRANK MILLER'S GRITTY REIMAGINING OF BATMAN, THE DARK KNIGHT RETURNS, AND ART SPIEGELMAN'S PULITZER PRIZE-WINNING MAUS.
Mets
NINE DECADES HAD PASSED SINCE THE YELLOW KID DEBUTED. "AMERICAN-STYLE" COMICS HAD AGED ALONG WITH THEIR AUDIENCE, BUT THEY HAD ALSO BEGUN TO EVOLVE, NOT MERELY REMAIN IN A STATE OF ARRESTED DEVELOPMENT.

OF COURSE MOST OF WHAT RESULTS FROM ANY GIVEN INSPIRATION WILL BE CRAP.
TO DECLARE AN ENTIRE MOVEMENT A FAILURE BECAUSE THE MAJORITY OF ITS OUTPUT IS FOUND WANTING IS LUDICROUS.
THE GOOD IS PRECIOUS AND VALUED BECAUSE IT IS RARE.
90%
10%
"STURGEON'S LAW"

FOR EXAMPLE, IT'S UNLIKELY NEIL GAIMAN'S BELOVED FANTASY EPIC *THE SANDMAN* COULD HAVE EXISTED WITHOUT **MOORE** FIRST PAVING THE WAY. GAIMAN ACTUALLY TOOK OVER SCRIPTING ***MIRACLEMAN*** FROM MOORE WHEN HE LEFT THE TITLE IN 1988. BUT THEIR PUBLISHER, ECLIPSE COMICS, WENT ***BANKRUPT*** IN 1993, LEAVING GAIMAN'S SERIES UNFINISHED. IN 1996, IMAGE COMICS COFOUNDER ***TODD MCFARLANE*** BOUGHT ECLIPSE'S ASSETS FOR ABOUT ***$50,000.*** HE CLAIMED THIS INCLUDED ECLIPSE'S PORTION OF THE *MIRACLEMAN* COPYRIGHT; GAIMAN DISAGREED, AND ***SUED*** MCFARLANE IN 2002 TO REGAIN THE CHARACTER!*

** ALAN MOORE HAD CEDED HIS INTEREST IN THE MIRACLEMAN COPYRIGHT TO GAIMAN & HIS ARTIST **MARK BUCKINGHAM** AFTER THEY TOOK OVER.*

BUT IN 2009, MARVEL COMICS CROSSED THE ATLANTIC AND BOUGHT THE RIGHTS TO **MARVEL**MAN FROM HIS ORIGINAL CREATOR, THE NOW-93 YEAR-OLD **MICK ANGLO!**
WHERE DOES THAT LEAVE THE LEGAL STATUS OF **MIRACLE**MAN?
WELL, IT'S QUITE **SIMPLE**, REALLY:
!?!?
I **SAY**, FACE **FRONT**, TRUE BELIEVERS!

MIRACLEMAN CAME TO BE BECAUSE **SUPERMAN** SAID THAT

CAPTAIN MARVEL WAS A COPYCAT, PUTTING HIM OUT OF BUSINESS, THUS

TURNING HIM INTO **MARVELMAN** SO HE COULD LIVE ON IN **BRITAIN**, BUT UPON COMING TO **AMERICA** 30 YEARS LATER

THE CHARACTER BECAME **MIRACLEMAN** TO PLACATE MARVEL COMICS, BUT NOW THAT **MARVEL** OWNS **MARVEL**MAN, THAT CLEARLY MEANS THAT...
UH...

?

THE GOD OF ALL COMICS

THOUGH THE FOCUS OF OUR HISTORY IS THE MEDIUM IN ***AMERICA***, IT MUST BE SAID THAT ***JAPAN*** IS INARGUABLY ***KING*** OF ALL COMICS CULTURES.

BUT ***WHY?***

SOME HAVE SUGGESTED THAT PART OF THE REASON THE JAPANESE HAVE SUCH AN AFFINITY FOR COMBINING ***WORDS AND PICTURES*** IS THAT MUCH OF THEIR ***WRITING*** IS ITSELF A KIND OF ***DRAWING***, IN THE FORM OF ***IDEOGRAMS***.

"MANGA" IS FORMED WITH TWO SUCH ***KANJI***:

"MAN" -- *"INVOLUNTARY"* OR *"UNCONSCIOUSLY"*...

...AND ***"GA,"*** OR *"PICTURE"* (REPRESENTED BY THE BORDERS OF A ***RICE FIELD***).

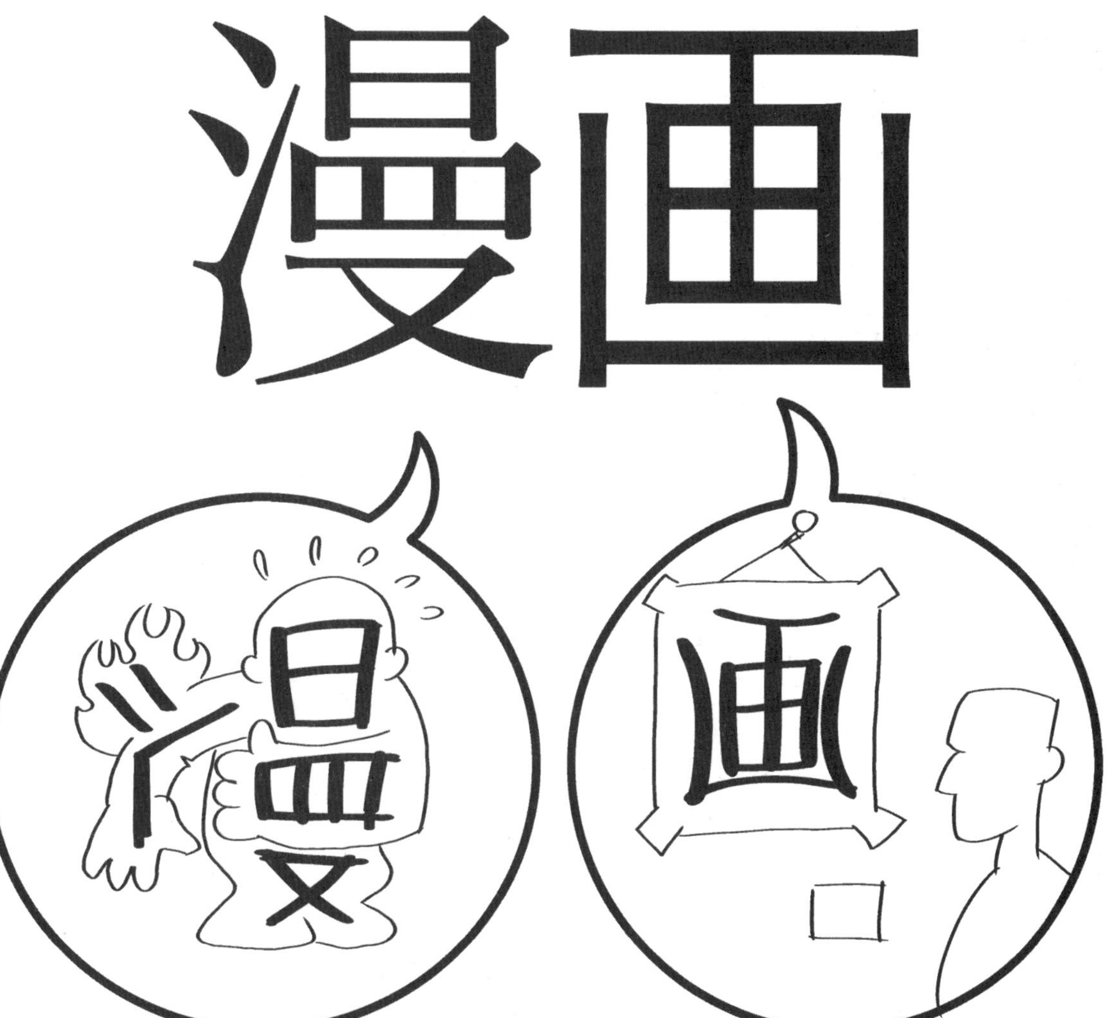
漫画

LEGENDARY PRINTMAKER ***KATSUSHIKA HOKUSAI*** (1760-1849) COINED THE TERM TO DESCRIBE A SERIES OF LEISURELY SKETCHES ON VARIOUS THEMES HE BEGAN PUBLISHING IN ***1814***.

"MANGA" EVENTUALLY CAME TO MEAN ***"HUMOROUS DRAWINGS,"*** BUT IT WAS NOT THE ***FIRST*** WAY THE JAPANESE DESCRIBED ***"KOMIKKUSU"*** (TO USE A POPULAR ADAPTATION OF THE ***ENGLISH*** WORD).

EARLIER SATIRIC CARICATURES HAD BEEN CALLED ***TOBA-E***, OR *"TOBA PICTURES,"* AFTER THE 12TH CENTURY BUDDHIST MONK WHO ALLEGEDLY DREW THE *CHŌJŪ-GIGA* NARRATIVE PICTURE SCROLL, WHICH USED ANIMALS TO ***MOCK*** HUMAN FOIBLES.
STOP HIM! I JUST MARRIED THAT STICK!
NO, I LOVE THAT STICK!
WHAT'S UP, DOC?
AM I TOO SEXY FOR THIS HAT?*
* NOTE: NOT ACTUAL DIALOGUE

THIS TYPE OF SCROLL IS SURPRISINGLY SIMILAR TO TODAY'S ***COMICS***.

THEY COULD BE UP TO ***EIGHTY FEET LONG*** UNFURLED, COMPRISED OF IMAGES PROGRESSING OVER TIME AND ***DISTANCE***.

EEK!

THE FORM ORIGINATED IN ***CHINA***, AND JAPAN CONTINUED TO ABSORB ***FOREIGN*** INFLUENCE FOR COMICS INSPIRATION.

WHEN THE WEST, LED BY AMERICAN NAVAL POWER, FORCED JAPAN OUT OF HER CULTURAL ISOLATION IN THE MID-19TH CENTURY, ***EUROPEANS*** CAME TO THE ISLANDS SEEKING FORTUNE AND ADVENTURE.

BRITISH CARTOONIST AND YOKOHAMA RESIDENT ***CHARLES WIRGMAN*** BEGAN *THE JAPAN PUNCH* IN 1862 FOR THE EX-PAT COMMUNITY, CONTAINING POLITICAL CARTOONS AND HUMOR SIMILAR TO THE UK MAGAZINE OF THE SAME NAME BACK HOME...

...BUT HIS ***JAPANESE*** FRIENDS LOVED IT TOO, AND SOON BEGAN PRINTING THEIR OWN HUMOR MAGAZINES FEATURING ONE-PANEL CARTOONS THEY CALLED ***PONCHI-E***, OR *"PUNCH PICTURES."*
MANY JAPANESE CONSIDER WIRGMAN THE ***FATHER*** OF MODERN MANGA AND HOLD AN ANNUAL CEREMONY AT HIS GRAVE IN YOKOHAMA.

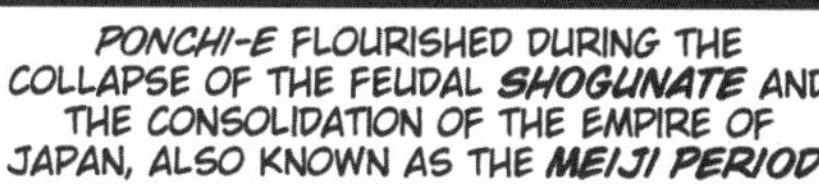
PONCHI-E FLOURISHED DURING THE COLLAPSE OF THE FEUDAL SHOGUNATE AND THE CONSOLIDATION OF THE EMPIRE OF JAPAN, ALSO KNOWN AS THE MEIJI PERIOD.

WHEN THE FIRST CHILD OF THE TEZUKAS OF OSAKA PREFECTURE WAS BORN ON MEIJI THE GREAT'S BIRTHDAY (NOVEMBER 3) IN 1928, THEY NAMED HIM WITH THE LAST CHARACTER IN THE EMPEROR'S NAME: OSAMU.

OSAMU'S PARENTS QUICKLY LEARNED THAT THE EASIEST WAY TO GET HIM TO STAY QUIET WAS TO HAND HIM PENCIL AND PAPER.
HE BEGAN DRAWING AT A YOUNG AGE AND CREATED HIS FIRST COMIC, PIN PIN SEI-CHAN, WHEN HE WAS NINE.

BUT OSAMU'S FIRST LOVE WAS UNDOUBTEDLY ANIMATION. HIS FATHER, YUTAKA, WAS AN AMATEUR PHOTOGRAPHER WHO BOUGHT A MOVIE PROJECTOR TO SCREEN CARTOONS FROM AROUND THE WORLD ON FAMILY FILM NIGHT.

WALT DISNEY'S WORK MADE THE STRONGEST IMPRESSION ON OSAMU AND HE WOULD WORSHIP THE FILMMAKER THROUGHOUT HIS LIFE.

OSAKA HAD ITS OWN COTTAGE COMICS INDUSTRY REVOLVING AROUND CHEAP AKAHON -- "RED BOOKS," AFTER THEIR COVERS' COLOR -- THAT WERE KIDS' FAVORITE READING MATERIAL.
NEWSPAPER STRIPS ALSO THRIVED DURING THIS PERIOD, AND OSAMU FORCED HIS PARENTS TO SUBSCRIBE TO ONE SO HE COULD FOLLOW THE STRAY PUP NORAKURO BY ARTIST SUIHŌ TAGAWA.

UNFORTUNATELY, OSAMU ALSO GREW UP ALONG WITH THE INCREASING MILITARIZATION OF THE IMPERIAL GOVERNMENT.
JAPANESE CARTOONISTS WERE SO FREQUENTLY ARRESTED BY THE RIGHT-WINGERS THEY CRITICIZED THAT MAGAZINE STAFF TOOK TURNS BEING "JAIL EDITOR" -- THE DESIGNATED FALL GUY TO BE HAULED AWAY WHEN THE COPS SHOWED UP.

IN 1937 JAPAN TOOK HER FIRST REAL STEPS TOWARD **WORLD WAR II** BY INVADING NEIGHBORING CHINA.
THE FOLLOWING YEAR STRICT LAWS REGULATING CHILDREN'S LITERATURE WERE PASSED, **BANNING** MOST *AKAHON* AS "POOR-QUALITY" AND "***HARMFUL.***"
IN THE RESULTING CRACKDOWN CARTOONISTS WHO CRITICIZED ***NATIONALIST IDEOLOGY*** WERE ARRESTED AND THEIR STRIPS CANCELLED.
COMIX

THE EMPIRE PRESSED MANY REMAINING ARTISTS INTO DRAWING ANTI-ALLIED PROPAGANDA LIKE ***EROTIC STRIPS*** AIRDROPPED ON WESTERN TROOPS THAT PREDICTED THEIR GIRLFRIENDS OR WIVES WERE ***CHEATING*** ON THEM BACK HOME.
?
Oh La La

DONNA... WITH ***MITCH?!*** ***NOOOO!!***
Oh La La

THE FIRST FEATURE-LENGTH "*ANIME*," IN FACT, WAS 1944'S ***MOMOTARŌ'S DIVINE SEA WARRIORS***, IN WHICH DISNEY-ESQUE ANIMALS DEFEND A PACIFIC ISLAND FROM U.S. FORCES.

"I ***WEPT***, AWED BY WHAT ***JAPANESE ANIMATION*** COULD DO," OSAMU TEZUKA WOULD WRITE LATER.
HE SAW *MOMOTARŌ* "IN A RUN-DOWN THEATER IN A BOMBED-OUT TOWN."

SIXTEEN-YEAR-OLD OSAMU WORKED IN A WARTIME ***ASBESTOS FACTORY*** WHERE HIS BOSSES ***BEAT*** HIM IF THEY CAUGHT HIM ***DRAWING.***
THE AMERICANS ***FIRE-BOMBED*** OSAKA THROUGHOUT THE SUMMER OF 1945. THE JUNE 1 ATTACK ALONE KILLED OVER ***4,000*** PEOPLE AND LEFT HUNDREDS OF THOUSANDS ***HOMELESS.***
ASBESTOS
OSAMU WITNESSED THE HORRIFIC ATTACK ***FIRSTHAND*** AND IT LEFT HIM AN ARDENT ***PACIFIST*** FOR LIFE. HE ENROLLED IN MEDICAL SCHOOL PARTLY BECAUSE OF HIS BELIEFS, PARTLY TO STAY OUT OF THE MILITARY, BUT ONLY A FEW WEEKS LATER, JAPAN ***SURRENDERED***, AND THE U.S. ***OCCUPATION*** BEGAN.

IT WAS DURING THIS CRUCIAL POSTWAR PERIOD THAT JAPAN TOOK DECISIVE STEPS AWAY FROM AMERICA TO ACHIEVE

TOTAL COMICS DOMINANCE

THE UNITED STATES BECAME ***SUBURBANIZED*** AFTER THE WAR, AND THE DOMINANCE OF ***AUTOMOBILES*** OVER PUBLIC TRANSPORTATION GREATLY REDUCED ***OPPORTUNITIES*** FOR ALL KINDS OF READING, BUT IT WAS PARTICULARLY DEADLY FOR ***COMICS***, WHOSE YOUNG, DRIVER LICENSE-LESS TARGET AUDIENCE HAD LESS ***DIRECT ACCESS*** TO THE PRODUCT!
NEWS

WHILE THE ISLANDS OF ***JAPAN***, WITH THEIR POPULATION CONCENTRATED ON SMALL LANDMASS(ES), REMAINED AND REMAINS A ***MASS TRANSIT*** SOCIETY -- ***PRIME*** READER MATERIAL!

THE INCREASING UBIQUITY OF ***TELEVISION*** IN AMERICA IN THIS PERIOD LEAD TO MASSIVE DECLINES IN MOVIE ATTENDANCE, NEWSPAPER CIRCULATION -- AND ***COMICS READERSHIP!***
WHILE TECHNOLOGY-STARVED ***JAPAN*** WOULDN'T EVEN ***BEGIN*** TV BROADCASTS UNTIL 1954-- WITH LESS THAN ***1,000 SETS*** IN THE WHOLE ***COUNTRY!***

INSTEAD, THEY MADE DO WITH THE ANCIENT ART OF ***KAMI-SHIBAI*** ("PAPER DRAMAS"): ITERANT STORY-TELLERS NARRATED TALES ILLUSTRATED WITH ***GEKIGA*** ("DRAMATIC PICTURES")! LOW-TECH ***COMICS*** ALSO FLOURISHED IN THE WAR TORN LAND!
(MANY FUTURE ***MANGA*** ARTISTS GOT STARTED PRODUCING GEKIGA FOR THE ***KAMI-SHIBAI*** MARKET.)

DURING THIS PERIOD THE ***AMERICAN OCCUPIERS*** TOOK OVER THE ***CENSOR OFFICE*** WITH A DIAMETRICALLY ***OPPOSITE*** AGENDA TO THEIR JAPANESE ***PREDECESSORS***.
SAM.
CENSOR
TOSHIRO.
THE U.S. WANTED TO ***BAN*** MILITARISTIC AND ***NATIONALIST*** IMAGES LIKE PERIOD SAMURAI DRAMA. CHILDREN'S BOOKS AND FANTASTICAL GENRES LIKE SCIENCE FICTION AND ADVENTURE WERE DEEMED HARMLESS--SO BOTH ***THRIVED*** IN THE NEW ERA!

AKAHON RETURNED WITH A ***VENGEANCE!*** MOST KIDS WERE TOO YOUNG OR HAD BEEN BORN TOO LATE TO SEE ANY COMICS ESPECIALLY DRAWN FOR ***THEM*** AND NOT THE EMPIRE BEFORE THE WAR!
PAY-LIBRARIES, IN WHICH CHILDREN TOO POOR TO BUY "RED BOOKS" ***RENTED*** THEM FOR A SMALL FEE, ***BOOMED***, PARTICULARLY IN ***OSAKA!***

YOUNG OSAMU DREW A "RED BOOK" IN BETWEEN MED SCHOOL COURSEWORK CALLED NEW TREASURE ISLAND.
IT PROVED IMMENSELY POPULAR, SELLING A STUNNING 400,000 COPIES IN 1947!
HIS DISNEY-INFLUENCED STYLE AND ATTENTION TO CINEMATIC ACTION STUNNED HIS AUDIENCE:

"THIS IS A STATIC COMIC PRINTED ON PAPER, BUT, THIS CAR IS RUNNING AT FULL SPEED! IT'S JUST LIKE I AM WATCHING A MOVIE!"
TEZUKA'S METERIC RISE SPAWNED HUNDREDS, IF NOT THOUSANDS OF IMITATORS.

"ONE OUT OF THREE PEOPLE HAD DREAMED OF BECOMING A CARTOONIST AT LEAST ONCE," RECALLS MANGA EDITOR AKIRA MARUYAMA ABOUT THIS PERIOD.
FUTURE BAREFOOT GEN AUTHOR KEIJI NAKAZAWA DEVOURED NTI IN THE ATOMIC-BOMBED RUINS OF HIROSHIMA.

OSAMU'S OUTPUT PROVED AS INSATIABLE AS THE DEMAND FOR IT. HE FOLLOWED HIS INITIAL SUCCESS WITH THE BLOCKBUSTERS LOST WORLD (1948), METROPOLIS (1949) AND JUNGLE EMPEROR (1950).
LOST WORLD
CINEMA-CRAZED TEZUKA BORROWED MANY TITLES FROM FAMOUS FOREIGN FILMS AND PRINTED THEM IN ENGLISH ON THE COVERS OF HIS "RED BOOKS." THE LANGUAGE OF JAPAN'S OCCUPIERS SIGNIFIED POWER AND NEWNESS TO HIS AUDIENCE!

TEZUKA FOUND INSPIRATION FROM AMERICA IN A VARIETY OF WAYS. TEZUKA'S JUNGLE EMPEROR IS BETTER KNOWN IN THIS COUNTRY AS (IN ITS 1960s ANIMATED FORM) KIMBA THE WHITE LION, THE INSPIRATION FOR THE LION KING.
BEER
TEZUKA'S MANGA WAS ACTUALLY INSPIRED BY DISNEY'S BAMBI--WHICH OSAMU WOULD SEE OVER EIGHTY TIMES AFTER ITS JAPANESE RELEASE!
OSAMU BELIEVED SELF-AWARE ANIMALS LIKE THUMPER & FRIENDS WOULD TRY TO BEFRIEND MAN RATHER THAN COWER IN THE FOREST.
AN ESSENTIAL EXPRESSION OF HIS CREATOR'S PACIFISM, THE HEROIC LION LEO IS RAISED BY HUMANS AND RETURNS TO THE JUNGLE TO TEACH BARBAROUS BEASTS CIVILIZED WAYS.

THE ALLIED OCCUPATION FORCES TRANSFERRED POWER BACK TO THE JAPANESE PEOPLE IN 1952.
AS THE COUNTRY REGAINED HER ECONOMIC MUSCLE, THE RENTAL MARKET FADED AND WEEKLY ***ANTHOLOGIES*** BECAME THE DOMINANT MEANS OF DISTRIBUTING COMICS.
THOUGH OSAMU EARNED HIS MEDICAL LICENSE, HE CHOSE TO MOVE TO ***TOKYO*** AND CONCENTRATE ON PRODUCING SERIALIZED STRIPS FOR THE MAGAZINE MARKET.
TOKYO

ANOTHER DISNEY INFLUENCE, ***PINOCCHIO,*** LED TEZUKA TO HIS MOST ***ENDURING*** CREATION: A HEROIC BOY ROBOT CREATED BY A SCIENTIST TO REPLACE HIS DEAD SON.

TETSUWAN ATOM *("IRON-ARMED ATOM")* PREMIERED IN 1952, THE SAME YEAR DISNEY'S FILM OPENED IN JAPAN. HIS ADVENTURES QUICKLY BECAME A ***SENSATION***, HEADLINING *SHŌNEN* MAGAZINE FOR THE NEXT ***SIXTEEN YEARS***.

ATOM PROVED SO POPULAR HE IS THE ONLY ***FICTIONAL*** PERSON TO BE GRANTED JAPANESE ***CITIZENSHIP*** -- ON HIS BIRTH DATE FROM THE COMIC, ***APRIL 7, 2003!***

MEANWHILE, THE JAPANESE TV INDUSTRY WAS MAKING UP FOR LOST TIME. ATOM STARRED IN A LIVE-ACTION TV SHOW IN 1959, BUT TEZUKA FELT AN ***ANIMATED*** PROGRAM WOULD TRANSLATE HIS MANGA BETTER.

HE ACHIEVED A LIFELONG DREAM BY FOUNDING MUSHI PRODUCTIONS TO PRODUCE ATOM CARTOONS-- BUT STRUGGLED WITH ***BUDGETS***. NOT EVEN ***DISNEY*** HAD FIGURED OUT A COST-EFFECTIVE WAY TO MAKE CARTOONS FOR THE TV MARKET.

INSTEAD, TEZUKA TURNED TO ***ANOTHER*** AMERICAN INFLUENCE. ***WILLIAM HANNA*** AND ***JOSEPH BARBERA*** PRODUCED THEIR HIT ***THE FLINTSTONES*** WITH LIMITED ANIMATION AT ABOUT 12 FRAMES PER SECOND -- ***HALF*** THE RATE OF A DISNEY CARTOON.
MUSHI ADAPTED THESE METHODS AND BROUGHT IN EACH *ATOM* EPISODE AT ***$5000!*** THE SHOW PREMIERED ON JANUARY 1, 1963 AND ***GALVANIZED*** JAPAN'S ANIMATION INDUSTRY!

WHEN *ATOM* WAS REDUBBED FOR BROADCAST ON NBC AS *ASTRO BOY*, TEZUKA EARNED FANS IN **AMERICA** AS WELL!

IN 1964, HE TRAVELED TO THE ***NEW YORK WORLD'S FAIR*** AND MET HIS IDOL FOR THE FIRST AND ONLY TIME AT THE *"IT'S A SMALL WORLD"* EXHIBIT. ***WALT DISNEY*** SAID HE KNEW AND ***ADMIRED*** *ASTRO BOY*, WHICH TEZUKA REMEMBERED FONDLY FOR LIFE.

PEPSI-COLA
WALT DISNEY

BACK IN JAPAN, HOWEVER, TEZUKA'S POPULARITY APPEARED TO HAVE ***PEAKED***.

FINANCIALLY SHAKY MUSHI PRODUCTIONS WENT ***BANKRUPT*** IN 1973. HIS NEW MANGA STRUGGLED TO FIND AN AUDIENCE AS THE KIDS WHO GREW UP ON HIS WORK WERE NOW TEENAGERS AND ADULTS WHO CRAVED NEW, MORE ***SOPHISTICATED*** COMICS.

ONLY FORTY-FIVE YEARS OLD, PEOPLE BEGAN TO CALL HIM *"THE OLD MAN OF MANGA."* HIS WORK HUNG PROUDLY IN ***MUSEUMS***, BUT A CONSENSUS GREW THAT HE WASN'T RELEVANT TO ***MODERN*** COMICS.

TEZUKA SUCCUMBED FROM TIME-TO-TIME TO HIS LIFELONG STRUGGLES WITH ***DEPRESSION.***

YOUNGER ARTISTS WHO ALSO GOT THEIR START IN OSAKA'S RENTAL TRADE ***CHALLENGED*** TEZUKA'S SUPREMACY.

THEY DISDAINED THE TERM "MANGA" AS TOO ***JUVENILE*** AND WANTED TO CHANGE IT TO ***GEKIGA***-- "DRAMATIC PICTURES," A TERM BORROWED FROM *KAMI-SHIBAI* -- TO DENOTE MORE ***MATURE*** WORKS.

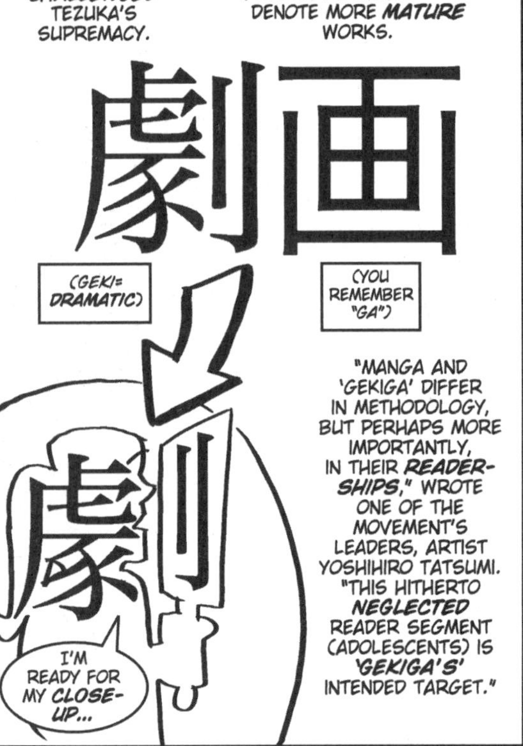

劇画
(*GEKI*= **DRAMATIC**)
(YOU REMEMBER "*GA*")
"MANGA AND 'GEKIGA' DIFFER IN METHODOLOGY, BUT PERHAPS MORE IMPORTANTLY, IN THEIR ***READER-SHIPS,*** " WROTE ONE OF THE MOVEMENT'S LEADERS, ARTIST YOSHIHIRO TATSUMI. "THIS HITHERTO ***NEGLECTED*** READER SEGMENT (ADOLESCENTS) IS ***'GEKIGA'S'*** INTENDED TARGET."
劇
I'M READY FOR MY ***CLOSE-UP...***

AKITA SHOTEN, PUBLISHER OF THE WEEKLY *SHŌNEN CHAMPION*, TOOK ***PITY*** ON THE FADING TEZUKA AND INVITED HIM TO DO "ANYTHING HE ***WISHED***" FOR THE MAGAZINE BEFORE ***RETIRING*** IN 1973.

TEZUKA TAPPED INTO HIS DOCTOR'S BACKGROUND TO CREATE ***BLACK JACK***, A REBEL SURGEON INVESTIGATING MEDICAL MYSTERIES.
CLEAR!
THE SERIES ***RESURRECTED*** TEZUKA'S CAREER AND LASTED OVER ***EIGHT YEARS!***

TEZUKA *MET* THE *GEKIGA* CHALLENGE BY ABSORBING *THEIR* METHODS INTO *HIS* WORK, EMBARKING ON EVER MORE *AMBITIOUS* PROJECTS, INCLUDING THE HISTORICAL EPICS *BUDDHA* (1972-1983) AND *ADOLF* (1983-1985).
HE ACHIEVED THIS NEW ***SOPHISTICATION DESPITE*** RETAINING THE SAME CUTESY DISNEY-INFLUENCED DRAWING STYLE.
OR... PERHAPS HE ACHIEVED IT ***BECAUSE*** HE RETAINED HIS STYLE!

FROM THE VERY BEGINNING, TEZUKA'S WORK EMPHASIZED ***THEATRICALITY*** -- HE GREW UP NEXT TO ***STAGE ACTRESSES*** AND PERFORMED OFTEN IN HIS YOUTH -- INCLUDING FOURTH-WALL-BREAKING ***ASIDES*** TO THE AUDIENCE, NEVER LETTING THEM FORGET THEY WERE READING A COMIC.

HE OFTEN DEPLOYED THE NON-SEQUITUR CHARACTER ***HYOTANTSUGI*** OUT OF NOWHERE TO BREAK NARRATIVE TENSION!

TEZUKA TREATED EACH OF HIS CHARACTERS AS ***ACTORS*** -- THEY COULD PLAY DIFFERENT PARTS IN ***DIFFERENT*** MANGA.

FOR EXAMPLE, ASTRO BOY "APPEARS" IN *BLACK JACK*, NOT ***AS*** ASTRO BOY BUT AS A ***PATIENT***. THE STOCK CHARACTER "DUKE RED" IS AN IMPORTANT FIGURE IN *METROPOLIS* ***AND*** *JUNGLE EMPEROR* ***AND*** *BLACK JACK* ***AND*** *BUDDHA*, ALL AS ***DIFFERENT PEOPLE.***

TEZUKA KEPT A LIST OF ALL THE CHARACTERS IN HIS ***"STAR SYSTEM"*** AND PERIODICALLY REVISED THEIR RANKINGS BY POPULARITY -- AND ***SALARY!***

THE ***MUTABILITY*** OF TEZUKA'S CHARACTERS SPEAKS TO THE UNDERLYING ***APPEAL*** OF CARTOONING ITSELF -- THE ABILITY OF TWO DOTS, A CIRCLE AND LINE TO BE ACCEPTED AS A ***HUMAN FACE!***

UNDERSTANDING COMICS AUTHOR SCOTT MCCLOUD CALLS THIS ***"AMPLIFICATION THROUGH SIMPLIFICATION."***

IT IS THE VERY ***ABSTRACTION*** OF TEZUKA'S STYLE THAT ENABLES WHAT IS HUMOROUS OR ***CHILDISH*** IN HIS ***MANGA*** TO TAKE ON A MORE SOPHISTICATED, ***PATHOS***-FILLED ROLE IN HIS ***GEKIGA!***
TEE HEE... ***FUNNY!***
-SOB-... ***POIGNANT!***

UNDER TEZUKA'S ***STAR SYSTEM***, THE CHARACTER ***DESIGN*** DOESN'T CHANGE-- THE ***CONTEXT*** CHANGES WITH THE GENRE ... AND THE ***AGING READER!***

HERE THE DIFFERENCES BETWEEN THE TWO COUNTRIES' STYLES IS EVEN MORE ***STARK***. AS MANGA SCHOLAR FREDERIK L. SCHODT HAS WRITTEN:
"IN CONTRAST TO THE ***AMERICAN*** COMIC, WHICH IS READ ***SLOWLY*** TO SAVOR LAVISHLY DETAILED PICTURES AND TO ABSORB A ***GREAT DEAL*** OF PRINTED INFORMATION...
USA

IRONICALLY, BY EMPHASIZING A MORE ***REALISTIC*** STYLE OF ART SINCE THE GOLDEN ERA OF ***ADVENTURE COMIC STRIPS*** (BY WAY OF SUPER HERO ARTISTS LIKE ***JACK KIRBY***), AMERICAN COMICS MAY HAVE ***DOOMED*** THEMSELVES TO BEING TRAPPED INTO ***ONE*** PARTICULAR KIND OF GENRE-- ENJOYED BY ***ONE*** PARTICULAR KIND OF PERSON!

AMERICAN COMICS ***STOPPED*** BEING A TRUE ***MASS*** MEDIUM IN THE MID-1950s AT THE SAME TIME JAPANESE COMICS ***BECAME*** ONE THANKS TO TEZUKA'S MORE ***EXPRESSIONISTIC*** CARTOONING!

"...THE JAPANESE COMIC IS ***SCANNED***. IN A SENSE IT DEMANDS ***MORE*** OF THE READER, BECAUSE HE MUST ***ACTIVELY*** SEEK OUT THE CLUES ON THE PAGE AND ***INTERPRET*** THEM."

VS.

JAPANESE POPULAR CULTURE HAS BEEN A MAINSTAY ON AMERICA'S SHORES SINCE GODZILLA ARRIVED HERE IN THE MID-1950S. SAMURAI MANGA INFLUENCED FRANK MILLER'S CLASSIC RUN ON MARVEL'S *DAREDEVIL*--
19
JAPAN POP
DUTY FREE
--WHICH IN ITSELF SPAWNED AMERICA'S MOST POPULAR HOME-GROWN MANGA DERIVATIVE, THE ***TEENAGE MUTANT NINJA TURTLES***, WHICH STARTED OUT AS A HUMBLE SELF-PUBLISHED COMIC FROM ARTISTS PETER LAIRD AND KEVIN EASTMAN IN 1984.

YET IT TOOK UNTIL THE ***TWENTY-FIRST*** CENTURY FOR MANGA ITSELF TO REALLY CATCH ON HERE. PARTLY THIS WAS A TRICKLE-DOWN EFFECT OF THE POPULARITY OF JAPANESE CARD & VIDEO GAMES, WITH THEIR STYLIZED, FRENETIC ICONOGRAPHY BORROWED ***FROM*** MANGA.

BY 2002, THE AMERICAN EDITION OF THE MANGA WEEKLY *SHŌNEN JUMP* OUTSOLD *AMAZING SPIDER-MAN* BY A ***2:1 MARGIN!***
BY 2006, SALES OF *TANKŌBON* (DIGEST-SIZED COLLECTIONS OF MAGAZINE SERIALS) COMPRISED ***TWO-THIRDS*** OF COMICS IN U.S. BOOKSTORES, MAKING JAPANESE IMPORTS AT LEAST ***AS POPULAR*** AS THEIR AMERICAN COUNTERPARTS!
PERHAPS ***MORE*** IMPORTANTLY, MANGA IS UNDOUBTEDLY THE MOST ***POPULAR*** FORM OF COMICS FOR THE ***YOUNGER*** GENERATION.
KIDS -- PARTICULARLY ***GIRLS*** -- FIND A WIDE ***VARIETY*** OF MANGA GENRES TO ENJOY -- AND BOOKS THAT SPEAK DIRECTLY TO ***THEM***, REFLECTING THE FACT THAT COMICS IN JAPAN ARE READ BY NO ***ONE*** DEMOGRAPHIC, BUT ***EVERYONE!***
BUT ***WHY?***
マンガの本

THE ***EXOTICNESS*** OF MANGA COULDN'T HAVE HURT EITHER, AS KIDS HAVE ALWAYS EMBRACED CULTURES THEIR PARENTS DON'T -- AND ***CAN'T*** -- UNDERSTAND.
MORE MANGA CREATORS ALLOWED THEIR WORK TO APPEAR IN ENGLISH AFTER U.S. PUBLISHERS DECIDED NOT TO TRANSLATE ***SOUND EFFECTS*** AND LEAVE THEIR EDITIONS ***"UNFLOPPED"*** IN THE ***RIGHT-TO-LEFT*** JAPANESE READING STYLE.
?
COMIC
THIS IS THE BACK COVER, IDIOT!

UPON OSAMU TEZUKA'S DEATH FROM STOMACH CANCER ON FEBRUARY 9, 1989, THE TOKYO DAILY *ASAHI SHINBUN* ASKED, "WHY DO THE JAPANESE LOVE **COMICS** SO MUCH? ... WHY HAVEN'T PEOPLE OF **OTHER** COUNTRIES BEEN READING COMICS?
"**ONE** OF THE ANSWERS IS, THEY DID NOT HAVE **OSAMU TEZUKA**."
EVEN A **CURSORY** LIST OF HIS **LIFELONG ACHIEVEMENTS** STRAINS **CREDULITY**:
WITH THE HELP OF THE ASSISTANTS IN HIS STUDIO, HE PRODUCED **170,000 PAGES** OF COMICS ACROSS **700 TITLES** COVERING MOST GENRES: HISTORY, SCIENCE FICTION, ADVENTURE, WAR, PHILOSOPHY, RELIGION, LITERARY ADAPTATIONS OF **GOETHE** AND **DOSTOEVSKY!**
IN ADDITION TO HIS PIONEERING WORK WITH *SHŌNEN* (**BOYS'**) MANGA, HE ALSO CREATED **RIBON NO KISHI** (*PRINCESS KNIGHT*), THE MOTHER OF ALL **SHŌJO (GIRLS')** MANGA, IN 1953!
IN ADDITION TO HIS **MEDICAL** DEGREE HE STUDIED FOR AND RECEIVED HIS **DOCTORATE** IN 1961! HIS DISSERTATION ON THE **SPERM PRODUCTION** OF THE **JAPANESE POND SNAIL** WAS ILLUSTRATED BY HIS STUDIO'S ARTISTS!
HE PRODUCED WELL OVER **110 ANIMATED FILMS**--IN ADDITION TO THE *ATOM* SHOW, HE CREATED JAPAN'S FIRST **COLOR** TV CARTOON, AN ADAPTATION OF *JUNGLE EMPEROR*, IN 1965!
IN 1989, THE EMPEROR CONVEYED UPON HIM THE ORDER OF THE SACRED TREASURE, OR *ZUIHŌSHO* (ESTABLISHED BY HIS NAMESAKE, EMPEROR **MEIJI**), FOR HIS SERVICE TO THE NATION.
IN 1971, THE PUBLISHER SHUEISHA ESTABLISHED THE **ONE MILLION YEN** TEZUKA AWARD, JAPAN'S HIGHEST HONOR FOR NEW COMICS ARTISTS!
AS SCHOLAR NATSU ONODA POWER HAS WRITTEN, "WHEN THE JAPANESE CALL TEZUKA '*MANGA NO KAMISAMA*,' THEY ARE NOT REFERRING TO TEZUKA AS THE GOD OF **MANGA**, THE SPECIFIC **GENRE** OF (JAPANESE) COMICS THAT IS ASSOCIATED WITH A SPECIFIC PICTORIAL OR NARRATIVE STYLE.
"THEY ARE CALLING HIM THE GOD OF ALL **COMICS**."

NO MORE WEDNESDAYS

HERE'S WHAT IT WAS LIKE TO BE A ***FAN*** BEFORE THE COMIC BOOK ***DIRECT MARKET:***

REMEMBERING HIS NEW JERSEY CHILDHOOD OF THE EARLY 1960s, FUTURE BATMAN AND SWAMP THING MOVIE PRODUCER MICHAEL USLAN SAYS HE AND HIS FRIENDS "HAD TO DOPE OUT FOR OURSELVES THAT COMIC BOOKS WERE BEING DELIVERED TO ALL THE DRUG STORES AND CANDY STORES ON THURSDAYS.
"EVERY THURSDAY AFTER SCHOOL WE WOULD RIDE OUR BIKES TO THEM AND ASK TO BUY THE NEW COMICS THAT CAME IN.
PHARMACY Since 1921
COMIX

"THE PHARMACISTS ALWAYS FOUND US TO BE PARTICULARLY ANNOYING, AS THEY USUALLY SAID THEY WERE TOO BUSY TO OPEN THE WIRED BUNDLES OF COMICS. SO WE WOULD SIT THERE IN THEIR STORES AND WAIT--SOMETIMES FOR HOURS."
WILL YOU OPEN THEM NOW?
NO.
WHAT ABOUT N--
NO!! WHY WON'T YOU KIDS JUST DIE?!
COMIX

"THE PROBLEM WAS THEN THAT EVERY DRUG STORE AND PHARMACY DID NOT RECEIVE EVERY COPY OF EVERY COMIC BOOK TITLE. WE HAD TO SEARCH STORES ALL AROUND OUR TOWNS BY BIKE, SEARCHING FOR WHAT WE BELIEVED WERE MISSING DCs AND ALMOST UNLOCATABLE ACGs* OR GOLD KEYS."
(* AMERICAN COMICS GROUP (1943-1967), BEST KNOWN FOR HERBIE, "THE FAT FURY"...)
Drugs

JERSEY'S DRUGGISTS TREATED COMICS (AND THEIR FANS) AS AN ANNOYANCE BECAUSE THEIR LOW, KID-FRIENDLY COVER PRICE ENSURED A RAZOR-THIN PROFIT MARGIN. TO THE RETAILER THEY WERE A "PENNIES BUSINESS" LIKE CANDY, GUM, OR ANY OTHER IMPULSE ITEM.
10¢
CHOC
CHOC
CHOC
10¢
GUM
10¢
10¢
COMICS CO.
PUBLISHERS SOLD COMICS AT A DISCOUNT OFF THE COVER PRICE TO NEWSSTAND DISTRIBUTORS WHO THEN SOLD THEM AT A SLIGHTLY HIGHER COST TO INDIVIDUAL SHOPS AND STANDS IN BULK -- BY AMOUNT, NOT TITLE, AS USLAN DISCOVERED.
TRUCK CO.
TO ENCOURAGE BULK ORDERING, PUBLISHERS MADE THEIR TITLES RETURNABLE. A DEALER SIMPLY HAD TO TEAR THE COVER OFF A COMIC (TO SAVE ON SHIPPING COSTS) AND SEND IT TO THE DISTRIBUTOR TO PROVE IT WAS UNSOLD SO THEY COULD OBTAIN A REFUND.
THUS FINANCIAL RISK RESTED ENTIRELY ON THE PUBLISHER'S SHOULDERS -- HE HAD TO MAKE SURE HE HAD SUFFICIENT CASH FLOW ON HAND TO COVER ANY AND ALL RETURNS.
IN THOSE DAYS, IF LESS THAN 65% OF COPIES WERE RETURNED (A "35% SELL-THROUGH," IN CIRCULATION PARLANCE) YOUR COMIC WAS A HIT.
BUT THE SYSTEM WAS RIFE WITH FRAUD AND WASTE, PARTICULARLY ON THE DISTRIBUTOR END.
READ CO.
LOVE
SUPER
FUN
KOOL
COMICS WERE REPORTED AS UNSOLD JUST BECAUSE THEY DIDN'T FIT ON THAT WEEK'S TRUCK; COVERLESS COMICS WERE SUPPOSED TO BE DESTROYED, BUT OFTEN THEY WERE SOLD TO FLEA MARKETS WITHOUT PUBLISHERS RECEIVING A DIME.
YEAH... UH...WE DIDN'T SELL NO COMICS THIS WEEK!
DELL
HARVEY
GOLD KEY
WHERE'S MY MONEY?!

AN ENGLISH TEACHER FROM CONEY ISLAND WOULD CHANGE ALL THAT.
PHIL SEULING, A LIFELONG FAN AND DEALER IN BACK ISSUES, VISITED DC COMICS AROUND 1973 AND WAS HORRIFIED TO SEE A PILE OF RIPPED-OFF COVERS IN ONE CORNER. WHEN TOLD WHAT HAPPENED TO UNSOLD TITLES, HE KNEW HE COULD DO BETTER.
"THAT'S CRAZY! THESE ARE COLLECTIBLE!"
DC
WONDER WOMAN
BATMAN
AQUAMAN
FLASH
JUSTICE LEAGUE
NEW GODS
HAWKMAN
ACTION
SEULING FOUNDED SEA GATE DISTRIBUTION, DEDICATED SOLELY TO GETTING NEW COMICS TO THE FAN MARKET, BYPASSING THE NEWSSTANDS ALTOGETHER.
AT THE TIME, THERE WERE PERHAPS THIRTY STORES SPECIALIZING IN COMICS IN ALL OF NORTH AMERICA.
BUT SEULING MADE THE PUBLISHERS A DEAL THEY COULDN'T REFUSE: HE WOULD BUY TITLES DIRECTLY FROM THEM AT 60% OFF COVER PRICE, SAME AS THE REGULAR DISTRIBUTORS...
COMIX CO.
NERD CO.
SEAGATE DISTRO.
COMIX
BACK ISSUES
...BUT THESE COMICS WOULD BE NON-RETURNABLE. HE SHIFTED THE FINANCIAL RISK FROM THE PUBLISHERS ONTO THE RETAILER.
LOCKED AS HE WAS INTO THE FAN NETWORK, SEULING DIDN'T SEE THIS AS A PROBLEM. HE WAS CERTAIN HE COULD SELL EVERY SINGLE COMIC HE BOUGHT, BECAUSE NEW COMICS THAT DIDN'T MOVE WITHIN A FEW WEEKS OF PUBLICATION WOULD BE SAVED AND PUT INTO HIS BACK ISSUE BINS TO BE SOLD TO COLLECTORS.
THIS NEW DIRECT RETAILING MARKET WAS SUPERIOR TO THE OLD NEWSSTAND MODEL IN PRETTY MUCH EVERY WAY CONCEIVABLE.
FANS NO LONGER HAD TO SCOUR DRUG SHOPS AND TOBACCO STORES IN A DESPERATE SEARCH FOR SPECIFIC TITLES. INSTEAD, THEY COULD GO TO THE COMICS SHOP TO GET ANY TITLE THEY WANTED, AS SOON AS IT CAME OUT!
COMIX
HERBIE
DEPENDABILITY + CONVENIENCE + TIMELINESS = SUCCESS!
CAPITALISM WORKS!
A FEW OF THE NOTORIOUSLY MOBBED-UP NEWSSTAND DISTRIBUTORS DID NOT TAKE TOO KINDLY TO THESE UPPITY GEEKS HORNING IN ON THEIR TERRITORY. SAN DIEGO RETAILERS HAD THEIR TIRES SLASHED AND BRICKS SENT THROUGH THEIR WINDOWS.
BUT BY THE MID-1970s, DENVER-AREA RETAILER CHUCK ROZANSKI REPORTS, THE OLD-SCHOOL WHOLESALERS "DIDN'T REALLY CARE THAT MUCH ABOUT COMICS ANYWAY. THE WHOLE ECONOMICS OF THE DISTRIBUTION BUSINESS WERE CHANGING AND THEY WERE TOO FOCUSED ON SAVING THEIR CORE BUSINESS TO GO AFTER COMICS BUSINESS."
COMIX

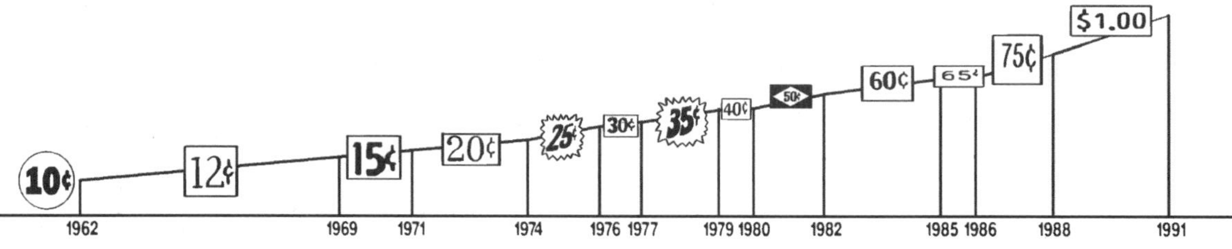
10¢
12¢
15¢
20¢
25¢
30¢
35¢
40¢
50¢
60¢
65¢
75¢
$1.00
1962
1969
1971
1974
1976
1977
1979
1980
1982
1985
1986
1988
1991

EVIDENCE OF THE NEWSSTAND'S GRADUAL ***DECLINE*** CAN BE TRACED THROUGH THE RISE IN COMICS' ***PRICE POINT.***

A ***"PENNIES BUSINESS"*** TURNS A PROFIT ONLY IF SOLD IN ***BULK.*** AS CIRCULATION ***DROPPED***, PUBLISHERS RAISED ***COVER PRICE*** TO MAKE UP THE LOSS IN REVENUE.

THE ***DIRECT MARKET*** ("DM") CAME ALONG JUST IN TIME TO ***SAVE*** THE INDUSTRY BY GIVING IT AN ALTERNATIVE, ***DEPENDABLE*** SOURCE OF CUSTOMERS.
MARVEL FULLY EMBRACED THE NEW RETAILING MODEL EARLY AND RELEASED ITS FIRST TITLE ***EXCLUSIVE*** TO THE DM, ***DAZZLER***, IN 1981. THE FIRST ISSUE SOLD ***400,000*** COPIES WHILE DC'S TOP SELLER ***SUPERMAN*** SOLD JUST ***235,000*** A FEW YEARS BEFORE ON THE NEWSSTANDS!
THE DIRECT MARKET WOULD GROW BY ***DOUBLE DIGITS*** EVERY ***YEAR*** FOR THE NEXT ***TWO DECADES.*** THE NUMBER OF COMICS SHOPS GREW FROM ***700*** IN THE 1970s TO ***3,000*** BY THE BEGINNING OF THE 1980s.
COMIX

WHOLE ***PUBLISHERS*** WERE CREATED JUST TO MEET ***DEMAND***. WEST COAST DISTRIBUTORS STEVE AND BILL SCHANES STARTED BRINGING OUT THEIR OWN TITLES UNDER THE ***PACIFIC COMICS*** IMPRINT "BECAUSE THERE WAS NOT ENOUGH PRODUCT FOR OUR ***STORES.***"
PACIFIC'S FIRST COMIC WAS ***CAPTAIN VICTORY AND THE GALACTIC RANGERS*** BY PERENNIAL PIONEER ***JACK KIRBY***, WHOSE POPULARITY HAD ***WANED*** ON THE NEWSSTAND... BUT STILL APPEALED TO THE ***OLDER FANS*** WHO FREQUENTED THE SPECIALTY SHOPS!
IT'S SAFE TO ***COME OUT***, JACK! THE NATIVES OF THE PLANET NERDIA ARE ***FRIENDLY!***
(...ALBEIT ***SOCIALLY AWKWARD...***)

NEW TALENT ALSO FLOURISHED IN THE SPECIALTY SHOPS--THANKS TO THE ECONOMIC SECURITY PROVIDED BY SUPER HERO FAN DOLLARS, RETAILERS WERE ABLE TO SUPPORT THE POST-PACIFIC WAVE OF ***INDEPENDENT PUBLISHERS*** LIKE FANTAGRAPHICS, FIRST AND ECLIPSE.

SELF-PUBLISHERS LIKE ***CEREBUS' DAVE SIM*** AND ***ELFQUEST'S RICHARD & WENDY PINI*** ALSO THRIVED IN ONE OF THE ***FEW*** INDUSTRIES WHERE TALENTED AND DEDICATED ***INDIVIDUALS*** COULD AFFORD TO PUT OUT THEIR OWN WORK TO A LARGE, BUILT-IN AUDIENCE--IN THE DM!

THE MOST SUCCESSFUL SELF-PUBLISHERS OF THIS ERA WERE ***KEVIN EASTMAN*** AND ***PETER LAIRD***, WHOSE FRANK MILLER PARODY ***TEENAGE MUTANT NINJA TURTLES*** PREMIERED AS A HUMBLE BLACK AND WHITE COMIC IN THE DIRECT MARKET IN 1984 AND WENT ON, THANKS TO THE BUSINESS ACUMEN OF THEIR SHREWD ***LICENSING AGENT***, TO BECOME A LUDICROUSLY SUCCESSFUL MULTIMEDIA FRANCHISE THAT MADE THEIR CREATORS ***MILLIONAIRES.***

THE UNEXPECTED POPULARITY OF *TEENAGE MUTANT NINJA TURTLES* CAUSED A RUN OF ***SPECULATION*** IN THE BACK ISSUE MARKET.

AS A SMALL SELF-PUBLISHED BOOK *TMNT* HAD A LIMITED PRINT RUN WHICH ***SOLD OUT*** RAPIDLY -- AND SO ***BACK ISSUES*** PRIZED BY COLLECTORS RATED ***HIGH PRICES***.

TURTLES
X MEN
WOW

RETAILERS BEGAN BUYING UP MORE AND MORE B&W INDEPENDENT BOOKS THAN EVER BEFORE -- THEN MARKED UP THE ***COVER PRICE*** IN THE HOPES SPECULATORS MIGHT THINK THEY'D BE THE NEXT ***TURTLES***. CREATORS AND PUBLISHERS WERE HAPPY TO OBLIGE BY ***FLOODING*** THE MARKET WITH AS MANY B&W TITLES AS THEY COULD -- THE VAST MAJORITY ***UNREADABLE DREK.***

AN INDY BOOK THAT MIGHT ENJOY A PRINT RUN OF 10,000 COPIES IN 1984 SHOT UP TO ***100,000*** IN 1986!

CRAP
BLEH
YECH MEN
TURD VERINE
STINK
CRUD
DUM
LAME
NO
WHAT
PUKE
MEH
DUH.

IT WAS A CLASSIC ***ECONOMIC BUBBLE*** IN ACTION: AN ISOLATED SUCCESS CAUSES A ***MISPERCEPTION*** OF DEMAND AND AN ***OVER-ABUNDANCE*** OF SUPPLY.

DEMAND DROPPED OFF SIGNIFICANTLY ONCE THE GULF IN ***QUALITY*** BETWEEN *TMNT* AND THE KNOCKOFFS BECAME ***CLEAR***.

UNDER THE OLD ***NEWSSTAND*** REGIME, ***NO PROBLEM***: JUST TEAR THE COVERS OFF THE UNSOLD PRODUCT AND RETURN THEM TO THE DISTRIBUTOR FOR A FULL REFUND!

BUT THE ENTIRE DIRECT MARKET IS BASED ON ***NON-RETURNABILITY***. THE RETAILER ***ATE*** WHATEVER HE COULDN'T SELL.

BY 1989, ALMOST ALL OF THE PUBLISHERS CREATED TO CASH IN ON THE B&W BOOM HAD GONE UNDER, TAKING MANY DISTRIBUTORS AND SPECIALTY SHOPS WITH THEM.

"THE BLACK AND WHITE BUST" WAS THE WORST CALAMITY TO HIT THE DIRECT MARKET...

...AT THE TIME.

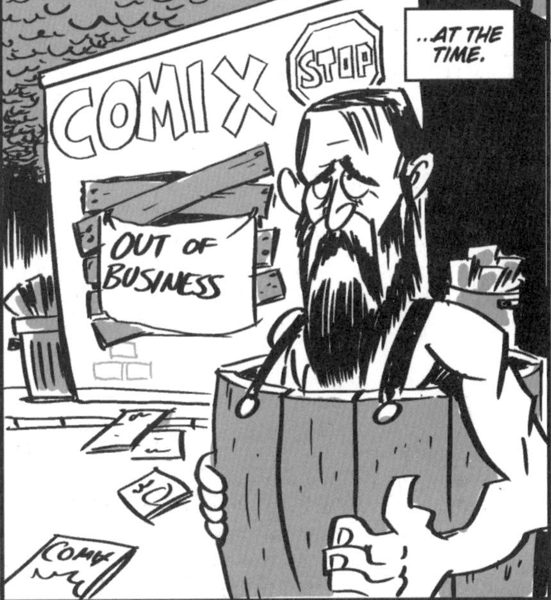

COMIX
STOP
OUT OF BUSINESS

MARKET INSTABILITY RATTLED MARVEL CORPORATE PARENT NEW WORLD ENTERTAINMENT, WHICH IN 1989 SOLD THE PUBLISHER AND ITS LIBRARY OF CHARACTERS TO INVESTOR RONALD O. PERELMAN, THE NOTORIOUS "WIZARD OF WALL STREET."
IN CLASSIC CORPORATE RAIDER STYLE, PERELMAN DOUBLED MARVEL'S NET INCOME BY LAYING OFF WORKERS AND SLASHING DIVISIONS, ENSURING A LUCRATIVE INITIAL PUBLIC OFFERING IN JULY 1991.
M

PERELMAN LEVERAGED MARVEL'S HIGH STOCK PRICE TO ISSUE A STAGGERING $900 MILLION IN HIGH-YIELD DEBT BONDS -- BETTER KNOWN AS JUNK BONDS -- TO LINE HIS OWN POCKETS, BYPASSING THE COMPANY ALTOGETHER.
THE WIZARD MADE SURE THE MARVEL BONDS WERE "ZERO COUPON" -- WHICH MEANT PERELMAN DIDN'T HAVE TO PAY A DIME IN INTEREST TO HOLDERS UP TO FIVE YEARS AFTER ISSUANCE -- BUT ON THE BOND'S FINAL MATURITY DATE, THE FULL SUM OF MONEY OWED WOULD HAVE TO BE PAID!
BOND
BOND

PERELMAN COVERED THE AMOUNT HE OWED HIS FIRST WAVE OF INVESTORS WITH A SECOND ISSUANCE OF JUNK BONDS!
BUT THIS HIGH-STAKES PONZI SCHEME ONLY WORKED IF MARVEL'S STOCK PRICE REMAINED SKY-HIGH!
MEMO
$

SUCH WAS THE CORPORATE CLIMATE IN DECEMBER 1991, WHEN MARVEL'S TOP THREE ARTISTS -- JIM (X-MEN) LEE, ROB (X-FORCE) LIEFELD AND TODD (SPIDER-MAN) MCFARLANE --
-- MARCHED INTO PRESIDENT TERRY STEWART'S OFFICE AND DEMANDED CREATIVE CONTROL OF THEIR MARVEL OUTPUT IN THE FORM OF A NEW LINE OF COMICS THEY OWNED OR THEY WOULD WALK.

FROM THE ARTISTS' PERSPECTIVE, THE DEMAND WAS A NATURAL OUTGROWTH OF THE CREATORS' RIGHTS MOVEMENT INSPIRED BY JACK KIRBY'S STRUGGLE TO GET HIS ARTWORK BACK THE DECADE BEFORE.
FROM THE CORPORATE STANDPOINT, THE REQUEST WAS NOTHING SHORT OF DISASTROUS. STEWART KNEW THAT IF THE ARTISTS WERE TAKEN OFF POPULAR MARVEL TITLES TO DO THEIR OWN BOOKS, IT SPELLED A HUGE LOSS IN REVENUE -- AND STOCK PRICE.
HE ALLEGEDLY TRIED TO DISSUADE THEM FROM THEIR COURSE OF ACTION BY MAKING SURE THEY FELT REPLACEABLE WITH AN UNFORTUNATE ANALOGY:
"THERE'LL ALWAYS BE SOMEBODY TO PICK THE COTTON!"
?
THE ARTISTS PROMPTLY LEFT WHAT MCFARLANE DUBBED "THE PLANTATION" TO FORM THEIR OWN PUBLISHER, IMAGE COMICS.
(IN FACT, MANY OF THEM PLANNED THIS FROM THE VERY BEGINNING, CORRECTLY PREDICTING THEIR ULTIMATUM WOULD BE ONE MARVEL COULDN'T ACCEPT.)

OWNING NO CHARACTERS OR INTELLECTUAL PROPERTY OTHER THAN THEIR "I" LOGO, IMAGE BEGAN PUBLISHING MCFARLANE'S SPAWN, LEE'S WILDC.A.T.S. AND LIEFELD'S YOUNGBLOOD IN 1992 TO HUGE SUCCESS.
READERS FOLLOWED THEIR FAVORITE ARTISTS FROM MARVEL TO IMAGE--ALMOST OVERNIGHT MARVEL'S MARKET SHARE DROPPED FIFTEEN PERCENT!

TO KEEP MARVEL'S STOCK PRICE LOFTY, PERELMAN'S PEOPLE LAUNCHED AN ORGY OF ACQUISITIONS WITH FUNDS BORROWED FROM A SYNDICATE OF BANKS LED BY CHASE MANHATTAN.
THE COMPANY GOT HEAVILY INTO THE SPORTS CARD MARKET BY BUYING FLEER CORPORATION (#2 IN THE WORLD NEXT TO TOPPS) FOR $286 MILLION IN JULY 1992...
...THEN DOUBLED-DOWN IN 1995 BY PURCHASING SKYBOX INTERNATIONAL, KNOWN FOR ITS NBA CARDS, FOR $150 MILLION.

SUDDENLY, NEW PLAYERS ENTERED THE DIRECT MARKET -- TRADING CARD RETAILERS WHO SAW A DEMAND FOR A DIFFERENT COLLECTIBLE FROM THEIR CUSTOMERS, LURED BY THE BUZZ SURROUNDING IMAGE.
THE NUMBER OF RETAILERS BALLOONED TO NEARLY TEN THOUSAND BY MID-1993!
SPORTS CARDS
& COMICS
A's

A GLOSSY FAN MAGAZINE, WIZARD, LAUNCHED IN 1991 AND BECAME THE VOICE OF THE NEW, SPECULATION-DRIVEN INDUSTRY, HYPING "HOT" ARTISTS AND CHARTING THE MONTH-TO-MONTH VALUE OF BACK ISSUES WITH A MONTHLY PRICE GUIDE.
THE WIZARD/IMAGE-FUELED SPECULATOR CRAZE OF 1992-4 WAS THE BLACK & WHITE BOOM ON STEROIDS. IMAGE COMICS' FIRST FEW TITLES HAD PRINT RUNS IN THE MILLIONS, AS SPECULATORS BOUGHT MULTIPLE COPIES FOR INVESTMENTS.
SPAWN
DO I HEAR TWO-FIFTY?
I'LL GIVE YOU TWO THOUSAND!!

BUT IMAGE'S FOUNDERS QUICKLY FELL VICTIM TO THEIR OWN SUCCESS. THEIR OWN BOSSES NOW, THERE WAS NO ONE TO FORCE THEM TO KEEP WORKING, AND THE DEADLINE BEAST BEGAN TO DEVOUR THEM.
IN APRIL 1993 -- ONE YEAR AFTER IMAGE BEGAN PUBLISHING -- ELEVEN OUT OF THIRTEEN SOLICITED TITLES FAILED TO SHIP ON TIME!

THE LONGER CUSTOMERS HAD TO WAIT FOR A GIVEN TITLE, THE MORE THEIR INTEREST WANED, AND SALES SUFFERED. DITTO WHEN LESS POPULAR ARTISTS WERE USED TO FILL IN FOR THE IMAGE FOUNDERS TO MEET DEADLINES. INNUMERABLE GIMMICKS LIKE MULTIPLE VARIANT COVERS CONTRIBUTED TO THE GLUT OF UNWANTED, UNRETURNABLE BOOKS ON THE STANDS!
SPORTS CARDS
OUT OF BUSINESS
IF ONLY THERE WAS SOME SORT OF HISTORICAL PRECEDENT THAT COULD HAVE WARNED ME AHEAD OF TIME!!

SENSING ***WEAKNESS*** IN IMAGE, PERELMAN BOUGHT MARVEL ITS OWN DISTRIBUTOR, THE NEW JERSEY-BASED ***HEROES WORLD*** (EST. 1989), IN DECEMBER 1994.

MARVEL SOON ANNOUNCED ITS COMICS WOULD BE DISTRIBUTED ***SOLELY*** BY HEROES WORLD, WHICH WOULD CARRY ***NO OTHER*** PUBLISHER'S TITLES.

HEROES WORLD

THE COMPANY WAS, IN ESSENCE, TRYING TO CREATE A ***MONOPOLY***, SQUEEZING OUT ALL OTHER COMPETITORS UNTIL IT DOMINATED THE DIRECT MARKET ***ALONE!***

THE ANNOUNCEMENT CAUSED SEVERAL DOMINOS TO FALL IN ***DEVASTATING*** SEQUENCE.

IN APRIL 1995, DC ANNOUNCED ITS OWN EXCLUSIVE RELATIONSHIP WITH BALTIMORE'S ***DIAMOND DISTRIBUTION***, ONE OF AMERICA'S LARGEST.

TAKING THE TWO BIGGEST COMPANIES (AND THE SALES THEY GENERATED) OFF THE TABLE ***DOOMED*** THE OTHER DISTRIBUTORS. FROM A HIGH OF ***SIXTEEN*** AT THE ZENITH OF THE DIRECT MARKET, THEY BEGAN DROPPING LIKE FLIES.

DC

EVEN WORSE, MARVEL'S TRANSITION TO EXCLUSIVE HEROES WORLD DISTRIBUTION, WHICH TOOK EFFECT JULY 1995, WAS A COMPLETE ***FIASCO.***

THE STAFF OF THE (FORMERLY) SMALL, REGIONAL HEROES WORLD WAS COMPLETELY ***OVERWHELMED*** BY GOING NATIONAL OVERNIGHT WITH MARVEL PRODUCT, WHICH RESULTED IN LATE, FORGOTTEN AND BUNGLED ORDERS.

THE DISTRIBUTION SCHEME HAD THE EXACT ***OPPOSITE*** OF ITS INTENDED EFFECT: MARVEL'S MARKET SHARE DROPPED TO AN UNTHINKABLE ***18.88%*** OF THE DM BY MAY 1996!

HEROES

THE PANIC COULDN'T HAVE COME AT A ***WORSE*** TIME. PAPER AND INK PRICES ***JUMPED*** AT THE WHOLESALE LEVEL IN 1995.

THE SPORTS CARD BUSINESS WAS ***TANKING*** -- BASEBALL CARDS, THE MOST ***POPULAR*** GENRE, WERE ALL BUT ***SLAIN*** BY FAN FURY AT THE 1994 ***PLAYERS' STRIKE***, WHICH HALTED MLB'S SEASON.

HEROES

THE CRUSHING LICENSING FEES SKYBOX HAD TO PAY THE NBA -- ALMOST ***$15 MILLION*** A YEAR -- RESULTED IN LOSSES FOR ***THAT*** DIVISION AS WELL.

THE DIRECT MARKET SUFFERED THE COLLAPSE OF SPORTS CARDS, THE SPECULATOR MARKET AND ITS DISTRIBUTION SYSTEM ***BACK-TO-BACK-TO-BACK***, AND THE EFFECT WAS NOTHING SHORT OF ***APOCALYPTIC***.

FROM A HEIGHT OF ***9,400*** IN 1993, THE NUMBER OF DIRECT MARKET RETAILERS DROPPED TO ***4,500*** BY MID-1996 -- NEARLY ***55%*** CLOSED THEIR DOORS DURING A ***THREE YEAR PERIOD***, NEVER TO RETURN.

PLUMMETING REVENUE JEOPARDIZED PERELMAN'S JUNK BOND EMPIRE. AT LAST, THE SYNDICATE OF BANKS THAT HAD BEEN THE WIZARD'S PRIMARY LENDERS DEMANDED A ***RECKONING***.

ON DECEMBER 27, 1996, MARVEL ENTERTAINMENT GROUP FILED FOR ***BANKRUPTCY*** IN FEDERAL COURT.

IN 1997, HEROES WORLD QUIETLY WENT OUT OF BUSINESS AND MARVEL SIGNED WITH DIAMOND DISTRIBUTION, THE ***SOLE REMAINING*** COMPANY IN THE BUSINESS OF DELIVERING COMIC BOOKS TO THE DIRECT MARKET.

IRONICALLY, IT WAS ONE OF PERELMAN'S MUCH-DERIDED ACQUISITIONS THAT ULTIMATELY SAVED MARVEL.
TOY BIZ
IN 1993, MARVEL TRADED WITH TOY BIZ THE EXCLUSIVE RIGHT TO MAKE TOYS BASED ON ITS CHARACTERS IN EXCHANGE FOR A 46% EQUITY STAKE IN THE MANUFACTURER.

TOY BIZ OWNER IKE PERLMUTTER OUTMANEUVERED PERELMAN AND ANOTHER WALL STREET HEAVY-WEIGHT, CARL ICAHN, WITH A RESTRUCTURING PLAN THE COURTS AND MARVEL'S CREDITORS COULD AGREE TO: IN ESSENCE, TOY BIZ ABSORBED THE BIGGER COMPANY!
THE TOY BIZ TEAM TURNED MARVEL AROUND, BEGAN MAKING THEIR OWN MOVIES BASED ON MARVEL CHARACTERS (STARTING WITH 2008'S IRON MAN) AND SOLD THE NEW, IMPROVED COMPANY TO DISNEY IN 2010!

CAN AI HAV
INTERNETZ COMMIX PLEEZE?

AT THE SAME TIME THE COMICS DISTRIBUTION WARS PLAYED THEMSELVES OUT, THE ***INTERNET*** WAS GAINING IN UBIQUITY -- AND ***BANDWIDTH***.

FANS WHO HAD BEEN TRADING FAVORITE COVERS AND/OR PANELS ON-LINE SOON HAD THE CAPACITY TO UPLOAD MUCH ***LARGER*** IMAGE FILES.

THE SCANNING OF ***COMPLETE*** COMICS BEGAN IN EARNEST AROUND ***1998*** WHEN SOMEONE WITH THE APT USERNAME OF ***"COMIX4ALL"*** POSTED AN ENTIRE ISSUE OF JOE LINSNER'S INDY COMIC HIT *CRY FOR DAWN* FOR FREE DOWNLOAD ON THE USENET NEWSGROUP *ALT.BINARIES.PICTURES.COMICS*.

THE ***MASS*** SCANNING OF COMICS STARTED ***INNOCENTLY*** ENOUGH. AT FIRST FANS ONLY SCANNED IN ***OUT-OF-PRINT*** BACK ISSUES TO SHARE WITH THEIR FRIENDS. A SMALL NETWORK OF SCANNERS ON THE IRC SERVER CHAT CHANNEL ***#COMICBOOKS*** AMASSED AN ***ENTIRE RUN*** OF MARVEL'S *DEFENDERS* THIS WAY.

COMIC
TO SCAN
EVERY COMIC EVER
THEY HAD CERTAIN RULES -- THERE WERE MANY RETAILERS AMONG THE EARLY SCANNERS, BELIEVE IT OR NOT -- AND THEY RECOMMENDED WAITING A YEAR TO SCAN IN NEW COMICS SO AS TO NOT CUT INTO STORES' PROFITS.

ONE OF THE SCANNERS WAS A FIXTURE IN COMICS' ***LETTER COLUMNS*** AND ALLEGEDLY TOLD A DC COMICS STAFFER ABOUT HIS ACTIVITIES WHILE ON A TOUR OF THE OFFICES.

THE STAFFER TOLD HIM (OR SO THE STORY ***GOES***) THAT DC WAS ***AWARE*** OF THE PRACTICE ALREADY, BUT DIDN'T ***CARE*** BECAUSE PEOPLE WERE SCANNING IN BOOKS THE COMPANY WOULD NEVER REPRINT ***ANYWAY***.

"(WHEN) SAID LETTER HACK/SCANNER ADVISED (THE OTHER SCANNERS) OF THIS, WE ALL THOUGHT, ***'OKAY! FULL SPEED AHEAD!'***" ONE EARLY SCANNER WROTE US. "WE FIGURED IF THEY ***WANTED*** US TO STOP THEY'D ***SAY*** SO."

AN FTP SITE CALLED THE ***CCA*** -- THE ***COMICS COPYING AUTHORITY*** -- BEGAN POSTING FREE DOWNLOADS OF COMICS ***THREE MONTHS OLD***.

ARRRRRRH! THESE BE SCANNABLE!
NEW THIS WEEK

RAWK
TEAM
COMIC SHOP
COMIX
COMIX
COMIX
BUT ONCE THE BIT TORRENT FILE FORMAT BECAME THE PREVALENT PEER-TO-PEER FILE SHARING PROTOCOL AFTER ITS INITIAL IMPLEMENTATION IN 2001, NEW COMICS WERE APPEARING FOR FREE ONLINE THE DAY THEY CAME OUT -- OR EARLIER, IF THE SCANNER HAD ACCESS TO COMICS BEFORE RETAILERS RACKED THEM.
TODAY, ONE CAN EASILY DOWNLOAD AN ENTIRE COMICS SHOP'S WORTH OF NEW TITLES FOR FREE IN A MATTER OF MINUTES AT ANY NUMBER OF TORRENT SITES.

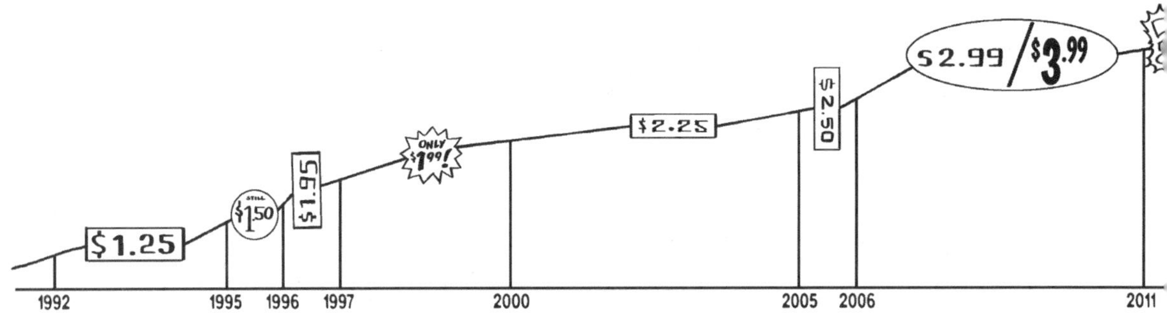
$1.25
STILL $1.50
$1.95
ONLY $1.99!
$2.25
$2.50
$2.99 / $3.99
1992
1995
1996
1997
2000
2005
2006
2011

MEANWHILE, COMICS' CIRCULATION HAS CONTINUED TO ***DROP*** AND PRICE POINT HAS CONTINUED TO ***RISE.***

THE DEMOGRAPHIC MOST SUPER HERO COMICS APPEAL TO -- YOUNG MEN BETWEEN THE AGES OF 18 TO 34 -- ARE THOSE ***HARDEST HIT*** BY THE GREAT RECESSION WHICH BEGAN IN 2007, WITH UNEMPLOYMENT RATES ***DOUBLE*** THE NATIONAL AVERAGE.
THE EXPENSE AND COMMITMENT TO A SHARED UNIVERSE -- NEEDING TO FOLLOW MULTIPLE TITLES SIMULTANEOUSLY, BUYING THEM THE WEDNESDAY THEY COME OUT SO ONE CAN TALK ABOUT THEM ONLINE INSTANTLY...
FOOD
COMICS

...MEANS THAT, IN MANY WAYS, AMERICAN SUPER HERO COMICS ARE THE ***PERFECT PIRATABLE MEDIUM!***
DEPENDABILITY + CONVENIENCE + TIMELINESS = SUCCESS!
+ FREE!
PIRACY WORKS!
HERBIE
AS WIDESPREAD AS DIGITAL PIRACY IS IN ***HERO*** COMICS, IN JAPANESE MANGA IT'S PRACTICALLY ***INSTITUTIONALIZED.***
"SCANLATORS" UPLOAD ENGLISH VERSIONS OF THE LATEST MANGA AS SOON AS THEY HIT JAPANESE STANDS, WELL BEFORE THEY REACH THE U.S. LEGALLY.
INDUSTRY ***BOOKSCAN*** DATA SHOWS A MASSIVE ***DROPOFF*** IN MANGA SALES IN THE U.S. STARTING AROUND THE END OF 2007 -- AT THE SAME TIME SCANLATION SITES EXPLODED IN POPULARITY.

MANGA PUBLISHERS HAVE AGGRESSIVELY PURSUED CRIMINAL COMPLAINTS AGAINST DIGITAL PIRATES -- BUT ONLY ***IN*** JAPAN.
THE COPYRIGHT HOLDERS HAVE LARGELY IGNORED ENGLISH-LANGUAGE SCANLATION, LEADING TO PSEUDO-***LEGITIMATE*** STATUS. TO ANYONE WHO VISITS PIRATE AGGREGATE SITES LIKE *ONE MANGA* OR *MANGA FOX*, THERE'S NOTHING ABOUT THEM THAT SEEMS THE LEAST BIT ***ILLICIT.***
AMERICAN MANGA PUBLISHERS CLAIM THEY HAVE HAD TO CUT BACK ON TITLES BECAUSE THEY CANNOT COMPETE WITH THE SCANLATORS.
(THOUGH PUBLISHERS' ***CRITICS*** CLAIM THAT MARKET WAS ALREADY ***SATURATED*** TO BEGIN WITH.)

COMIX
ARRRRH! LIES!! YE CAN'T PROVE PIRACY HAS HAD ANY IMPACT ON COMICS SALES!
I TELLS YE LUBBERS, ME TORRENTS BE THE NEW "SPINNER RACK" -- BRINGING IN THE CASUAL READER WHO CAN'T GET TO OR IS TURNED OFF BY A COMIC BOOK STORE!
AND THAT MAY VERY WELL BE TRUE...
...BUT TO WHAT DEGREE?

A YOUNGER GENERATION IS GROWING UP HAVING FIRST EXPERIENCED COMICS THROUGH FREE ILLEGAL DOWNLOADS.
OBVIOUSLY, THOUGH, SOMEWHERE ALONG THE SUPPLY CHAIN, SOMEBODY HAS TO BE ACTUALLY PAYING FOR THIS STUFF.
WE LIVE IN A CAPITALIST SOCIETY. MEDIA DOESN'T GROW ON TREES.
DVD
COMIX
POPULAR CULTURE THAT DOESN'T MAKE MONEY CEASES TO EXIST.

EVEN IF, AS PIRATES CLAIM, THEY MOSTLY PIRATE WHAT THEY PROBABLY WOULDN'T BUY OR USE TORRENTS JUST TO SAMPLE COMICS THEY MAY BUY IN THE FUTURE...
...THE DIRECT MARKET ISN'T THE MUSIC INDUSTRY OR HOLLYWOOD. A NICHE MARKET RUNNING A PENNIES BUSINESS FEELS ANY LOSS IN REVENUE, NO MATTER HOW SLIGHT, NO MATTER WHAT THE SOURCE.
THOUGH NO STATISTICS CAN BE PRODUCED TO PROVE PIRACY IS HAVING A NEGATIVE IMPACT ON THE DM--
--THE CONTINUING DECLINE OF DM SALES WOULD INDICATE IT'S NOT HAVING MUCH OF A POSITIVE IMPACT, EITHER.
MOM POP

COMICS-LOVERS ARE SUSCEPTIBLE TO THE MYTH OF THE "VAST UNTAPPED AUDIENCE." IF PUBLISHERS JUST SPENT ENOUGH ON ADVERTISING AND/OR PUT EVERY TITLE ONLINE IMMEDIATELY THE MONEY WOULD JUST START ROLLING IN.
READ COMIX!
I HAVE THIS SUDDEN URGE TO READ WOLVERINE FOR SOME REASON...
CX8 COMIX TOWN EXPRESS
READ COMIX!!!
BUT IF PIRATES' LOGIC IS CORRECT, AND THEY'RE BRINGING NEW, PAYING READERS INTO THE INDUSTRY, GIVEN THE MILLIONS OF COMICS DOWNLOADED FOR FREE DAILY...
...WHY HAVEN'T WE SEEN A SIGNIFICANT UPSWING IN COMICS SALES ALREADY?
P.R. TIMES

THOUGH PUBLISHERS WERE SLOW TO EMBRACE LEGITIMATE ON-LINE DISTRIBUTION, BY 2011 THE SALE OF DIGITAL COMICS TRIPLED TO $25 MILLION ANNUALLY!
THE MOVEMENT TO DIGITAL RETAILING HAS, IN ALL OTHER MEDIA, NEARLY CRIPPLED THE BRICK-AND-MORTAR VERSION.
SEE YOU NEXT WEEK!
GULP!
BOX OFFICE RENTAL
DISC JOCKEY
ARCADE
BEST BOOKS
COMIX TOWN
IS IT REALISTIC TO EXPECT COMIC BOOK STORES TO BE THE EXCEPTION?
CAN THE DIRECT MARKET SURVIVE? AND, PERHAPS MORE IMPORTANTLY ...
...SHOULD IT SURVIVE?

TO THE DIRECT MARKET'S ***CRITICS***, ITS STRUGGLES ARE SIMPLY ***CHICKENS COMING HOME TO ROOST***-- THE INEVITABLE RESULT OF ABANDONING ***CASUAL*** READERS IN ITS ***RETREAT*** TO THE GEEKS-ONLY ***FAN*** MARKET.

DO YOU HAVE STRANGERS IN PARADI-- AAHHH!!

NO SALE

AAAGH! A GIRL!

GET YOUR DIRTY PILLOWS OUT OF MY STORE!!

TITS

BOOBS

MORE TITS

BUTT

BUT THAT RETREAT WAS OUT OF ***NECESSITY*** FOLLOWING THE COLLAPSE OF THE NEWSSTAND MARKET. THE DM (AND ***SUPER HERO DOLLARS***) REMAINS THE ECONOMIC ENGINE THAT FUELS THE ***ENTIRE*** INDUSTRY, MAINSTREAM AND INDEPENDENT ALIKE. IF IT ***FAILS***, AN ENTIRELY ***NEW*** DISTRIBUTION PARADIGM, DIGITAL OR OTHERWISE, MUST ARISE TO TAKE ITS PLACE.

IT'S DOUBTFUL THE COMICS RETAILER CAN FLOURISH WITH THE SAME "PENNIES BUSINESS" MODEL THAT DRUGGISTS AND NEWSIES BEGAN IN 1933.
AND UNLESS THE VAST, UNTAPPED AUDIENCE CHOOSES TO GRACE US WITH ITS PRESENCE, IT'S HARD TO SEE HOW ENOUGH COMICS CAN SELL IN BULK AT THE DIGITAL-FRIENDLY $0.99 PRICE POINT TO SUPPORT AN ENTIRE INDUSTRY.

ONE ALTERNATIVE COULD BE SWITCHING TO A "NO PENNIES BUSINESS."
COMIC
A FEW ONLINE CARTOONISTS HAVE FOUND FINANCIAL SUCCESS OFFERING THEIR POPULAR WEBCOMICS FOR FREE TO THE PUBLIC, MAKING ALL THEIR MONEY ON ADVERTISING AND MERCHANDISING.
MATTHEW INMAN, CREATOR OF ONE OF THE MOST POPULAR ONLINE STRIPS, THE OATMEAL, TOLD THE ECONOMIST IN 2010 THAT HE GROSSES AN AVERAGE OF $1,000 A DAY FROM MERCH SALES... HE MADE $70,000 OVER ONE THANKSGIVING WEEKEND!
CREATORS FLYING SOLO HAVE LOW OVERHEAD: INMAN ONLY HAS TO PAY HIMSELF AND THE HANDFUL OF PART-TIMERS HE HIRED TO FILL ORDERS.

PIRATE SITES GROSS THOUSANDS MONTHLY BY SELLING ADVERTISING -- PERHAPS LEGIT PUBLISHERS CAN GET SOME OF THIS ACTION BY BECOMING TORRENTERS THEMSELVES, CUTTING OUT THE SCANNERS AND OFFERING THEIR COMICS AS FREE DOWNLOADABLE FILES WITH ADS EMBEDDED RIGHT IN THE PAGES!
OF COURSE, PIRATE SITES PROFIT THIS WAY BECAUSE THEY HAVE NO OVERHEAD. (THAT'S THE MAIN ADVANTAGE TO STEALING STUFF.) TO PAY EVERYONE THEY NEED TO, PUBLISHERS MUST HAVE MULTIPLE REVENUE STREAMS...
Gulf
at&t
Ford
Arby's
Wii

...INCLUDING PRINT, AND THIS IS WHERE THE DM COMES IN.
ANOTHER WAY OF REJECTING THE "PENNIES BUSINESS" IS TO STOP THINKING OF COMICS AS DISPOSABLE OR SOMETHING TO RUSH TO READ IMMEDIATELY ON THE WEDNESDAY THEY COME OUT, BUT RATHER AS PHYSICAL ARTIFACTS... WITH THE PRICE POINT TO MATCH.
THIS HAS ALREADY BEGUN WITH THE GRAPHIC NOVEL REVOLUTION -- AND THE PEOPLE MOST QUALIFIED TO SELL THESE BOOKS ARE THE RETAILERS OF THE DM.

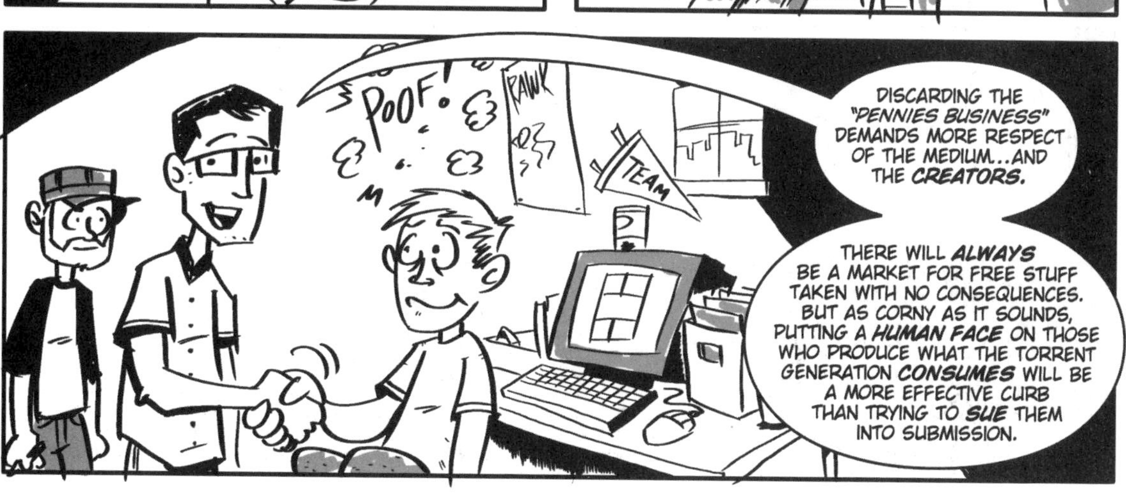
POOF!
RAWK
TEAM
DISCARDING THE "PENNIES BUSINESS" DEMANDS MORE RESPECT OF THE MEDIUM...AND THE CREATORS.
THERE WILL ALWAYS BE A MARKET FOR FREE STUFF TAKEN WITH NO CONSEQUENCES. BUT AS CORNY AS IT SOUNDS, PUTTING A HUMAN FACE ON THOSE WHO PRODUCE WHAT THE TORRENT GENERATION CONSUMES WILL BE A MORE EFFECTIVE CURB THAN TRYING TO SUE THEM INTO SUBMISSION.

WOULD-BE SAGES HAVE BEEN TRUMPETING THE *"DEATH OF COMICS"* SINCE ***1955***.

BUT AS LONG AS WRITERS & ARTISTS WANT TO TELL STORIES THROUGH PICTURES, THE MEDIUM WILL ***NEVER*** DIE.

THE END IS HERE!

WILL FIGHT CRIME FOR "EXPOSURE"

THE ***DIVERSITY*** OF THE COMICS MEDIUM IN THE MODERN ERA -- ***UNTHINKABLE*** WITHOUT THE DIRECT MARKET -- MAY ***SAVE*** IT! COMICS ARE NOW PRODUCED FOR ALL INTERESTS -- AT ALL ***AGES!***

THE END IS HERE!

PRE-READERS USE WORDLESS GRAPHIC NOVELS TO IMPROVE VERBAL NARRATIVE SKILLS!
YOU TELL ME THE STORY...
OKAY... WELL... THE GIRL AND HER DOG ARE GOING UP THE HILL...
GOOD! AND WHAT HAPPENS NEXT...?
KORGI

WE THINK VISUALLY. COMICS REINFORCE PROCESS, AS IN THE DECODING OF SYMBOLS REQUIRED FOR LITERACY.
R-A-T-T-H-I-N-G...

THE NEW "SPINNER RACK" MAY IN FACT BE THE SCHOOLS THEMSELVES AS MORE AND MORE TEACHERS ENTHUSIASTICALLY EMBRACE THE MEDIUM!
PLATO'S THEORY OF FORMS...IT'S KIND OF LIKE A MOVIE THEATER!
I THINK I GOT IT, NOW!
ACTION
PHILOS

THE FUTURE FOR COMICS -- ONLINE, IN THE DM, ARTISTICALLY, AND COMMERICALLY -- WILL BE SET BY THIS UP-AND-COMING GENERATION!
PERSEPOLIS
PERSEPOLIS
PERSEPOLIS

...AND WE CAN'T
WAIT TO SEE
WHAT COMES
NEXT!
NEW

NOTES ON SOURCES

A MORE EXTENSIVE, HYPERLINKED VERSION OF THESE NOTES MAY BE FOUND AT HTTP://WWW.EVILTWINCOMICS.COM/CBC_NOTES.HTML

"Funnies Get Famous"

The designation of October 18, 1896 as the date of the tectonic shift in comic art comes from Bill Blackbeard and Martin Williams, Eds. *The Smithsonian Collection of Newspaper Comics.* Washington: Smithsonian Institution Press & Harry N. Abrams, Inc., 1977. 14. All events cited on Page 1 were gleaned from the October 19, 1896 *New York Times.* See also RC Harvey. *Children of the Yellow Kid: The Evolution of the American Comic Strip.* Seattle: Frye Art Museum, 1998. 13, 17-20.

Schon vs. Luther: Craig Yoe. *Craig Yoe's Weird But True Toon Factoids.* New York: Gramercy Books, 1999. 93.

Kant discusses the connection between sequence and time in Section II of "Transcendental Aesthetic," Part First of the "Transcendental Doctrine of Elements" in *Critique of Pure Reason* (1781). Eisner coined the term "sequential art" in *Comics & Sequential Art* (1985).

"Yellow journalism": Harvey 20; Yoe 77.

Bud Fisher and his innovations: Yoe 15; Blackbeard 15-16, 58-59; Harvey 23-26; **"prominent position across the top"**: Harvey 34.

Birth of King Features: Don Markstein's Toonopedia: http://www.toonopedia.com/king.htm.

Winsor McCay: Harvey 23; JVJ Publishing site (http://www.bpib.com/illustrat/mccay.htm) and John Canemaker's 1976 documentary "Remembering Winsor McCay" on Image Entertainment's excellent DVD collection *Winsor McCay: The Master Edition.* When I curated the exhibit *Toon Town: New York City in Comic and Cartoon Art* for New York's Museum of Comic and Cartoon Art (MoCCA) in 2004, I was priviledged to hold in my hand an original cel from *Gertie* generously lent by Bob West, the voice of Barney, via Heidi Leigh and Animazing Gallery, and up close McCay's linework is so fine it's still astounding almost 100 years since it was drawn.

"Max, you're a bright young man": Richard Fleischer. *Out of the Inkwell: Max Fleischer and the Animation Revolution.* Lexington: University of Kentucky Press, 2005. 15.

"Amazing Spicy Science Mystery Stories"

"I spotted this magazine": Greg Theakston, Ed. *The Complete Jack Kirby Volume One: 1917-1940.* Atlanta: Pure Imagination, 1997. 12.

"Story is worth more": ThePulp.Net: http://www.thepulp.net/pulp-info/pulp-history/.

Pulp vital statistics: "The Bloody Pulps" by Jim Steranko (originally printed in *Steranko's History of Comics, Vol. 1*, 1971). http://homepage.mac.com/cdkalb/the86floor/novels/thepulps.html

The Hugo Gernsback story: Ron Goulart. *Cheap Thrills: An Informal History of the Pulp Magazines.* New Rochelle, NY: Arlington House, 1972. Ch. 11. Gerard Jones. *Men of Tomorrow: Geeks, Gangsters, and the Birth of the Comic Book.* New York: Basic Books, 2004. 55-56. **"The present order of civilization"**: Hugo Gernsback. "Wonders of Technocracy." *Wonder Stories Vol. 4, #10.* March 1933. Reprinted by *The* (now defunct) *Pulp Zone* web site.

Illustration vs. cartooning: Harvey 76, 95.

Jack Kirby's childhood: Glenn B. Fleming. "The House That Jack Built." John Morrow, Ed. *The Collected Jack Kirby Collector, Vol. 2.* Raleigh, NC: TwoMorrows Publishing, 1998-2000. 15. References to the *Collected Jack Kirby Collector* will hereafter be abbreviated to "CJKC" [volume number]:[page number]. Ergo, reference to Fleming, here, would read CJKC 2:15.

See also Kirby biography in "Lord of Light" promotional package (reproduced CJKC 2:102-3). Ken Viola. "Jack Kirby: Master of Comic Book Art." CJKC 1:130-1. Jack Kirby. "Street Code." Jon B. Cooke and John Morrow, Eds. *Streetwise: Autobiographical Stories by Comic Book Professionals.* Raleigh, NC: TwoMorrows Publishing, 2000. 14-23.

Many thanks also to Eric Evans and Gary Groth of *The Comics Journal*, who kindly provided me with a copy of the raw transcript of Groth's 1989 interview with Jack and Rosalind ("Roz") Kirby. The comprehensive interview covers most of Kirby's life and career and filled in many gaps in the artist's early years.

Siegel background: Jones 37-38, 72, 77-79, 82-85. Also Les Daniels. *DC: Sixty Years of the World's Greatest Heroes.* Boston: Little, Brown & Co., 1995. 20-21.

"Toon Feud"

Fleischer/Disney rivalry: Leonard Maltin. *Of Mice and Magic: A History of American Animated Cartoons.* New York: McGraw Hill, 1980. See also Leslie Cabarga. *The Fleischer Story.* New York: De Capo Press, 1998. Fleischer comes up with spinach: R. Fleischer 54-5.

Fleischer childhood: R. Fleischer 2-3. Disney childhood: Anthony Lane. "Wonderful World." *The New Yorker.* December 11, 2006: 67-75. Nat Gerbler. *Walt Disney: The Triumph of the American Imagination.* New York: Alfred A. Knopf, 2006. 19-22. **"You can't eat medals"**: R. Fleischer 74.

Head animator system: Maltin 92-95. **"I hated it"**: Theakston, *Kirby Volume One*, 17.

"The super-strength and action": Jones 116.

1937 Fleischer Strike: R. Fleischer 90-92. "14 Pickets Seized in Broadway Fight." *The New York Times:* May 8, 1937: 5. "Movie Studio Strike Voted by 100 Workers." *The New York Times*. May 7, 1937: 9. **"I'm Popeye the Union Man"**: R. Fleischer 91.

Making of *Snow White*: Gabler Ch. 6; rejected dwarf ideas: Ibid 220; casting animators: Ibid 233; rotoscoping: Ibid 262-3; Reaction: Ibid 272-273, R. Fleischer 93-4.

Fleischer moves to Florida: R. Fleischer 95-96. Kirby would claim (CJKC 2:112, for example) to have left Fleischer Studios a few months before the 1937 strike, but also always gives as the primary reason for his leaving (CJKC 2:15, et al) their transfer to Florida, which happened almost a full year later. Also in CJKC 2:15, however, Kirby says that **"it's fortunate I didn't go [to Florida] because soon after [the studio] moved, they all went on strike and men were laid off."** I am operating on the assumption that while in later life Kirby mistakenly believed that the strike and the move were coterminous occurrences, events did indeed unfold as we present them in this story.

"New Action Fun"

The birth of the comic book: Mike Benton. *The Comic Book in America: An Illustrated History*. Dallas: Taylor Publishing, 1989. 14-17. Coulton Waugh. *The Comics*. Brooklyn: Luna Press, 1974. 335-342. Jones 98-101. Gaines' contribution: Frank Jacobs. *The Mad World of William M. Gaines*. Secaucus, NJ: Lyle Stuart, 1972. 54-6.

Poor Major Malcolm Wheeler-Nicholson: Jones 101-102; Benton 17-18; Daniels, *DC*, 14-15.

Early Siegel and Shuster comics & Superman's creation: Daniels, *DC*, 16-17, 20-23; Jones 38, 109, 113-116. Many thanks to *Comics Should Be Good*'s Brian Cronin for turning me on to an essay by Gregory Feeley in *Science Fiction Studies* #95, *Volume I, Part 5* (March 2005), which discusses on Wylie's influence (or lack thereof) on Siegel and emphasizing the John Carter of Mars connection.

"Demmed, elusive Pimpernel": Baronness Orczy. *The Scarlet Pimpernel* (1905 novel). Ch.12. **"Señor Zorro has paid a visit"**: Johnston McCulley. *The Curse of Capistrano* (1919). Ch. 4. Zorro background is from the 2000 documentary *The Many Faces of Zorro*, written by Philip Dye.

The Wonderman debacle: Bob Andelman. *Will Eisner: A Spirited Life*. Milwaukie, OR: M Press, 2005. 43-45. Eisner thinly fictionalizes the Wonderman story in his autobiographical graphic novel *The Dreamer*. Princeton, WI: Kitchen Sink, 1986.

Kirby meets Fox, Simon meets Kirby: Joe Simon with Jim Simon. *The Comic Book Makers*. Lebanon, NJ: Vanguard Press, 2003. 29-33. **"I'm the King of the Comics!"**: Simon 30 (Simon writes [33], "Every artist got the Fox monologue treatment."). **"Don't want no Rembrandts!"**: Pierce Rice in *The Comics Journal #219*. January 2000: 86. Simon's Art Background: Theakston, *Kirby Volume One*, 99-100.

1940 comic book statistics: Benton 32; Kurtzberg Becomes "Kirby": Simon 41.

"America [Hearts] Comics"

"Artists sat lumped": Jules Feiffer. *The Great Comic Book Heroes*. New York: Dial Press, 1965. 50-1.

Comics shop stories: Pimp: Gil Kane in *The Comics Journal #186*. April 1996: 57; **"Well how much do you need?"**: Joe Kubert in *The Comics Journal #172*. November 1994: 64; **"below digging ditches... get to do a syndicated strip"**: Ibid 67.

Martin Goodman and Funnies, Inc.: Les Daniels. *Marvel: Five Fabulous Decades of the World's Greatest Comics*. New York: Harry N. Abrams, Inc., 1993. 17-23. See also Theakston, *The Complete Jack Kirby Volume Two: 1940-1941*. Atlanta: Pure Imagination, 1997. 11-13. Writing "Roman" backwards: *Marvel Comics Vol. 1 No. 1*. New York: Marvel, 1990. 39.

Simon & Kirby at Timely: Daniels, *Marvel*, 32-52; Theakston, *Kirby Volume Two*, 236-245; Simon 42-57, 52-53. **"Started with the villain"**: CJKC 1:54. **"The bastard is alive"**: Simon 43. **"The pressure was t776rememndous ... needed a superpatriot"**: Theakston, *Kirby Volume Two*, 238. Lamppost threat: CJKC 1:181. La Guardia Help: Simon 45. Sentinels of Liberty ad copy: Joe Simon and Jack Kirby. *Captain America: The Classic Years 2*. New York: Marvel Comics, 2000. 42.

Stan Lee, née Lieber: Stan Lee. *Excelsior!* New York: Simon & Schuser, 2002. Ch. 2; Simon 46.

The spread Siegel mentions would be "Up, Up and Awa-a-y! The Rise of Superman, Inc." John Kobler. *Saturday Evening Post*. June 21, 1941. 14-15, 70-78. **"Aw, I told you"**: Kobler 14. **"The businessmen have made an even better thing"**: Ibid 15.

Walt Disney's Comics and Stories: Benton, *America*, 30, 158.

S&K defect to DC: Daniels, *DC*, 64. Simon 53, 58-61. **"I'm your man ... Martin is furious"**: Simon 53. **"I'm gonna kill him"**: "More Than Your Average Joe: Excerpts from Joe Simon's Panels at the 1998 Comicon International: San Diego." *Jack Kirby Collector #25* (Downloaded from TwoMorrows web site 4/14/00).

"Our Artists At War"

"Inventive Israelite...Colorado beetle": *Das Schwarze Korps*. April 25, 1940. 8. Translated by Randall Bytwerk on Calvin College web site: http://www.calvin.edu/academic/cas/gpa/superman.htm.

Comic creators' service records: Simon 63-7; Lee, *Excelsior!*, Ch. 3; Andelman Ch. 3.

Read "How to Spot a Jap" in its entirety at Ethan Person's web site: http://www.ep.tc/howtospotajap/howto03.html.

"Images demonstrated process": Andelman 85.

Disney goes to war: Gabler Ch. 8; **"for everybody but himself"**: Ibid 365; **"as invisible as possible"**: Ibid 379; ship and plane emblems: *Disney Goes to War* site. http://www.skylighters.org/disney/.

Minute Man Bert Christman: Andrew Glaess. "Remembering Bert Christman." http://www.warbirdforum.com/scorchy.htm.

Our Kirby at War: Ray Wyman, Jr. "Jack Kirby on: World War II Influences." *The Jack Kirby Collector #27*. February 2000: 16-23; 1989 Groth interview; Greg Theakston. "Kirby's War." *Jack Kirby Quarterly*. Spring 1999: 6-13. **"Jack Kirby, the artist? ... nice guys don't get scout duty"**: Wyman 20.

Mickey Mouse password: *Toons at War* web site. http://toonsatwar.blogspot.com/2010/05/mickey-mouse-d-day-invasion-password.html.

Comics sales at WWII post exchanges (PXs): Waugh 334.

"All You Need Is Love"

Captain Marvel's circulation woes: Benton 43.

The Archie Comics story: Don Markstein's *Toonopedia* (online); Benton 93-5, 181-3.

The best survey of romance comics may be found in Trina Robbins. *From Girls to Grrrlz: A History of Women's Comics from Teens to Zines.* San Francisco: Chronicle Books, 1999. Ch. 2.

The birth of *Young Romance*: Robbins 50-52; Simon 109-112; Benton 141-2; Robert Greenberger. "Comics Find True Love." *Millennium Edition: Young Romance Comics #1.* April 2000: inside covers. Richard Howell. "Kirby's Romance Women: Tough Enough?" CJKC 5:64-66. Genre statistics: Benton 46.

"I hope they put out more ... borders on pornography": Simon 112.

1947 comic book industry statistics: Waugh 334. Greg Theakston. *The Complete Jack Kirby: March-May 1947.* Atlanta: Pure Imagination, 1998. 107.

"Crime...Does It *Pay!*"

Biro meets voyeur: Simon 56-57. Mike Benton. *The Illustrated History of Crime Comics.* Dallas: Taylor Publishing Co., 1993. 20.

Gil Kane tells the Western Union girls' locker room story in *The Comics Journal #186*: 48.

The Lev Gleason Story: Benton, *America,* 124-125; *Crime,* 19-22; Jones, 193, 235. Everything I know about the Lev Gleason *Daredevil* comes from Don Markstein's *Toonopedia* (online).

CDNP letters practices: Benton, *Crime*, 29. Origin of Mr. Crime: Ibid 27-28. CDNP Sales Figures: Benton, *America* 125; *Crime* 35.

Titles that magically turned into crime comics once the trend began include Fox super heroes *Blue Beetle* and *Phantom Lady*, Marvel's venerable *Sub-Mariner* (which was re-titled *Official All-True Crime Cases*) and, under the guidance of Simon & Kirby, Crestwood's *Headline Comics.*

Chicago crime comics ban: Theakston, *Kirby March-May 1947*, 108. Other anti-crime comics legislation and Gleason's reaction: Benton, *Crime*, 75-76.

Post-Code fate of *CDNP* & its creators: Benton, *Crime,* 85-87; Jones 281-282; Simon 151-153; Yoe 106.

Bob Wood, murderer: Kermit Jaediker. "Gramercy Park Gets the Horrors." *New York Daily News.* September 14, 1958: 3. "Cartoonist Held as Slayer." *The New York Times.* August 28, 1958.

"The House of Fear"

Early comics criticism: Amy Kiste Nyberg. *Seal of Approval: The History of the Comics Code.* Jackson: University of Mississippi Press, 1998. Chs. 1-2.

That big weirdo, William Moulton Marston: Daniels, *DC*, 58-61; Jones 205-211; Nick Gillespie. "William Marston's Secret Identity: The strange private life of the creator of Wonder Woman." *Reason.* May 2001. http://reason.com/archives/2001/05/01/william-marstons-secret-identi. Marguerite Lamb. "Who Was Wonder Woman 1?" *Bostonia.* Fall 2001. http://www.bu.edu/bostonia/fall01/woman/.

"Blood-curdling masculinity ... cynical enough": Daniels, *DC*, 58. **"When women rule ... preference in story strips"**: Olive Richard (aka Olive Byrne). "Our Women Are Our Future." *Family Circle.* August 14, 1942. http://www.wonderwoman-online.com/articles/fc-marston.html. **"Psychological propaganda"**: Les Daniels. *Wonder Woman: The Complete History.* New York: Chronicle Books, 2000. 22. **"Willing slaves"**: Daniels, *DC*, 58. **"Sold more comics"**: Daniels, *DC*, 61. **"Enjoy submission"**: Lamb.

All-American Comics: Daniels, *DC*, 48-63; Jacobs Ch. 3; **"Where's Bill?"**: Ibid 56-7. **"How long it took Moses"**: Ibid 59-60;

EC's New Trend: Jacobs Chs. 4-7; Benton 112-114. **"Old man's stockroom boy"**: Ibid 63. Pencil sharpener suggestion: Ibid 78.

"Evil twin brother": Dick DeBartolo. *Good Days and MAD: A Hysterical Tour Behind the Scenes at MAD Magazine.* New York: Thunder's Mouth Press, 1994. 192-3.

"Americans are good guys": Greg Sadowski, Ed. *The Comics Journal Library Vol. 7: Harvey Kurtzman.* Seattle: Fantagraphics, 2006. 104. **"If I was going to tell kids anything about war"**: Ibid 24. **"To the right of the sulpha"**: Jacobs 82. **"The average comic-book guy"** Sadowski 43. **"I wasn't making any money"**: Ibid 111. Protesting horror comics: Ibid 108.

"Important contributing factor": Wertham's Senate testimony, from the transcript in Maurice Horn, Ed. *The World Encyclopedia of Comics.* Philadelphia: Chelsea House Publishers, 1999. 871.

"Madness"

"No child should be diagnosed": HL Mosse. "The Misuse of the Diagnosis Childhood Schizophrenia." *American Journal of Psychiatry.* March 1958: 114(9):791-4. http://www.neurodiversity.com/library_mosse_1958.html. Wertham biography: Nyberg Ch. 4.

"Easier to sentence a child to life": Nyberg 33. Revenue quote: Benton 48.

"Lack of modulation": Richard Warshow. "Paul, the Horror Comics, and Dr. Wertham." *Commentary Vol. 17* (1954). Reprinted in Jeet Heer and Kent Worcester. *Arguing Comics: Literary Masters on a Popular Medium.* Jackson: University of Mississippi Press, 2004. 69. Warshow's praise of *Krazy Kat*, "Woofed with Dreams" from *The Parisian Review* (1946), may be found on 63-66.

"Distinction between 'bad' and 'good'": Ibid 76. **"Irritated pleasure"**: Ibid 68.

"You're a humorist": Jacobs 85.

"Indiscriminate anarchy": Heer & Worcester 68.

"I was pretty bitter": Sadowski 44.

"Desecrated Christmas": David Hajdu. *The Ten-Cent Plague: The Great Comic-Book Scare and How It Changed America.* New York: Farrar, Straus and Giroux, 2008. 220.

"If you open the door": Attributed to Anthony Comstock (1844-1915).

"Crime comic book for parents": Heer & Worcester 77.

"The group most anxious to destroy comics": William M. Gaines and Jack Davis. "Are You a Red Dupe?" *The Haunt of Fear #26.* July-August 1954: Inside front cover.

"Hitler was a beginner": Horn 880.

"Good taste": Jacobs 109.

"Stupid, stupid, stupid": Hajdu 271.

"No Harm": Peter Kihss. "No Harm in Horror, Comics Issuer Says." *The New York Times*. April 25, 1954: A1.

"It was like the plague": Hajdu 326.

"Most severe set of principles": Nyberg 112.

"Too violent": Lee, *Excelsior*, 96.

"Comics were a bastard form": Jacobs 117.

"Russian beatnik": Marshall McLuhan. *Understanding Media*. 1964. Reprinted in Heer & Worcester 109.

"Unsuitable for reproduction": Nyberg 81.

"Not the cause": Ibid 83.

"Fanbase Presents..."

The full story on EC fandom can be found in Ch. 1 of Bill Schelly's *The Golden Age of Comics Fandom*. Seattle: Hamster Press, 1995.

R. Crumb's Childhood: The film *Crumb*, directed by Terry Zwigoff (1994). Chs. 1-2 of R. Crumb and Peter Poplaski. *The R. Crumb Handbook*. London: MQ Publications Ltd., 2005.

"Forced me to draw": Peter Poplaski, Ed. *The R. Crumb Coffee Table Art Book*. Boston: A Kitchen Sink Book for Little, Brown and Company, 1997. 3. See also R. Crumb. "Treasure Island Days" (1978). Reprinted in *Crumb Coffee Table*, 20-21.

Disneyland (the TV show): Gabler 511-513.

"I lived, breathed and ate": Sadowski 14.

"The real importance of *Foo*": *Crumb Handbook* 100.

Science Fiction/Double Feature: Julius Schwartz with Brian M. Thomsen. *Man of Two Worlds: My Life in Science Fiction and Comics*. New York: Harper Collins, 2000. Benton 171-174. Michael Uslin, Ed. *Mysteries in Space: The Best of DC Science Fiction Comics*. New York: Fireside, 1980.

"A whole new audience": Schwartz 87.

"Spread disease": Schelly 23. **"Fantastic Coincidence"**: Ibid 24.

Kirby v. Schiff: Jon B. Cooke. "The Story Behind Sky Masters." CJKC 3:147-151.

"Tales to Marvel (at)"

Atlas Shrugged: Jim Vadeboncoeur, based on a story uncovered by Brad Elliott. "The Great Atlas Implosion." CJKC 4:134-7; Lee, *Excelsior*, Ch. 8; Daniels, *Marvel*, Ch. 3. Patsy Walker crosshatch: Al Jaffe in *The Comics Journal* #225. July 2000: 41.

American News anti-trust case: Nyberg 125-6; **"on the *Titanic*"**: *Excelsior* 99. "Sixteen titles" meant eight titles per month, or, in practice, 16 bi-monthly titles published every other month.

"Quite a novel idea": Schwartz 97; Lee's monologue is adapted from Ch. 1 of his *Origins of Marvel Comics*. New York: Fireside, 1974.

"I wrote an outline": *Excelsior* 114-5. I read a reproduction of the original outline for *Fantastic Four #1* on display at the MoCCA exhibit *Stan Lee: A Retrospective* in 2007.

"I'd be writing a story for Kirby ... lazy man's device": CJKC 4:143.

"The best thing": R.C. Harvey. *The Art of the Comic Book: An Aesthetic History*. Jackson: Mississippi Press, 1996. 44.

"The Twentieth-Century Mythology": "OK, You Passed the 2-S Test—Now You're Smart Enough for Comic Books." *Esquire*. September 1966: 115. It's worth noting that this article, one of the earliest mainstream pieces on Marvel, describes Stan Lee as "the *author* of Marvel's ten super-hero comics" (emphasis mine) and though Jack Kirby provides the illustrations for the tongue-in-cheek piece, his name (other than his signature on his art), or Ditko's, or any other artist's, is not mentioned anywhere in the article.

"Stan Lee was being foisted on me": Alex Ross in *The Comics Journal #224*. June 2000. 78.

"I like very much": Nat Freedland. "Super-Heroes with Super Problems." *The New York Herald Tribune Sunday Magazine*. January 9, 1966. Reprinted CJKC 4:156.

"ESP sessions": Ibid 159. Roy Thomas, Lee's assistant, who was called in to witness the same session the reporter observered, reports on Kirby being upset about it — and Stan being embarrassed — in an interview in CJKC 4:148.

"I'm gonna blow": Gil Kane interview, *Comics Journal #186*. April 1996: 95.

Ditko and Ayn Rand: Blake Bell. *Strange and Stranger: The World of Steve Ditko*. Seattle: Fantagraphics, 2008. Ch. 6.

"Mysticism": Ayn Rand. *The Virtue of Selfishness*. New York: Signet, 1964. 29.

"They are all abstractions": Steve Ditko. *The Avenging Mind*. Bellingham, WA: Robin Snyder and Steve Ditko, 2008. 9. **"Executing is creating"**: Ibid 10. **"Like someone wanting a building"**: Ibid 11.

Ditko departs: Bell 94-5.

Lee himself admits Kirby was the sole creator of the Silver Surfer in CJKC 4:143 and in his own 1975 book *Son of Origins of Marvel Comics* (p206).

"The backbone of Marvel": CJKC 4:181.

"POP"

"A very strong afterimage": Janis Hendrickson. *Roy Lichtenstein*. Köln, Germany: Taschen, 2006. 10.

"More as an observer": Ibid 20.

Lichtenstein's process is described in detail in "Is He the Worst Artist in the U.S.?" *Life Magazine*. January 31, 1964. http://www.lichtensteinfoundation.org/lifemagroy.htm.

Beer cans as art: Klaus Honnef. *Pop Art*. Koln: Taschen, 2004. 21.

"How can you like exploitation?": Hendrickson 39.

"A wish dream": Dr. Fredric Wertham. *Seduction of the Innocent*. New York: Rinehart, 1954. 190.

It's a Bird! It's a Plane! It's Superman!: Daniels, *DC*, 146-7.

"I thought they were crazy ... like an idiot": Joel Eisner. *The Official Batman Batbook*. Chicago: Contemporary Books, Inc., 1986. 6.

"I loathed the word 'camp'": Adam West with Jeff Rovin. *Back to the Batcave*. New York: Berkeley Books, 1994. 98-100.

"The Texas Mafia"

Jack Jackson background: Patrick Rosenkranz. "Jack Jackson's Long Rough Ride Comes to an End." *The Comics Journal #278*. October 2006: 20-26; Rosenkranz. *Rebel Visions: The Underground Comix Revolution, 1963-1975*. Seattle: Fantagraphics, 2002.

16-26. **"putting one over on the bigwigs"**: "Ride" 22.

Chet Helms, aka Family Dog: Joel Selvin. "Chet Helms, aka Family Dog, celebrated along with his era." *San Francisco Chronicle.* October 31, 2005. B-1.

"Medically unfit": Frank Stack's interview of Gilbert Shelton in *The Comics Journal #187.*

Birth of Rip-Off Press: Patrick Rosenkranz. "Underground Publishers." *The Comics Journal #264*; Jack Jackson. "Rip-Off Press: The Golden Era." 1988. Reprinted in *The Comics Journal #278.* October 2006: 29-32. See also *Rebel,* 90-94; 132-4. **"Texas Mafia"**: "Ride" 22-3.

"Feed Your Head"

Crumb in New York: Rosenkranz 53-56.

"The only thing we had in common": Documentary *The Confessions of Robert Crumb*, written by Crumb.

"My mind was a garbage receptacle": *Crumb Handbook* 60. ***"'What the hell does it all mean?'"***: Ibid 132.

Help! as **"first underground comic"**: Jay Lynch, attributed in Rosenkranz 27.

"A Tribtue to Dr. Strange": Bell 78.

"Crazy and helpless ... egoless state": *Handbook* 132.

"Got room for one more?": Ibid 127.

"Some of that free love action ... I couldn't get with it": *Crumb* (Zwigoff).

"I thought he must be an old man": Rosenkranz 69.

"Turning up in all the windows in Haight Street": *Crumb* (Zwigoff).

"The real big vision": Rosenkranz 71.

"Masses of humanity being gassed": Ibid 120.

"'I'm beautiful, I'm spiritual'": Ibid 67.

"Completely biltzkrieged": Dez Skinn. *Comix: The Underground Revolution.* New York: Thunder's Mouth Press, 2004. 49.

"I got too much love": Rosenkranz 137.

"Internment camps": Ibid 143.

"We can't stop you": Ibid 162.

"Dependent on no outside force": Ibid 182.

Spider-Man vs. the Comics Code: Daniels, *Marvel,* 152-154.

"That was supposed to be a joke": *Handbook* 172.

"I was the meat": Ibid 189, 194.

"'Til the bubble bursts": Rosenkranz 170.

"You can't win!": *Confessions of R. Crumb.*

"Mouse Pirates"

Much of the information in this story comes from the work of Bob Levin, specifically "The Pirate and the Mouse: Part 2." *The Comics Journal #239.* November 2001: 34-63; and "Disney's War Against the Counterculture." *Reason.* December 2004. http://reason.com/archives/2004/12/01/disneys-war-against-the-counte. See also Rosenkranz 197-204.

"Rape our sisters": Robert L. Garland. "The Sky River III Story": http://skyriverlives.com/page10.php.

"Pair of hands for the counterculture": Levin, "Pirate," 35.

"Outrage at '50s America": Ibid 38.

"Living Grimm Brother": Rosenkranz 202.

"Why have a fight if no one comes?": Levin, "Pirate," 40.

"Are you Dan O'Neill?": Ibid 41.

"It's still a line ... deal with the image ... Jonathan Swift ... obliterating copyright protection": Levin, "Disney's War."

"If you do something stupid twice": Levin, "Pirate," 52.

The 2 Live Crew 1994 Supreme Court case is *Campbell v. Acuff-Rose Music.*

"Heavy Mettle"

Le Journal de Mickey at Disney Comics Worldwide site: http://www.wolfstad.com/dcw/france/le-journal-de-mickey/. "The Deadly Side of French Comics History" by Spider Rocket (2003): http://www.miltonknight.net/frenchcomics.html

Tintin's Nazi Troubles: Michael Farr. *The Adventures of Hergé, Creator of Tintin.* San Francisco: Last Gasp, 2007. Ch. 3.

Heavy Metal: Dave Cail's HM fan site: http://www.heavymetalmagazinefanpage.com/history.html. Gary Groth and Kim Thompson. "'We're All Lunatics.': The *Heavy Metal* Interview." *The Comics Journal #49.* September 1979: 42-50. Gary Groth. "A Life on the Fringe of Comics: The Ted White Interview." *The Comics Journal #59.* October 1980: 56-81.

"Another outlet": Groth and Thompson, "*Heavy Metal,*" 43.

Comics Implosion: Benton, *America,* 77, 80; "The DC Implosion" by David R. Black in *Fanzig #27* (July 2000). http://www.fanzing.com/mag/fanzing27/feature1.shtml.

Star Wars, Epic Illustrated: Daniels, *Marvel*, 177, 183-4. **"The way it works in the real world"**: "Rick Marschall on EPIC: 'Every Comic Book Publisher Should Be Doing This...'" *The Comics Journal #40.* September 1979: 9-10.

"The Grabbers"

Many thanks to Jeff Trexler of uncivilsociety.com, a lawyer, professor and blogger on legal issues in comics, for reviewing this story for Ryan and me.

"An employee who hires another": Playboy v. Dumas, 53 F.3rd 549 (2d. Cir. 1995).

"To have and to hold forever": Joanne Siegel and Laurel Siegel Larson v. Warner Bros. Entertainment, Inc., Time-Warner, Inc., and DC Comics, Inc. ORDER GRANTING IN PART AND DENYING IN PART PLAINTIFFS' MOTION FOR PARTIAL SUMMARY JUDGMENT; ORDER GRANTING IN PART AND DENYING IN PART DEFENDANTS' MOTION FOR PARTIAL SUMMARY JUDGMENT. Central District of California 2008. 10. The copyright notices cited are part of the defendants' exhibits in this legal action. The acrimony between Siegel and various DC employees, including Liebowitz, is nakedly evident from the correspondence included in same.

"Employees of a Work Made for Hire": National Peridoical Publications, Inc. Certificate of a Registration of a Claim to Renewal Copyright dated May 18, 1939. R. #388937. Siegel & Shuster vs. DC, Round 1: Jones 225-6, 244-9.

Robinson discusses his contributions to *Batman* in his interview with *The Comics Journal #271.* October 2005: 82-3.

Siegel & Shuster vs. DC, Round 2: Mary Breasted. "Superman's Creators, Nearly Destitute, Invoke His Spirit." *The New York Times.* November 22,

1975: 31. Siegel's reaction to Puzo deal: Jones xi-xiii.

Jack Kirby's legal troubles with Marvel Comics, over Joe Simon and his art, are summarized by John Morrow. "Art vs. Commerce." *The Jack Kirby Collector #24.* April 1999: 28-31.

Robinson & Adams fight for Siegel & Shuster: Jones 319-323.

The sorry state of the Marvel original art storage facility from 1975 to 1980 is delineated by ex-employee Irene Vartanoff to Tom Heintjes. "Where did all the art go?" *The Comics Journal #105.* February 1986: 16-22.

"Asks for a Jack Kirby": Tom Heintjes. "The Negotiations: Jack Kirby discusses his efforts to retrieve his art from Marvel Comics." *The Comics Journal #105.* February 1986: 59. **"I sold them stories"**: Ibid 58.

"Provide as a gift": The complete text of the agreement Marvel originally wanted Kirby to sign may be found on the inside front cover of *The Comics Journal #105.*

"I can't sign it ... I have more respect for you": Heintjes, "Negotiations," 54. **"They're grabbers"**: Ibid 59.

"More money for creating Darkseid": *Hour Twenty-Five* radio talk show transcript (1986). CJKC 4:209.

Howard the Duck suit: John Morrow. "The Other Duck Man." CJKC 2:72-75.

Blade suit: The trial transcripts are reprinted (in part) in "Creators Rights on Trial: Marv vs. Marvel, Part 2." *The Comics Journal #239.* November 2001: 68-112.

DeCarlo vs. Archie: Eric Walsh. "Dan DeCarlo, Archie Artist and Creator of *Josie and the Pussycats*, Is Dead at 82." *The New York Times.* December 23, 2001. http://www.nytimes.com/2001/12/23/nyregion/dan-decarlo-archie-artist-and-creator-of-josie-and-the-pussycats-is-dead-at-82.html.

Simon vs. Marvel, Round 2: Michael Dean. "Joe Simon Claims Cap Copyright." *The Comics Journal #219.* January 2000: 8-10.

"Subject to termination ... after seventy years": ORDER GRANTING IN PART...:. 48, 72.

"It Rhymes with Traffic Hovel"

"The most fertile inventor of combinations": David Kunzle. *Father of the Comic Strip: Rodolphe Töpffer.* Jackson: University Press of Mississippi, 2007. Kindle Edition, Ch. 2. **"The drawings, without this text"**: Ibid Ch. 3.

"Bringing details out of darkness": Lynd Ward. "On 'Gods' Man'." *Lynd Ward: Six Novels in Woodcuts, Vol. 1.* New York: Library of America, 2010. 783.

The *Classics Illustrated* Story: Benton 123-124. William B. Jones, Jr. "Alfred Lewis Kanter." http://www.jacklakeproductions.com/File22.html. **"We were the best"**: Benton 123.

"*Batman* to *Beowulf*": Arnold Drake. "The Graphic Novel — and How It Grew." Arnold Drake, Leslie Waller & Matt Baker. *It Rhymes with Lust.* Milwaukie, OR: Dark Horse Books replica edition, 2007. 129.

"Turning out a pornographic book": Mike Craton, Gary Groth, and Gil Kane. "Kane on Savage: An Interview with the Creator." *Gil Kane's Savage!* Stamford, CT: Fantagraphics Books, 1982. 50.

"The best thing he ever saw": Gil Kane in *The Comics Journal #186.* 87.

"The shape of the '60s": Art Spiegelman. "Intro." *Harvey Kurtzman's Jungle Book.* Princeton, WI: Kitchen Sink Press, 1988. ix.

"Two years after meeting Lynd Ward": Art Spiegelman. "Reading Pictures." *Lynd Ward: Six Novels in Woodcuts. Vol. 1.* xxiv.

"Mouse as the oppressed": Rosenkranz 189-190.

"You the guy who does those pictures?": Andelman 150. **"That sounds interesting"**: Ibid 290.

"Absolute shock of an oxymoron": Art Spiegelman in *The Comics Journal #180.* September 1995: 76.

"One thing that's irritating": Christopher Irving. "Art Spiegelman: Still Movin' With Comix." *Graphic NYC.* http://www.nycgraphicnovelists.com/2010/11/art-spiegelman-still-movin-with-comix.html.

"Hard to classify": Alessandra Stanley. "'Thousand Acres' Wins Fiction As 21 Pulitzer Prizes Are Given." *The New York Times.* April 8, 1992. http://www.nytimes.com/1992/04/08/nyregion/thousand-acres-wins-fiction-as-21-pulitzer-prizes-are-given.html.

"1986 AD"

The Looking Glass: Paul Gravett & Peter Stanbury. *Great British Comics.* London: Aurum Press Ltd., 2006. 8.

"The boy's concentration": Martin Barker. *A Haunt of Fears: The Strange History of the British Horror Comics Campaign.* London: Pluto Press Ltd., 1984. 11. Communist Party involvement in UK comics campaign: Barker Ch. 3. **"This American vulgarisation"**: Ibid 25. Text of the Children and Young Persons (Harmful Publications) Act: Ibid. 16.

National Comics Publications v. Fawcett Publications: Jacobs 262.

"Anonymous British backdrop ... this became a preoccupation": The film *The Mindscape of Alan Moore*, written, produced and directed by Dez Vylenz (2003).

"World's most inept LSD dealer": *Inside Out East*, BBC, airdate March 31, 2008. http://www.youtube.com/watch?v=NYkQJ_2K0dY.

"Better about an English superhero": George Khoury, Ed. *Kimota! The Miracleman Companion.* Raleigh, NC: TwoMorrows Publishing, 2001. 11.

"Dead and buried": Gravett & Stanbury 109.

"Do what you like": Khoury 10. For Skinn's side of the story, see Khoury 41.

"Thirty people in anoraks": *Mindscape of Alan Moore* (Vylenz).

"Applying real world logic": Khoury 23.

"Put in a taxicab": Dave Gibbons. *Watching the Watchmen.* London: Titan Books, 2008. 124. **"Batman and Robin!"**: Ibid 241.

"It's like a Xerox": Interview with Neil Gaiman. Conducted October 26, 1989 12:30 am. by Brian Hibbs, Owner of San Francisco's Comix Experience. Transcribed by Brian Hibbs. Edited by Brian Hibbs and Neil Gaiman. http://www.holycow.com/dreaming/lore/interview/gaiman-interview-with-brian-hibbs/.

"A dog riding a bicycle ... doomed the mainstream": Adam Rogers. "Legendary Comics Writer Alan Moore on Superheroes, The League, and Making Magic." *Wired.* February 23, 2009. http://www.wired.com/entertainment/hollywood/magazine/17-03/ff_moore_qa?currentPage=all.

This account of the post-Eclipse battle for

Miracleman comes from Hank Wagner, Christopher Golden and Stephen R. Bissette. *Prince of Stories: The Many Worlds of Neil Gaiman.* New York: St. Martin's Press, 2008. 224-230.

"The God of All Comics"

Etymology of "manga": Frederik L. Schodt. *Manga! Manga! The World of Japanese Comics.* Tokyo: Kodansha International, 1986. 18. Also Natsu Onoda Power. *God of Comics: Osamu Tezuka and the Creation of Post-World War II Manga.* Jackson: University Press of Mississippi 2009, Kindle ed. Ch. 1.

Tezuka's early years: Helen McCarthy. *The Art of Osamu Tezuka: God of Manga.* New York: Abrams, 2009. Ch1.

"Jail editor": Schodt 51. **"Poor-quality, harmful"**: McCarthy 20.

"I wept": Power Ch. 7.

"It's just like I am watching a movie!": Fujuko Fujio A, in *Futari de shonen manga bakari kaite ita (All We Ever Did Was Draw Boys' Comics)*, quoted by Power Ch. 3. **"One in three"**: Ibid Ch. 5.

"News: Astro Boy a Japanese Citizen?" AnimeNewsNetwork. March 30, 2003. http://www.animenewsnetwork.com/news/2003-03-20/astro-boy-a-japanese-citizen.

Disney meets Tezuka: McCarthy 158.

"'*Gekiga's*' intended target":The entire text of "Introduction to the Gekiga Workshop" (aka Gekiga Manifesto) may be found on page 730 (in Japanese) and 852 (in English) of Yoshihiro Tatsumi. *A Drifting Life.* Translated by Taro Nettleton. Montreal: Drawn & Quarterly, 2009.

"Anything he wished": Power Ch. 3.

The Star System: McCarthy Ch. 2; Power Ch. 4.

"Amplification through simplification": Scott McCloud. *Understanding Comics.* Northhampton, MA: Tundra Press, 1993. 30.

"In contrast to the American comic": Schodt 23.

American manga statistics: Jason Thompson. "How Manga Conquered the U.S., a Graphic Guide to Japan's Coolest Export." *Wired.* October 23, 2007. http://www.wired.com/special_multimedia/2007/1511_ff_manga. Many thanks to Kurt Hassler, the buyer mentioned in the article, who helped spearhead the manga bookstore revolution in the US. Now with Hachette, he kindly spoke with me about past and present issues in American manga publishing.

"One of the answers": Power Ch. 8. **"The God of All Comics"**: Ibid Ch. 1.

"No More Wednesdays"

"Dope out for ourselves": Maggie Thompson. "A quarter century of delivering comics: Steve Geppi's company gets comics to stores." *Comics Buyer's Guide #1628.* May 2007: 27.

"That's crazy!": Michael Dean. "Fine Young Cannibals: How Phil Seuling and a Generation of Teenage Entrepreneurs Created the Direct Market and Changed the Face of Comics." *The Comics Journal #277.* July 2006: 56. **"Didn't really care"**: Ibid 53.

Dazzler's stats come from Benton 82; Supes' from Joe Brancatelli. "The Comic Books: Death by the Numbers." *Eerie #96.* October 1978: 17.

Direct Market growth statistics: Dean 53, 54. **"Not enough product"**: Ibid 57. See also "Jack Kirby Returns to Comics with Cosmic Hero." *The Comics Journal #65.* August 1981: 23.

The B&W Boom & Bust: Gary Groth. "Black and White and Dead All Over." *The Comics Journal #277.* July 2006: 60-67.

The Perelman Marvel Saga: Dan Raviv. *Comic Wars.* New York: Broadway Books, 2002. R. Walker and Josh Neufeld. "The Comic Book Villain." *Titans of Finance.* Alternative Comics. 2001. iBooks edition.

The Speculator Fiasco of the '90s: Dirk Deppey. "Suicide Club: How Greed and Stupidity Disemboweled the American Comic-Book Industry in the 1990s." *The Comics Journal #277.* July 2006: 69-75. **"Pick the cotton ... The Plantation"**: Michael Dean. "The Image Story, Part One: Forming an Image." *The Comics Journal #222.* April 2000: 12.

As a Marvel freelancer at the time, I actually received the court notice announcing Marvel's bankruptcy in 1996.

Thanks again to Hachette's Kurt Hassler as well as Orbit's Alex Lencicki for discussing the challenge of digital piracy and scanlation to American manga publishing with me.

Much of our discussion of piracy was inspired and informed by self-identified pirates themselves. Via Twitter and our Evil Twin Comics blog, Ryan and I asked people to tell us why they did or didn't torrent comics via our web site and anonymous email. The source for much of the historical perspective of scanning and piracy comes from an ex-scanner by the name of Jamie Coville, who gave us permission to name him as a source. **"Okay! Full steam ahead!"** comes from an email he wrote us on April 14, 2011. You can read many of their responses at our web site at: http://eviltwincomics.blogspot.com/2011/03/normal.html.

Inman interview: GF. "Pease porridge hot." *The Economist.* December 29, 2010. http://www.economist.com/blogs/babbage/2010/12/online_cartoons.

ABOUT THE AUTHORS

FRED VAN LENTE (writer) has written too many comics, including *The New York Times* bestsellers *Cowboys & Aliens* (with Andrew Foley), *Incredible Hercules* (with Greg Pak), and *Marvel Zombies* (with just himself), as well as *Taskmaster, Hulk: Season One, MODOK's 11, X-Men Noir, Amazing Spider-Man* and *Archer & Armstrong*. His favorite, though, remains *Action Philosophers*, drawn by *Comic Book History of Comics* co-conspirator Ryan Dunlavey.

You may find him on the Internet in the usual places under his own name.

RYAN DUNLAVEY (artist) is the cartoonist responsible for such sequential attrocites as *MODOK: Reign Delay, Tommy Atomic, Bad Guy, The Dirt Candy Cookbook* (with Chef Amanda Cohen) and *Action Philosophers* (with longtime collaborator Fred Van Lente, who once described Ryan as "history's greatest monster").

Drawing this book was a lot harder than he thought it would be.

More of his artwork and his irresponsible abuse of the internet can be witnessed at **ryandartist.com.**